P9-DNR-648

SMITHSONIAN
BASEBALL

INSIDE THE WORLD'S FINEST PRIVATE COLLECTIONS

SMITHSONIAN
BASEBALL

INSIDE THE WORLD'S FINEST PRIVATE COLLECTIONS

BY STEPHEN WONG

PHOTOGRAPHS BY SUSAN EINSTEIN

SMITHSONIAN BOOKS

Collins

An Imprint of HarperCollinsPublishers

HarperCollins books may be purchased for educational, business, or sales promotional use. For information, please write: Special Markets Department, HarperCollins Publishers, 10 East 53rd Street, New York, NY 10022

FIRST EDITION

Library of Congress Cataloging-in-Publication Data has been applied for.

ISBN-10: 0-06-083851-5
ISBN-13: 978-0-06-083851-5

05 06 07 08 09 10 9 8 7 6 5 4 3 2 1

Grateful acknowledgment is made to the following for permission to reprint previously published material:

Excerpt from THE BOYS OF SUMMER by Roger Kahn. Copyright © 1971, 1972, 1998 Roger Kahn. Reprinted by Permission of Roger Kahn. All Rights Reserved. Available wherever books are sold.

Excerpt from THE TEAMMATES by David Halberstam. Copyright © 2003 The Amateurs, Inc. Reprinted by Permission of Hyperion. All Rights Reserved. Available wherever books are sold.

COVER: Official American League Ban Johnson baseball autographed by Babe Ruth and Lou Gehrig circa 1927. Courtesy of Dr. Kevin Chan. Circa 1930s store-model baseball glove. The Gary Cypres Collection. Ted Williams's game-used bat from the 1946 season. The Wong Family Archives Collection.

PHOTOGRAPHS BY SUSAN EINSTEIN

Prepared by
BISHOP PUBLISHING
777 Westchester Avenue
White Plains, New York 10604

EDITORS: Morin Bishop, John Bolster, Reed Richardson
Designed by Barbara Chilenskas

DEDICATION

For my parents
Dr. Andrew Wing Hung Wong
and
Catherine Po Kiu Wong

And in memory of my paternal grandparents
The late Dr. and Mrs. Min Sam Wong

And for my maternal grandparents
Professor and Mrs. H. C. Ho

BOLDEN SANTOP WINTERS CURRIE LEE CARR C.JOHNSON J.JOHNSON RYAN MACKEY ALLEN CAMPBELL LEWIS THOMAS COCKRELL BRIGGS WARFIELD STEVENS LAMBERT

CONTENTS

Among the many treasures gathered by our featured collectors are a panoramic photograph of the 1924 inaugural Negro League World Series (top). Satchel Paige's autographed game-worn glove from the 1940s (above), and the famous T206 Honus Wagner Baseball card (left).

Half Title page: Official National League baseball autographed by each member of the 1955 Brooklyn Dodgers.

Title page: Original panoramic photograph taken on October 13, 1906, by George R. Lawrence, the father of aerial photography, of the 1906 World Series between the Chicago Cubs and the Chicago White Sox.

One of the unique qualities of the game of baseball is that the vast array of objects associated with it lends itself so easily to collecting. In fact, a baseball fan has a veritable cornucopia of choices to consider when beginning a collection. Uniforms; equipment such as bats, balls, or gloves; relics from baseball stadiums of the past; trophies and awards; sheet music of baseball songs; baseball cards and autographs; ticket stubs and World Series and All-Star Game programs; even baseball-themed jewelry—any one of these categories may yield a treasure trove of objects and evoke powerful memories for the true fan.

Many of these collectibles have a historical significance that transcends the sport as well. The reason is simple: The history of baseball has mirrored the history of America and its artifacts reflect that fact. Social issues such as segregation and integration; economic developments such as the rise of organized labor, and the evolution of marketing and mass merchandising; technological and scientific inventions and advancements; and cultural phenomena in music, art, and literature have all challenged and affected the national pastime.

Since 1939, the National Baseball Hall of Fame and Museum in Cooperstown, New York, has served as a sanctuary dedicated to preserving and celebrating this rich heritage through its world-renowned collection of rare and historically significant baseball artifacts. Nowhere is this heritage more respected than at the National Baseball Hall of Fame and Museum.

Virtually all of our nearly 400,000 annual visitors have their own individual memories of baseball, many of which are powerfully stirred by the Museum's thousands of artifacts. Lazy sunny days in the stands with mom or dad, the dramatic home run that clinched the pennant, the improbable diving catch in the outfield, the sheer wonder on the faces of one's fellow fans when a sure loss is transformed into golden triumph and wild exultation—these are the shared moments the Museum recalls for generations of fans, who find in our collection that magic the game has so often embodied for them. In this way, our collection connects families, honors playing excellence, and preserves the remarkable history of the game we love.

The Museum contains nearly 200,000 bats, balls, gloves, caps, helmets, shoes, trophies, awards, and baseball cards.

The Hall of Fame's Research Library possesses an additional 2.6 million items, including books, records, correspondence, and photographs, while the library's film, video, and recorded sounds archive contains more than 10,000 hours of footage. Once we add an object to our collection, we handle, store, and display it with the utmost care. Considerable time and expense is involved in making certain that the environment in which an object is stored or displayed is strictly controlled, ensuring that it is permanently preserved for future generations of visitors and researchers.

The vast majority of baseball fans know about the National Baseball Hall of Fame, but few are aware of the extraordinary private collections of baseball memorabilia, filled with historically significant artifacts, many of which have never been seen by the general public. In the exceptional new book you are holding in your hands, author Stephen Wong presents 21 of the finest and most specialized such collections. In addition to spectacular photographs of some of the sport's most historically significant uniforms, balls, bats, early equipment, advertising ephemera, etc., Wong has written insightful essays and detailed captions, which present the stories behind the collectors and their collections, and place the artifacts in their historical, social, and cultural contexts. For those wishing to join Wong's merry band of collectors, the book also offers a series of "collecting tips" essays from renowned hobby experts and collectors explaining how to tell whether a particular item is authentic, how to develop different collection themes, where to find these treasured items, and much more.

The time and effort required to complete this project was surely immense. Stephen Wong is to be complimented for his investigation and presentation of these never-before-seen collections and for the thorough research with which he has supplemented his exposition. His decision to move beyond simple description towards a more sophisticated historically-informed perspective makes this book a compelling read for any baseball fan and a must-have for anyone who has ever visited or plans to visit the National Baseball Hall of Fame and Museum.

JANE FORBES CLARK
Chairman
The National Baseball Hall of Fame and Museum

THE VERY SOUL OF BASEBALL

> "Few things survive in these cynical days to remind us of the Union from which so many of our personal and collective blessings flow, and it is hard not to wonder, in an age when the present moment consumes and overshadows all else—our bright past and our dim unknown future—what finally does endure? What encodes and stores the genetic material of our civilization—passing down to the next generation the best of us, what we hope will mutate into betterness for our children and our posterity? Baseball provides one answer. Nothing in our daily life offers more of the comfort of continuity, the generational connection of belonging to a vast and complicated American family, the powerful sense of home, the freedom from time's constraints and the great gift of accumulated memory than does our National Pastime."
>
> —*KEN BURNS AND LYNN NOVICK*
> *from* Baseball: An Illustrated History

Not long after Ty Cobb died in 1961, Lawrence Ritter, an economist at New York University, began a journey that would last five years and take him more than 75,000 miles across the United States and Canada. He was looking for old-time baseball players who could tell him about their lives in the big leagues in the 1890s and the early years of the 20th century. According to Ritter, "It seemed to me then that someone should do something, and do it quickly, to record for the future the remembrances of a sport that has played such a significant role in American life." Ritter recorded conversations with 22 ballplayers, including Rube Marquard, "Wahoo Sam" Crawford, Fred Snodgrass, Smokey Joe Wood, Babe Herman, Paul Waner, and Lefty O'Doul. Each one of them, in talking to Ritter, vividly re-created what it was like to play in the majors during the era of Cobb, Honus Wagner, Tris Speaker, and Christy Mathewson, as well as later legends such as Babe Ruth, Lou Gehrig, and Jimmie Foxx. Ritter compiled his interviews in *The Glory of Their Times: The Story of the Early Days of Baseball Told by the Men Who Played It* (1966), one of baseball's landmark literary masterpieces.

I first read and was captivated by the book in the autumn of 1982, when I was a sophomore in high school and a beginning collector of baseball memorabilia (see Chapter XXI, "The Wong Family Archives Collection"). More than 20 years later, *The Glory of Their Times* surfaced again as a major inspiration for this book. In February 2003, with war looming in Iraq and Severe Acute Respiratory Syndrome (SARS) on the rise in Hong Kong where my family has lived since the 1980s, my personal world was in crisis as well. Burnt out after six and a half years as an investment banker, I had left my job and was at loose ends about my future. One evening during this time, I decided to cheer myself up (once again) with baseball and Duke Ellington. I pulled out *The Glory of Their Times* from the bookshelf and sat down with a glass of wine and the Duke's *Creole Rhapsody* purring softly in the background. While reading the book's original preface, I kept thinking how rewarding those five years on the road must have been for Ritter, and how exciting it must have been to travel all those miles in pursuit of a dream.

Slowly it dawned on me that I might consider a baseball journey of my own. The timing seemed ideal. Only seven months earlier, baseball and America had lost one of their beloved icons, Ted Williams, and 2003 was the year in which baseball would celebrate the 100th anniversary of the World Series, the 70th anniversary of the All-Star Game, and the 80th anniversary of the opening of Yankee Stadium. I thought how wonderful it would be, as a passionate collector of baseball memorabilia, to visit, professionally photograph, and write about some of the world's finest private collections of rare and important artifacts from baseball's rich history. What a delight it would be to meet with people who, like me, have dedicated a significant part of their lives to collecting and preserving some of the game's most precious relics; to learn more about, and share in, their joy and fascination with the objects in their collections; to listen to their stories about

The Wong Family Archives Collection includes (page 1) a game-worn jersey and cap, a game-used bat, a pennant celebrating the Yankees' 1937 American League title, and a 1939 World Series program, all related to the great Lou Gehrig, whose entire Hall of Fame career was spent in Yankee Stadium (below).

how they got started in collecting and why they chose particular themes or types of artifacts in which to specialize; to reminisce with them about special moments in baseball history, both on and off the field.

That evening's epiphany led me to develop a proposal for this book. I wanted to shine a spotlight on some of the finest and most comprehensive private collections in each major segment of baseball memorabilia. My primary focus would be on the period starting before the Civil War and ending in the 1960s. For the most part, artifacts from this period are significantly scarcer and more valuable than those from later eras.

In all, there are 21 private collections featured in the following pages. Some are all-encompassing, consisting of a diverse array of memorabilia. Others focus on a specific era or type of memorabilia: 19th-century baseball, game-used bats, game-worn jerseys, and World Series programs, to name only a few. I chose some collections because of their unique themes. For example, one collection is dedicated to the evolution of the baseball, glove, bat, and catcher's gear. Another comprises items from baseball's overseas exhibition tours of the late 19th and early 20th centuries.

Some of the chapters highlight the chronological progression of certain types of memorabilia and artifacts, and how those types affected other forms of memorabilia. For example, some of the 19th-century advertising displays and prints featured in the collections of Corey R. Shanus and Gary Cypres are the antecedents of some of the 20th-century displays and prints that appear in the collections of Marshall Fogel and Bill Mastro. The styles and shapes of the game-used baseball bats featured in the Dr. Richard C. Angrist Collection were largely derived from the bats featured in the Greg John Gallacher Collection.

Yet while the book traces the broad history of collecting, each chapter also seeks to capture the essence of the collection it describes. The heart of any collection lies in the historical background of the artifacts it contains. But the collector's history or character can invest his or her collection with special significance.

Along with many of the stunning featured artifacts, which speak for themselves, there is a treasure trove of complementary information in the captions, which not only describe the objects and memorabilia, but also provide insight into the players or events they commemorate, or the era from which they originate. In this way, for neophytes and aficionados alike, the book offers an entertaining lens through which to view the history of the game.

I have always been amazed that some of the game's most historically significant artifacts reside in private collections. When I first visited the Baseball Hall of Fame and Museum in Cooperstown, in the early 1980s, I thought that every baseball-related object of any historical significance either was already at the Museum or would eventually end up there. Even today, I find it surprising that many of the compelling objects featured in this book remain in private hands. These treasures include the only known photographic image of baseball's first organized team (a circa 1846 daguerreotype of six of the original members of the New York Knickerbocker Base Ball Club); the oldest known trophy ball in existence, from a game on July 5, 1853, between the Knickerbockers and the Gotham Club of New York; Shoeless Joe Jackson's game-used bat from the very early days of his career; the game-worn jerseys from the 1909 season of the Chicago Cubs' celebrated infield trio of Joe Tinker, Johnny Evers, and Frank Chance; Ty Cobb's game-worn jersey from his last year in the majors (1928); the jersey that Babe Ruth wore during the 1932 World Series, in which he hit his alleged "called shot" home run; Satchel Paige's game-worn glove from the 1940s; Jackie Robinson's game-worn jersey from his second year in the majors (1948); the jersey Roger Maris wore when he hit his 61st home run of the 1961 season, breaking Babe Ruth's 34-year-old record for home runs in a season; Roy Campanella's Most Valuable Player Award trophy from the 1955 season; the ball caught by Yogi Berra for the last out in Don Larsen's perfect game in the 1956 World Series; and Mark McGwire's 70th home run ball from the 1998 season.

In addition to these one-of-a-kind objects, this book features private collections containing the game-worn jerseys and/or game-used bats of an impressive array of baseball's legendary players, including Napoleon Lajoie, Lou Gehrig, Rogers Hornsby, Jimmie Foxx, Lefty Grove, Dizzy Dean, Hack Wilson, Ted Williams, Hank Aaron, and many others. You will see extraordinary 19th-century memorabilia, from the dawn of the national pastime; rare advertising posters and ephemera ranging from the 1880s to the 1960s; original first-generation photographs from the early part of the 20th century; and the most valuable baseball cards in the world, including the celebrated T206 Honus Wagner, once owned by hockey superstar Wayne Gretzky. All of the artifacts have been reviewed and professionally authenticated by the world's leading experts on historical baseball memorabilia.

Complementing the collections are essays by leading collectors and experts outlining how to collect the major types of baseball memorabilia. You'll learn how to distinguish between an original first-generation photograph and a wire photo, between a vintage game-worn jersey in original form and one that has been restored, and between a bat once used by a professional ballplayer and one made for retail sale. There is advice on how to collect baseball folk art and the many types of 19th-century memorabilia, and a discussion of the benefits of having a "general" collection versus a narrow one. Readers can learn whether, or when, to acquire items in their original form as opposed to items that have been restored. Lastly, the essays offer advice about how to store and display a collection.

By July of 2003, when Smithsonian Books expressed interest in publishing this book, professional photographer Susan Einstein and I were on our way to the first photo shoot in Los Angeles. During the next six months, we traveled to 19 other cities and towns throughout the country. Drives from Haddonfield, New Jersey, to Pittsburgh; Cincinnati to St. Louis via Louisville; and Memphis to Clarksdale, Mississippi, were long but always rewarding. Although I enjoyed every aspect of the work, my greatest joy came from spending time with each of the collectors and their families. Every collector we visited was exceedingly gracious and hospitable during our stay.

In January 2004, I flew back to Hong Kong to finish the research and the writing. The passenger sitting next to me on the plane, a man who looked to be in his mid-40s, introduced himself and we started chatting. When he asked what I did for a living, I told him that I had been writing a book on private collections of historical baseball artifacts. He asked me what kind of objects would be featured. When I told him a few of the highlights, his eyes widened in disbelief. Across the aisle, I noticed an elderly gentleman wearing a Boston Red Sox cap so weathered it looked as though its prime coincided with Carl Yastrzemski's. Seated next to him was a young boy, probably his grandson, also wearing a Red Sox cap. The boy kept tugging at the man's sleeves to show him his baseball cards. I turned back to my window and thought about all the miles I had traveled during the past six months, and about why I had taken such a chunk out of my life (eventually more than two

Baseball's first All-Star Game took place at Comiskey Park on July 6, 1933, as part of Chicago's Exposition. But its antecedents go back 22 years. On July 24, 1911, "the greatest collection of All-Star players who ever appeared on the field in the history of the game," as one newspaper wrote, played the Cleveland Naps (now called the Indians) in the Addie Joss Benefit Game. The ball that was used in the game (right) was signed that day in black ink by 19 of the famous participants in that celebrated game, including Shoeless Joe Jackson, Ty Cobb, Larry Napoleon Lajoie, Cy Young, Eddie Collins, Sam Crawford, Frank "Home Run" Baker, and Walter Johnson. One of the ball's side panels shows the following notation in period black ink. "Game Ball – Cleveland Naps 3 – Joss All Star 5." A second panel reads. "Benefit – All-Stars vs. Cleveland A.L. Addie Joss Day 7-24-11." This is one of only two baseballs known to exist from that game. Next to the ball is a rare T205 baseball card of Addie Joss that was issued in 1911 by the American Tobacco Company. The Wong Family Archives Collection.

and a half years) to complete this book. I realized then that my journey was not only about commemorating these astounding collections. It was about being part of the very soul of baseball. As author Tom Stanton wrote in *The Road to Cooperstown:* "Baseball's appeal isn't complicated or confusing. It's about the beauty of a game; it's about heroes and family and friends; it's about being part of something larger than yourself, about belonging; it's about tradition—receiving it and passing it; and it's about holding on to a bit of your childhood."

That is how we baseball collectors feel. The collections are our way of expressing it.

STEPHEN WONG
Hong Kong
August 10, 2004

baseball Centennial
NEW YORK
MALONE · HADLEY
POWELL
DICKEY
PEARSON
GOMEZ
GEHRIG
MURPHY
TRADE MARK
REG. U.S. PAT. OFF.
ORLD SER
YANKEE STADIUM
NEW YORK
YANKEES
VS
CINCINNATI
REDS
SOUVENIR PROGRAM 25

GENESIS

BY-LAWS AND RULES

OF THE

Knickerbocker Base Ball Club.

~~~~~~~~

Article I.

OF THE CLUB.

Sec. 1. THIS Club shall be designated by the name of the KNICKERBOCKER BASE BALL CLUB.

Sec. 2. The Club shall consist of not more than forty Members.

Sec, 3. Honorary Members may be elected by an unanimous vote.

Article II.

OF MEMBERSHIP.

Sec. 1. Gentlemen desirous of becoming Members of this Club, may, at any time, be proposed to the Committee on Membership. The proposition must be in writing, stating the name, resi-

" . . . there is nothing now heard of, in our leisure hours, but ball—ball—ball."
—*HENRY WADSWORTH LONGFELLOW*
from a letter to his father written at
Bowdoin College, April 11, 1824

Corey R. Shanus fondly recalls sitting at his desk in fourth grade and watching the clock slowly grind its way toward three o'clock—the hour the local candy man named Sam parked his blue station wagon at the back of the school. Corey and his buddies would sprint across the football field to see if Sam had the latest series of Topps baseball cards and whether it included Mickey Mantle. Corey, who had started collecting cards at age six in 1963, continued his passionate pursuit into his college years. In the late 1980s, he ventured into 19th-century baseball memorabilia, a new area of collecting animated by a galaxy of stars with peculiar sobriquets such as "Old Reliable," "Ace of the Staff," "King Kelly," "Old Hoss," and "Cyclone." Corey was hooked, and the extraordinary treasures he has unearthed since then provide an illuminating glimpse into the origins of the national pastime.

The objects comprising Shanus's collection of significant 19th-century baseball artifacts connect us viscerally with the game's neglected if not forgotten early era. Baseball's formative years involve unfamiliar individuals, and events far removed from the game we know today. Noted baseball historian John Thorn suggests that the history of this particular era has been "left to academicians who have interpreted the game rather than reveled in it." He goes on, "By viewing the period through such prisms as class and culture, urban modernization, and labor-management strife, they have reduced the grand old game to simply another socioeconomic microcosm of America at

An circa-1846 half-plate daguerreotype (right) from Shanus's collection depicts six of the original members of the New York Knickerbocker Base Ball Club. Alexander Joy Cartwright, who helped draft the first written rules in modern baseball, stands in the center of the back row. Daniel Lucius "Doc" Adams, who pioneered the position of shortstop, sits in the center of the front row with a cigar in his mouth. To his right is Duncan F. Curry, the club's first president. This is the only known photographic image of baseball's first organized team. The image sits in a velvet-lined thermoplastic case. (4½" x 5½")

The New York Knickerbocker Base Ball Club rules and bylaws (inset) contain, among other strictures, the rules governing play under the "New York game," which was started by the Knickerbockers. The booklet, which was printed in 1848, constitutes the first written rules of modern baseball. (5" x 3½")

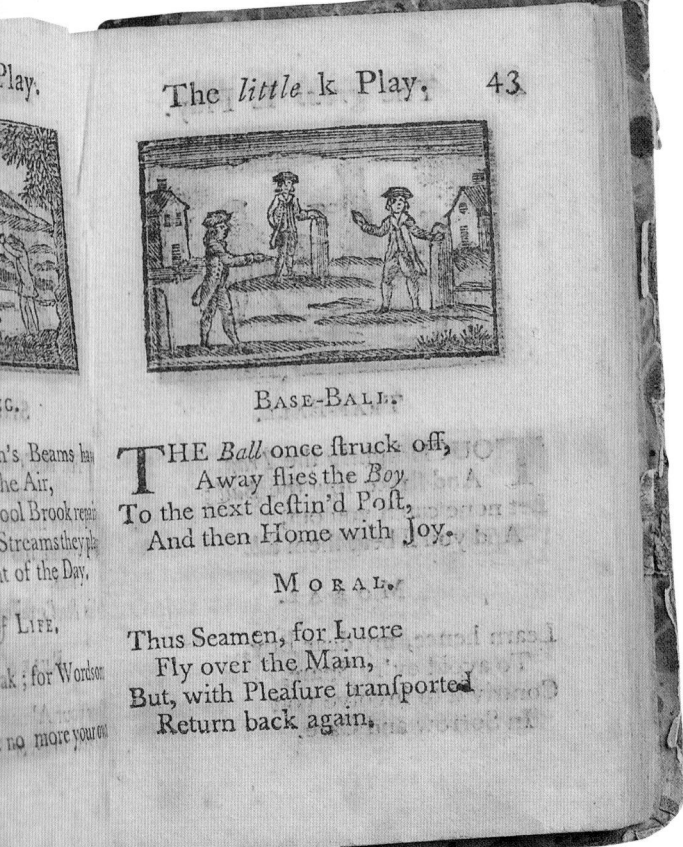

large." Shanus's remarkable collection reanimates the culture and the characters of that era, making the old game grand again.

Another factor contributing to the disconnect between modern fans and the game's earliest days may be the overall scarcity of 19th-century baseball memorabilia. Apart from the collection at the National Baseball Hall of Fame and Museum at Cooperstown, New York, few objects from this particular era have survived, and many of those that have are one of a kind. Most fans, therefore, are deprived of a physical connection to the invaluable contributions made by the pioneers who graced the diamond more than 130 years ago. But if it's an important 19th-century baseball artifact, and it's not in Cooperstown, there's a good chance it's in Shanus's world-class collection.

The items he's compiled come primarily from the the 1840s to the dawn of the 20th century, some of the most fascinating years in baseball's rich history. This was the era during which baseball became organized, evolved into a professional team sport, and

John Bachman, who was renowned for drawings of northeastern American cities, created the spectacular lithographic panorama of greater New York City (above) for the Knickerbocker Mutual Life Insurance Company. Issued in 1868, the print represents one of the earliest attempts to incorporate baseball in advertising, very subtly depicting, in its lower left corner, two games of "base ball" at the Elysian Fields in Hoboken, New Jersey. The irony of this image is that the "Massachusetts game"—which is illustrated on the left side of the refreshment pavilion—was almost obsolete in New England by the time this print was issued. (33" x 44")

Shanus owns the earliest known illustration of baseball, an English woodcut depicting the game (opposite) in A Little Pretty Pocket Book (Worcester, 1787), an American reprint of the 1744 London edition published by John Newbery. Popular in England at the time, the book also contains a rhymed description of "base-ball." (3½" x 2")

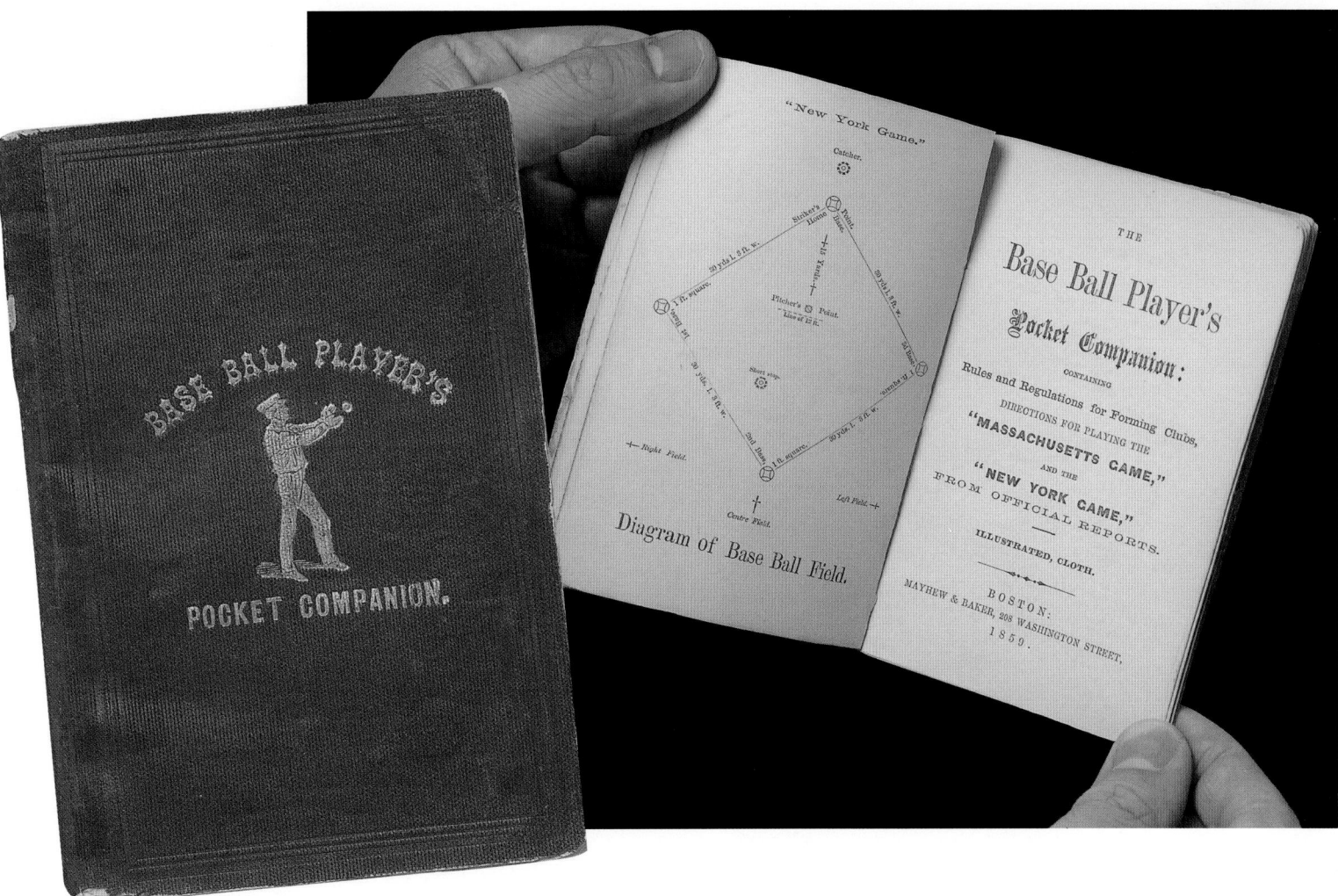

produced a cavalcade of colorful stars. Indeed, this was when baseball was transformed from a pastoral recreation into the national pastime.

According to baseball historian Harold Seymour, "The game's phenomenal growth in the postwar years was reflected in the National Association, whose membership skyrocketed from a relatively few clubs within a 25-mile radius of New York City to hundreds all over the nation." Baseball was on almost everyone's mind, and, as Seymour describes it, "all classes were succumbing to the baseball 'furor.'"

The sudden growth in the game's popularity sparked significant innovations in rules and equipment, many of which still apply today. The composition and design of the balls, bats, gloves, catcher's gear, and uniforms used by 20th-century legends such as Ty Cobb, Babe Ruth, and Willie Mays have their origins in this period.

"I see great things in baseball," Walt Whitman wrote in 1846. "It's our game—the American game. It will take our people out-of-doors, fill them with oxygen, give them a larger physical stoicism. Tend to relieve us from being a nervous, dyspeptic set. Repair these losses, and be a blessing to us." Imagine what it must have been like to experience the "furor" of baseball at the dawn of its development as a professional sport. With the remarkable objects in Shanus's collection, we begin to do just that.

The journey begins with six gentlemen in straw boater hats, captured in an original daguerreotype (an early form of photography based on an invention by French painter Louis Jacques Mande Daguerre) circa 1846 (see page 3). Much as Daguerre's new medium would "revolutionize picture making," these six men, who were members of the original New York Knickerbocker Base Ball Club, would revolutionize the game of "base ball." At the instigation of a shipping clerk named Alexander Joy Cartwright—who stands at the center of the back row of the daguerreotype—28 young men formed the Knickerbocker Club, baseball's first organized team, on September 23, 1845.

The Base Ball Player's Pocket Companion (above) is the first book dedicated entirely to baseball. Shanus's first edition from 1859 is one of only a handful of copies known to exist, and it provides details on the New York rules as well as the rules for the Massachusetts game, which was still popular in New England at the time. (5" x 3½")

Cartwright, along with fellow teammate Daniel Lucius "Doc" Adams—who would eventually invent the position of shortstop—helped draft the first written rules in modern baseball, an original copy of which is pictured on page 2. Many of these rules are still in play: the infield was to be diamond-shaped, rather than square, with three bases and a home plate; foul lines and 90-foot base paths were to be established; each side was to consist of nine-man teams with each player covering a specific position; batting was to be conducted in rotation; three outs were to retire a side; and runners were to be tagged or thrown out, not thrown *at*—a rule that changed an earlier custom known as "soaking."

In addition to Cartwright and Doc Adams, who was a physician, the Knickerbockers' roster included merchants, clerks, Wall Street brokers, insurance men, professional men, a bank teller, and a cigar dealer. If the team resembled a highbrow social club, that was no accident: In addition to baseball skills, a certain level of social standing was a prerequisite for admission as a member. It was only fitting, then, that games were often followed by lavish post-dinner banquets.

Initially, the Knickerbockers gathered to play during weekends in various Manhattan neighborhoods. But the city streets soon proved to be too congested, so they began taking the Barclay Street Ferry across the Hudson River to the Elysian Fields of Hoboken, New Jersey, where they rented a field. A portion of the Elysian Fields is visible in the bottom left corner of the spectacular advertising print on page 4. Part of Shanus's collection, the lithographic print was issued in 1868 by the Knickerbocker Mutual Life Insurance Company of New York, which had no relation to the baseball club.

Close examination of the image reveals

In the 1850s and 1860s, games between clubs were typically arranged through formal "challenge letters" (above). In the one on the left, prepared on June 5, 1860, the Star Base Ball Club of Brooklyn challenges the Knickerbockers of New York to a "best two-out-of-three" match. The letter, which was prepared by the club secretary, also refers to "balls to be taken on the fly," which means that a ball caught on the fly constituted an out. The Knickerbockers proposed this rule in 1857, but other teams opposed it, fearing injury to unprotected hands, since baseball players did not wear gloves at the time. The fly rule was not universally adopted until 1864. Before then, a batter could be counted out if a fielder caught his batted ball on one bounce. (8" x 6½")

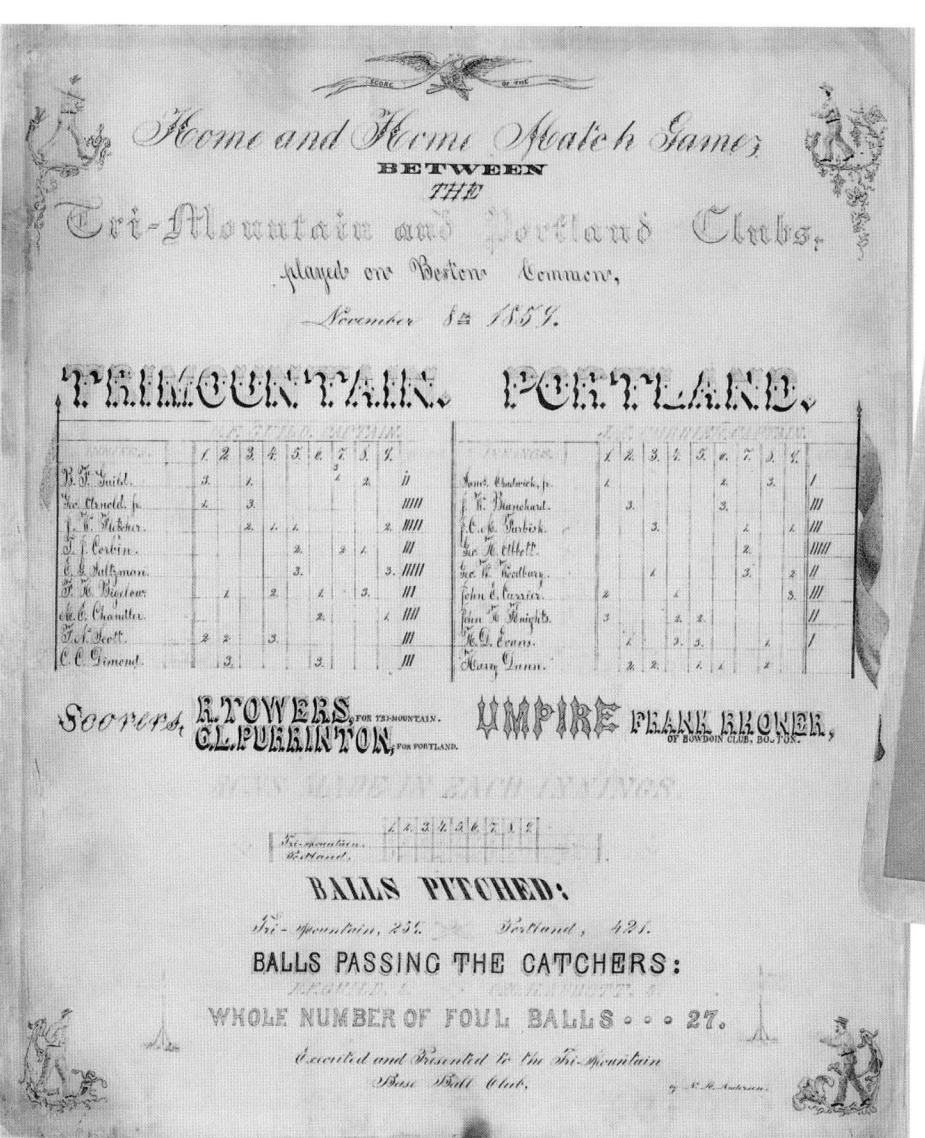

The scorecard (above) of a match game at Boston Common between the Tri-Mountain Club of Boston and the Portland Club of Maine, played on November 8, 1859, has been transformed into a presentation piece and now resides in Shanus's collection. It is one of the oldest baseball scorecards known to exist. Both the Tri-Mountains and the Portland Club played by the New York rules and helped popularize the New York game in New England, which eventually led to the extinction of the Massachusetts game. (12½" x 15")

The autographed cabinet photograph of Henry Chadwick (above right) dates to 1874. For more than five decades, Chadwick, referred to as the "Father of Baseball" by his contemporaries, served as the game's chief arbiter, foremost statistician, and consummate publicist. He is the only sportswriter enshrined in the Hall of Fame. (4" x 6")

not only two baseball fields separated by a refreshment pavilion, but also a turning point in the evolution of the game. The field to the left of the pavilion is square, and a batter stands in the middle of what would be referred to today as a base path. The two teams depicted on this field are playing the "Massachusetts game," an early version of baseball evolved from "town ball," which was an Americanized version of the English game of rounders. Popular in New England, the Massachusetts game was played with teams of twelve to twenty on each side. A smaller ball was used and runners were put out by soaking. On the field to the right of the pavilion, the batter and runners appear to be positioned at the corners of the field. This suggests that these teams are playing according to the rules of the "New York game" pioneered by the Knickerbockers.

By the late 1850s, the New York game

The ball used in the landmark match game between the New York Knickerbocker Club and the Gotham Club of New York on July 5, 1853, was transformed into a trophy (below) and presented to Henry Chadwick on the 50th anniversary of the historic game. The trophy ball, the earliest of its kind known to be in existence, commemorates the historic meeting at the Elysian Fields in Hoboken, and the Knickerbocker's 21–12 victory. There is an engraved tribute to Chadwick on its base. (Base: 8½" in diameter. Height: 10½")

Captured in a circa 1860 carte-de-visite (CDV), the Brooklyn Atlantics (right) were the preeminent team of the 1860s, winning five championships during the decade. This carte pre-dates by three to four years the next earliest known baseball CDV. (2½" x 4")

The 1865 Brooklyn Atlantics (below, in a mammoth plate salt print) were in the midst of a three-year run as "whip-pennant" champions, bolstered by three of their perennial stars—Joe Start, fourth from the left, Jack Chapman, fourth from the right, and Dickey Pearce, third from the left. (28½" x 24½")

"ATLANTIC TEN,"
CHAMPIONS OF AMERICA.
Photographed by C.H.Williamson, Brooklyn, 1865.

Mills. Zettlen. Pearce.
THE ATL

SMITHSONIAN BASEBALL: INSIDE THE WORLD'S FINEST PRIVATE COLLECTIONS

Hurley, Sub.; G. Wright, S.S.; Allison, C.; McVey, R. F.; Leonard, L. F.
Sweasy, 2d B.; Waterman, 3d B.; H. Wright, C. F.; Brainard, P.; Gould 1st B.

RED STOCKING B. B. CLUB OF CINCINNATI.

...art. Smith. Ferguson. Crane. Pratt. Chapman.

...ANTIC NINE. 1868.

Peck & Snyder, a prominent New York sporting goods and novelties merchant, was quick to see the value of baseball trade cards as an advertising medium. The company's 1868 Brooklyn Atlantics card (below left) and its 1869 Cincinnati Red Stockings card (left) each features an original photograph of the team, with the players' names printed below it, and a black-and-white Peck & Snyder advertisement on the reverse side. Asa Brainard, the Red Stockings' one and only pitcher, who was known as "Ace of the Staff," sits next to Harry Wright in the first row. (Atlantics trade card: 3" x 4") (Red Stocking trade card: 3½" x 4½")

On June 14, 1870, the Brooklyn Atlantics ended the Cincinnati Red Stockings' 92-game winning streak, scoring three runs in the bottom of the 11th inning to defeat the Cincinnati club 8–7, as reflected in the scorecard of the game (left inset) from Shanus's collection. The Red Stockings had barnstormed the country in 1869, going undefeated. The following year, they won another 27 consecutive games, extending their streak to 92 games without a loss before their fateful mid-June meeting with the Atlantics at the Capitoline Grounds in Brooklyn. This is the only scorecard from that historic contest known to be in existence. (8½" x 7")

would begin to displace the Massachusetts game, largely because the New York rules were more favorable to spectators: foul lines in the New York game allowed fans to get closer to the field; three outs per inning, rather than one, permitted more action; and limiting play to nine innings (by 1857) meant that games would conclude within about three hours, as opposed to the substantially longer time it would take for the winning team to score a hundred runs as required by the Massachusetts game. The changeover began in 1857 when a newly formed club from Boston called the Tri-Mountains decided to follow the New York rules. A year later, another New England team called the Portland Club of Maine also adopted the New York rules and agreed to play the Tri-Mountains on Boston Common. On November 8, 1859, these two teams met again—Shanus's original score-

JAMES CREIGHTON,

Pitcher of the EXCELSIOR BASE BALL CLUB of Brooklyn, N. Y.

LIVE OA[...]

Composed by

J. H. KALBFLEISCH.

ENDICOTT & CO. LITH. N.Y.

Ent'd according to Act of Congress in the year 1860 by J.P. Shaw

PUBLISHED BY JOS. P. S[...]

ROCHEST[...]

James Creighton, one of baseball's first superstars, appeared on an 1863 Peck & Snyder trade card (above). The picture is one of only two known photographic images of Creighton. (4" x 2½")

On October 21, 1861, pitcher James Creighton led an all-star team from Brooklyn against one from New York at Hoboken's Elysian Fields. The ball that Creighton pitched during the game (left) was hand-made by Al Reach, who also played in the game, and went on to become a sporting goods magnate. Reach would go on to display the ball on a trophy at the 1876 Centennial Exposition in Philadelphia. In addition to Creighton and Reach, that landmark game in Hoboken featured Harry Wright, who went on to manage the 1869 Red Stockings, and Dickey Pearce, the celebrated shortstop for the Atlantics during the 1860s. (Base: 8½" in diameter. Height: 4")

card from that game appears on page 7. The New York game was spreading throughout New England.

The Knickerbockers played their first official match game at the Elysian Fields on June 19, 1846, against a team that referred to itself as the New York Base Ball Club. Although the Knickerbockers lost 23–1, they would go on to dominate baseball in the New York area for the next decade. In a game played on July 5, 1853, at the Elysian Fields, the Knickerbockers defeated the Gotham Club of New York 21–12. The ball used in this game has miraculously survived the vagaries of time, and rests in Shanus's collection, as the centerpiece of a trophy, underneath three

In 1888, the E. & J. Burke ale brewing company issued a lithographic advertising poster (above) featuring the likenesses of Adrian C. "Cap" Anson of the Chicago White Stockings and Buck Ewing of the New York Giants. With its painterly graphic design and rich color palette, the poster is one of the most visually captivating 19th-century advertising prints, and the stature of the two players adds to its allure: Anson batted over .300 for 20 straight seasons and was the first player to accumulate 3,000 hits. He later became manager of the White Stockings. Ewing had a throwing arm so strong it was said that he could "have handed the ball to the second baseman from the batter's box." (23½" x 18")

Baseball was alive and well in Rochester, New York, in 1860, as evidenced by the sheet music for Mr. J. H. Kalbfleisch's "Live Oak Polka" (above), published that year. The song commemorates the Live Oak Base Ball Club of Rochester and the sheet music is the first to feature baseball in chromolithographic art. (12" x 9½").

crossed bats and on top of a metal-and-wood circular base (see page 7). The ball has been coated with what appears to be lead-based paint, and inscribed with the date of the game, the score, and the contestants in black, handwritten print. During this era, it was common for the winning team to claim the ball used in the game and then record the outcome on it.

The historic Elysian Fields ball, which is the earliest known trophy ball in existence, remained in the care of the Knickerbocker Club until 1903, when it was presented to Henry Chadwick on the 50th anniversary of that match game. Chadwick, a British-born journalist who helped popularize and develop the sport during the 19th century,

introduced, among other things, statistical benchmarks like batting averages and earned runs, as well as the newspaper box score. He published and edited a number of baseball guides and yearbooks and was widely referred to by his contemporaries as the "Father of Baseball."

The Gotham Club appeared around 1850, and until 1852 it represented the Knickerbockers only serious competitor. The excitement generated from games played between these two teams inspired others to form clubs of their own. By 1854, New York had two more well-organized clubs—the Eagles and the Empires—and by the end of the decade, the four New York clubs were joined by one from the Bronx

They may look peculiar to contemporary eyes, but the uniforms worn by the "Atwaters" (above), captured in a full-plate tintype photograph from 1859, were customary for the period. Ten years later, the Cincinnati Red Stockings' Harry Wright introduced "knickers" to replace the long pants. (10" x 8½")

(Unions of Morrisania) and four from Brooklyn (the Excelsiors, Putnams, Eckfords, and Atlantics).

The 1860s were auspicious times for organized baseball in Brooklyn. Up until 1867, a club from Brooklyn won the series championship (known as the "whip pennant") every year: the Eckfords in 1862 and 1863, and the Atlantics every other year. The decade also saw the rise of clubs comprised of men other than those of "higher social standing." The Eckfords were dockworkers; the Atlantics, working-class men. The Atlantics were bolstered by talent like that of first baseman Joe Start, who earned his nickname, "Old Reliable," for his ability to catch even the most errant throws. Outfielder Jack Chapman was just as accomplished, especially at catching balls over his shoulder, and he was known as "Death to Flying Things." Shanus's collection includes three diverse examples of 19th-century photographs featuring the Atlantics during their decade of reign: an 1860 carte de visite (CDV)—a paper print pasted on a mount

measuring 4" x 2½"; an 1865 mammoth-plate salt print (a large print made with salt solution and silver nitrate); and an 1868 trade card issued in conjunction with advertising by Peck & Snyder, a prominent New York sporting goods and novelties merchant.

Despite the recognition bestowed on Start and Chapman, Brooklyn's—and in fact baseball's—first real superstar was pitcher James Creighton, who started his career at the age of 17 and went on to national renown with the Brooklyn Excelsiors. In an 1863 Peck & Snyder trade card (see page 10), Creighton is portrayed throwing a ball underhand, as the rules required at the time. The rules also required pitchers to toss the ball gently over the plate without snapping their wrist during delivery. But Creighton managed to snap his wrist without being detected, generating speed on the ball "as swift as [if] sent from a cannon." He bewildered most of his opposing batsmen, who stood only 45 feet from the pitcher's box—another rule at the time.

During a barnstorming tour with the

UNION PRISONERS AT SALISBURY, N.C.

DRAWN FROM NATURE BY ACT. MAJOR OTTO BOETTCHER

Excelsiors in 1860, Creighton proved to be the game's first big draw. Fans in upstate New York, Pennsylvania, Maryland, and Delaware came out in droves to see him pitch. Creighton's dominance continued into the following year at the Grand Match, the first baseball match game to be played for a trophy. On November 21, 1861, at the Elysian Fields, an "all-star" team from Brooklyn took on an all-star team from New York. Creighton pitched Brooklyn to an 18–6 win. The lemon peel–style baseball used in this game is mounted on a circular black wooden base in Shanus's collection—thrown by the game's first star, it's a glorious relic (see page 10). Tragically, Creighton's reign was cut short the following

year, when he died from a ruptured bladder after hitting a home run against the Unions of Morrisania. His stature was so widespread by then that the president of the Excelsiors, concerned that American mothers would deem baseball too dangerous for their sons, told reporters that the accident had happened while Creighton was playing cricket, not baseball.

By 1861, the popularity of the New York game had spread beyond the region. The convention of the National Association of Base Ball Players that year drew delegates from as far as Philadelphia, New Haven, Baltimore, Detroit, and Washington, D.C. Although the Civil War temporarily slowed the overall pace of baseball's growth, it actually

An 1863 lithographic print (above) from Shanus's collection is one of the earliest color displays featuring baseball: The piece depicts Union soldiers playing the game at Salisbury Prison in North Carolina. Salisbury began housing Civil War prisoners in December 1861, and its population swelled to approximately 1,400 by the following May. It was then, reportedly, that baseball was first played on the grounds, introduced by POWs captured during battles in New Orleans and Tuscaloosa. The men played in the prison's large open courtyard, getting a much-needed respite from prison life. (21" x 37½")

THE POLO GROUNDS
NEW YORK

NEW YORK

SEASON OF 1887.

HOME GAMES OF THE NEW YORK BALL CLUB FOR THE LEAGUE CHAMPIONSHIP.

April 28, 29,	with Philadelphia,	June 9, 10, 11,	with Washington,	Aug. 22, 23,	with Pittsburg,
May 5, 6, 7,	" Boston,	" 13, 14, 15,	" Philadelphia,	" 25, 26, 27,	" Chicago,
" 9, 10, 11,	" Washington,	July 7, 8, 9,	" Detroit,	" 29, 30, 31,	" Indianapolis,
" 14,	" Philadelphia,	" 11, 12, 13,	" Pittsburg,	Sept. 1, 2, 3,	" Detroit,
" 16, 17, 18,	" Indianapolis,	" 15, 16, 18,	" Chicago.	" 5, 6, 7,	" Washington,
" 20, 21, 23, 24,	" Pittsburg,	" 19, 20, 21,	" Indianapolis,	" 26, 27, 28,	" Boston,
" 26, 27, 28,	" Detroit,	" 23, 25, 26,	" Boston,	Oct. 5. 6. 8.	" Philadelphia
Decoration Day " 30 A.M.&P.M., 31,	" Chicago.				

helped entrench the game's popularity in the South, chiefly because Northern prisoners played baseball in Southern Confederate prison camps, as illustrated in the magnificent lithographic print on the previous page, entitled *Union Prisoners at Salisbury, N.C.* The illustration, drawn "from nature" by Acting Major Otto Boetticher in 1862, depicts Union prisoners playing baseball under the watchful eye of Confederate guards at North Carolina's Salisbury Confederate Prison.

Baseball's amateur status was slowly yielding to the rise of professionalism by the late 1860s. As ballplayers started to receive salaries for their services, they began to focus on becoming experts in one particular position—be it pitcher, infielder, or outfielder—and the overall standard of play rose considerably, a development that attracted more paying customers. The catalyst for this evolution was a man named Harry Wright, who was no stranger to the baseball phenomenon in New York: He had played with the Knickerbockers in 1858. Wright foresaw baseball's potential as a paying profession and would eventually become manager of the game's first all-professional club, the 1869 Cincinnati Red Stockings, each of whose players received a

A stunning 1887 lithographic print (left) from the Shanus collection presents a delightful tableau of the Old Polo Grounds. The home schedule of the New York Ball Club appears beneath the print, whose detail, size, and classic folk-art qualities make it an extraordinary example of 19th-century American graphic art. There are only two examples of this print known to exist; the other is housed in the collection of The Library of Congress. (43½" x 39")

Counting second-stringers, the Hudson River Nine in Shanus's mammoth plate hand-colored salt print from 1865 (below) actually number 18. One of the earliest known examples of this panoramic style of baseball team photographs, the portrait is composed of three attached 12" x 12" photographs, and the entire image, including the floor and the background, was painted to maintain an image of continuity. The 18 men in the portrait comprised one team out of approximately 20 that played relatively regular schedules in New York's Hudson Valley at the time. This team represented Newburgh and competed against nines from towns like Troy and Albany. Many of the players were paid to play, a practice that would lead to the formation of the all-professional 1869 Cincinnati Red Stockings. (36" x 12")

salary. The 10-man squad, pictured in an 1869 Peck & Snyder trade card (see page 9), finished the season with 65 wins and no losses, a victory for the concept of professional squads. But the team disbanded the following year after losing to the Brooklyn Atlantics and seeing its 92-game winning streak halted.

Wright nevertheless remained committed to his vision of professionalizing the game, and he moved the Red Stockings to Boston. Before his death in 1895, Wright instituted a number of key innovations, including hand signals, pregame batting practice, and the drill of hitting fungo fly balls to outfielders before a game. Wright also helped design the face mask for catchers and introduced flannel knickers as part of a ballplayer's uniform—a style used, with some variations, by major-league baseball to this day.

By the 1880s, baseball was not only an established professional sport, it was also big business. Companies exploited the game's genteel, recreational character to promote their products. American cigarette makers like Allen & Ginter and Goodwin & Company produced tobacco cards and posters (examples of the latter appear in Chapter IV, "The Gary Cypres Collection"). E. & J. Burke, a renowned Irish brewery, issued a beautiful lithographic advertising print in 1888. To promote its "Finest Pale Ale" and "Extra Foreign Stout,"

Burke chose wisely, tapping future Hall of Famers Adrian C. "Cap" Anson of the Chicago White Stockings and Buck Ewing of the New York Giants. Anson had led his team to five pennants between 1880 and 1886; and Ewing, widely companynsidered the best all-around player of the 19th century, led the New York Giants to their first National League pennant, in 1888. The poster, which appears on page 11, portrays Anson and Ewing leisurely sipping their brew in front of a tent, with a baseball game going on behind them.

Another companylor lithographic print (see opposite page) bears a schedule of the 1887 Giants' home games and features a stylized illustration of a game at the club's ballpark, the Polo Grounds on 110th Street. With its pennants fluttering in the breeze, and rows of horse-drawn carriages standing in wait for lavishly dressed men and women, the scene has a festive, fanciful air. Even in the sport's earliest days, a baseball game was an event.

In the many years since then, grass has obscured the base paths at the Elysian Fields, and a housing development has taken the place of the Polo Grounds. And though the days of the Knickerbockers are long gone, and the Giants have moved to California, the ingenuity and spirit of the baseball they played remain vividly alive in Shanus's fine collection.

19TH-CENTURY MEMORABILIA

BY COREY R. SHANUS AND BARRY SLOATE

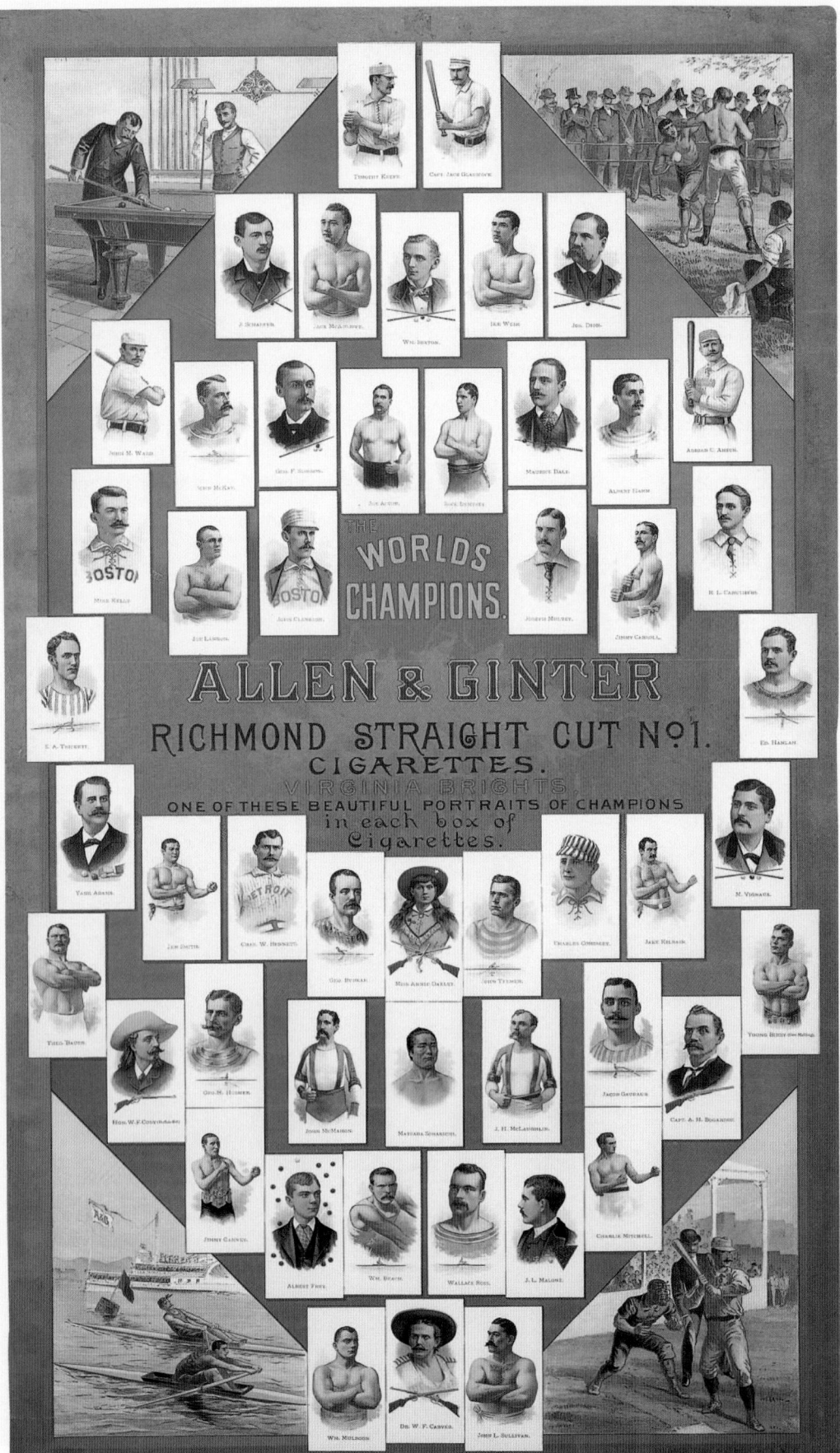

Collecting 19th-century baseball memorabilia is a multifaceted undertaking. While the most conventional and widely known items from this period are baseball cards, the array of collecting possibilities is vast and includes photographs, sheet music, trophy bats and balls, and lithographic prints and posters. Let's consider each one in turn.

BASEBALL CARDS

Baseball cards are an important part of any 19th-century collection, especially those from 1886 to 1890, a period collectors often call "the first golden age" of baseball-card production. More than 25 issues, encompassing thousands of cards, flooded the marketplace. Produced primarily by cigarette and tobacco companies and marketed as inserts with their goods, the intriguing swatches of cardboard featured either state-of-the-art color lithography or handsome sepia-toned photographs of the most notable players of the era. The surprisingly large number of these cards that survives today can be loosely divided into three categories: 1) relatively common items, for which it would not be overly challenging to obtain every card of a given set; 2) rare pieces, for which a single example from an issue would suffice (this popular approach is known as "type" collecting); and 3) the ultra-rare collectibles, for which there remain no more than five cards, or even as few as one. Few of the cards in this third category will ever become available, even to the most advanced collector.

In 1887, Allen & Ginter issued the first full color set of tobacco cards, inserted inside packs of their cigarettes. The cards depicted all kinds of sports champions, from boxers, rowers, and wrestlers, to marksmen, billiard players, and baseball players. To augment sales, the company produced spectacular color chromolithographic posters (left) for display at tobacconist stores. Part of Gary Cypres's collection, the poster is one of only six of its kind known to exist. (16" x 28")

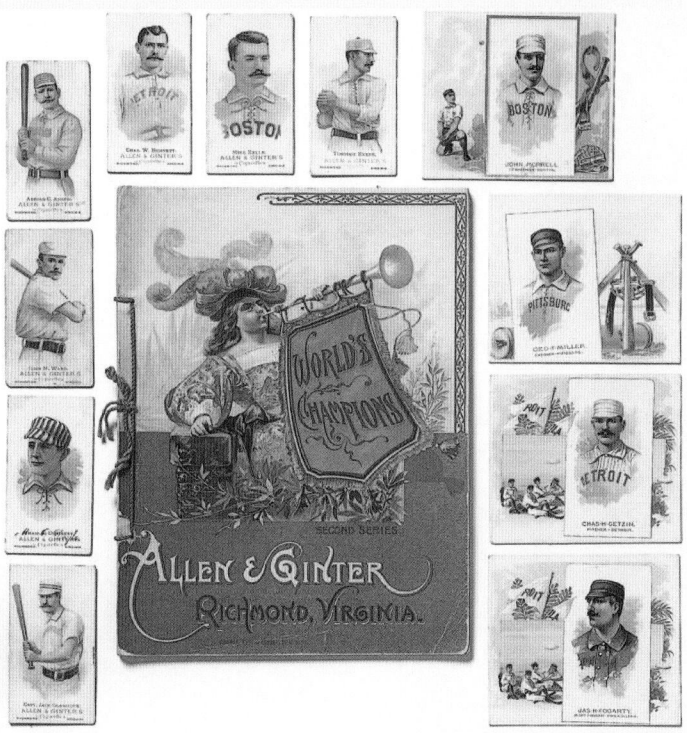

In conjunction with its N28 and N29 tobacco-card issues, Allen & Ginter produced premium color lithographic sports albums. Gary Cypres owns an album (above) from the N29 series, and its interior pages feature exact replicas of all 50 of the N29 cards produced in 1888. To acquire the album, customers needed to accumulate coupons from Allen & Ginter cigarette products. To the right of the album are examples of Allen & Ginter's N43 cards.

In 1887, Old Judge Cigarettes converted some of its uncut sheets of N172 baseball cards into advertising displays. Shanus owns a particularly interesting one (right) that features the cards of several legendary 19th-century Hall of Famers, including Dan Brouthers, Ned Hanlon, Mike "King" Kelly, Charles Comiskey, and John Ward. (13½" x 9¾")

The first major issue of baseball cards was produced in 1887 by the tobacco firm of Goodwin & Company and distributed in packages of Old Judge cigarettes. They have an American Card Catalog (ACC, the first reference and pricing source on baseball cards) designation of N172 (the "N" signifies 19th century in the ACC, and the 172 is an arbitrary number assigned to that card issue). These small cards consisted of sepia toned photographs glued onto thick cardboard mounts. They depicted well over 500 different subjects, including all the stars of the day from both the major and the minor leagues. Because nearly all of the players appeared in multiple poses, there are more than 2,000 cards from this issue. Although collecting the entire issue is almost impossible, compiling formidable groupings is a popular challenge for collectors. Many collectors seek to acquire a single example of each Hall of Famer

from this period, for example. The most sought-after subjects include Cap Anson, Mike Kelly, Buck Ewing, John Ward, Connie Mack, John Clarkson, Dan Brouthers, Pud Galvin, Amos Rusie, Harry Wright, Tim Keefe, and Charles Comiskey.

Other collectors strive to procure cards featuring each player from a favorite team, cards that show players in unusual poses, portrait cards (since nearly all are N172s are full-length studio poses), multiplayer cards, or cards of umpires and managers. Collection subsets range from world champion St. Louis Browns players to New York Metropolitans sporting their fancy spotted ties. Whatever the substantive goal of an Old Judge collection may be, the budget invariably helps determine its scope.

Examples of these cards are shown above right on a rare advertising sign made of an uncut sheet of 24 N172s glued onto thick cardboard. The edges

were stamped with bright red lettering touting the baseball cards. The signs, which hung in tobacconists' stores, heralded the set and encouraged smokers to buy Old Judge cigarettes.

Goodwin also issued a group of large cabinet photographs, known as N173, which reproduced many of the photos from N172. These special items were acquired directly from the company by redeeming coupons that came with the cigarettes.

In 1887 and 1888, the Allen & Ginter Company produced three full-color 50-card sets of sports champions, including baseball stars (see poster, opposite). These sets are extremely popular with collectors today. The first, cataloged as N28, features 10 baseball players, six of whom are members of the Hall of Fame. The second series, designated N29 and issued the following year, contains only six ballplayers, with Buck Ewing as the lone Hall of Famer. The third series, N43, displays images that

are identical to those in N29 but in a larger and more ornate format (see above left). The N28 and N29 sets can be completed with a bit of patience, but the N43 is a great challenge to assemble.

Many other issues appeared in the last four years of the 1880s, among them the Kimball, Goodwin's Champions, and Buchner gold coin releases. Each of these issues featured beautiful color images. In the mid-1890s, Mayo and Company issued a 48-card set, designated N300, with sepia portraits of many of the day's stars. They are classics of the period.

Many collectors try to obtain a single example of the era's scarcer issues, which include Lone Jack, Yum Yum, Kalamazoo Bats, S. F. Hess, and G & B chewing gum (one of the few period issues that is not tobacco-related). Perhaps the most popular of these was the Kalamazoo Bats, issued by Charles Gross and cataloged as N690. This large issue of about

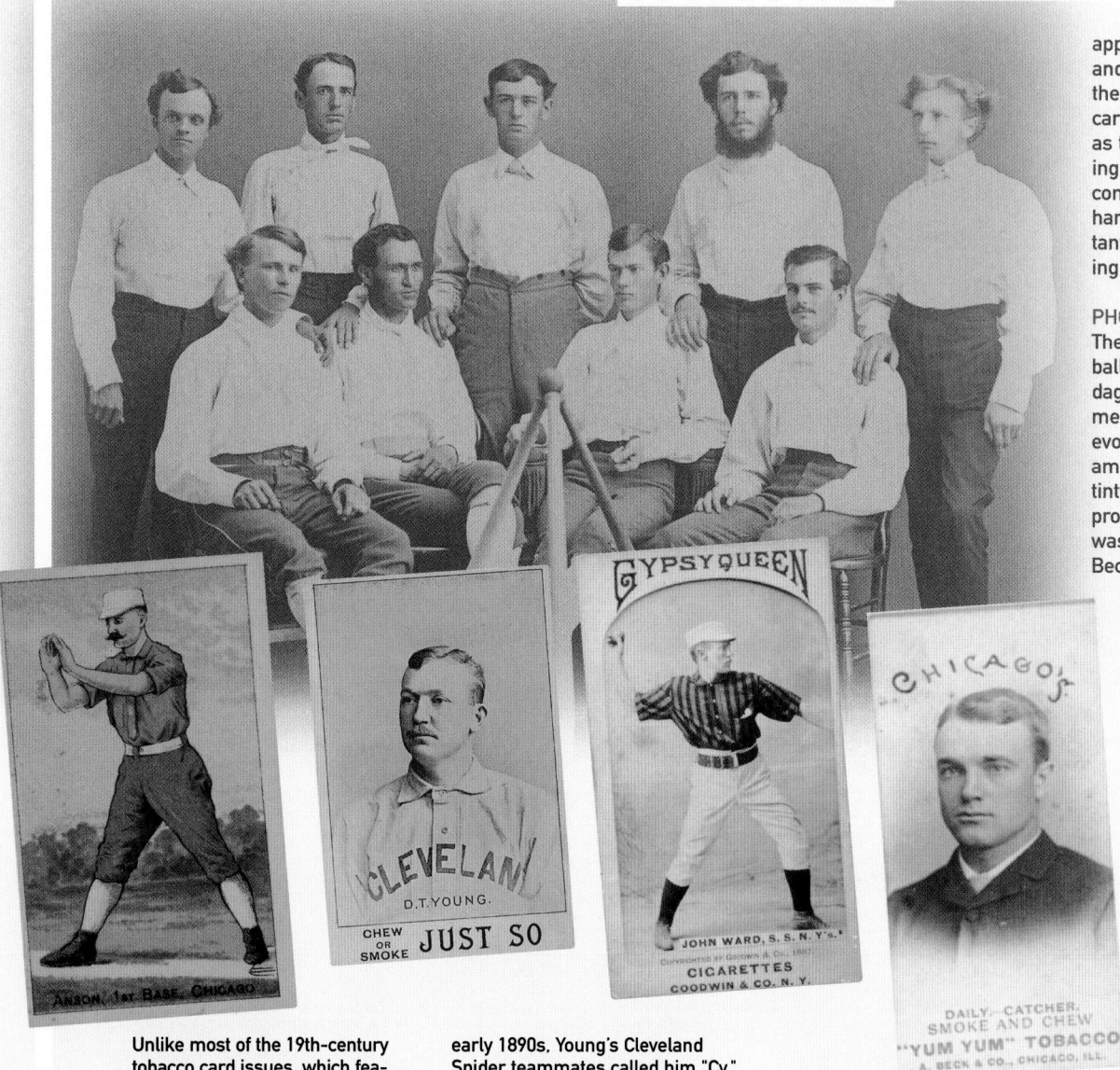

appearance on a baseball card, and there is only one example of the immortal pitcher's Just So card known to exist. Cards such as these are the stuff of collecting legend. They may never come up for sale, but the die-hard collector lives for the ever-tantalizing possibility of acquiring one.

PHOTOGRAPHS

The earliest 19th-century baseball photographic images are daguerreotypes ("dags"). As the medium of photography rapidly evolved, dags were replaced by ambrotypes ("ambros") and then tintypes. With each of these processes, every image created was, by definition, unique. Because the negative itself was the image—a reverse rendering, in fact—no prints could be made. In a dag, the image appears on a silver-coated copper plate. An ambro image is created with a collodion binder (a chemical process) on a glass plate (with a black background to bring out the image). A tintype image uses a collodion binder on a tin plate. A particularly outstanding example of a baseball tintype is the full-plate of the circa 1859 Atwaters, resplendent in their period baseball attire (see page 12). Dags, ambros, and tintypes come in various sizes. The largest is a full-plate measuring 6" x 8". Other sizes are half-plates (4" x 5"), quarter-plates (3" x 4"), sixth-plates (2" x 3"), and ninth-plates (2" x 2"). Not surprisingly, all other considerations being equal, the larger the image, the greater its value. Only three confirmed baseball dags exist: a half-plate of six members of the 1840s New York Knickerbockers, and a quarter-plate and a sixth-plate of Alexander Cartwright (who helped draft the first written rules in modern baseball) with an unidentified gentleman, taken in Hawaii in the 1850s. The value of a baseball dag is many times more than that of a baseball ambro or tintype.

By the mid- to late-1850s, positive photographic images generated from negatives began to appear. Although this means that, technically, the images are

Unlike most of the 19th-century tobacco card issues, which featured sepia-toned images, the 1887 N284 Buchner gold coin cards, including Cap Anson's (above) were produced in color lithography. Courtesy of MastroNet, Inc.

In Shanus's cabinet-sized team photograph of the 1868 Marshalltown, Iowa, club (top), Anson stands in the back row, far right. (4" x 6")

The 1893 Just So tobacco card for legendary pitcher Cy Young (above inset) lists the initials of his real name: Denton True Young. In the

early 1890s. Young's Cleveland Spider teammates called him "Cy," a pejorative nickname for an out-of-place farmboy from Ohio, though another story has it that Young's nickname was short for "cyclone," due to the speed of his pitches. The winningest pitcher in baseball history, Young once told his teammates, "All us Youngs could throw. I used to kill squirrels with a stone when I was a kid, and my granddad once killed a turkey buzzard on the fly with a rock." With 511 career wins, Young leads his nearest competitor in the category, Walter Johnson, by 94 victories. (2½" x 3⅞")

An 1887 N175 Large Gypsy Queen cigarettes card (above) shows Hall of Famer shortstop John Montgomery Ward, a graduate of Columbia Law School who helped found the Brotherhood of Professional Base Ball Players to fight the reserve clause. This was the first time players attempted to organize for a cause. (2" x 3⁷⁄₁₆") Image courtesy of MastroNet, Inc.

1888 N403 Yum Yum tobacco card. (1⅜" x 2¹¹⁄₁₆") Image courtesy of MastroNet, Inc.

50 cards can be divided into four groups. The first three feature shots of individual players on the Philadelphia Athletics, the New York Giants, and the New York Metropolitans. The fourth contains full-team poses. Each of the four types is distinctive. The Philadelphia players, all of whom appear in outdoor photographs, are by far the most commonly found, but the set is

all but impossible to complete. A collection of even six different cards would be considered an achievement. Gross also issued a group of even larger cabinet images. One of these, an image of baseball pioneer Harry Wright, is extremely rare and particularly desirable.

Extremely rare card issues, such as Four Base Hits, Just So, and the Large Gypsy Queens,

represent a formidable challenge to collectors looking for just a single example. Two of the great rarities of this group are the Four Base Hits collectible of legendary player Mike Kelly, of which only two examples are known to exist, and the Just So card of Cy Young (above; the Just So set included only Cleveland Spiders, Young's team from 1890 to 1898). This was Young's first

An 1890 hand-colored full-plate tintype of George Davis (above). (15¼" x 13"). The Corey R. Shanus Collection.

William Arthur "Candy" Cummings, who is credited with inventing the curve ball, appears in Shanus's composite mammoth plate of the 1873 Baltimore Base Ball Club

(right). Legend has it that Cummings got the idea from watching thrown clam shells in flight. To his left is Lipman Pike, one of the first noteworthy Jewish pro ballplayers. (28½" x 24½")

The sheet music for "The Base Ball Quadrille" (below right) was published in 1867. (10" x 13")

not unique, there is rarely more than one known original print of them in existence today. The chemical media used to produce positive photographic prints evolved over time. First came salt prints, then albumen prints. These were followed in order by collodion prints and silver gelatin prints. With each change, picture quality improved, and the cost of producing prints went down.

The smallest prints were the cartes de visite (CDVs), which appeared around 1860. They consisted of an albumen photograph attached to a cardboard mount measuring approximately 2½" x 4". Typically, the photographic studio of origin was identified on verso (backside) of the CDV, often with copyright information noted as well. In the mid-1860s, sporting goods manufacturers such as the prominent firm of Peck & Snyder introduced photographic trade cards that were slightly larger than CDVs. Like CDVs, trade cards consisted of albumen photographs on cardboard mounts. The front of the cards depicted important teams of the era while the verso served as

advertising space for the sporting goods manufacturer. Most of the known examples of trade cards were at some point trimmed to CDV size, undoubtedly to allow them to be inserted in CDV-size frames and albums of the period.

The earliest known trade card portrays James Creighton, the renowned pitcher for the Brooklyn Excelsiors (see page **10**). The card dates to around 1863 and was issued by Peck & Snyder in response to the player's untimely death. It is the only known trade card depicting an individual ballplayer. By contrast, seven team trade cards are known to exist. They represent the 1868 Lowells of Boston, the 1868 Brooklyn Atlantics, the 1869 Cincinnati Red Stockings, the 1870 New York Mutuals, the 1870 Chicago White Stockings, the 1870 Philadelphia Athletics, and the 1872 Philadelphia Athletics.

"Cabinet" cards appeared in the late 1860s. These, too, are albumen prints, but their cardboard mounts are approximately 4" x 6". A good example is the circa-1868 Marshalltown team photo on page **18**. Its image is

especially significant as it contains the earliest known baseball likeness of Adrian C. "Cap" Anson, arguably the greatest player of the 19th century. Photographs affixed to mounts larger than the standard cabinet are referred to as "imperial" cabinets (they vary in size, with a number of examples reaching 8" x 10"). "Mammoth" plates constitute the largest photographic images and can be more than twice the size of

THE AMERICAN NATIONAL GAME OF BASE BALL.
GRAND MATCH FOR THE CHAMPIONSHIP AT THE ELYSIAN FIELDS, HOBOKEN, N.J.

In a striking lithographic print (above, from Bill DeWitt's collection), Nathaniel Currier and James Merritt Ives reproduced a scene from the first Grand Match for the Championship of the United States on August 3, 1865. The Brooklyn Atlantics won the game, which was played at the Elysian Fields in Hoboken, New Jersey, defeating the New York Mutuals 13–12. In the print, the Atlantics are at bat, the Mutuals are in the field, and Henry Chadwick, overseeing the game, stands just in front of the crowd. Later that month, the Atlantics won the second game of the series 40–28, becoming organized baseball's first national champion. (20" x 30")

Corey Shanus owns the bat (left) that was given to the Tri-Mountain Base Ball Club of Boston in 1867 and is depicted on the cover of "The Base Ball Quadrille" sheet music.

imperial cabinets. Imperial cabinets and mammoth plates are not limited to albumen prints. Some are salt prints, collodion prints, and silver gelatin prints. The 1873 Baltimore Baseball Club composite mammoth plate (on page 19) is particularly interesting. Individual CDVs of each player were mounted onto a backing. An overlay with oval cutouts displays the player portraits, and calligraphy identifies the players and the team. This particular composite was probably a "proof" of a CDV of the 1873 Baltimore team. A photograph of this composite affixed to a CDV mount constituted the "final" CDV.

While dags and ambros began to disappear when positive photographic images came into being, tintypes persisted into the 1890s. They were less expensive than dags, and a great deal more durable than the glass ambros. Sometimes a tintype would be colored by hand to enhance its appearance. The circa 1890 full-plate tintype of Hall of Famer George Davis on page 19 is an example of a hand-colored tintype.

BASEBALL SHEET MUSIC

Sheet music is an important aspect of 19th-century Americana. With baseball's growing popularity in the 1860s, baseball images began to appear on the covers of selected sheet music. By far the most desirable examples of collectible sheet music are those with chromolithographic baseball images. The four earliest known sheet music covers are the "Live Oak Polka" (1860; see page 11), "The Home Run Quick Step" (1861), "The Base Ball Polka" (1867), and "The Base Ball Quadrille" (1867, see previous page). "The Base Ball Quadrille" is particularly interesting, because the song was dedicated to the Tri-Mountain Base Ball Club of Boston, which won the New England Championship of 1867. A rendering of the trophy bat appears on the sheet music's cover. Like other baseball memorabilia, sheet music can be collected according to teams. Although sheet music associated with specific teams was not produced in color, the engravings have plenty of aesthetic merit. The most popular and valuable sheet music of this kind is The Red Stockings', dating from 1869. The cover features each member of the 1869 Cincinnati Red Stockings, baseball's first professional team.

TROPHY BATS AND BALLS

Trophy bats and balls constitute an extremely popular area of 19th-century baseball memorabilia. The most valuable trophy balls are from the 1850s and 1860s. Before the birth of baseball's first professional league, the National Association, in 1871, baseball matches were arranged through interclub correspondence called "challenge letters." After the match, the losing team customarily presented the game ball to the winning team, often at a formal banquet. Teams commonly made a trophy ball by painting the game ball and inscribing the date and the score on it. Usually, a trophy ball was mounted on a base or affixed in the winning club's trophy case, so most trophy balls have some type of hole, usually in an inconspicuous location, out of view of the inscription. Because of their eye-

Premium sports photo albums were a popular form of 19th-century baseball-oriented promotional items. In 1888, the tobacco firm of Goodwin & Company produced a circular album (far right) to complement their more traditional album (near right). Both of them were available by mail only in exchange for coupons (right, below) that came with Goodwin tobacco products. The Gary Cypres Collection.

Shanus's remarkable collection includes an 1896 color print

(below) commemorating the inaugural "Temple Cup" in 1894 between the Baltimore Orioles and the New York Giants. A precursor to the modern World Series, which began in 1903, the Temple Cup came about when Pittsburgh entrepeneur William C. Temple donated an $800 trophy cup to the winner of a seven-game, postseason series between the first- and second-place team in the National League. (30½" x 44")

catching qualities, gold-painted trophy balls are among the most coveted collectors' items. Silver-plated balls were presented to the winner of a tournament or championship game, also with the game information engraved on the ball.

Trophy bats are particularly rare, even by the standards of 19th-century baseball memorabilia. Most were prizes awarded to the winners of tournament or championship games, or to players for specific, noteworthy achievements. A truly outstanding example is the bat, visible on the opposite page, given to the Tri-Mountain club of Boston after it won the 1867 New England Base Ball Tournament. Silver mounts identifying the scores of the tournament's games are attached to the bat, which itself is constructed of various historically significant woods from the 1860s. The different woods are labeled KEARSAGE and ALABAMA (Civil War battleships), BOSTON ELM, HANCOCK HOUSE, TREE UNDER WHICH GEN. LEE SURRENDERED, and

LINCOLN CABIN. The bat is housed in a custom-made wooden case from the period, which is adorned with illustrations of crossed bats, a cap, and a ball. As we've said, this trophy bat appears on "The Base Ball Quadrille" sheet music cover from the same year.

LITHOGRAPHIC PRINTS AND POSTERS

Lithographic prints and posters represent baseball art at its finest. The earliest examples are hand-colored lithographs from the 1860s. Four such lithographs are known to exist: *Union Prisoners at Salisbury, N.C.*, by Otto Boetticher (1863; see page 13), which shows Union prisoners playing baseball at the Salisbury prisoner-of-war camp in North Carolina; *The American National Game of Base Ball*, by Currier and Ives (1866; opposite page), which depicts an 1865 championship game between the Brooklyn Atlantics and the New York Mutuals; *The Second Great Match for the Championship*, by

J. L. Magee (1867), a depiction of an 1866 championship game between the Brooklyn Atlantics and the Philadelphia Athletics; and *Panorama of New York and Vicinity*, by J. Bachman (1866, reprinted 1868; see page 4), which shows the Elysian Fields in Hoboken. A version of this last print without the hand-coloring also exists. All of these prints are extremely rare and highly sought after by collectors.

Among the most valuable baseball posters are spectacular color stone lithographs that were created for advertising purposes. Among the items and events that these posters advertise are baseball card sets (such as those from Allen & Ginter, Old Judge, and Buchner gold coins), the Old Judge Round Album (a color, premium album, above, depicting famous baseball

players), baseball's World Tour in 1888–89 (organized by Albert Spalding), New York's Polo Grounds (where the Giants played) and such commodities as ale and cigars. As you might expect, these posters, most of which date from the 1880s, are extremely rare and highly coveted.

Another desirable print from the period is one made in 1896 by Boussod, Valadon and Company. Taken from an 1894 painting by Hy Sandham, the print (below left) depicts that year's Temple Cup series between the Baltimore Orioles and the New York Giants. Above and below the game scene are portraits of key baseball players and executives from the period. Almost all copies of the print are black-and-white, although there is one known version that shows the game scene in color (with the portraits in black-and-white) and another version that shows both the game scene and the portraits in color. In 1897, the print was reissued without the portraits. This later version is in color, although the hues are less vibrant than in the 1896 color version.

As you can see, some very special baseball relics survive from the 19th century. Items from this period are guaranteed to enhance any collection and engage the imagination of enthusiasts who seek to acquire them. Given their rarity and uniqueness, 19th-century relics are found primarily at major sports memorabilia auctions.

WHEN IT WAS A GAME

RULES FOR PLAYING
THE NEW
Parlor Game of Base Ball.

RULE FIRST.

RULE SECOND.

RULE THIRD.

RULE FOURTH.

RULE FIFTH.

Issued by N. B. Sumner in 1869, the New Parlor Game of Base Ball (left) is the earliest baseball game known to exist. The game's illustration reflects the style of baseball at the time: There are no players' benches, the fielders are not wearing gloves, and they are dressed in the bib uniforms customary for the era. (17" x 12")

McLoughlin Brothers produced Zimmer's Base Ball Game (right) in 1893. The game took its name from Charles "Chief" Zimmer, who revolutionized the catcher's position in 1887, when he crouched directly behind home plate for every pitch. (Before then, catchers positioned themselves several feet away, fearing injury from foul tips.) Six years later, Zimmer helped revolutionize player-endorsed baseball games by lending his name and likeness to a stunning board game that featured 17 other player endorsements, by far the most of any similar product of its time. The field of play contained nine spring "catches" to catch the wooden ball off of the swivel-mounted bat. The ball was pitched by a spring-loaded device in the center of the board. (20" x 20")

> " Baseball's time is seamless and invisible, a bubble within which players move at exactly the same pace and rhythms as all their predecessors. This is the way the game was played in our youth and in our fathers' youth, and even back then— back in the country days—there must have been the same feeling that time could be stopped."
>
> —ROGER ANGELL, *The Interior Stadium*

Long before Monopoly, Scrabble, and Twister reached the living rooms of American households, games and toys related to the national pastime provided adults and children with a great source of home recreation and an entertaining survey of baseball, its rules, and its history.

Baseball is the ideal sport to capture in a board game, card game, or action game, because in each of these games, as in baseball, time is not a factor. This sense of timelessness underlies the beauty and unique quality of Mark Cooper's collection of baseball artifacts. As a child, growing up in Philadelphia in the late 1950s through the 1960s, Mark spent idyllic afternoons rolling the dice, spinning the tin wheels, and flipping the cards of baseball-based games and toys. He was playing out his big-league fantasies of fielding a sharply hit grounder like Brooks Robinson, hitting a

home run like Mickey Mantle, or throwing a knee-high slider like Sandy Koufax. With every spin of the wheel or roll of the dice, he could imagine seeing 19th-century Hall of Famer Dan Brouthers blast a homer over the rightfield wall at Congress Street Grounds with a "ring bat," or Tris Speaker line a double off the wall at Fenway Park. Playing these colorful, baseball-themed games, young Mark could picture Carl Hubbell fanning Ducky Medwick with a screwball at the Polo Grounds, or Frank Robinson robbing Willie McCovey of a late-inning homer, snagging a line drive against the wall at Candlestick Park. Mark could bring the Miracle Braves, the Gashouse Gang, or the 1969 Amazing Mets back to life.

He was part of a generation of children who nurtured their baseball fantasies through board games and toys. The oldest baseball board game known to exist, the New Parlor Game of Base Ball, was issued by N. B. Sumner in 1869, before baseball was a professionally organized sport. These games and toys represent more than a symbolic relic of childhood and baseball dreams. They embody the rich traditions of family life and portray the evolution of organized baseball through several generations after the Civil War.

Cooper's collection includes a number of

McLoughlin's Game of Base-Ball (above), issued in 1886, featured two spinners and was the company's only game involving metal figurines. (17" x 9½")

The 1899 version of McLoughlin's Game of Base Ball (right) included a lush color illustration of late 1890s baseball on its box top. (22" x 13")

With the prevailing rules of the game printed on the concentric circles of its board, Edward B. Pierce's Parlor Base Ball Game (above) appeared in 1878. It featured a color lithograph design mounted on wood with a metal spinner. Both the manufactured version that was sold in stores and the prototype are shown here, with the game's original patent papers. (10½" x 21," opened)

artifacts from the 19th century, a period during which America underwent dramatic social change. The growth of giant industrial monopolies transformed a rural society into a crowded urban one. The rise of immigration, industrialization, and urbanization provided new opportunities for the growing middle class. Coping with such changes and trying to capitalize on the new opportunities added stress and anxiety to family life. Family recreation and relaxation in the comfort of the home became a crucial retreat from the hustle and bustle of a coun-

try on the move. The parlor became an oasis of tranquility, where family members could enjoy board games, card games, and toys.

While organized baseball was evolving in America during the 1860s, game companies pondered how to recast the characteristics of the sport in board and card games. The production of baseball-themed board games that had started soon after the Civil War increased substantially in the 1880s and 1890s, as baseball grew even more popular. Nineteenth-century board games are especially intriguing because they chart the evolution of baseball's rules. Cooper's editions of the New Parlor Game and Parlor Base Ball Game (the latter of which was issued by Edward B. Pierce of Lowell, Massachusetts, in 1878) show a diamond-shaped infield with foul lines, a pitcher throwing underhand to a catcher, and nine players standing in designated positions—all characteristics of the "New York game" promulgated by baseball's first organized team, the New York Knickerbocker Base Ball Club, in the late 1840s.

One of the first player-endorsed games of the 19th century, the Sporting Life Game of Base-ball (right), which appeared in 1887, featured a W. P. Snyder woodcut on the cover of its box. The image, titled "A Double Play-First League Game, New York Against Boston, April 29, 1886," had appeared in *Harper's Weekly* on May 8 of that year. (12" x 12")

To commemorate Albert Goodwill Spalding's 1888–89 World Tour (see Chapter XV), McLoughlin produced The World's Game of Base Ball (below) in 1889. A spinner game that featured color lithographic images of Charles Comiskey—one of the co-sponsors of the World Tour—and Robert Ferguson, whose career included stints as a player, a manager, an umpire, and president of the National Association (1872–75). (12½" x 8")

From a baseball-themed game whose rules and manufacturer are unknown, these Base Ball Playing Cards (below) are dated February 28, 1888. They display action portraits of professional ballplayers from the era, with the player's name and position printed below his portrait, and his team above. The letters in the upper left corner are the team initials. The full deck consists of 72 cards. (2½" x 3½").

A number of baseball rules that no longer exist can be glimpsed in these 19th-century board games. The New Parlor Game featured a wooden spinner on a dial with the numbers 1 through 30. Each number corresponded to a rule listed on the "umpire card." If the player spun the number one, for example, he referred to the number 1 on the umpire card, which read "out on a foul bound." Before 1883, a foul ball caught on a single bounce constituted an out. The number 14 read, "A safe hit over short stop takes a base." Number 6, "Three called balls takes a base," referred to a rule in which three pitches that were not strikes were considered one ball, and three of

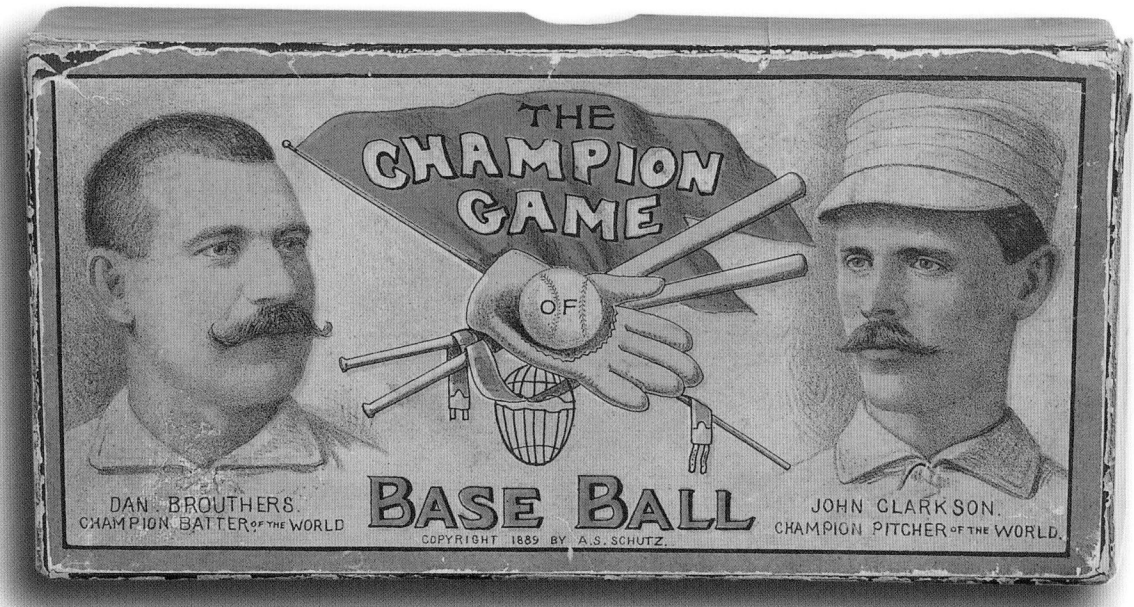

these balls constituted a walk. This rule was standard until 1881. Most board games also included pamphlets that listed the current rules of baseball. A pamphlet from the New Parlor Game's accessories appears on page 22. A child could also learn rules simply by looking at the illustrations on the games' box tops and game boards. Games like the New Parlor Game, the Parlor Base Ball Game, and the Game of Base-Ball (issued in 1886 by McLoughlin Brothers of New York, the most successful game manufacturer of the 19th century) depicted the first and third basemen standing in or near foul territory so that they can play a foul ball. Indeed, until 1887, the

"fair-foul rule" stipulated that a batted ball that touched in fair territory but went foul before reaching first or third base was in play.

As its rules were refined and improved, baseball became faster and more exciting. Then as now, the stewards of the game tried to strike an appropriate balance between offense and defense, so baseball's rules tended to oscillate between favoring pitchers and favoring batters. One 1884 ruling boosted pitchers by allowing them to throw with any motion, instead of only underhand, as previously required. The box top of the 1886 McLoughlin Game of Base-Ball reflects this rule change with an illustration of a pitcher

The Schultz company tapped Dan Brouthers and John Clarkson to endorse its Champion Game of Base Ball (above) from 1889, dubbing the two ballplayers "champion batter of the world" and "champion pitcher of the world," respectively. Brouthers won more major-league batting titles (five) than any other 19th-century ballplayer, and Clarkson won the 1889 pitching Triple Crown by leading the National League in wins (49), strikeouts (284), and ERA (2.73). The double-spinner game featuring their likenesses was one of only three player-endorsed board games of the 19th century. (7½" x 3½")

The Philadelphia Game Manufacturing Company's Major League Indoor Base Ball (right) came with a beautifully finished wood frame and a sturdy cardboard cover and back. Produced in 1913, the game featured a hinged box top that opened up to reveal a color lithographic illustration of a baseball diamond and grandstand filled to capacity (below). The interior bottom por-

tion features a large metal spinner, which dictated the action when spun. The game also included lineup cards for each of the 16 major-league teams at the time, and painted wooden pegs, which represented runners on base. Every season the manufacturer published new lineups that could be purchased separately. (2 ⅝" x 19 ⅜" x 13¼").

throwing in what looks like a side-armed, if not overhand, motion. In 1899, McLoughlin produced another board game called The Game of Base Ball. Its cover (see page 25) wonderfully depicts the version of baseball played at the turn of the century, with many aspects that modern fans will recognize. A coach stands in a box in foul territory near third base, as required under a rule passed in 1886. A runner takes a daring lead off second base, engaging in aggressive base running—a common practice by the 1880s and 1890s. The catcher stands directly behind home plate (compare this with where the catcher stands in the New Parlor Game cover, on page 22), wearing a mask (designed in 1875) and a chest protector (introduced in the 1880s). The batters hold ring bats, which were common by this time. And home plate, which would become a pentagon the following year, is still diamond-shaped.

The sale of player-endorsed products was already well under way by the late 1880s, with cards featuring images of ballplayers included in packs of cigarettes. Game manufacturers quickly joined the trend, producing intriguing and striking board and card games that used cross-promotion. In 1887, the Sporting Life Game of Baseball— which was conceived to help advertise the new Sporting Life newspaper—featured

"BABE RUTH" WITCH-E BASE-BALL GAME

(PATENT PENDING)

MANUFACTURED BY
BALTIMORE NOVELTY CO., INC.
215 N. FREDERICK STREET
BALTIMORE, MD.

STRIKE

FLY OUT

FOUL OUT

SACRIFICE HIT

HOME RUN

3 BASE HIT

"BABE" RUTH IN ACTION

When the "Babe Ruth" Witch-E Base-Ball Game (left) was released in 1918, the Bambino was already a big-league sensation—not for his hitting, but for his pitching. Between 1915 and 1918, Ruth was arguably the best lefthander in the majors, winning 18 games in 1915, 23 in 1916, and 24 in 1917 for the Boston Red Sox. By the eighth inning of Game 4 of the 1918 World Series, Ruth had pitched 23⅔ consecutive scoreless innings in Series play, a record that stood until 1961. The Baltimore Novelty Co. chose the star pitcher to help sell this game, the first one, as far as anyone knows, to feature Ruth in a Red Sox uniform. (6½" x 5")

Released in 1918, Christy Mathewson's Base Ball Game (below) was produced by the star pitcher's own game manufacturing company, which he had formed earlier that year. He also managed the Cincinnati Reds for the first half of the 1918 season, but left baseball, and the gaming business, at midseason to join the army as a captain on the Western Front in World War I. Exposure to poison gas on the battlefield eventually led to Mathewson's death in 1925. (23" x 17")

an eight-inch wooden figure of famous pitcher Timothy Keefe and star backstop Buck Ewing of the New York Giants. Two years later, A. S. Schultz introduced The Champion Game of Base Ball, which had color lithographic head shots of future Hall of Famers Dan Brouthers and John Clarkson on its box cover. And in 1893, McLoughlin Brothers produced Zimmer's Base Ball Game (see page 23), widely considered to be the most significant of all board games because it was the first to feature a large number of ballplayer endorsements. Its board bears chromolithographic images of 18 of the era's top stars, including Ed Delahanty, George Davis, and Cy Young.

In the early 20th century, following the success of the Zimmer's game, the use of ballplayers' names and images in board and card games became more prevalent. The trend reached a high point in 1913, when the Philadelphia Game Manufacturing Company placed 16 black-and-white cameo portrait photographs of the era's famous ballplayers on the box cover of its Major League Indoor Base Ball game. All of the portraits were taken by Carl Horner, one of the most prominent early-20th-cen-

tury photographers. His photos had been used a few years earlier by the American Tobacco Company on tobacco card inserts (known today as T206 White Border Series cards). Player endorsement has roots stretching to the 19th century, and of course it remains an integral sales catalyst to this day. For collectors like Cooper, the value of

CHRISTY MATHEWSON'S BASE BALL GAME

"PLAY BALL WITH ME"

Christy Mathewson

PRICE $1.00

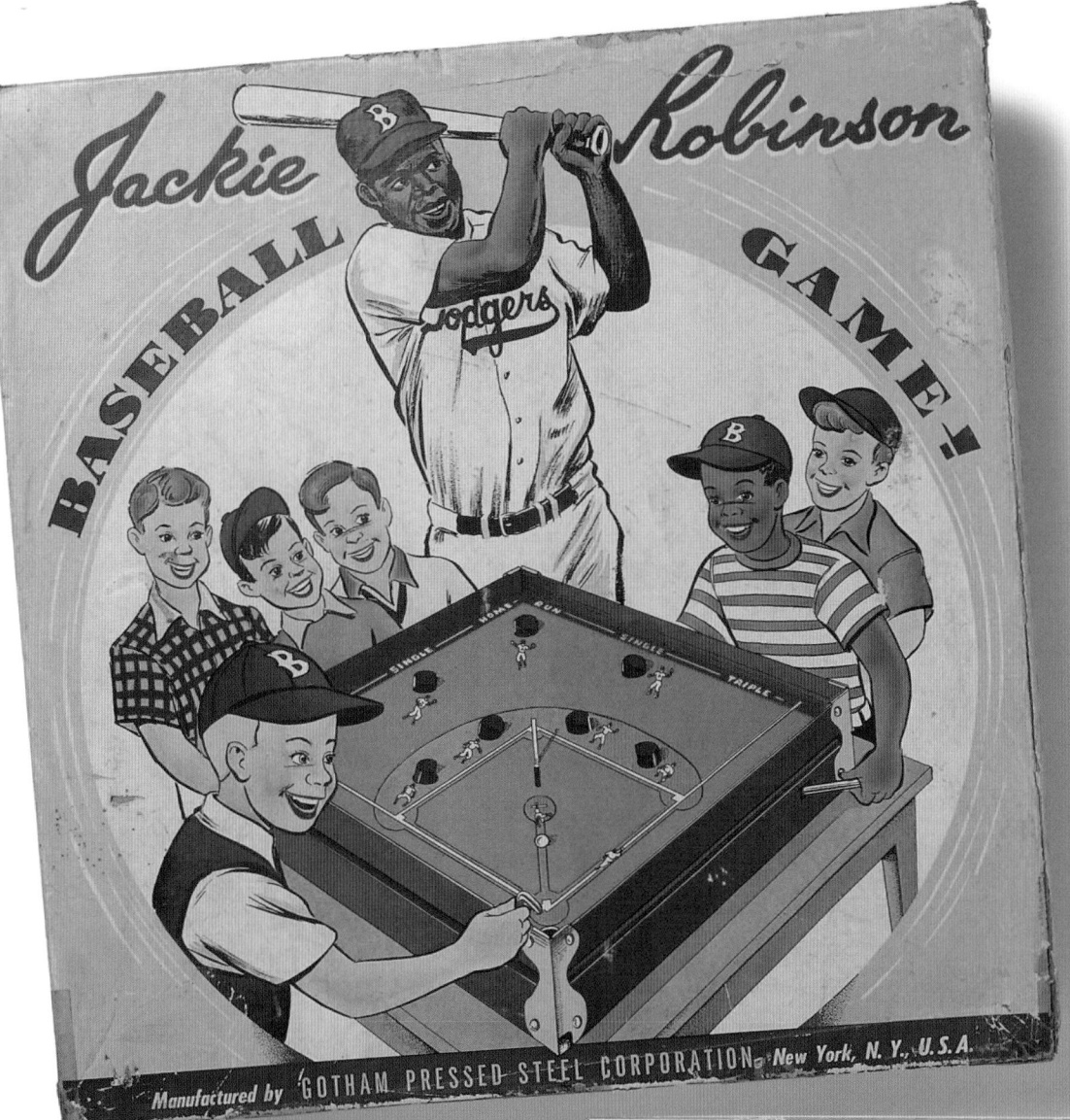

player-endorsed board games typically exceeds that of nonendorsed games.

Game manufacturers in the first half of the 20th century did not rely solely on board and card games to stimulate their customers' imaginations. They also produced a variety of baseball-related "action games" and toys that ranged from a ball and string attached to a paddle, to windup toys, bagatelle games, pinball games, and dartboard games (see page 32). The contrast in design between late 19th- or early-20th-century action games and toys and their contemporary counterparts is remarkable. The very primitiveness of the bygone games and toys only adds to their allure. Consider the Edwards Big League Table Baseball Game, produced in 1905 by the Edwards Manufacturing Company of Cincinnati (see page 33). A knob behind home plate moves the runners around the bases by a chain-driven mecha-

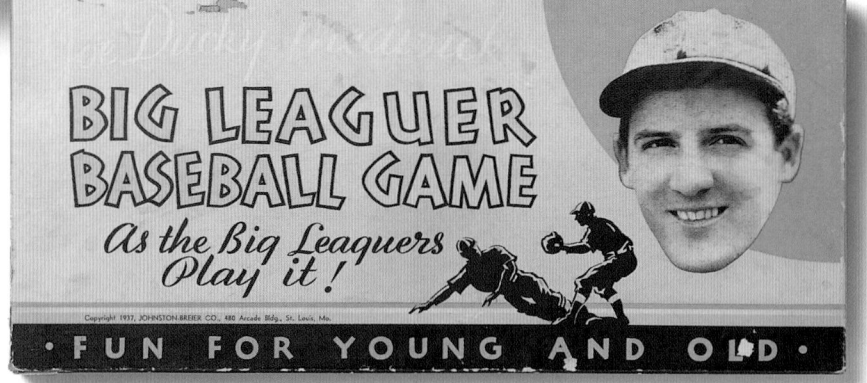

nism. It's not exactly the most refined contraption, but that is part of its charm. The difference in safety standards (or lack thereof) is also striking. In the Edwards game, pressing one button makes the pitcher fling a metal ball, the size of a large pearl, into the air; pressing another button releases the batter's swing, potentially sending the ball in flight. You can imagine the hazards, with children playing the game!

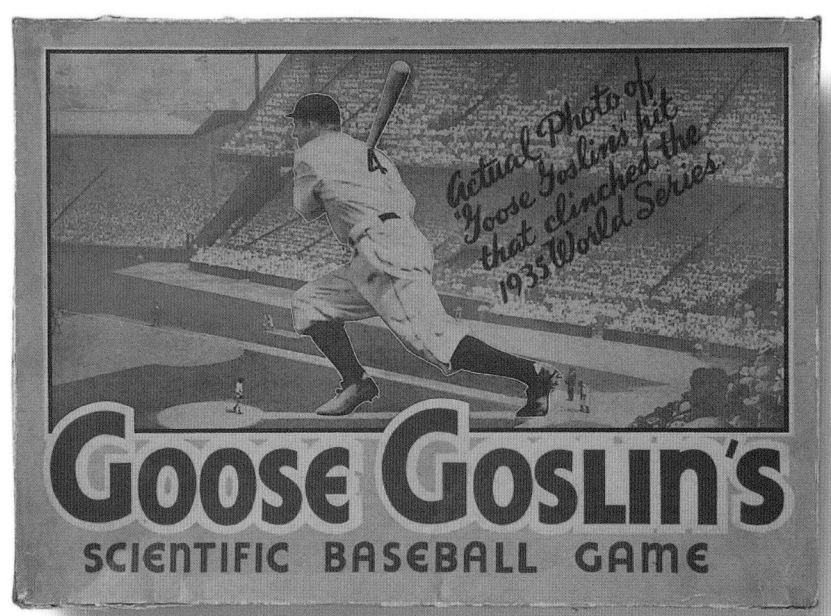

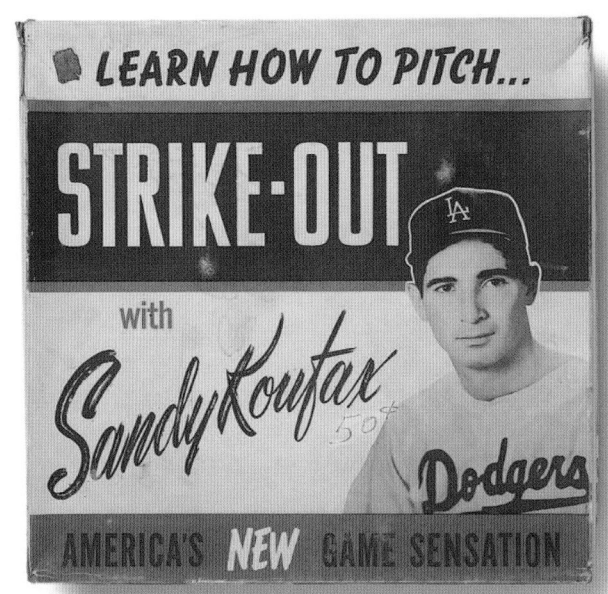

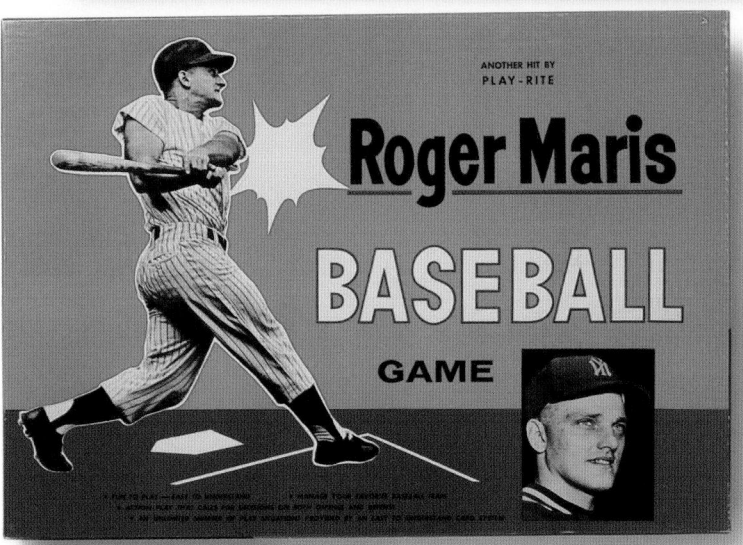

Goose Goslin's Scientific Baseball Game (top left) featured a photograph of its namesake's World Series–winning single from 1935 on its cover. Released that year, the game could scarcely have done better in its choice of endorser, but why the Wheeler Toy Company called this standard spinner game "scientif-ic" remains a mystery. Goslin's single came with two outs in the bottom of the ninth, and scored Mickey Cochrane, clinching the Detroit Tigers' six-game Series triumph over the Chicago Cubs. (15" x 11")

Instructo Sports released Strike Out with Sandy Koufax (above right) in 1963, the year the Dodgers lefthander won the first of his three pitching triple crowns, leading the National League in strikeouts, wins, and ERA. One of the rarest games

from the postwar era, it came with Styrofoam balls that were thrown at targets equipped with plastic spikes to catch them. (16" x 16")

A card game with die-cut field-ers placed at various points on the diamond, Play-Rite's Roger Maris Baseball Game (above) came out in 1962. If the "batter" drew a card that placed him in a spot occupied by a defensive player, he was out. One might think that the manufacturer of this game scored a marketing coup, signing Roger Maris one year after he broke Babe Ruth's single-season home run record, but the picture is not quite so rosy: At the 1980 All-Star Game, Maris was still angry about how the public and the press had treated him in 1961. "They acted as though I was doing something wrong,

poisoning the record books or something," he said. "Do you know what I have to show for 61 home runs? Nothing. Exactly nothing." (19" x 11")

No less an authority than Sandy Koufax described Willie Mays as "probably the best all-around player" in baseball his-tory, but as good as Mays was at baseball, he was terrible at remembering other people's

names. To cover for this failing, he developed a customary greeting, "Say hey," which quickly became part of his nickname. By the time Centennial Games issued the Willie Mays "Say Hey" Baseball Game (above) in 1958, the "Say Hey Kid" already had a well-stocked trophy case: Rookie of the Year (1951), National league MVP (1954), and two Gold Gloves (1957, 1958). (17" x 17")

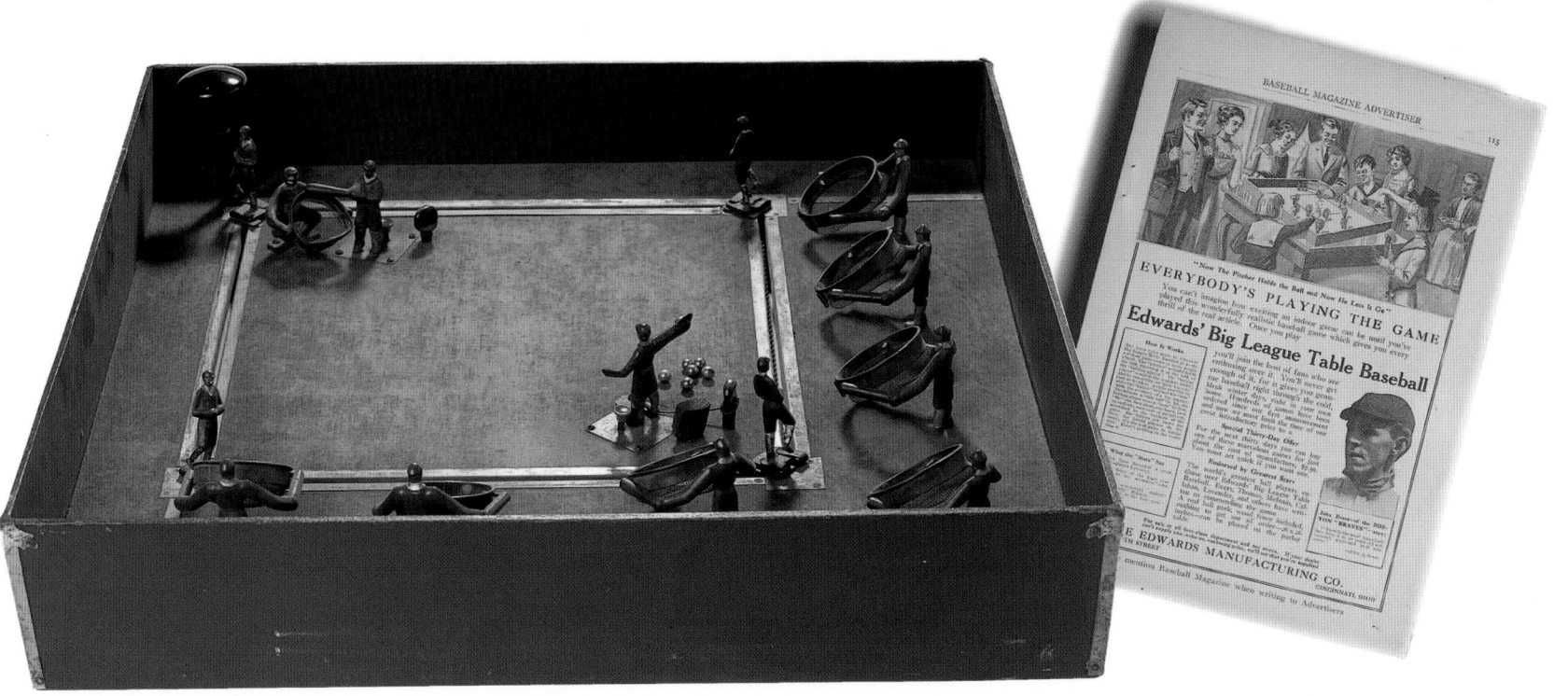

Composed of wood, metal, and felt, with leatherette covering the sides, the Edwards Manufacturing Company's Big League Table Baseball Game (above) appeared in 1905, and was the most sophisticated of all action games of the period. The game's popularity endured for years, and its magazine advertisements (above right) appeared in periodicals as late as 1914. (27" x 27")

Some of the most aesthetically captivating baseball action games and toys came from the late 19th century and first half of the 20th century, including the Ives Manufacturing Company's large-mouthed Champion Base Ball Catcher (opposite page, near left). Issued in 1888, the game invited participants to throw a rubber

ball into one of the figure's three pockets, each of which had a different point value. In 1885, the Clarkes Company produced the Fortune Teller (left, in front of the "Catcher"), a dark wooden box containing the figures of three players. The key on the outside wound the bat, whose final position—first base, second base, third base, or home plate—determined the player's fortune. Other artifacts from the period include wooden 10-pins in the form of ballplayers (far left), which were produced in 1888; a 1905 paddle game endorsed by Philadelphia Athletics stars Rube Waddell and Harry Davis; an action game from 1925 (far left, figure with bat); three toys from the 1920s and 1930s; and a pocket pinball game from the 1940s.

Produced continuously between 1941 and 1993, Cadaco's All-Star Baseball Game (right) was one of the most popular baseball board games ever created, and the first popular statistics-based game. It was designed by former major-league outfielder and Yale University coach Ethan Allen. The game reproduces realistic baseball results by representing a major leaguer's statistical performance on a cardboard player disc. When fitted to a spinner device, the individual player discs produced a variety of results, such as a single, a home run, a walk, a double play, etc. By grouping the discs into teams, children and adults could manage their own all-star team. The version pictured here is a special

edition that was issued in 1950 and includes discs of all-time greats and a three dimensional pop-up grandstand. (14" x 22")

Just as baseball has evolved over time, so have the many replica games it spawned. We've come a long way from the simple invitation to "Play ball with me" on the cover of Christy Mathewson's Base Ball Game (1918), to the high-speed graphics of today's All-Star Baseball Game by PlayStation. So the next time you play Strat-O-Matic, Pursue the Pennant, or Rotisserie-league baseball, remember that you are participating in a pastime almost as old as baseball itself—and that the inspiration for these modern-day marvels of fantasy baseball started more than 130 years ago with a wooden spinner.

THE DR. MARK W. COOPER COLLECTION

33

20TH-CENTURY COIN-OPERATED GAMES

By the 1890s, manufacturers of coin-operated machines—which include slot machines, trade stimulators, vending machines, and arcade games—had joined board-game manufacturers in capitalizing on baseball's popularity. Along with horse racing and card playing, baseball was the most popular theme exploited by makers of these devices. Few patents were available for coin-operated machines because the U.S. Patent Office generally considered them to be gambling-related, and, by law, patents could not be issued for gambling devices.

In 1893, however, a coin-operated-machine maker named J. D. Latimer was awarded a patent for a device that he referred to on his application as a "Game of Skill Amusement Toy." By defining his invention as a "toy," Latimer circumvented the legal hurdle and pioneered the strategy of using baseball and other themes to conceal the reality that most of these contraptions were, in fact, gambling devices.

How Latimer slipped this by the U.S. Patent Office remains unclear, but his was the first of a series of inventions that, in their own peculiar way, pay tribute to the national pastime.

Manufactured in 1908, the Caille Base-Ball Trade Stimulator (below) had nothing to do with prodding baseball owners to swap, say, Ty Cobb for Christy Mathewson. No, the game was placed in general stores to stimulate business by offering a chance to win a token for merchandise credit. It cost a penny, and with its baseball theme, moving parts, and amusing challenge, a Caille machine was a valuable device for merchants, certainly worth whatever it paid out in tokens. (20" tall, 12" x 15" base)

The Play Ball Vendor Machine (right) from 1927 was not a vending machine as we know the term today. It promoted a gum that "aids digestion" and "preserves the teeth," and contained a game whose object was to shoot four colored balls into the matching colored slots that corresponded to four different flavors of the gum. If you were successful, the clerk paid you off in merchandise. (19" tall, 15" x 6¾" base)

Produced in 1926, the Paupa Hochriem Baseball Game (left) blended the features of a vending machine and an arcade game, offering both chewing gum and a challenging, amusing game of skill for the price of a coin. (20" tall, 16" x 7" base)

Daycom's Reel-O-Ball slot machine (above), from the early 1930s, was exactly that—a slot machine, but one ingeniously disguised by a baseball-themed facade. The ruse was necessary to fool the local constable, because slot machines were illegal in venues that were not licensed to provide gambling-related entertainment. Between 1929 and 1940, a number of manufacturers employed similar deceptions. At the cost of a penny, the Daycom machine gave players a spin of the rotary-style wheel of fortune, where single, double, strike, ball, and home run were all possible outcomes. For impressive spins, the machine rang an interior bell and paid out a token that could be redeemed for a prize. And if the pleasure of chance was not incentive enough to play, each penny bought one of the rainbow of gumballs displayed in the window above the lever. (17" tall, 13" x 16" base)

EVOLUTION

> "We used no mattress on our hands,
> No cage upon our face;
> We stood right up and caught the ball
> With courage and with grace."
> —*GEORGE ELLARD*
> *Member of the undefeated 1869*
> *Cincinnati Red Stockings*

Gregory John Gallacher of Wantagh, Long Island, is a devout family man who enjoys a simple diet of meat and potatoes, prefers his occasional whiskey straight up, and steadfastly hews to a conservative line on politics. He owns a curved-dash Oldsmobile manufac-

tured in 1903 and has traveled to Africa to hunt wild game. His ideal vacation is a week of deer hunting at his Adirondack Mountains lodge, with a wood-burning stove and no running water. Gallacher's old–New York accent, stocky physique, and thick, well-groomed mustache recall an old-fashioned pugilist or a ballplayer from a 19th-century tobacco card. It seems fitting that he has become one of baseball's foremost archaeologists, with a collection that focuses on the evolution of the game's equipment (balls, gloves, bats, and catcher's gear) dating to the Civil War.

During the two decades leading up to the

Striking a pose identical to the one Hall of Fame catcher Buck Ewing assumed for his 1888 Old Judge cabinet card (above right). collector Gallacher (above left) wears a 19th-century baseball uniform and leans on a "ring bat." These bats, popular in the 1880s. took their name from the black rings encircling their barrels.

A solid-oak Spalding bat rack (opposite) was a common feature of early-20th-century sporting goods stores, as it could display an entire line of the company's bats in one impressive setting.

War between the States, baseball gained tremendous momentum as America's most popular team sport. It was a time of rapid innovation and creativity in the game. Inventors, leather and wood craftsmen, and, eventually, equipment retailers, all vied to make their mark in designing, manufacturing, and selling the tools of the baseball trade. Baseball equipment tells a unique story about American ingenuity, a story that started nearly a century and a half ago. As the chief curator of that story, Gallacher looks and behaves as though he actually witnessed its unfolding.

BALLS

In 1861, the National Association of Base Ball Players (NABBP)—the game's first official league, which grew out of a meeting between the Knickerbockers and 15 other clubs in 1857—determined that a baseball's circumference be between 9½" and 9¾", and its weight between 5½ and 5¾ ounces. Before this decision, the size, composition, and design of a ball had undergone a series of modifications. Balls from the 1830s and 1840s were typically smaller, and the method of constructing them varied, depending on the available materials and the background of the maker. Many of the early balls were made with four strips of leather stretched and stitched over a compound of string and India rubber strips. They are known today as "lemon-peel" baseballs. Typically homemade or produced by leather craftsmen such as saddlers and shoemakers, these balls were relatively soft, to permit "soaking" (retiring a base runner by hitting him with the ball). Soaking was allowed in early versions of baseball, including "town ball," a game derived from the English game of rounders. The lemon-peel stitch ball prevailed until the late 1860s or early 1870s. Before the 1861 NABBP decision, the circumference of a baseball could be as large as 10" to 10¼", as was the case with the balls made by Daniel Lucius "Doc" Adams of the Knickerbockers. Adams was known to make a ball for his team by gathering three or four ounces of rubber cuttings, winding yarn around them, and then covering the layers with leather.

Other kinds of balls during this period included the "belt ball," which was fashioned from one piece of leather that was cut and stitched to form a sphere. The belt ball featured an "H" pattern of stitching that left one hemisphere of the ball completely without stitches. Variations on the belt ball in the 1870s led to the now familiar two-panel, figure-eight pattern found on today's Rawlings official model baseballs. The center of the belt ball contained string and India rubber strips, as opposed to the cork and two layers of rubber encasing that Rawlings uses today.

GLOVES

The baseball glove went through several incarnations during the second half of the 19th century. Although some ballplayers, including Dave Birdsall and Doug Allison, used gloves as early as the 1860s, most fielders played the game without a glove until the mid-1870s. Wearing

Gallacher owns a handmade lemon-peel baseball (left, top), circa 1850s. Its circumference of 7 ¼" is significantly smaller than the official 1861 ruling of 9½" to 9¾".

A belt ball (left, middle), circa 1870s, was fashioned from one strip of leather, cut and stitched in "H" pattern to form a sphere.

Gallacher's pigskin ball (left, bottom) features a figure-eight stitching pattern, which had become standard by the mid-1870s and is still used today.

Early-20th-century factory workers used a vise like apparatus (below) to hold a ball in place while they stitched together its two strips of leather.

A fingerless glove from 1880 (above) helps chart the evolution of baseball equipment.

In an original photograph from the 1880s, a ballplayer from Long Island (left) wears a fingerless glove on his throwing hand and a workman's glove on his other one, a fairly common setup for players of the era.

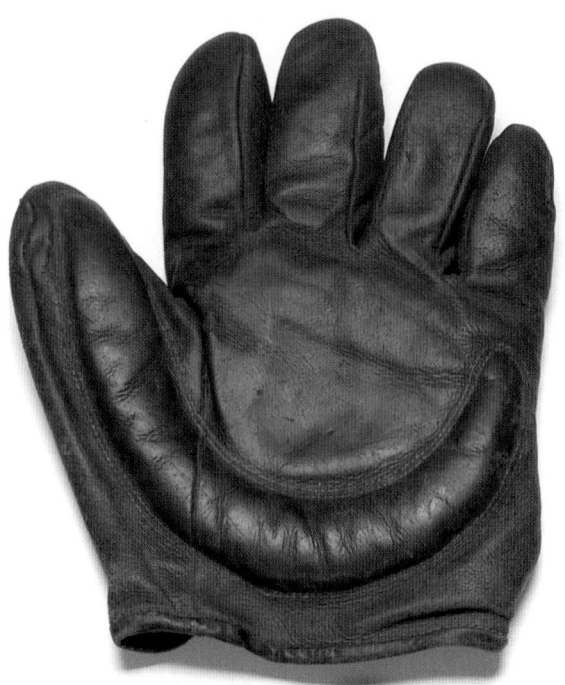

The crescent-heel glove, from the 1890s, takes its name from the heavy padding at its base.

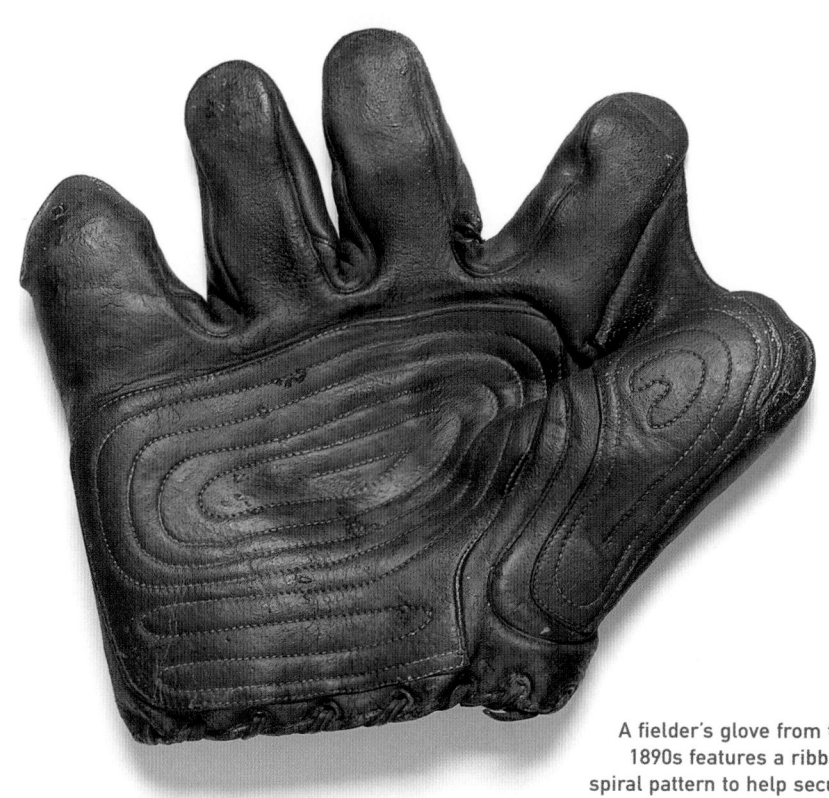

A fielder's glove from the 1890s features a ribbed, spiral pattern to help secure the ball in the pocket.

A Rawlings fielder's glove from the 1980s demonstrates how much fielders' gloves have evolved since Cardinals spitballer Bill Doak introduced webbing in the early 1920s.

a glove was considered unmanly, except in the case of catchers, who typically wore them. This started to change in 1875, when St. Louis first baseman Charles C. Waitt began to wear a flesh-colored, skin-tight glove with the fingertips cut off. Known as the fingerless glove, it covered only the palm of his hand, and was relatively thin and inconspicuous. In 1877, Albert Goodwill Spalding, the Chicago first baseman whose name would later become synonymous with sporting goods, started to wear a fingerless glove, believing it would help the sale of gloves in his sporting goods business. Spalding's belief was well founded, as gloves gradually became de rigueur for baseball players. From 1877 to 1882, players at other positions began to wear gloves—infielders first, followed by outfielders, and then pitchers. In 1882, Philadelphia shortstop Arthur Irwin became the first player to use padding in a glove when he did so to protect his injured hand. Moderately padded finger-style gloves, known today as workman's gloves, became more popular in the late 1880s, when fielders realized that gloves made it possible to handle hard-hit balls.

But the workman's glove was nothing more than a "small leather pillow," its pri-mary purpose to protect the player, not improve his fielding. By the 1890s, though, gloves included several other features that transformed them into significant defensive aids. Some models had raised, crescent-shaped padding in the palm area, which helped players cradle the ball as they caught it. Other turn-of-the-century gloves came with a ribbed, spiral design in the palm that improved the fielder's ability to grip the ball.

In the early 1920s, Bill Doak, a spitball pitcher for the St. Louis Cardinals, designed a fielder's glove that quickly became the era's ideal defensive tool. Doak's design included not only a pocket area, but also a lattice of leather strips between the thumb and forefinger that helped a ballplayer snag the ball. The Doak model eventually evolved into today's large, padded and webbed glove.

In addition to a fingerless glove, a crescent-heel glove, a spiral-palm glove, and an early 1930s fielder's glove, Gallacher's collection contains a crescent-pad first baseman's mitt (circa 1900), which was the prototype for today's oversized first-baseman's mitt. He also owns some bizarre models that illustrate the period's trial-and-error phase of glove making. These include an ambidextrous glove (which could be worn on either hand, circa 1900), an odd-shaped "pita

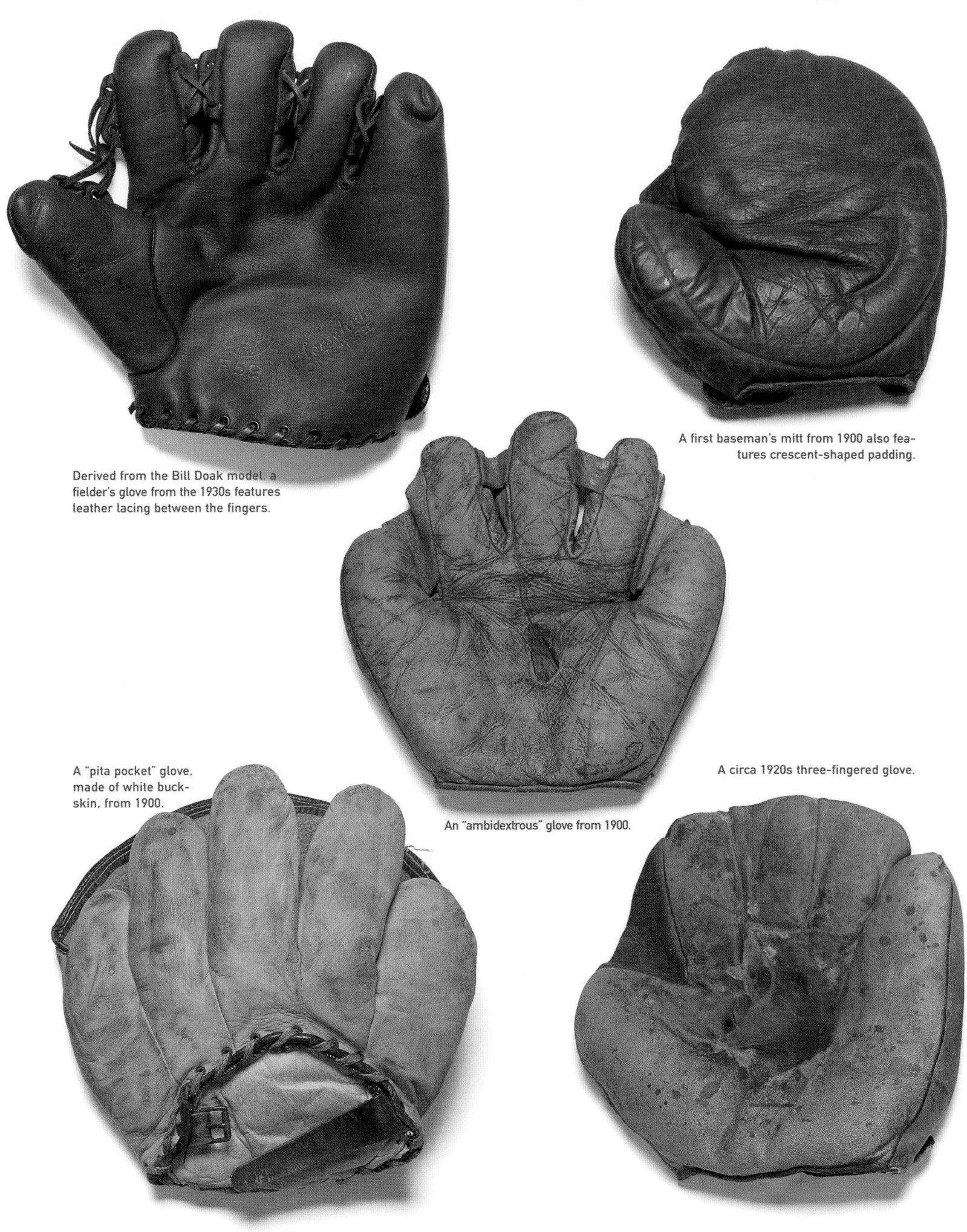

Derived from the Bill Doak model, a fielder's glove from the 1930s features leather lacing between the fingers.

A first baseman's mitt from 1900 also features crescent-shaped padding.

A "pita pocket" glove, made of white buckskin, from 1900.

An "ambidextrous" glove from 1900.

A circa 1920s three-fingered glove.

pocket" glove (consisting of a large pocket with finger sections hidden behind the pocket area, circa 1900), and a three-fingered glove (which contained four pocket sections for placement of three fingers and a thumb,. circa 1920–1940).

BATS

The bat is the only piece of baseball equipment that predates the game. "Trap bats" (small, cricket-style paddles) and spherical bats were used in the English children's games of trap-ball and rounders, respectively. (Examples of both bats are below.) Trap-ball—which can be traced to the early 14th century and was played in parts of northern England until as late as 1825—was played with a wooden trap bat and a hard wooden ball about the size of a walnut. One player pitched the ball and another swung at it with the trap bat. Players could swing the bats, as shown in the lithographic card below, with one hand. The object of the game was to hit the ball as far as possible, either in one stroke or a series of strokes.

Rounders was played on a field with a diamond-shaped area delineated by four stones, or wooden posts, placed from 12 to 20 yards apart. The number of players on a team was generally not specified. Players in the field had no assigned positions, except for the "feeder" (pitcher), who gently tossed the ball to the opposing team's striker (batter) from a designated spot marked by another stone or post. If the striker hit the ball, he ran the bases clockwise as far as he could go without being soaked (hit with the ball). The striker could also be called out if he missed three swings, hit the ball behind his position, or had his batted ball caught. The team at bat continued hitting until each of its members had been put out.

Early versions of American baseball bats were slightly more primitive looking than rounders bats. One example is a "Massachusetts-style" bat from the 1840s, which was made from a wooden axe handle. One end of the axe handle was chiseled down to create a knob that prevented the bat from slipping out of the player's hands. This relatively small bat resembled a large stick and was used to play the "Massachusetts game" (see Chapter I).

Bat design innovations accelerated between 1880 and 1910. As long as bat

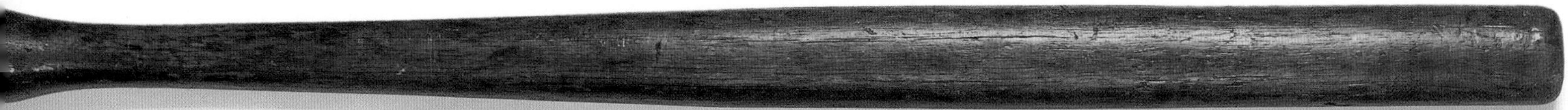

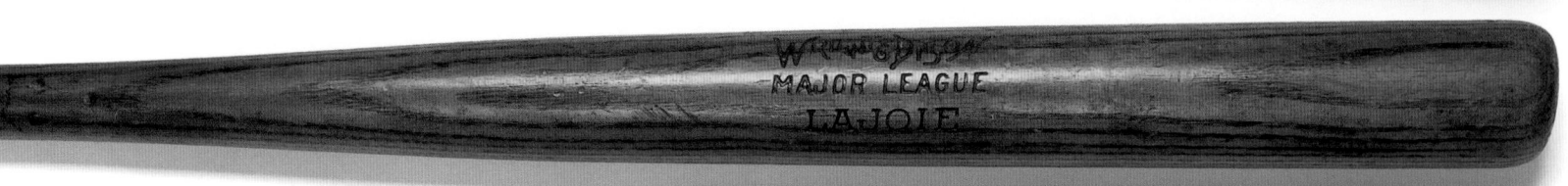

A circa-1840s "Massachusetts-style" bat made from an axe handle.

A circa-1885 "flat bat," designed to aid hit-and-run batting techniques, like bunting.

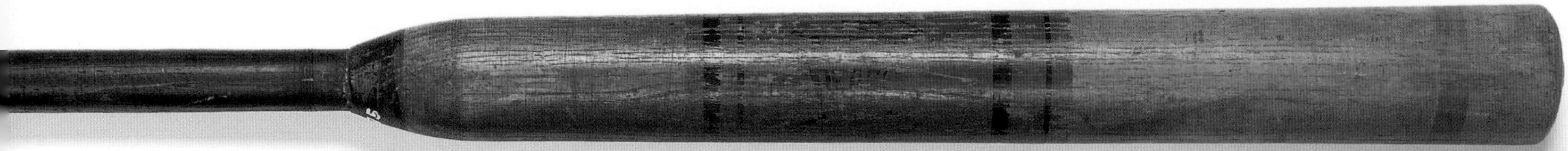

The short-lived "spring-handled" bat appeared at the dawn of the 20th century.

Gallacher's Spalding "mushroom" bat dates to around 1906, and was designed to give hitters "a more even distribution of weight."

J. F. Hillerich & Son, maker of the famous Louisville Slugger, issued this "ball-balanced" bat—clearly influenced by the mushroom bat—circa 1908.

Named for Hall of Fame second baseman Nap Lajoie, Gallacher's Wright & Ditson double-handle bat dates to about 1910.

In a framed color lithographic card (opposite) children are depicted playing the English game of trap-ball, which used a cricket-style trap bat (left, bottom). Behind the card is a bat that was used in the game of rounders.

makers kept within the limits specified by the NABBP rules—no greater than 2" in diameter and 42" in length—they could vary a bat's design as much as they pleased. Bats that were flattened along the barrel, known as "flat bats" or "sacrifice bats," allowed more accurate placement of the ball. The flat bat was legalized for major-league play in 1885, but by

the following year it had fallen out of favor because a fast pitch caused the bat to turn in a batter's hands, often resulting in a weak dribbler out of the batter's box. By 1893, flat bats had disappeared entirely. In the early 1900s, bat manufacturers focused their attention on creating unique designs along the bat's handle, an effort that yielded the "spring-handled"

The Tools of Ignorance, early-20th-century version: Catcher's gear (above) developed rapidly after its debut in the 1870s, offering steadily increasing protection to backstoppers. Note the catcher's mask—a far cry from the one James Tyng wore at Harvard in 1876 (see opposite page).

bat (circa 1900). The narrower bat-handle area and wider hitting surface combined to generate more whip-action, for enhanced power. The effort was misplaced, though, since power hitting would not become an integral part of the game until the arrival of Babe Ruth in the early 1920s.

Until then, overall bat speed was not nearly as important as simply making contact with the ball. The key objective on offense was to advance runners through base hits, not home runs. This strategy, popularized by the hit-and-run play of the legendary Baltimore Orioles of the 1890s, was referred to as the "scientific game." Batters typically choked up on the bat, gripped it with their hands separated, and poked or punched at the ball. A bat with evenly distributed weight allowed more control through the hitting zone, which in turn made it easier for a hitter to make contact with the ball. The "mushroom" bat, patented by the A. J. Reach Company on August 1, 1905, featured an unusually large knob at the handle that was intended to "enable the batsman to get a more even distribution of weight than was possible under the old construction," according to the company's 1905 Fall catalog. "Ball-balanced" bats also featured large knobs, as did the Wright & Ditson Company's "Lajoie" double-handle bat, which was named after Cleveland's Napoleon Lajoie, the legendary second baseman.

CATCHER'S GEAR

Before the 1870s, a rubber mouthpiece was the only protection a catcher had against the flurry of fastballs headed his way. In 1875, Fred Thayer, captain of the Harvard University Base Ball Club, designed the first catcher's mask, which he modeled on masks used by the Harvard fencing team. Thayer's teammate, catcher James Tyng, first wore the mask in 1876 during an exhibition game between Harvard and the Boston Red Stockings. Tyng insisted on wearing the mask because of "the high risk of disfigurement" from catching fastballs without protective gear. Because there was almost no padding on Thayer-style masks, a foul tip to the mask must have felt like a punch in the face. To make matters worse, the pitcher's mound was only 45 feet from home plate until 1893, when it was moved back to the 60-foot 6-inch distance that is standard today. The catcher's masks quickly evolved from something resembling a medieval torture device into the more refined apparatus that currently protects the face, head, and neck of every backstop from neighborhood sandlots to major-league ballparks.

James "Deacon" White, the catcher for the 1870 Boston Red Stockings, devised the first chest protectors. His design included a canvas-covered rubber bladder pumped full of air. Padding eventually replaced the air tubes, as the circa-1910 chest protector on the opposite page demonstrates. The chest protector has remained almost unchanged to this day.

In 1907, Roger Bresnahan of the New York Giants became the first major-league catcher to use shin guards. Commonly used by cricket players, these guards consisted of wood slats covered by canvas. During the 1920s, plastics began to replace the "reed" guards, providing more protection for the catcher's knees and feet.

A tour of the balls, gloves, bats, and catcher's gear in Gallacher's display room drives home the collector's devotion to preserving an integral part of baseball's origins. For Gallacher, the century of progress and

Gallacher's circa-1878 Fred Thayer–style catcher's mask is one of only four surviving Thayer-style masks. Each example differs slightly from Thayer's original patent drawings, indicating that the masks were handmade and most likely modified with each subsequent production. Thayer successfully sued Spalding in 1886 to prevent the sporting goods company from mass-producing his mask, hence the very limited number of them in existence today.

the impact of modernization have, to some degree, eroded the game's charm and innocence. He seems to be a man born in the wrong century, someone who deeply yearns for the simpler ways of the old world, and someone who would take great pride in being a leather or wood craftsman in a 19th-century equipment factory. Those days may be long gone, but Gallacher can rest assured that his treasured relics keep alive a timeless quality from the old world: the spirit of American ingenuity.

A MUSEUM OF DREAMS

For the quality of its art-work, the array of ballplayers depicted on it, and its scarcity (only one other copy of the poster is known to exist), Cypres's 1888 Old Judge Cigarettes advertising display poster (opposite), is widely considered to be one of the most significant advertising displays to come to light in the history of the hobby. (41 ½" x 28")

Attributed to the workshop of renowned tobac-conist carver Samuel Anderson Robb, Cypres's 1880s Virgin Cigars wooden baseball show figure (left) stands 48 inches high atop a 16-inch base.

> " John: Is this heaven?
> Ray: It's Iowa.
> John: Iowa? I could have sworn this was heaven.
> Ray: Is there a heaven?
> John: Oh yeah. It's the place where dreams come true."
> —*Excerpt from the movie*
> **Field of Dreams**

In W. P. Kinsella's novel *Shoeless Joe*—the basis for the classic baseball movie *Field of Dreams*—a young Iowa farmer named Ray one day hears a voice telling him: "If you build it, he will come." Ray eventually figures out that "it" refers to a baseball diamond in his cornfield and "he" refers to Shoeless Joe Jackson, who, along with seven of his Chicago White Sox teammates, was banished from baseball for throwing the 1919 World Series. Ray builds the diamond, and Jackson and his teammates turn up to play baseball in their White Sox uniforms one last time. The game fulfills Jackson's dream of having one last chance to play the game that was once the center of his life.

Gary Mark Cypres has created his own field of dreams, or, more accurately, his own museum of dreams. His extensive collection of baseball, football, and basketball relics has outgrown the confines of his home. It now takes up more than half of a 45,000-square-foot building in downtown Los Angeles. The collection shares space with Cypres's travel and mortgage brokerage business that caters to the Hispanic community throughout the United States. Many of Cypres's employees and local customers don't have the option of bringing their children to Cooperstown, New York; Can-ton, Ohio; or Springfield, Massachusetts, to see the baseball, football or basketball Halls of Fame, so Gary brought a sports museum to them.

Visitors of all ages can see and learn about baseball bats, gloves, uniforms, and catcher's gear; football helmets, shoulder pads, and jerseys; basketball rims and jerseys, and balls used throughout the history of each sport. In addition to his extensive sports memorabilia, Cypres owns some of the hobby's most colorful and visually attractive baseball-related advertising signs, movie posters, and paintings. This last category of items makes Cypres's collection unique.

American producers of tobacco products, soft drinks, candy, ice cream, chewing gum, and a host of other items have spent generations incorporating baseball into their advertising. Although the marriage between baseball and advertising can be traced to the late 1860s and 1870s (with trade cards and scorecards), the trend really took off in the mid-1880s, with a big boost from the tobacco industry.

A machine developed in the early 1880s increased the speed and cost-effectiveness of cigarette production. But because the packets were flimsy, cigarettes often sustained damage. Tobacco companies responded by putting cardboard "stiffeners" between rows of cigarettes. Legend has it that James Buchanan Duke, one of the pioneers of the American cigarette industry, witnessed a smoker throwing his stiffener on the sidewalk. According to the story, seeing the stiffener treated as a separate object made Duke recognize its marketing potential. In the late 1880s, he joined Allen &

Building on the success of its 1887 "World's Champions" set of insert cards, Allen & Ginter issued a new series, with 50 additional stars, in 1888. As it did in 1887, the company produced a spectacular advertising display (right) to accompany the new set of cards. Printed in vibrant chromolithographic color, the poster was to be displayed at tobacco shops and featured reproductions of all 50 cards from the 1888 set, including images of boxers, track stars, and six baseball players—Hall of Famer Buck Ewing of New York, "Honest John" Morrill of Boston, James "Pony" Ryan of Chicago, George "Doggie" Miller of Pittsburgh, Charles "Pretzel" Getzein of Detroit, and James Fogarty of Philadelphia. (16" x 28")

In 1912, Hassan Cigarettes produced a set of baseball cards known as the T202 Triple Folders. Each card featured two color portraits of ballplayers, on either side of a black-and-white center panel, which contained a baseball action shot. The reverse of the card contained the two players' bios and a caption for the center panel image. Cypres owns an advertising poster for the set featuring Christy Mathewson (below). (35" x 15")

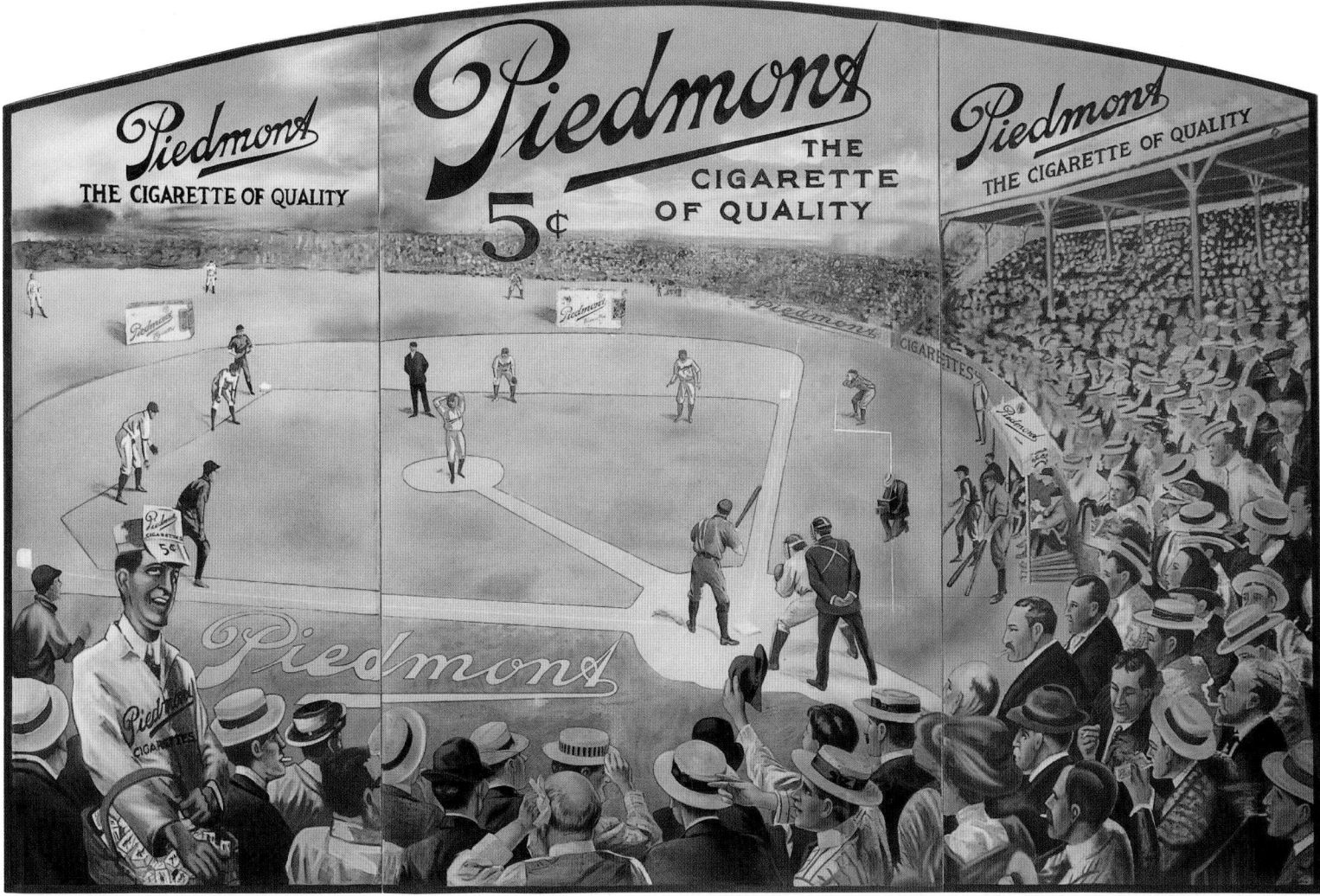

Ginter (one of the big four U.S. cigarette makers) and others in a campaign to increase sales by printing cigarette brand names, coupons, and images of baseball players and other professional athletes on the stiffeners. Thus began the first era of tobacco cards. (See examples of such cards in Chapter I, "Collecting 19th-Century Memorabilia.")

In 1887, Allen & Ginter began to produce advertising posters encouraging smokers to purchase their brands. (For the "First Series" poster, produced in 1887, see Chapter I, "Collecting 19th-Century Memorabilia"; the 1888 "Second Series" poster is opposite, near left.) The campaign paid off: Demand for cigarettes increased so greatly that annual domestic production jumped from one billion units in 1885 to 2.4 billion units in 1889.

The cigarette companies brilliantly exploited baseball's pastoral and genteel characteristics in their advertising materials. Another poster in Cypres's collection, called "Old Judge Cigarettes," features a series of portraits of the era's greatest stars, including Hall of Famers Adrian C. "Cap" Anson, Mike "King" Kelly, Charles "Old Hoss" Radbourn, and many others. Produced in 1888 by Goodwin & Co., another one of the four big U.S. cigarette makers, the portraits surround a magnificent color lithographic image of a game in progress, with rows of gentry smoking cigarettes and cigars in their suits, top hats, derby hats, and boaters. An usher plies the crowd with a tray of spirits. Pastel blue skies extend beyond the emerald-green field. A majestic wooden double-deck grandstand with conical pagodas stretches along the left field line. Another advertisement, a circa 1910 triptych for Piedmont Cigarettes (one of 16 brands advertised on the backs of T206 baseball tobacco cards), evokes a similar mood.

The depth and exceptionally rich, multi-layered tones that characterize the advertising art of Allen & Ginter, Old Judge, Piedmont, and some of the other early-20th-century examples in this chapter come from a

Cypres's Piedmont Cigarettes advertising display triptych (above), produced around 1910, features an interesting tidbit: The spectator smoking a Piedmont in the lower right corner of the triptych bears a striking resemblance to Honus Wagner, who disapproved of tobacco companies' using his name and likeness to promote their products. (The story of Wagner's association with tobacco products is discussed in Chapter V, "The Brian Seigel Collection.") (38" x 50")

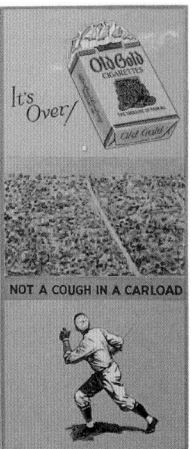

Old Gold joined other tobacco firms in capitalizing on the genteel aspects of baseball, as Cypres's colorful 1930s advertising piece (left) attests. The poster's dubious (not to mention humorous) "Not a Cough in a Carload" slogan was a common promotional tack of the time, as tobacco companies routinely, and baselessly, claimed that their brand was less harmful than the brands of their competitors. (38" x 51")

Lucky Strike went all out to secure baseball's "cream of the crop" to endorse the company's advertising triptych from 1928 (left). All four players depicted in the piece would end up in the Hall of Fame, and they had just completed banner seasons: Detroit's Harry Heilmann won the 1927 batting title with a .398 average; Pittsburgh's Lloyd Waner and the Yankees' Tony Lazzeri met in the '27 Fall Classic (a 4–0 Yankees sweep); and Philadelphia's young Lefty Grove produced his first 20-win season in 1927. He would reach the 20-win mark seven more times in his career. (61" x 40")

In 1912, the sporting goods firm of Draper & Maynard produced one of the most visually striking advertising displays of its kind (above). In addition to the artistic detail in the image of the company factory, the piece boasts two side panels featuring composite team photographic portraits of the 1911 Philadelphia Athletics and New York Giants, who squared off in the World Series that year. Each portrait was taken by renowned early-20th-century baseball photographer Carl Horner. (46" x 22")

Cypres owns a colorful and dynamic 1913 advertising poster from the Reach sporting goods company (near right). The piece was used by selected sporting-goods merchants to create a storefront window display to dazzle customers with the company's array of new baseball products. (68" x 45")

printing technique called stone lithography. Invented in 1798 by a German named Alois Senefelder, stone lithography was based on the principle that grease and water do not mix. Artists and illustrators drew on a slab of limestone with a greasy substance such as chalk, litho crayons, or pencils that contained wax, pigment, soap, and shellac. After the image was drawn, the limestone was dampened with water, and an oily ink was applied with a roller. The greasy image repelled the water and held the ink while the rest of the stone's surface did the opposite. The finished limestone was then placed on a tray and put through a lithography press. Printing craftsmen typically used a separate limestone slab for each color and, in certain lithographs, as many as 28 stones were required to achieve the dense, rich tones that set litho posters apart from other printing processes.

* * *

In 1890, James Duke masterminded the merger of all the large-scale tobacco companies into the American Tobacco Company, or ATC. As ATC's monopoly grew, advertising began to drop off substantially. In 1907, ATC acquired Butler & Butler, owner of Sovereign and Pall Mall brand cigarettes. The move prompted Teddy Roosevelt's Justice Department to file an antitrust lawsuit against ATC in July of that year. On November 16, 1911, ATC was split up into four entities: Liggett & Myers, P. Lorillard, R. J. Reynolds, and a much smaller ATC.

Intense competition among these companies gave rise to a new era in advertising that produced some extraordinary display pieces that rival the aesthetic appeal of Allen & Ginter and Old Judge signs of the late 1880s. Cypres's collection includes a magnificent cardboard color lithographic advertising poster produced in 1912 by Hassan Cigarettes (a brand under ATC). The poster promoted Hassan Cigarettes' T202

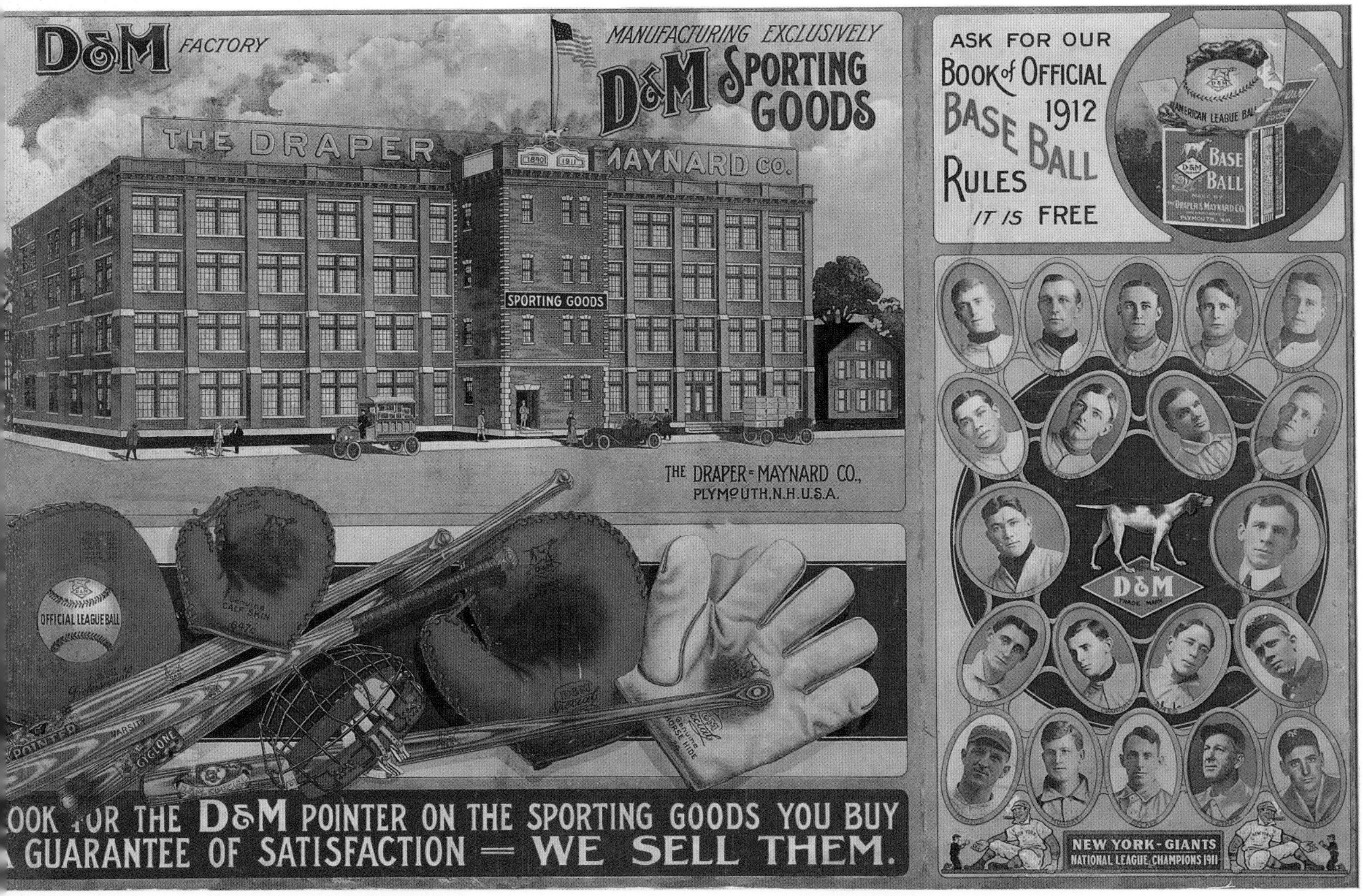

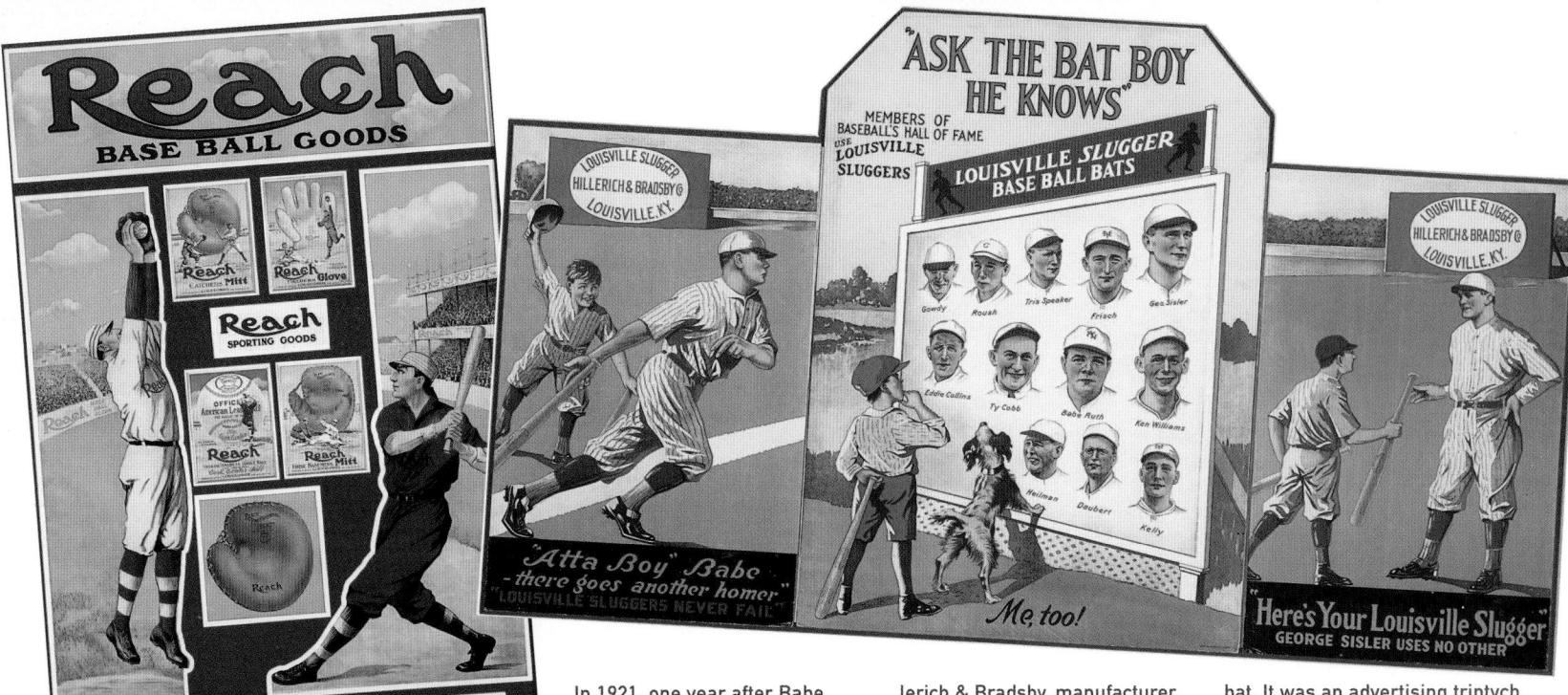

In 1921, one year after Babe Ruth's unprecedented first season with the Yankees and George Sisler's successful assault on the .400 plateau, Hillerich & Bradsby, manufacturer of the iconic Louisville Slugger bat, produced one of the finest items ever created in the history of the company, and it wasn't a bat. It was an advertising triptych (above) that featured skillfully rendered portraits of Ruth, Sisler, and 10 other big-league stars. (28" x 48")

PARAMOUNT-MACK SENNETT COMEDY

"You Get First Pick!"

'THOSE ATHLETIC GIRLS'
WITH
LOUISE FAZENDA

Whenever top silent-screen comedienne Mabel Normand griped to slapstick director Mack Sennett that she wanted classier roles, Sennett always retorted, "I'll send for Fazenda," referring to Louise Fazenda, another leading comedienne of the era. In 1918, Fazenda appeared in Sennett's *Those Athletic Girls*; the one-sheet poster from the film (above) is one of the first to depict women and baseball. (27" x 41")

Mike Donlin batted .333 lifetime in his 12-year major-league career, and in the fall of 1908, he made a hit on Broadway, too, starring in a vaudeville production called *Stealing Home*. Seven years later, Donlin would move to the silver screen and make history, along with John J. McGraw, in *Right Off the Bat* (right) as the first baseball stars to play themselves in a fictional feature film. (81" x 41")

Triple Folders baseball card set, which was endorsed by legendary hurler Christy Mathewson. The war for cigarette market share continued to escalate in the 1920s. In 1921, R. J. Reynolds spent $8 million in advertising, mostly to promote its Camel brand, and inaugurated the I'D WALK A MILE FOR A CAMEL slogan. By 1923, Camel controlled 45 percent of the U.S. cigarette market. In an attempt to steal market share from Camel in 1927, P. Lorillard launched its OLD GOLD CIGARETTES . . . NOT A COUGH IN A CARLOAD campaign, as shown on a triptych in Cypres's collection. ATC, maker of the Lucky Strike brand, bolstered its advertising campaign with some of the game's

CONTROLLED BY
ALL FEATURE BOOKING AGENCY
71 W. 23RD ST. N.Y.C.

MIKE DONLIN
IN
RIGHT OFF THE BAT
AN ORIGINAL COMEDY DRAMA IN 5 PARTS=
BY ALBERT S. LE VINO
WITH
JOHN J. McGRAW
STAR CAST

greatest stars: images of Hall of Famers Harry Heilmann, Lloyd Waner, Tony Lazzeri, and Lefty Grove, adorn a Lucky Strike triptych issued in 1928.

Prominent early-20th-century sporting goods franchises like Reach, Draper & Maynard Company, and Hillerich & Bradsby also saw the benefits of eye-catching advertising signs. Cypres's collection has three examples, the most interesting of which was produced by Reach. In 1913, selected sporting goods merchants dressed up their storefront windows with a color lithographic advertising display. The Reach company logo, which measured 46" x 12", was flanked by images of a Reach glove and ball at the top of the window. Images of the batter and fielder (each 49" tall) occupied the window's lower corners. A Reach salesman's catalog

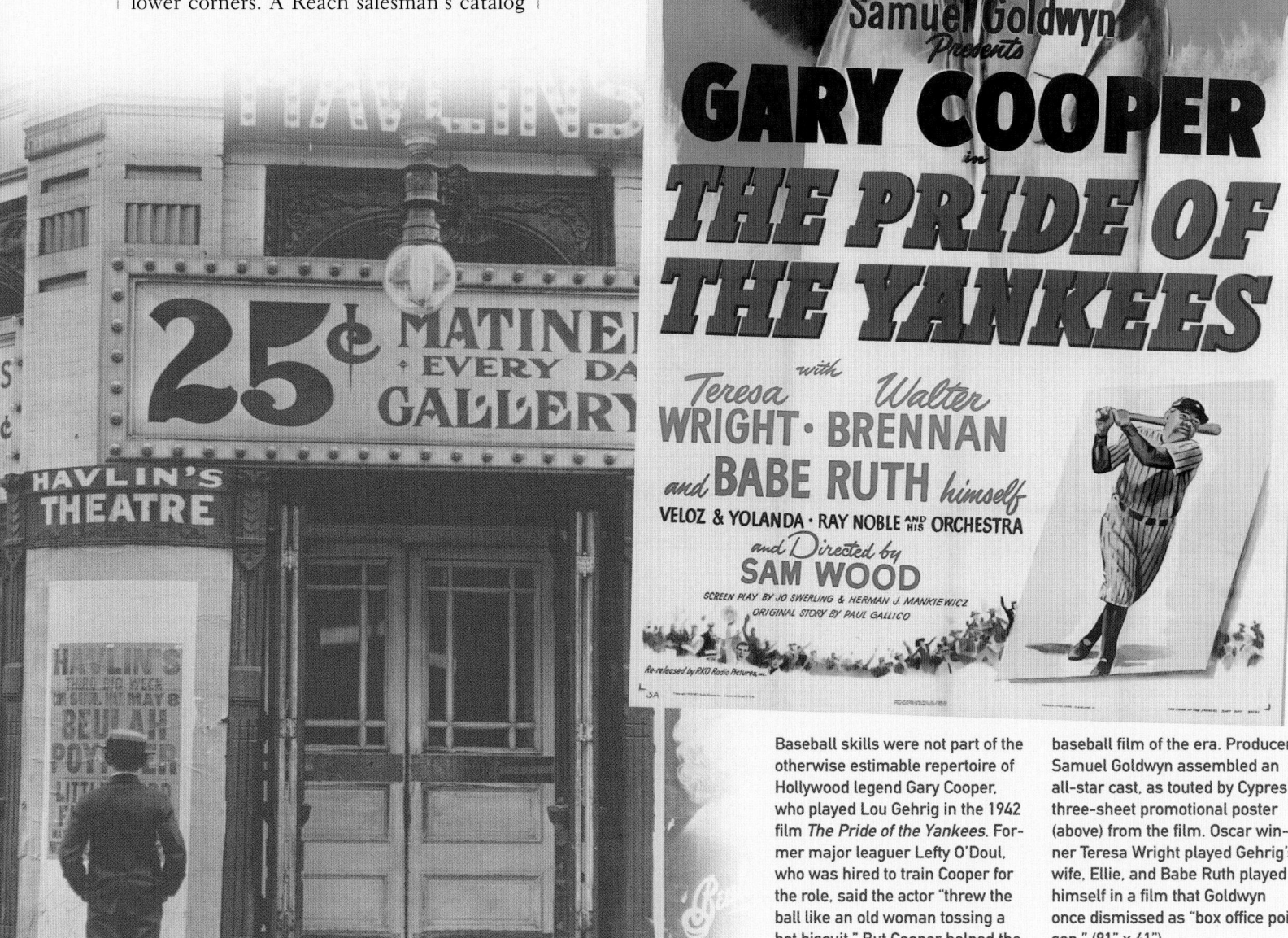

Baseball skills were not part of the otherwise estimable repertoire of Hollywood legend Gary Cooper, who played Lou Gehrig in the 1942 film *The Pride of the Yankees*. Former major leaguer Lefty O'Doul, who was hired to train Cooper for the role, said the actor "threw the ball like an old woman tossing a hot biscuit." But Cooper helped the movie become the most profitable baseball film of the era. Producer Samuel Goldwyn assembled an all-star cast, as touted by Cypres's three-sheet promotional poster (above) from the film. Oscar winner Teresa Wright played Gehrig's wife, Ellie, and Babe Ruth played himself in a film that Goldwyn once dismissed as "box office poison." (81" x 41")

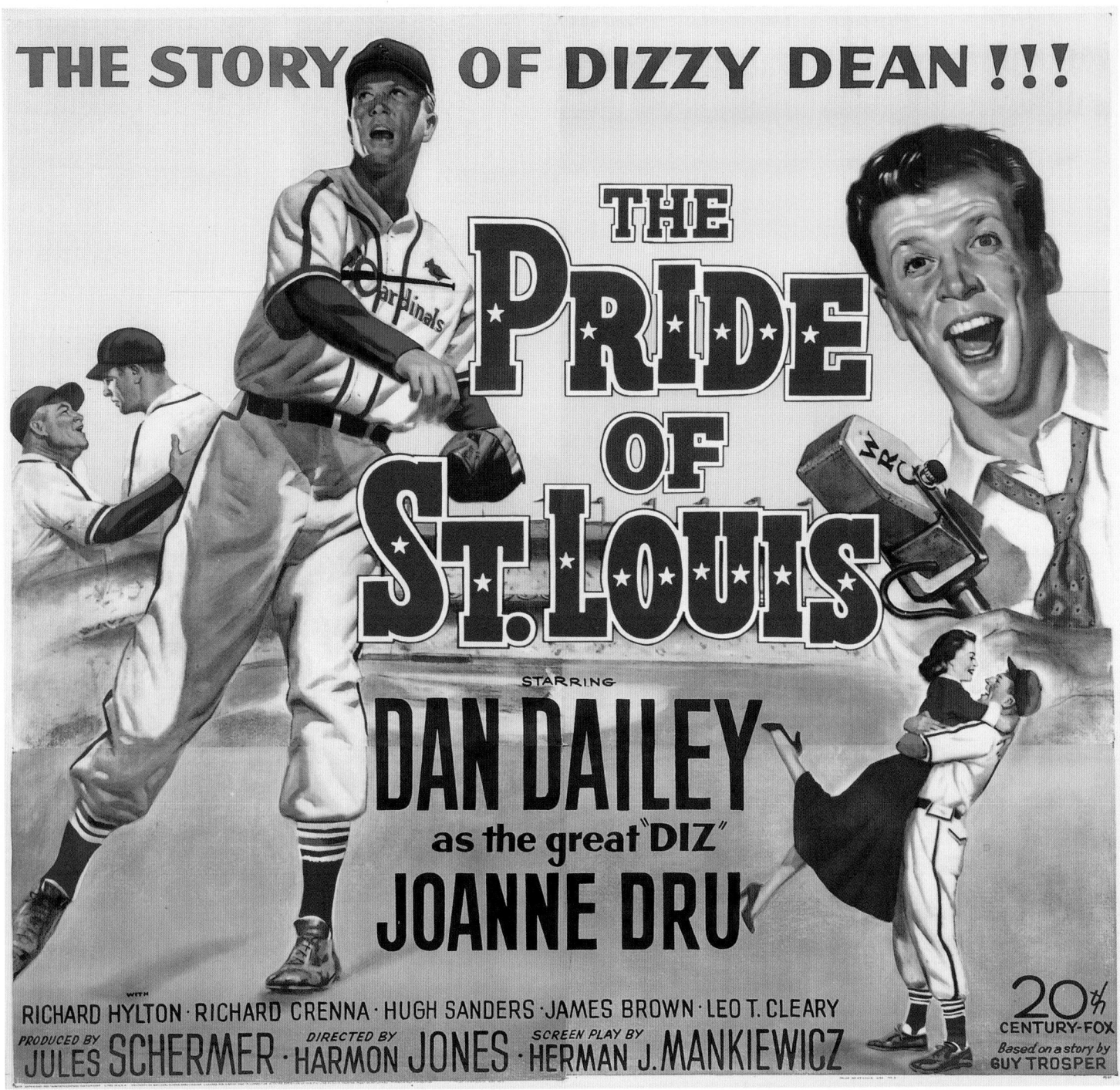

accompanied the display, along with two more Reach logo displays, and four framed show cards, each promoting a different Reach product (catcher's mitt, fielder's glove, first baseman's mitt, and a baseball).

* * *

Even Hollywood created baseball-related advertising art. Major production houses such as Samuel Goldwyn, Columbia Pictures, Paramount Pictures, and 20th Century-Fox issued movie posters. Like most forms of advertising art, they were designed to entice ticket buyers where it most counted: at the point of sale. Artists and

A 1952 six-sheet promotional poster heralds the *The Pride of St. Louis* (above), the story of Cardinals pitcher Dizzy Dean. Baseball executive Branch Rickey once said, "I completed college courses in three and a third years. I was in the top 10% of my class in law school. I am a doctor of jurisprudence. I'm an honorary doctor of laws. And I like to believe I'm an intelligent man. . . . Then will you please tell me why in the name of common sense I spent four hours today conversing with a person named Dizzy Dean?"

Rickey's opinion of its subject aside, the film received an Oscar nomination for Best Motion Picture Story. (81" x 81")

Hollywood portrayed all facets of baseball, including the life of the men who called the shots behind home plate. Cypres's striking three-sheet promotional poster for the 1950 film *Kill the Umpire* (opposite) demonstrates that, even for average films, illustrators and artists remained dedicated to "selling the sizzle, not the steak." (81" x 41")

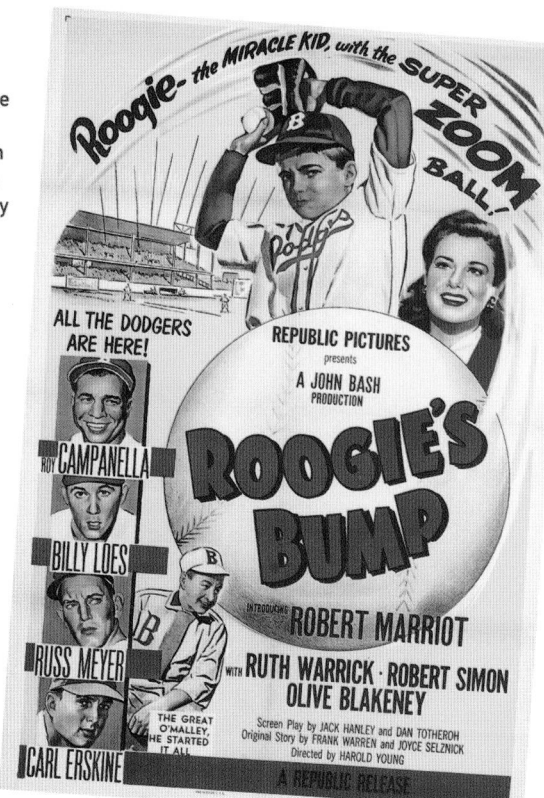

Some critics dismissed *Roogie's Bump* as "the sort of movie destined from the start for church basement showings," but Republic, the movie's producer, hoped that youngsters would still buy a ticket to see young Roogie Rigsby pitch alongside some of Brooklyn's Boys of Summer, who received billing on the film's one-sheet poster (right). (27" x 41")

Thirty-seven years before Mark McGwire and Sammy Sosa enthralled the nation with their home-run derby in 1998, Mickey Mantle and Roger Maris staged one of their own. In 1961, the M&M boys were chasing Babe Ruth's magical mark of 60 home runs in a single season (which Maris broke) and the excitement generated during that unforgettable summer was not lost on Hollywood's top brass. Columbia Pictures quickly signed the two Yankee immortals to star in *Safe at Home*, whose one-sheet (top) featured the two star outfielders. The movie was filmed during the off-season and released the following year. (27" x 41")

Peanuts and baseball have always gone hand in hand, as the song "Take Me Out to the Ballgame" says, and Cypres's original turn-of-the-century roasted-peanut machine (above) attests. (width: 3½' x 2'; height: 5¾')

Cypres's baseball museum includes an exact-replica wooden model (top center) of the original Polo Grounds, which stood at 110th Street and Sixth Avenue (now Lenox Avenue) in Manhattan from the 1870s to 1888. (width: 5' x 6'; height: 12½')

illustrators sought to capture a film's essence, whether it was romance, drama, or slapstick comedy, and magnify it for effect. According to movie poster historians Stephen Rebello and Richard Allen, "Posters were designed to sell the sizzle, not the steak. From the teens through the '40s, movies competed for the same spare change as a variety of other entertainment forms—fairs, circuses, stage shows, vaudeville, radio, and, from 1950 on, television. Posters needed to be sensational." The early-20th-century posters were produced by stone lithography, while those from the 1940s and 1950s were mostly run through an "offset printing" process, which was far cheaper than lithography.

The fact that these posters managed to survive gives them great appeal, especially the posters that originated before World War II, such as *Right Off the Bat* (1915) (see page 52) and *Those Athletic Girls* (1918) (see page 52). Before 1940, the printer would ship the posters to one of the many exchanges operated by National Screen Service, a poster accessories distributor, in every major city throughout the country. The exchanges would distribute them to surrounding theaters for display. Most theaters showed a film for only three or four days, after which the posters were taken down and then sent, along with the film, by bus to the next theater. A film and its posters typically traveled to a number of theaters before returning to the exchange, from where they would be sent out to still more theaters. This constant putting up and taking down destroyed many of the pre-1940s posters. Sometimes, when posters from the 1910s and 1920s made their way into private hands, they were put into walls and under floors of homes to serve as insulation, which obviously removed them completely from circulation.

* * *

Visitors to Cypres's museum can also enjoy some fabulous pieces of baseball folk art. (For an explanation of baseball folk art, see

LEROY (Satchel) PAIGE
PITCHER

When Satch was finally admitted in the MAJORS, he was 42 years of age!- This AMAZING RECORD was made during the age of 42 through 47.... An age when most Ball Players have retired.

MAJOR LEAGUE RECORD

	Games	ShO	Wins	LOST
1948-Cleveland---A.L.	21	2	6	1
1949-	" "	31	0	4	7
1951-St. Louis	" "	23	0	3	4
1952-	" "	46	2	12	10
1953-	" "	57	0	3	9
Totals	178	4	28	31

Beginning in 1924 in Semi-Pro as in Mobile Alabama. Tigers-he pitched many games for One Dollar! Winning 90% of games. Many shut outs, often striking out 14-16 Batters! In 1948 age-42-became the FIRST NEGRO PITCHER in the MAJORS. He reached $25,000 a season. Satch was FIRST NEGRO to pitch in WORLD SERIES (⅔ inning)

Carl Tolpo's original color oil painting of Satchel Paige (above right) belonged to 1930s infielder Tony Piet before Cypres acquired it. (6' x 3')

Former major-league catcher Fred Hofmann constructed a bench (below) out of game-used bats and autographed balls from his personal collection. (width: 51⅛", height: 34", depth: 32")

Chapter XII.) One example is a four-foot wooden show figure of a 19th-century baseball player that stood outside a tobacco shop in the 1880s, inviting customers to enter. According to Frederick Fried, an expert on 19th-century tobacconist figures and author of the definitive book on the subject, *Artists in Wood*, this figure probably came from the

workshop of Samuel Anderson Robb (1851–1928), who is widely considered to be the most accomplished carver of tobacconist figures in American history. Robb, like many show-figure carvers, descended from a family of ship carvers who turned to creating show figures like this one when demand for figureheads and other ship decorations subsided in the middle of the 19th century.

Another folk-art item in Cypres's collection is a bench made of game-used bats and balls. This one-of-a-kind relic was created by Fred Hofmann, who played for the Yankees and Red Sox from 1919 to 1928, and continued his involvement with baseball for an additional 27 years as a minor-league manager and coach for the St. Louis Browns. During his years in baseball, Hofmann amassed a personal collection of game-used bats and balls autographed by the sport's biggest names, including Cy Young, Babe Ruth, and Jimmie Foxx. In the late 1950s, Hofmann used many of these bats and balls to make the bench.

One wing of Cypres's museum contains more than 25 6' x 3' oil paintings of baseball's top stars. The collection once belonged to former big-league second baseman Tony Piet and includes a portrait of the legendary Satchel Paige. Piet had commissioned painter and sculptor Carl Tolpo (1901–1976) to create these massive oil paintings in 1963 so he could display them in his car dealership showroom.

An adjacent gallery in the museum houses an original roasted-peanut machine from the turn of the century, as well as large-scale wooden models, assembled in excruciating detail, of baseball's legendary ballparks, from New York's old Polo Grounds to Boston's Fenway Park.

Cypres's museum is Los Angeles's first sports museum. It opens a door to professional sports history for the city, and sheds light on a vivid and colorful era of American culture.

5

THE LEGEND OF HONUS

> **❝ I don't want my picture in any cigarettes, but I also don't want you to lose the 10 dollars, so I'm enclosing my check for that sum."**
>
> —HONUS WAGNER,
> *in a letter to Pittsburgh sportswriter
> John Gruber (circa 1908/1909)*

In a famous scene from one of Hollywood's most celebrated sci-fi movies, *Close Encounters of the Third Kind,* a power-company employee played by Richard Dreyfuss stands, along with hundreds of his peers, in slackjawed wonder as a group of aliens descends from a flying saucer that has just landed on Earth. The captivated expression on Dreyfuss's face is on a par with the one Brian Seigel wore in the midst a memorabilia auction on July 14, 2000, when his wife, Lorrie, told him he would be foolish to allow the famous T206 Honus Wagner baseball card—once owned by hockey legend Wayne Gretzky and former Los Angeles Kings owner Bruce McNall—to be captured by another bidder. "This is an opportunity of a lifetime for you, honey," Lorrie said to her baffled husband. "You love collecting T206 cards, and if you miss out now, how many years might pass before you have an opportunity to own it?"

Eventually, Seigel snapped out of the awestruck state these words had put him in, and the following day, he won the card for an unprecedented sum of $1.265 million. As the only example of this card graded in near-mint-to-mint "8" condition (on a scale of one to 10 with 10 being the highest grade possible) by Professional Sports Authenticator (PSA), a prominent third-party sports-card grading service, this Wagner T206 card

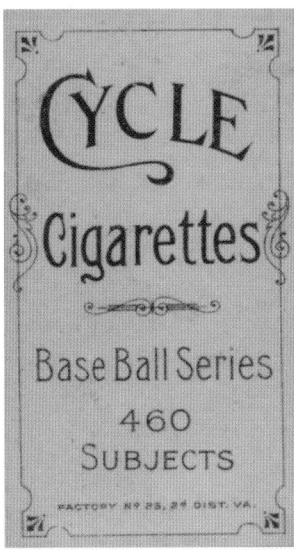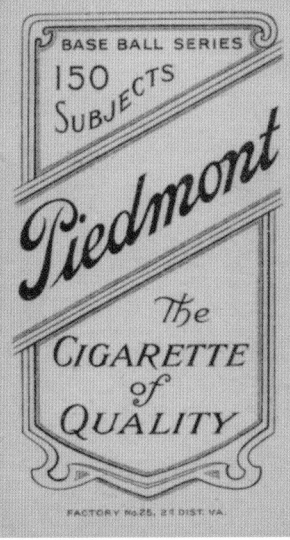

is the highest graded example known, and the most expensive baseball card in the world.

For most baseball card–loving husbands, the kind of support Lorrie showed is nearly incomprehensible, as many of them have spent their entire married lives trying to downplay, if not conceal from their wives, the large fortunes channeled into their cardboard treasures—a habit no doubt connected to their childhoods, when moms threw away entire shoeboxes full of baseball cards. But Lorrie is no ordinary wife, and the T206 Honus Wagner is no ordinary baseball card.

In 1907, the American Tobacco Company (ATC), under the leadership of George Washington Hill (who would serve as president of ATC from 1925 until his death in 1946), revived the use of inserts, premiums, and coupons in packs of cigarettes. The move was designed to advertise ATC products, and it did that, but it also ushered in the second great era of American

The famous Honus Wagner T206 card (opposite) was once owned by hockey legend Wayne Gretzky and former Los Angeles Kings owner Bruce McNall, as its PSA identification tag indicates. "There was something endearing—yes, winning—about Honus Wagner," baseball historian John Thorn has said. "It wasn't just that he was big and ungainly, with a blacksmith's forearms, a cowboy's bowed legs, and the huge hands of a stevedore. It wasn't just that he was quiet and unassuming, though not exactly shy. And it wasn't that he was good, very good, some said better than Cobb. It was all of these things together, his utter unlikeliness, and his utter likeability, his clumsiness and his speed, his power and his modesty, that made him a workingman's hero."

The T206 set features attractive advertisements of the 16 cigarette brands on the backs of the cards. Those for El Principe de Gales, Cycle, and Piedmont are shown above.

Professionally Graded Baseball Cards

Baseball cards that have been professionally authenticated and graded by third-party sports-card grading services constitute a key segment for sports memorabilia collectors. (See "Collecting Vintage Baseball Cards (1915-70s)" by Kevin Struss and Stephen Wong, in Chapter XIII.)

One of the primary determinants of the market value of any item of baseball memorabilia is its condition. An object that shows creases, stains, scratches, holes, etc., commands substantially lower value than an object in pristine condition. For certain kinds of memorabilia, such as advertising displays, movie posters, and photographs, a minor amount of restoration usually will not substantially diminish the object's value. This is not the case for baseball cards. Any form of restoration whatsoever on a baseball card substantially diminishes its market value. One of the objectives of sports-card grading services is to determine whether a submitted card has undergone any restoration and/or doctoring. Any card that has will be identified as such and will not receive a designated grade. All of the cards featured in the Seigel collection have been authenticated and graded by one of the leading services, Professional Sports Authenticator (PSA). PSA authenticates and grades sports cards on a scale from 1 to 10, with 10 being the highest grade. Baseball cards from the early 20th century that have been awarded a grade of 5 or higher by PSA are considered rare.

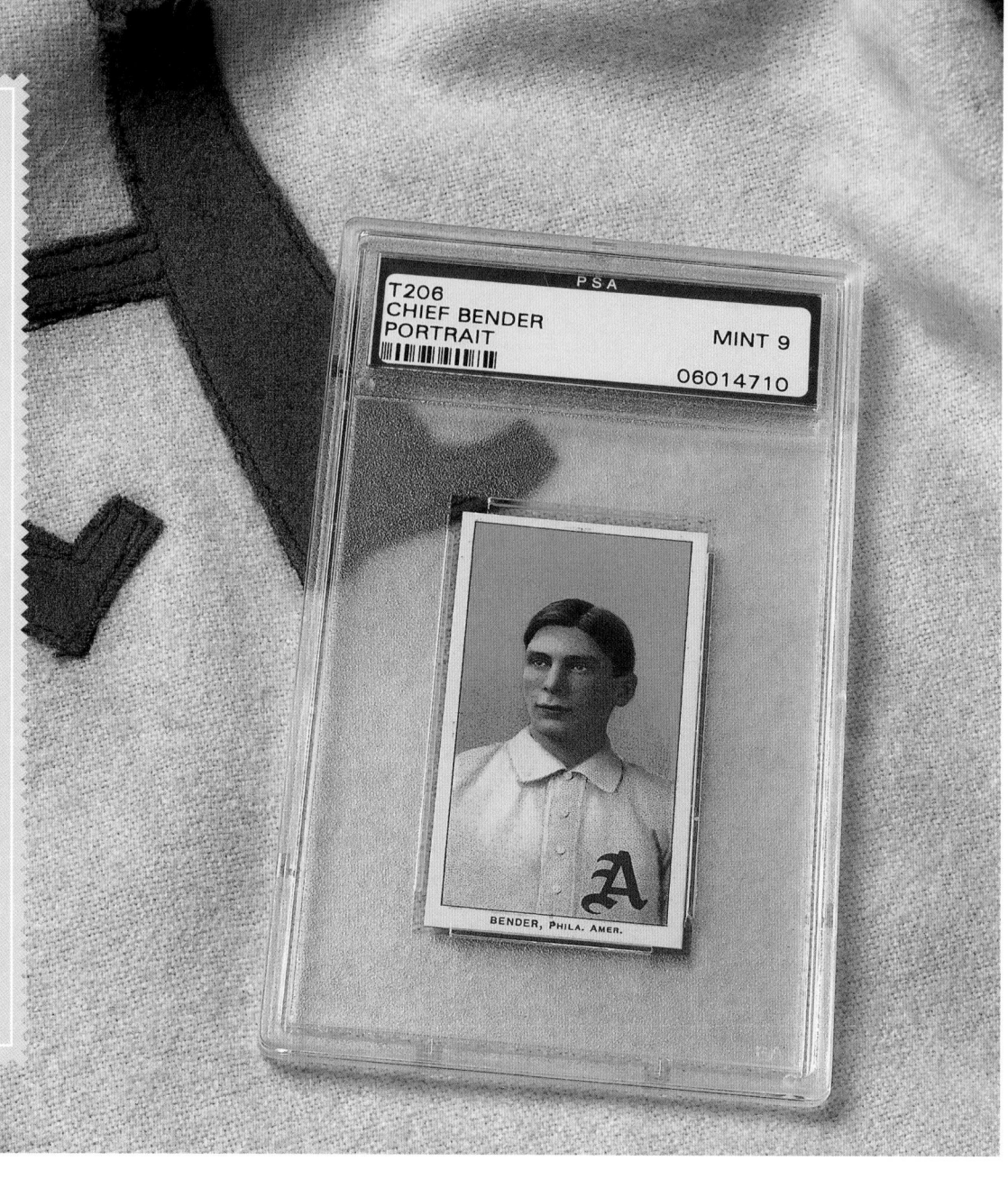

Seigel's T206 portrait card of Charles Albert "Chief" Bender (above) has a PSA rating of "Mint 9." One-quarter Chippewa and a graduate of the Carlisle Indian School in Pennsylvania—whose most famous alum is Jim Thorpe—Bender overcame discriminatory jeering (war whoops, rain dances, and the "Chief" epithet) to become one of the top pitchers for Connie Mack's Philadelphia Athletics. He led the American League in winning percentage three times and was one of the first stars in World Series play, winning six games and producing a 2.44 ERA in five trips to the Fall Classic. Looking back on his legendary managerial career, Mack said, "If I had all the men I've ever handled and they were all in their prime and there was one game I wanted to win above all others—Albert would be my man."

tobacco cards. In 1909, the ATC issued a landmark set of 523 cards (referred to today as "T206" or "white border set"), which are certainly among the most important and popular card sets ever produced. One card, measuring $1\,^{7}/_{16}$" x $2\,^{5}/_{8}$", was inserted into each pack of cigarettes to promote smoking and loyalty to one of the 16 brands advertised on the back of the cards, brands with names like American Beauty, Broad Leaf, Carolina Brights, and El Principe De Gales, to name a few. The set was issued during a three-year period from 1909 to 1911, and its cards feature superb color lithographic images of almost every ballplayer of the era.

The American Lithographic Company of New York (ALC) produced the images for the set from selected photographs of major-league players. A number of the set's portraits—including those of Walter Johnson, Frank Chance, Ed Walsh, Joe Tinker, and Addie Joss—are based on the outstanding photographic work of Carl Horner, one of the most renowned baseball photographers of the early 20th century. Many of the action poses are based on the work of another early-20th-century master photographer, Charles M. Conlon. The lithograph process involved printing in layers, and adding a variety of colors in stages, with high-quality dyes imported from Germany.

The card of Honus Wagner—star shortstop of the Pittsburgh Pirates from 1900 to 1917 and a member of the inaugural class of five at the Hall of Fame—was one of the featured cards in the 1909 set, and it has since achieved a mythical status, transcending the hobby to become an icon of Americana. A partial explanation of the Wagner card's status comes from the well-known legend sur-

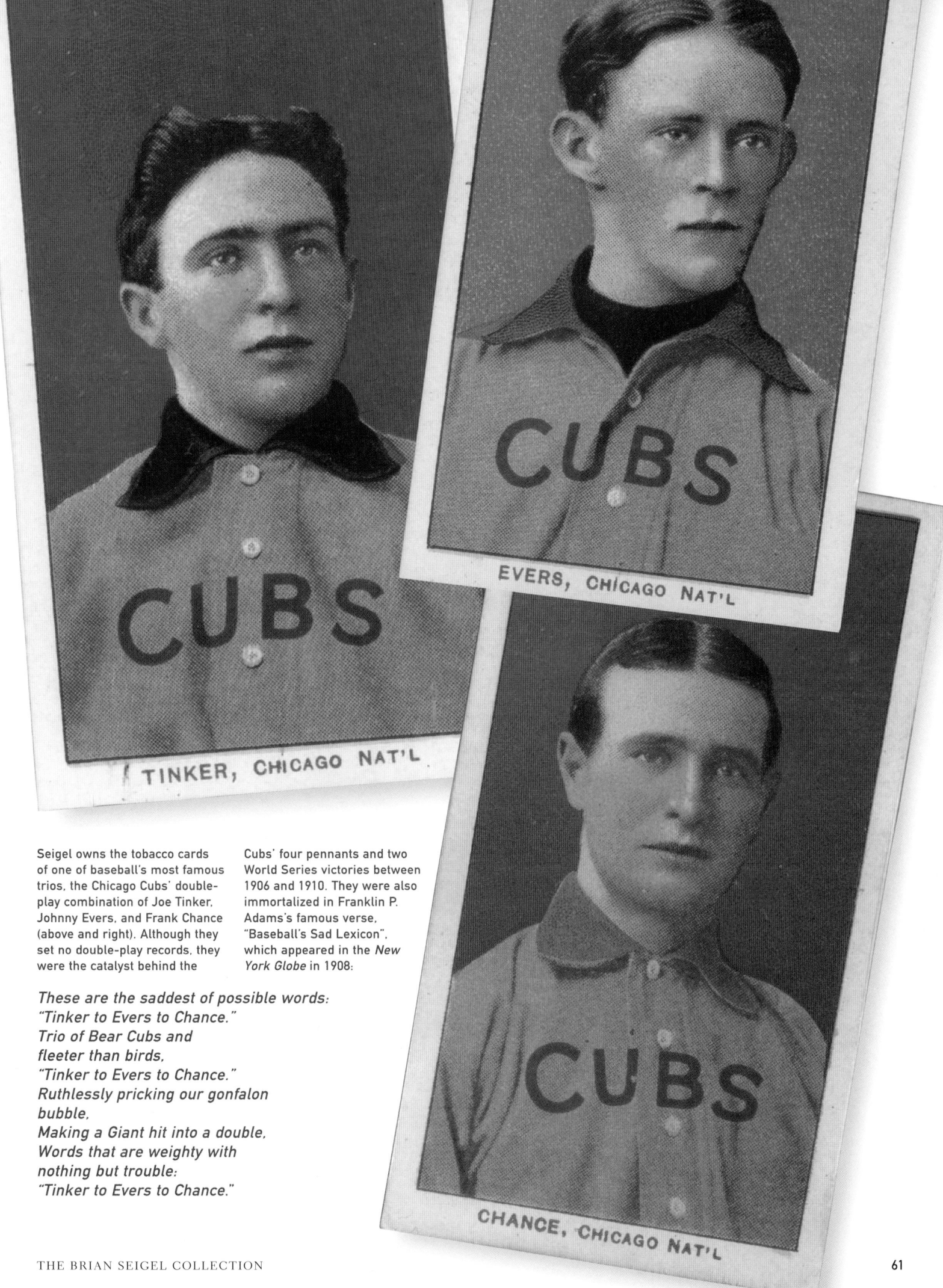

Seigel owns the tobacco cards of one of baseball's most famous trios, the Chicago Cubs' double-play combination of Joe Tinker, Johnny Evers, and Frank Chance (above and right). Although they set no double-play records, they were the catalyst behind the Cubs' four pennants and two World Series victories between 1906 and 1910. They were also immortalized in Franklin P. Adams's famous verse, "Baseball's Sad Lexicon", which appeared in the *New York Globe* in 1908:

These are the saddest of possible words:
"Tinker to Evers to Chance."
Trio of Bear Cubs and
fleeter than birds,
"Tinker to Evers to Chance."
Ruthlessly pricking our gonfalon
bubble,
Making a Giant hit into a double,
Words that are weighty with
nothing but trouble:
"Tinker to Evers to Chance."

Seigel owns three T206 cards of Hall of Fame righthander Cy Young (left). In his first major-league game, Young held Cap Anson's Chicago White Stockings to only three hits. After the game, Anson approached the Cleveland Spiders' club secretary, David Hawley, telling him, "Funny about that big rube of yours beating us today. He's too green to do your club much good, but I believe if I taught him what I know, I might make a pitcher out of him in a couple of years. He's not worth it now, but I'm willing to give you a $1,000 for him."

"Cap," said Hawley, "you can keep your thousand and we'll keep the rube." The rube finished his career with an astonishing 511 big-league wins. Only Walter Johnson, with 417, is within a hundred career victories of Young's total.

rounding the card's origins.

As the story goes, Wagner demanded that the ATC stop issuing his card because he did not want to endorse products that encouraged America's youngsters to smoke. For years, however, this account was disputed by naysayers who pointed to Wagner's well-known taste for cigars during his playing days, and his use of chewing tobacco later in his career. Indeed, Wagner's image appears on a circa-1897 cigar-box lid, as well as on an advertising card produced by Henry Reccius, a Louisville cigar merchant and manufacturer of none other than Hans Wagner cigars. During the 1909 World Series, an advertisement for Murad cigarettes ran in Pittsburgh newspapers, featuring an action pose of Wagner along with the baseball-related slogan, A HIT EVERY TIME. His image appears again on a box lid for another brand of cigars sold in 1910 and called Hans Wagner—King of the Diamond. On a 1948 bubble gum card produced by Leaf Gum, Inc., and featuring Wagner in his later years, when he was a Pittsburgh Pirates coach, the great player is pictured with a huge wad of chewing tobacco in his mouth and a pack of the stuff in his hands.

Needless to say, there is considerable evidence of both Wagner's affinity for tobacco and his willingness to endorse the product. Such evidence prompted speculation that the real reason his card was pulled from the T206 set was because he wanted more money to cooperate with the ATC—not because he was opposed to smoking.

But an article from *The Sporting News*, one of baseball's leading publications, lends credence to the hoary legend. According to the article, which ran in the October 24, 1912, edition, Wagner was so opposed to having his picture associated with tobacco products, that he offered money to prevent it. The article states that the ATC offered a Pittsburgh sportswriter named John Gruber a "liberal fee" (10 dollars) to arrange for the images of Wagner and some of his Pirates teammates to be included in the T206 set. But when the sportswriter sought Wagner's permission,

COBB, DETROIT

JOHNSON, WASHINGTON

COLLINS, PHILA AMER.

When the photograph for Eddie Collins's rookie card (above) was shot by Carl Horner in 1906, Collins was not yet a full-time player for the Philadelphia A's. Indeed, Collins was still a junior at Columbia University, where he went by the name of Edward T. Sullivan to protect his eligibility. "Sullivan" was a star quarterback for the Columbia football team and a crackerjack infielder on the baseball team. The sixth big-leaguer to reach 3,000 career hits, Collins finished with a .333 lifetime batting average.

The T206 set featured four different Ty Cobb cards, of which the green-background portrait of him in his Detroit Tigers uniform (above) is the rarest. The irascible Cobb was one of only four players in the set to have more than three different card variations. In 1910, *The Sporting News* wrote, "Cobb . . . is unpopular with the masses in general, and especially with the players, and it is all brought about by his great love for Ty Cobb himself. But withal, you have to acknowledge that he is the greatest ballplayer in the game today and possibly the greatest of all time."

Walter Johnson's card (above, middle) was inserted into packs of Sweet Caporal cigarettes, whose advertisement appears on the card's reverse. From 1910 to 1919, the Washington Senators righthander won 20 or more games every season and led the American League in strikeouts in all but one. With his gangly arms and sidearm motion, Johnson fired a fastball that Ty Cobb described as "speed, raw speed, blinding speed, too much speed."

Seigel's T206 card of Rube Waddell (right) comes from the latter stages of the lefthander's career, when he played for the St. Louis Browns. Babe Ruth had nothing on Waddell in terms of a lust for life and adventure. According to historian Lee Allen, Waddell began the 1903 season "sleeping in a firehouse in Camden, New Jersey, and ended it tending bar in a saloon in Wheeling, West Virginia. In between those events he won 22 games for the Philadelphia Athletics, played left end for the Business Men's Rugby Football Club of Grand Rapids, Michigan, toured the nation in a melodrama called *The Stain of Guilt*, courted, married and became separated from May Wynne Skinner of Lynn, Massachusetts, saved a woman from drowning, accidentally shot a friend through the hand, and was bitten by a lion." Whew! But as volatile as he was off the field, Waddell was steady as could be on it: He led the American League in strikeouts for six straight years

WADDELL, ST. LOUIS AMER.

SPEAKER, BOSTON AMER.

LAJOIE, CLEVELAND

(1902-07) and his record of 349 strikeouts in 1904 lasted 61 years.

The T206 card for Tris Speaker (above, middle)—and there is only one—came before the Boston outfielder's career truly took off. Had the set been issued a few years later, Speaker might have joined Ty Cobb with four T206 poses, because in addition to being Cobb's equal in the batter's box—a .345 lifetime average and a record 792 doubles—Speaker was the "greatest centerfielder of his day," as his Hall of Fame plaque states. His customary shallow positioning in centerfield and lightning-quick jump on any batted ball resulted in 448 outfield assists, which is still a major-league record.

A Nap Lajoie T206 card (above, right) shows the Cleveland infielder in his follow-through motion after a throw. In addition to being a .338 lifetime hitter (who batted .426 in 1901), Lajoie was, according to his Hall of Fame plaque, the "most graceful and effective second-baseman of his era."

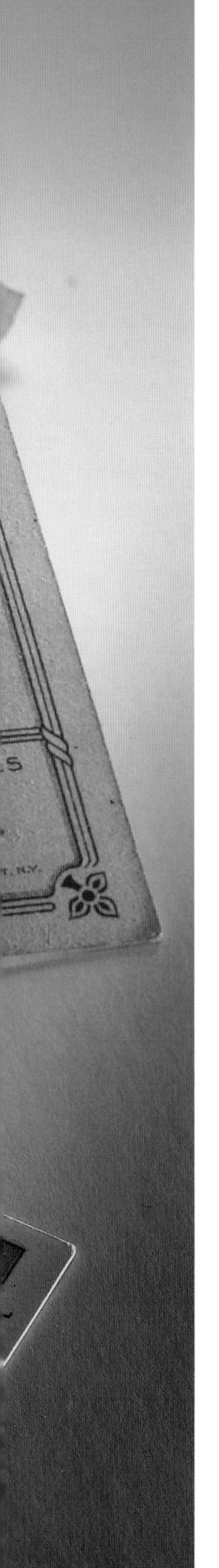

KEELER, N. Y. AMER.

JOSS, CLEVELAND

JENNINGS, DETROIT

M. BROWN, CHICAGO NAT'L

In 1910, a Johnny Evers T206 card (opposite, bottom) could be found in a pack of Sweet Caporal cigarettes, one of the 16 brands of smokes advertised on the backs of the cards.

"Wee Willie" Keeler's T206 card (above) shows him in the uniform of the New York Giants, the team with whom he bookended his career, sandwiching stints with the Giants around spells with Baltimore and Brooklyn. At 5-foot-4 and 140 pounds, "Wee Willie" was one of the smallest men ever to play in the majors, and he used the smallest bat in big-league history: a 29-ounce, 30-inch stick. But what he lacked in physique, he made up for in skill: Keeler retired with a lifetime batting average of .341 (12th-best all-time), and his record 44-game hitting streak stood for 44 years, until Joe DiMaggio broke it in 1941. When a *Brooklyn Eagle* newspaperman asked Keeler to explain his hitting technique, he said, "Keep a clear eye, and hit 'em where they ain't," a phrase that has become one of the game's time-honored maxims.

Addie Joss—whose T206 card (above, second from left) shows him in the beginning stages of the pinwheel pitching windup that gave him his nickname, "the

Human Hairpin"—was involved in one of the great pitching duels in baseball history. With a week left in the 1908 season, and his Cleveland team in a fierce pennant race with the White Sox and the Tigers, Joss squared off against Chicago's "Big Ed" Walsh. Walsh was excellent, allowing only four hits while striking out 15, but Joss was spectacular, setting down 27 consecutive White Sox—a perfect game—and leading Cleveland to a 1–0 win.

Seigel's T206 card for Hughie Jennings (above, second from right) depicts the legendary Detroit Tigers manager in a distinctive pose, one which was often accompanied by an eardrum-splitting scream that echoed through every American League ballpark in which the Tigers played for 30 seasons. "I used to say, 'That's the way!'" Jennings once recalled. "Then I found that it was too dull and tiresome. I wanted something with snap and go to it. So I changed it to 'That's the way-ah!' Finally I found I was just yelling 'Ee-yaah!'"

Mordecai "Three Finger" Brown, whose T206 card is shown above (far right), deserves recognition for more than his colorful nickname, a result of childhood accidents on his uncle's farm that

left him with part of his index finger gone and two other fingers severly misshapen. His lifetime ERA of 2.06 is third best of all time, behind only Walsh and Joss. Ty Cobb described his breaking ball as "the most devastating pitch I ever faced."

Wagner kindly refused, and then sent the sportswriter a 10-dollar check to reimburse him for the money he would have earned if he had secured Wagner's cooperation. Gruber refused to cash the check, and was left with an even greater impression of Wagner as a gentleman after this incident. All of the other uses of Wagner's image in service of tobacco products, it seems, were either without his permission, or for products not directly aimed at children.

More stories and tales have been written about the T206 Wagner than about all other baseball cards combined. But what about the card's current humble owner? Besides having an extraordinarily supportive wife, what would drive someone to spend a seven-digit sum on a baseball card, particularly since this price is nearly $1 million more than the $325,000 paid for the second highest graded example a year earlier (graded as a very good "4" condition by PSA)? Seigel's answer is that his appreciation for the history behind American business conglomerates, early-20th-century baseball, and rarity all converge in his extensive early-20th-century sports card collection—of which his remarkably high-grade T206 Hall of Fame set (a collection that took more than 10 years to assemble) is the crown jewel.

F. CLARKE, PITTSBURG

MC GRAW, NEW YORK NAT'L

MARQUARD, N. Y. NAT'L

WHEAT, BROOKLYN

In addition to symbolizing a significant revival in advertising within the U.S. tobacco industry, T206 cards coincided with a landmark shift in the way the industry was permitted to do business. From 1904 to 1910, companies under the ATC produced 88 percent of the nation's cigarettes, 75 percent of its smoking tobacco, and 90 percent of its snuff. In 1907, the U.S. government began a court battle to dismantle the ATC, claiming it was in violation of the 1890 Sherman Antitrust Act. On May 16, 1911, the U.S. Supreme Court ruled that the ATC was in "restraint of trade and an attempt to monopolize." ATC was given six months to dissolve. On November 16, 1911, the ATC was split up, with new companies Liggett & Myers and P. Lorillard being granted 28 percent and 15 percent of the cigarette business, respectively. ATC retained 37 percent of the cigarette business.

T206 cards also celebrate an entire generation of some of the most recognizable names in baseball lore, many of whom still remain as recognized today as they were nearly a century ago. Seigel's magnificent T206 collection features 75 of the 76 Hall of Fame ballplayers featured in the set. Amazingly, all of these cards have been graded in near-mint-to-mint 8 condition or higher by PSA. They thus represent among the highest\-conditioned examples known. Many constitute only one of two to three examples in that condition.

But T206s, and other early-20th-century Hall of Fame cards, mean more to Seigel than just a world-class collection. They form a con-

nection to one of his most memorable moments as a child. During the summer of 1965, five-year-old Brian, along with his nine-year-old brother Mitch and a dozen buddies, gathered at a neighborhood cul-de-sac in Orange, California, for a biweekly game of street baseball. Standing over the manhole cover that served as home plate, the youngsters began their pregame preparations—determining the batting order, fielding positions, and designated retriever of foul balls. Mitch, whose dream was to be a radio broadcaster in the major leagues, would announce the batting lineup and call the games pretending he was Vin Scully, the golden voice of the Dodgers since 1950.

The boys' idols were the Sandy Koufax–Don Drysdale Dodgers of the mid-1960s, and they could name every ballplayer on that team, as well as the benchwarmers and farm-team hopefuls. But Mitch didn't stop there. To make it as a big-league announcer, he knew he had to polish his knowledge of baseball history. So he practiced his delivery by announcing a lineup that included the game's heroes from as far back as the 1900s. As the kids came up to bat, Mitch stood erect, cupped his hands over his mouth, and boldly announced the names of early-20th-century stars like Honus Wagner, Ty Cobb, Cy Young, Christy Mathewson, and others, all of whom were featured in the T206 set. And when Mitch really wanted to show off, he threw in the ballplayers' nicknames like "the Flying Dutchman," "Georgia Peach," and "Three-Finger Brown."

Fred Clarke of the Pittsburgh Pirates wears a Mona Lisa smile and cradles a bat in his T206 card (above, left). Perhaps he was smiling at the memory of another .300 season with that bat, of which he had 11 in his 21 years. Clarke, who hit .315 lifetime, was a player-manager for 16 years, leading his clubs to 14 first-place finishes.

"There has been only one manager, and his name is John McGraw," Connie Mack once said of the pugnacious New York Giants manager, who wears a catcher's mitt in his T206 card (above, middle). Known as the Little Napoleon for his command of baseball strategy,. McGraw joined the last-place Giants in 1902, led them to the NL pennant in '04, and the World Series title a year after that. He would win three Series and 10 pennants in 29 years.

As unassuming as he looks in his T206 card (above, middle), Richard "Rube" Marquard may have been surprised when the New York Giants paid $11,000 for him in 1908. The *Giants* must have been surprised when Marquard hit the first batter he faced, walked the next two, and then gave up a grand slam to the Reds' Hans Lobert. Sports writers quickly dubbed him the "$11,000 Lemon." Three years later, Marquard became known as the "$11,000 Beauty" when he won a record 19 straight games.

When Zack Wheat posed for the image on his circa-1909 card (above, right), he was fresh from semi-pro ball in the Southern League, where he had hit only .246.

MATHEWSON, N. Y. NAT'L

DUFFY, CHICAGO AMER.

At 5-foot 7-inches, Hugh Duffy's small frame did not impress his first major-league manager, Chicago's Cap Anson. "Where's the rest of you?" the tactless Anson sneered when he first saw Duffy. As was the case with "Wee Willie" Keeler, physique did not seem to impede Duffy's success at the plate. He won the Triple Crown in 1894 when he batted an incredible .440, with 145 RBIs and eighteen home runs. No other player in baseball history has ever batted .440 in a single season.

Surprisingly, as the leftfielder for the Brooklyn Superbas (later renamed the Dodgers), Wheat batted .300 or better for 14 seasons, leading Brooklyn to its first two World Series appearances (1916 and 1920). Wheat was also incorporated in stadium advertising, as a sign on the outfield wall declared ZACK WHEAT CAUGHT 300 FLIES LAST YEAR; TANGLEFOOT FLYPAPER CAUGHT 10 MILLION.

If Horace Fogel, an advisor to New York Giants owner Andrew Freedman, had had his way, the pose on Christy Mathewson's

T206 card (above) would have been different: Fogel advised moving Mathewson from the mound to first base in 1902, prompting manager John McGraw to say, "You can get rid of Fogel. Anybody who doesn't know any more about baseball than that doesn't have a right to the ballpark. Trying to make a first baseman out of Mathewson! There's a kid with as fine a pitching motion as I ever saw. . . . He'll pitch from now on." And so he did, winning 373 games in his career, tying him for first on the all-time NL victories list.

These were the powerful formative memories that instilled in Seigel a love for the game, for its history, and its legends of yore. He sometimes returns to his childhood home, which is approximately three miles from his current residence. The manhole cover is still there, partially buried in layers of asphalt accumulated over the years. He stands over it, closes his eyes, takes a few practice swings, and imagines Mitch announcing a lineup of a dozen T206 stars. If Honus Wagner only knew what his T206 card would mean to passionate card collectors like Seigel, more than 90 years after it was issued, the Flying Dutchman may have reconsidered his opinion about the set—and held off on sending that 10-dollar check to the Pittsburgh sportswriter!

THE ESSENCE OF PROVENANCE

Hallowed relics: Angrist owns the baseball caps (left, l to r) of Joe DiMaggio from the late 1930s, Lou Gehrig from the early '30s, and Babe Ruth from the late 1920s. (Note Ruth's name stitched into the leather sweatband.)

Eight Babe Ruth Louisville Sluggers (opposite) form the centerpiece of Angrist's bat collection and are among the most coveted game-used bats in the hobby. They all show extensive game use and have been side-written, and/or vault-marked, or autographed by Ruth. These elements verify that Ruth used the bats, and tell us when he did—during some of the most astonishing seasons of his one-of-a-kind career:

The bat at the bottom of the photograph is autographed and dated "1920," a season in which Ruth hit 54 homers, *35* more than his nearest competitor.

Side writing on the barrel of the bat second from the bottom confrims that Ruth used it during the 1923 season, when he was the AL MVP and led the Yankees to their first World Series title.

An "R43" vault mark on the knob of the bat third from the bottom indicates that Ruth used it during his epic 1927 season, when he hit .356 with 60 homers and 164 RBI.

The small notches above the center-brand oval on the bat fourth from the bottom verify that Ruth walloped a handful of homers with it. In 1926 and '27, the Babe carved such notches into his bats to mark his home runs.

The POWERIZED AND BONE RUBBED stamp near the centerbrand on the bat second from the top, along with notarized letters of provenance, prove that Ruth used this bat in 1932, when he hit his legendary "called shot" in the World Series.

> " This refutes Gertrude Stein's claim 'a rose is a rose is a rose': that it has become a different object if Napoleon wore it on his uniform. A key is no longer a key if it belonged to the Bastille. A knitting needle is an object with a special aura if Marie Antoinette made it rattle, and a shaving kit will evoke horrible associations if it was once owned by Danton."
>
> —LORENZ TOMERIUS, *"Das Gluck, zu finden. Die Lust, zu zeigen"*

If Lorenz Tomerius, a renowned German music and literary critic, had held Babe Ruth's "side-written" and "notched" home run baseball bat—one of the crown jewels in Dr. Richard Angrist's treasury of historically significant game-used bats and uniforms—his observation about Danton's shaving kit might have been followed by: "A baseball bat will send chills down your spine if it was once used to hit a home run by the incomparable Babe Ruth." But how can one be sure that the rose was actually affixed to Napoleon's uniform, or that Ms. Antoinette really rattled the needle, or that Babe Ruth definitely hit a home run with this particular bat?

Unlike baseball cards, vintage photography, and advertising posters—which are primarily mainstream display items—game-used items of equipment, including bats, uniforms, and other forms of apparel, derive their appeal, importance, and, hence, value from the certainty that they were once owned and used by particular ballplayers. The challenge for game-used-equipment collectors, therefore, is to verify provenance, i.e. an object's origin. And through such provenance, one can determine, often with pinpoint accuracy, whether the item was, in fact, actually used or worn by a given ballplayer.

TRADE MARK
George "Babe" Ruth
REG. U.S. PAT. OFF.
LOUISVILLE SLUGGER
125
HILLERICH & BRADSBY Co.
MADE IN U.S.A.
LOUISVILLE. KY.
"Babe" Ruth

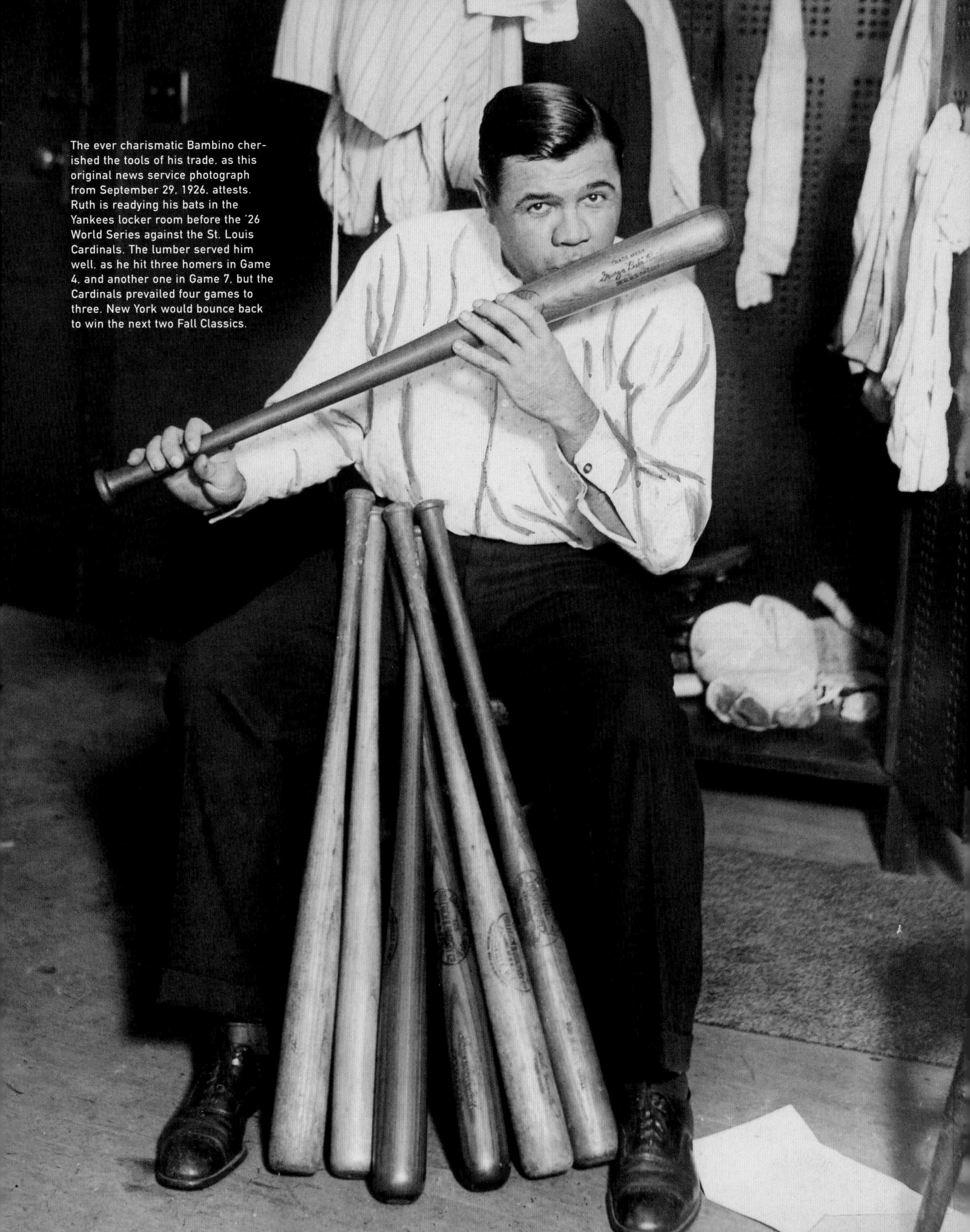

The ever charismatic Bambino cherished the tools of his trade, as this original news service photograph from September 29, 1926, attests. Ruth is readying his bats in the Yankees locker room before the '26 World Series against the St. Louis Cardinals. The lumber served him well, as he hit three homers in Game 4, and another one in Game 7, but the Cardinals prevailed four games to three. New York would bounce back to win the next two Fall Classics.

The Wazir of Wham

The grease pencil side-writing on the barrel of Joe DiMaggio's bat from 1938 (above) implies that this piece of lumber was one of the Yankee Clipper's favorites. Reading JOE DIMAGGIO 8-16-38 NEW YORK AMERICANS 36 INCHES, 34.6 OUNCES, the side-writing proves that after Joe D. cracked the bat, he returned it to H&B to have duplicates made.

H&B applied the vault mark "F3" to the bat knob of Hall of Fame slugger Jimmie Foxx's bat (left). The designation means that this bat served as the prototype for all future Jimmie Foxx bats made with the same weight and length specifications. A .325 lifetime hitter with 534 home runs, Foxx, like many legendary hitters, was justifiably particular about his bats.

Angrist approaches collecting with much the same precision that he applies to his ophthalmic plastic and reconstructive surgery practice. He considers it sacrilegious to purchase any item unless questions of provenance can be answered with unequivocal evidence. In fact, trying to definitively establish provenance has been the catalyst behind Angrist's drive to assemble his peerless collection of some of the world's finest game-used bats. Who else in the world would hire a private investigator to locate a family in order to verify the authenticity of a bat autographed by Babe Ruth? Who else would require laboratory forensic testing to determine whether the markings on a Shoeless Joe Jackson gamer are, in fact, authentic for the period? Some may say Angrist's approach to bat collecting is eccentric. Others view it as the authoritative model of how to collect vintage game-used baseball bats.

It is not overwhelmingly difficult to establish that a ballplayer actually wore a jersey, as the ballplayer's name and/or uniform number typically appear on the garment. The case is slightly more complex for game-used bats. Many ballplayers emulated legendary sluggers like Babe Ruth, Hank Aaron, Lou Gehrig, Willie Mays, and Jimmie Foxx, by ordering and using the same "signature" models used by these players. Hence, the fact that Babe Ruth's name is imprinted on a bat's barrel does not prove that the Sultan of Swat actually used it.

Bat collectors typically focus on three factors to determine whether a player actually swung a particular bat. First is whether or not the physical markings on the bat reveal personal traits associated with use by that ballplayer—the singular pattern of taping on the handle of a Duke Snider or Johnny Mize bat, or the peculiarly scored handle on a Hank Greenberg gamer. (Greenberg used to scratch the handle of his bat with a bottle cap, roughing it up to improve his grip.) Second is whether a bat is autographed by the player or was obtained directly from someone with a firsthand connection to the player, i.e. his family, a fellow teammate, or a scout, manager, or bat boy from the player's team. And last, for those bats manufactured from 1930 onwards by Hillerich & Bradsby Company (H&B, maker of the famous Louisville Slugger baseball

The game-worn home jerseys of Lou Gehrig (opposite, far left) and Babe Ruth (3) from the 1932 season reside in Angrist's impressive collection, along with an autographed photograph of the legendary teammates shaking hands (opposite; Gehrig is on the left) and a ball autographed by both of them. "It was commonly said at the time that Lou Gehrig lived in Ruth's shadow." sportswriter Fred Lieb once recalled. "Such talk never bothered Lou. 'It's a pretty big shadow.' he said. 'It gives me lots of room to spread myself.'" Gehrig spread himself magnificently in 1932—when the Yanks swept Chicago in the Series—batting .349 with 151 RBIs, and becoming the first American Leaguer to hit four home runs in a single game, which he did on June 3. Ruth, for his part, hit .341 with 41 homers and 137 RBIs.

bat since 1884), collectors can look at H&B's shipping records, which document every bat that H&B produced and subsequently sent to a ballplayer.

These factors are generally quite reliable in establishing game-use by a specific batter. But Angrist has taken verification a step closer to absolute certainty by focusing his collection predominantly on "side-written" and/or "vault-marked" bats. Such bats are extremely rare (they constitute less than 0.1 percent of all game-used bats) and are the most coveted in the hobby because their game-use can be traced directly and definitively to a particular player's hands.

In 1943, H&B introduced model numbers that represented a bat's weight and length specifications and were catalogued in factory shipping records. Before that, baseball players would return their favorite game-used bats (usually cracked) to the H&B factory in order to have more of them made with the same weight and length specifications. These returned bats were marked on the side of the barrel in grease pencil, typically with the name of the player who had returned the bat, the date on which H&B had received the bat, the player's team, and the bat's weight and length. Hence the designation "side-written" bats. The grease-pencil markings represent virtually incontrovertible proof that the bat was used by the player who returned it. If a Joe DiMaggio signature-model bat, for example, was returned by one of DiMaggio's teammates (like Tommy Henrich), then the side writing would bear Henrich's name instead of DiMaggio's, and game-use would

Side-writing notations along the barrel of Shoeless Joe Jackson's bat (top), and a "J13" vault mark on both the knob and the barrel end verify that the bat was Jackson's and that he used it during his first few years in the majors, including part of the 1911 season, in which he hit .408. Before Jackson entered the majors, his hometown fans in Greenville, South Carolina, marveled at his blistering, rising line drives, which they called "blue darters," because some locals swore they saw a comet-like blue flame trailing behind the ball. Ty Cobb called Jackson "the greatest natural hitter I ever saw," and Babe Ruth would later admit that he modeled his swing after Jackson's.

Displayed at sporting goods stores during the 1930s and '40s as part of a promotional stunt to augment store-model bat sales, a Nap Lajoie bat from 1903 and '04 (above) is affixed with a typed notation explaining its provenance. The Hillerich & Bradsby Co. organized the campaign, displaying a number of bats that had been used by former big-league stars in stores around the country. Lajoie was the first player in the 20th century to win the Triple Crown, and he won consecutive American League batting titles in '03 and '04, with .355 and .381 averages, respectively. This is the only bat known to exist from Lajoie's playing days.

GAME-USED BASEBALL BATS

BY DAVID BUSHING AND STEPHEN WONG

In the early part of the 20th century, bat makers used tools such as calipers and chisels (above) to produce handcrafted beauties like the bats used by Frank "Home Run" Baker (above left) and Ty Cobb from 1911 to 1916. Franz Bickel, who started working at Hillerich & Bradsby in 1912 and eventually became the foreman of its bat department, was one such worker. During his 50-year tenure with H&B, he made bats for Cobb, Baker, Tris Speaker, and Lou Gehrig. "I had to hold my calipers in one hand and my tools in the other," Bickel has said. "I'd caliper all the way down the bat, then slough it off. I could put my calipers over the turning bat, then check it with the model one. I could just feel when it was right."

Game-used bats constitute one of the fastest-growing areas of concentration in the baseball memorabilia industry. Apart from the sheer historical appeal of any bat that was once used by a famous ballplayer, there are two reasons behind this. First, there have been several books about game-used bats published in recent years, a development that has legitimized the specialty in the public's eye and provided much-needed definitive information. Second, shipping records from famous batmaker Hillerich & Bradsby have become available, and they have provided reliable historical information about which bats were

shipped to which players. As a result of these developments, our knowledge about game-used bats in general, and certain game-used bats in particular, has increased tremendously during the last decade.

What is a "game-used bat"? Which features differentiate such a collectible from a "store model," a retail, over-the-counter bat with similar attributes? Apart from the obvious implication of the term, a game-used bat is a specially ordered and factory-documented bat made specifically for a professional player and not otherwise available to the over-the-counter, retail-store trade. By contrast, a store-model bat is one that has

been manufactured specifically for public sale and/or use. (A major leaguer's bat that never saw game action is known as a professional-model bat, and does not qualify as game-used.)

What sometimes muddies this distinction is the existence of store-model bats endorsed by pro ballplayers. As far back as 1905, the Hillerich & Bradsby marketing team concluded that association with a superstar player, such as Pittsburgh's Honus Wagner, would increase sales of bats among youngsters. The immediate popularity of bats endorsed by Ty Cobb, Napoleon Lajoie, and Tris Speaker, among others, con-

the season with the Hartford Club of the Eastern League. Gehrig became a full-time Yankee in 1925. (Courtesy of the Louisville Slugger Museum)

Above are five marvelous store-model decal bats, the kind of bats that American youngsters commonly wielded more than 90 years ago. Dead Ball–era stars Shoeless Joe Jackson, Tris Speaker, Hank Gowdy, and Eddie Collins are pictured on the decals, which, miraculously (considering the bats' intended use) are still intact. (The Greg John Gallacher Collection)

Babe Ruth (below, left) and Lou Gehrig select their Louisville Sluggers outside the visitors' dugout at Pittsburgh's Forbes Field during the 1927 World Series.

firmed the hunch, and the trend caught on. But these bats were never actually used by the players whose names they bore.

Both player-endorsed and non-player-endorsed store-model bats came with colorful names such as Heavy Hitter Model, Big Leaguer, and The Texas Swatter inscribed on the barrel. They were commercially produced, cleverly marketed, and sold for 50 cents to a couple of bucks. Some of the most popular store-model bats were known as decal bats—they had color decals affixed to their barrels. Almost every store-model bat made by H&B from 1910 through the '20s—a popular period for store-model bat collectors—has a code (such as 40W) imprinted within the centerbrand above "Hillerich & Bradsby Co." Store-model bats can be identified by this code. The letters match the initials of the ballplayer whose name is stamped on the barrel (e.g., Wagner), and the number represents the bat's length in inches. Any H&B bat with markings on the knob indicating bat length is also a store-model bat.

Store-model bats have their charms, but few collectors will dispute that a genuine, game-used bat has an allure unmatched by any mass-produced product. Most firms that made store models also sought to make bats for professional ballplayers, since a contract with a star athlete boosted the company's profile and, consequently, its sales. Since the majority of game-used bats in private collections are Louisville Sluggers, the rest of this essay will focus only on this particular brand.

To ascertain whether a game-used bat is authentic, you need to consider a number of factors, including manufacturer markings, signs of game use, and label dating.

MANUFACTURER MARKINGS ON GAME-USED LOUISVILLE SLUGGERS

• 1. Centerbrand: Since 1917, just about every game-used H&B bat has had the professional model number "125" prominently burned into its centerbrand. A few models had "40" and "250" imprinted instead of "125," but

Starting in the 1910s, professional bat-order records were kept in ledgers (above) containing handwritten dates, names, and notes. These pages show that Walter Johnson ordered a bat on February 20, 1915, and that Lou Gehrig ordered one on July 5, 1924, when he spent most of

these represent only a fraction of post-1917 gamers. Bats dating from 1897 to 1911 have "MADE BY" instead of "125," and gamers from 1911 to 1916 have a "–.–" symbol.

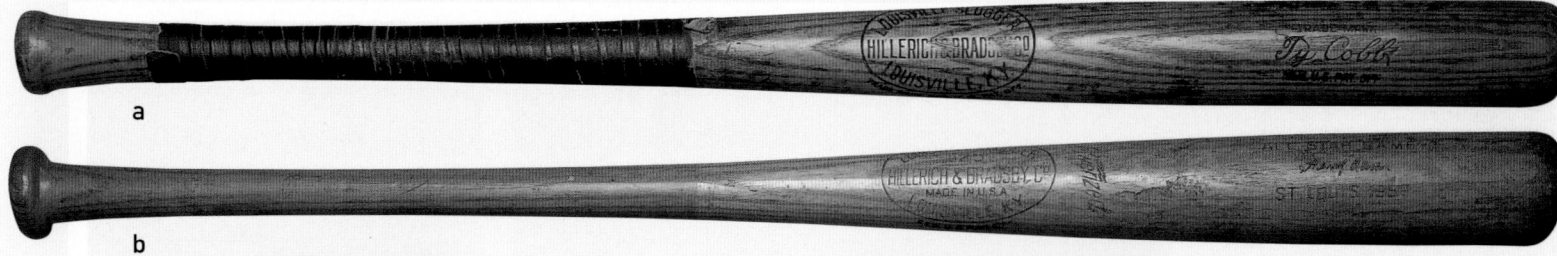

a

b

c

d

e

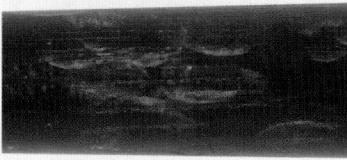

f

g

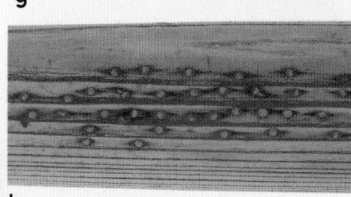

h

a. Ty Cobb usually applied black tape to the handles of his bats, as he did to this gamer that he used during the 1916 season.

b. Judging by the extensive markings on this 1957 Hank Aaron All-Star gamer, it's clear that Hammerin' Hank continued to use it for the remainder of the season. And it served him well: Aaron won the National League MVP award and led his Milwaukee Braves to a World Series title over the Yankees, batting .393 in the Series. The Wong Family Archives Collection.

c. Professional model number "125" was stamped into the centerbrand of this game-used H&B bat from the 1917- 21 period.

d. An Adirondak black foil-tape center-brand stamp.

e. A professional model number from the 1943- 75 period.

f. Ball and stitch marks.

g Rack marks.

h. Small nails applied to repair a crack.

• 2. Labels: For a bat to be a genuine H&B game-used bat, its labels must have been "burned in" by a process in which a die is heated and then pressed into the bat. Game-used bats produced by one of H&B's competitors, Adirondak, employed a method in which "foil-tape" was heated and pressed into the bats. The foil-tape system left a light impression beneath the foil, which is often found flaked to some degree. H&B did not use this foil-tape method until 1985. Any vintage Louisville Slugger bat with a shallow, heat-impressed black foil is not a genuine H&B gamer.

• 3. Model Numbers: These numbers identify the style, dimensions, and weights of bats used by individual pros. Each Louisville Slugger made in or after 1943 has a professional model number stamped onto the knob (1943– 75) or the barrel (1976- present). A model number consists of a letter followed by one to three numbers and sometimes a second letter, such as "L" (large knob), "S" (small knob) or "C" (cupped). Mickey Mantle preferred the M110 model. Willie Mays, Ernie Banks, and Eddie Matthews preferred the "S2" model. Before 1943, a game-used H&B bat usually had nothing stamped on its knob, unless it was one of the rare vault-marked bats that had been returned to the factory by a player.

SIGNS OF GAME USE

In addition to the manufacturer markings mentioned above, you should check factory records to confirm that the bat was shipped to the ballplayer whose name is stamped on the barrel. Factory records exist for any H&B bat shipped after 1930. Second, the bat must show signs of game use, the following of which are the most common:

• 1. Ball and Stitch Marks: A ball mark is an imprint of smears left by a baseball when the bat connects with it. Because such marks often fade over time, most vintage gamers will not bear ball marks. A stitch mark is a seam imprint left on the bat by a baseball. Many vintage gamers retain stitch marks, typically along the bat's barrel.

• 2. Rack Marks: Rack marks are long friction marks (often colored) caused by a bat being repeatedly pulled from team bat racks. Bats used by New York Giants Hall of Famer Mel Ott, for example, typically show green rack marks because the bat rack at the Polo Grounds, home of the Giants, was painted green.

• 3. Other Markings: If a player was concerned that his bat was subject to "checking" (the seams in the wood grain becoming loose), he might "bone" the bat— rub a hard object against it—to toughen the bat's surface. In the old days, players sometimes repaired dead wood or a slight crack in a bat with small finishing nails. Even a severely cracked bat might be tossed to a batboy, who would apply nails to fix the crack. Such markings are rare and can be highly valued by collectors.

• 4. Personal Attributes: Characteristics of certain ballplayers link them to the bat they used. Collectors prize bats with such personal traits. Ty Cobb, for example, preferred bats with knots in the wood, and black handle tape. A Duke Snider bat can also be recognized by its taping: He always wrapped his tape in a criss-cross pattern. Ted Williams sometimes painted his uniform number (9) in black on his bat's knob. After 1968, Roberto Clemente almost always had his number (21) written in black marker on his bat's knob. To improve his grip, Clemente, like Hank Greenberg before him, used a bottle cap to scrape grooves into his bat (referred to as "scoring").

• 5. Side Writing and Vault Marks: "Side writing" and/or "vault marks" on a bat provide airtight evidence of game use by the ballplayer who returned the bat to the H&B factory. Bats with these markings are among the most coveted bats in existence, and they are exceedingly scarce, constituting less than 0.1 percent of all game-used bats. (See page 71 for more detail on these types of markings.)

SPECIAL BATS

In 1949, H&B started to make bats especially for use in the All-Star Game. The following year, the company began producing special World Series bats as well. But players received only two All-Star bats and two World Series bats each per event, so these items are very rare today. Other special bats include those that have been autographed, and bats that can be identified as having been used to hit a specific home run or reach a certain milestone. Such a bat is typically far more valuable than a standard game-used bat, depending on the landmark it commemorates, its condition, and its rarity.

BAT LABEL DATING

Distinguishing factors on a bat's label often allow collectors to pinpoint the year in which it was made. For a comprehensive discussion of dating by means of bat labels, see *MastroNet Reference and Price Guide for Collecting Game-Used Bats* (2001).

GAME-USED BAT AUTHENTICATION AND GRADING

Maybe the game bat you have is in gem mint condition, and has never connected with a baseball. If a player or friend asked Stan Musial for a game bat, more often

a

b

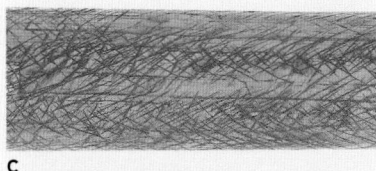

c

WORLD SERIES 1955
Mickey Mantle
NEW YORK YANKEES

d

a. This vault-marked Jimmie Foxx bat, returned to H&B in 1931, bears its owner's cleat marks along the barrel. (The Dr. Richard C. Angrist Collection)

b. A 1950s game-used Duke Snider bat displays the criss-cross taping pattern Snider usually put on the handle of his bats.

c. The rough-hewn scoring on the bat handle of this 1930s Hank Greenberg gamer is one piece of evidence of its authenticity.

d. Twenty-four-year-old Mickey Mantle used this specially made World Series bat against the Brooklyn Dodgers in the 1955 Fall Classic. Some World Series bats were never used because players preferred to stick with their regular-season bats. Not so with this bat, which is riddled with stitch marks along the sweet spot of the barrel.. The Ron Leff Family Collection

than not he would give them a brand-new example straight from the rack. Collectors today, however, want bats with verified, identifiable game use (as opposed to baseball card collectors, who value pristine items). A genuine used bat could win the rarefied grade of 7 or higher, while the "gem," factory-documented Stan Musial gamer—the one that looks like it was made yesterday—might grade 5.

How is a game-used bat graded? Factory records, evidence of game use, the importance of the player, the condition of the bat, an autograph (especially of a deceased Hall of Famer), and scarcity all contribute to the analysis. An overall grade takes into account every factor but assigns a value based mostly on market appeal and scarcity. Both SCD Authentic (SCD) and Professional Sports Authenticator (PSA) are renowned professional third-party grading services for game-used bats. SCD, however, also awards a numeric grade to a bat based on an assessment of the aforementioned criteria. While addressing each criterion, the company's evaluation is designed to yield a definitive summary of all pertinent physical, subjective, and historical aspects of the bat. SCD's grading scale, ranging from A10 (highest) to A1, provides a useful framework for collectors to distinguish an outstanding

gamer from an average one.

Even with the advent of strictly codified grading, though, collector preferences will still be important in ascribing value to particular bats. A bat used by a Hall of Famer who is not recognized for his hitting prowess, such as Walter Johnson, Satchel Paige, or Sandy Koufax, will sometimes bring a price far above a bat that was used by one of the game's great sluggers like Jimmie Foxx or Babe Ruth, just because it is rarer. Yet the rarest, finest game-used bat of Billy Rogell will never approach the value of a common Ted Williams gamer. And of course any post-1980 game-used bat will be hundreds of times less valuable than any bat made before 1950. With each passing decade, game bats become easier to obtain. There are so many game-used bats made after 1980 in circulation that you could literally build a house from the available supply! By contrast, for almost any pre-war Hall of Famer, there are fewer than six truly verifiable game-used bats.

COLLECTING THEMES

There are a number of themes on which you can base a collection of game-used bats. You might strive to acquire a game-used bat of every player with at least 500 career home runs, or 3,000 career hits, or a lifetime batting average of at least .300. Other themes include bats of Hall of Famers from a particular era, or bats of players from touchstone teams such as the 1929 Philadelphia Athletics, 1955 Brooklyn Dodgers, 1961 New York Yankees, or the 1975 Cincinnati Reds.

Whatever theme you choose, you'll no doubt bear in mind that owning a bat once gripped by a professional ballplayer is a special privilege. According to author Bob Hill, who has written a wonderful book on the history of Louisville Slugger, "no piece of equipment in sport has ever excited a more personal response from its user than a baseball bat." Ted Williams often visited the H&B factory and climbed around stacks of drying white ash to pick out the best wood for his bats. That is the spirit that makes these relics so treasured. To own one is to possess not only a piece of American history, but also some of the heart and soul of a ballplayer.

In 1938, a little boy received a game-used bat from the great Lou Gehrig, who inscribed it, To Jimmy, may you use this to better advantage than I did. Unaware of the amyotrophic lateral sclerosis—still known as Lou Gehrig's disease—that was killing him, Gehrig hit only .250 that season. Marshall Fogel owns the inscribed bat (below) as well as an autographed ball, and the program from the game on May 2, 1939, when Gehrig took himself out of the New York lineup for the first time since 1925, ending his then record streak of 2,130 consecutive games played.

Seven decades of New York Yankees glory are enshrined in Angrist's display cabinet in the form of the home-game-worn jerseys (below) of every Bronx Bomber Hall of Famer who has had his number retired by the storied franchise. Stitched into the collars of the hallowed garments are the indelible names of their former owners, starting with Babe Ruth and Lou Gehrig, and concluding with Whitey Ford, Casey Stengel, and Reggie Jackson. Between them, the 10 Yankees who wore these jerseys won 33 pennants and 22 World Series titles.

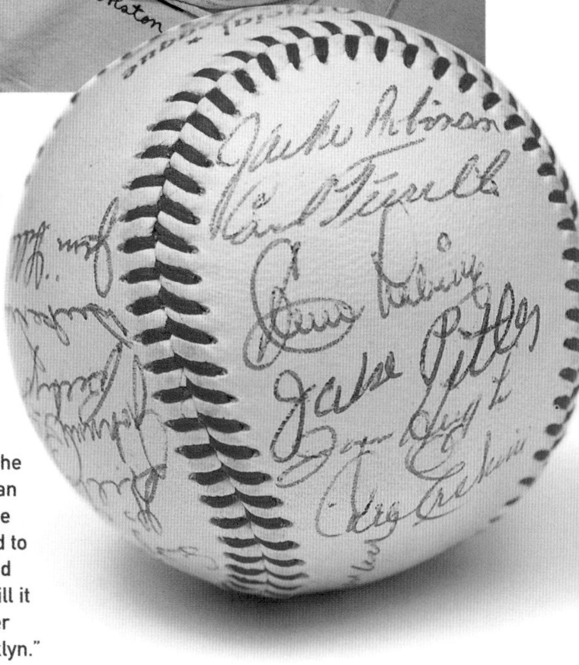

More jewels in the Angrist collection include the home-game-worn jerseys (above) of several icons of the Brooklyn Dodgers of the 1940s and '50s, including Gil Hodges, Pee Wee Reese, Jackie Robinson, Roy Campanella, and an autographed Duke Snider flannel. "You may glory in a team triumphant," wrote Roger Kahn in his Dodgers classic, *The Boys of Summer*, "but you fall in love with a team in defeat." The Dodgers certainly had their share of heartbreaking defeat between 1949 and 1953: They lost the NL pennant two times on a home run in the final inning of the season, and they fell to the dreaded Yankees three times in the World Series.

Twenty-five members of the 1955 Dodgers, the team that finally broke through and won a World Series for Brooklyn, signed an Official National League baseball (right), which now resides in Angrist's collection. Brooklyn ace Johnny Podres beat the Yankees twice in that Series, wrapping it up with a 2–0 shutout in Game 7, and unleashing pandemonium in the borough. Podres recalled, "I can remember that the champagne was really flowing. All you had to do was hold out your glass and somebody would be there to fill it up. . . . I doubt if there had ever been a night like that in Brooklyn."

be attributed to Henrich, not DiMaggio.

Vault-marked bats were also returned to the H&B factory by specific players for duplication. These returned bats, however, were assigned a vault-mark on the butt end (and sometimes at the end of the bat's barrel as well) in the form of a letter from the alphabet followed by a one to three-digit number. H&B, for example, designated the "F3" vault mark to a bat returned by Jimmie Foxx in 1931; "F3" stands for the third type of variation in a bat's length and weight, for a ballplayer whose last name begins with the letter "F." After the vault mark was applied to the bat—by burning it into the wood and then, usually, filling it with white paint—the bat was placed in the factory tool room to serve as the prototype for all future bats made with "F3"-designated weight and length specifications.

Many of H&B's side-written and vault-

FROM BUTTER CHURNS TO BASEBALL BATS

BY ANNE JEWELL

Some of the most significant moments in baseball history took fire in the split-second when leather met lumber. That unmistakable sound, a percussive collision between ball and bat, is an indelible part of the game and has remained relatively unchanged since baseball's beginning. The same holds true for Louisville Slugger baseball bats. Since 1884, many of the greatest hitters in baseball have used Louisville Sluggers, making these sticks a coveted artifact for collectors. But when J. Michael Hillerich and his family of woodworkers sailed into Baltimore harbor in 1842 from Baden-Baden, Germany, they never dreamed of the impact their family would have on their new homeland's favorite pastime.

The Hillerichs settled in Louisville, a busy river town that was then one of the nation's largest cities. In 1859, one of Michael's sons, J. Frederick Hillerich, established his own woodworking shop there. Some debate surrounds the origin of the very first Louisville Slugger bat. The company contends that J. Frederick's 17-year-old son, John A. "Bud" Hillerich, crafted a bat for Pete "The Old Gladiator" Browning in 1884, after the great slugger's bat broke during a game in Louisville. But other theories have been advanced. Arlie Latham, a player for the St. Louis Browns, claimed that the company's first bat was made for him. Bud Hillerich's recollection in 1914 was that he simply carved a ring around Browning's bat, putting a "home run in it," which satisfied Browning's superstitions. Yet another tale has Bud, an amateur ballplayer, making his own bats, which attracted the attention and admiration of his teammates.

Whatever the circumstances, one thing is certain—J. Frederick wanted nothing to do with making bats. His core business had always been bedposts, wooden bowling balls, and swinging butter churns. He believed there was little profit in producing baseball bats, and he considered the players requesting them a nuisance. But Bud, who had a passion for the game and a commitment to customer service, persevered with bat making. As the reputation of the Hillerich bats grew, so did the family's business.

In 1911, Frank Bradsby joined the Hillerich family business, coming over from Simmons Hardware in St. Louis, where he managed the sales of athletic goods. Bradsby was already familiar with Louisville Slugger baseball bats, and his sales and marketing talents had a dramatic and dynamic impact on the batmaking company. In 1916, the business name became Hillerich & Bradsby Co., as it is still known today.

For many years, the company handcrafted bats to specific weights, lengths, and styles. Making a bat by hand requires great concentration, infinite patience, and an impeccable eye for detail. Wood chips fly from the timber as it spins on the lathe. The worker meticulously applies just enough pressure with his hand tools to coax the bat shape out of a hunk of white ash. Sliver by sliver, ounce by ounce, a bat emerges. As the bat takes shape from the lumber, the craftsman hovers over it, running his experienced hands along the length of the whirling wood. He dutifully checks at least a dozen measurement points against the model he is re-creating, sanding off a fraction here or perfecting a taper there.

Archive photos in the Hillerich & Bradsby Co. collection show bins of bats in the Hand Turning Room with workers standing at their steam-powered lathes. Wood shavings from the bats are sprinkled on their clothes and piled knee-high on the factory floor. While it once took 30 minutes to create a bat by hand, it now takes about 30 *seconds*. Louisville Sluggers are currently produced on automatic lathes, which provide a more consistent and precise bat. But several factory workers practice and preserve the art of hand turning by demonstrating the process for visitors at the Louisville Slugger Museum in Louisville, Kentucky. Visitors to the Museum can also observe another step in the batmaking process that has changed little since the early years—the branding of the bats. Each bat is carefully placed by hand next to the branding plate, then rolled over it. With a sizzling kiss, the red-hot plate greets the timber. As the smoke clears, the bat rolls off the plate bearing the company's oval trademark, along with the player's name or signature. On colored bats, gold or silver foil brands are used instead of burned-in brands, because they show up more clearly than burned wood on a colored background.

The current bat factory and museum are not far from the site where the very first Louisville Slugger baseball bat was allegedly created in 1884. More than 100 years later, the company no longer makes butter churns, but it is still churning out baseball bats.

marked bats, some of which were used by ballplayers as early as in the 1910s, were kept for over 40 years in storage barns at the H&B factory. Some of the most precious examples include those returned by Dead Ball–era legends like Shoeless Joe Jackson, Ty Cobb, and Tris Speaker, as well as legendary sluggerss from the 1920s and 1930s like Babe Ruth, Lou Gehrig, and Rogers Hornsby.

In the mid-1980s, almost all of the side-written and vault-marked bats from the H&B storage barns were made available to the public. Many of them now reside in Angrist's remarkable collection, vaulting his assortment of exquisite lumber into the pantheon of Americana holdings. Angrist owns side-written, vault-marked, and autographed gamers of every batter who has attained one of baseball's loftiest benchmarks, from hitting .400 for a season to winning the Triple Crown (the league's season leader in batting average, home runs, and runs batted in), to smacking 3,000 lifetime hits to belting 500 career home runs. His magnificent collection also pays tribute to Babe Ruth with a side-written, vault-marked, and/or autographed game-used bat from virtually every stage of the one-and-only Bambino's astounding career.

But Angrist's passion for collecting does not end with the game's legendary lumber. Some of the game's most treasured wool-flannel relics complement his bat collection. These include Ruth's home Yankees game-worn jersey from the 1932 World Series against the Chicago Cubs, the series in which he allegedly pointed to the centerfield bleachers of Wrigley Field and, "calling his shot," belted an 0-2 pitch for a home run into the very same centerfield seats. This jersey is accompanied by a game-used home jersey, hat, and bat of every other player who has had his number retired by the Yankees, including Gehrig (#4), DiMaggio (#5), Mickey Mantle (#7), and Reggie Jackson (#44), among many others. Angrist also owns a plethora of some of the finest vintage team-signed baseballs and photographs from every significant era in Yankees history.

He has also devoted a portion of his collection to the Bronx Bombers' crosstown rivals, the Brooklyn Dodgers. The spirit of Ebbets Field lives on in an assortment of team-signed baseballs from the halcyon days of Brooklyn (the late 1940s and 1950s) along with game-worn home jerseys right off the backs of Brooklyn's famed Boys of Summer, including Jackie Robinson, Duke Snider, Roy Campanella, Gil Hodges, Pee Wee Reese, and Walt Alston. In addition

It would be difficult to find artifacts in the hobby than Angrist's New York Yankees team-signed baseballs from 1927 (above left) and 1932 (above right). Twenty-three members of the '27 New York Yankees—arguably the greatest team in baseball history—signed the Official American League baseball in black fountain pen, and Byron Bancroft "Ban" Johnson, who founded the American League and served as its president from 1900 to 1927, placed his official stamp on the ball. The ball from 1932 is signed in black fountain pen by 22 members of that season's Yankees, who won 107 regular-season games and swept the Chicago Cubs in the World Series. It is also an Official American League baseball, and Johnson's successor as AL President, Ernest S. Barnard, placed his official stamp on it.

Angrist owns a Lefty Grove game-worn uniform (shirt and pants), a photograph of the pitcher posing with his father and his son, and a ticket to the 1931 World Series (left) between Grove's Philadelphia Athletics and the St. Louis Cardinals. Widely regarded as the greatest lefthander of all time, Grove produced a spectacular season in 1931, going 31–4 and leading the American League in wins, shutouts, strikeouts, ERA, and complete games, accomplishments good enough to earn him the league MVP award. Grove led the league in strikeouts in his first seven seasons in the majors, and he won 20 games or more seven times. For nine seasons, his ERA was the lowest in the league, and during Philadelphia's pennant-winning years (1929–31), his won-lost record was 79–15. Baseball analyst Bill James called him "the greatest pitcher of all time, period."

Roberto Clemente's game-used bat and jersey from the 1959 season (opposite above) reside in Angrist's sparkling store of baseball memorabilia. Clemente played baseball with uncommon passion, brilliance, and intensity. Baseball writer Roger Angell described him as "playing a kind of baseball that none of us had really seen before—throwing and running and hitting at something close to the level of absolute perfection, playing to win but also playing the game almost as if it were a form of punishment for everyone else on the field." But Clemente will always be remembered for his dedication and passion beyond the playing field. In December 1972, having heard that some of the donations for earthquake survivors in Nicaragua were being pirated, Clemente took matters into his own hands, boarding a cargo plane headed for Nicaragua to oversee the distribution of donations. The plane crashed shortly after takeoff, killing everyone on board. Thirty-two years after his untimely death, he is still referred to in Pittsburgh as "The Great One."

to his artifacts commemorating stellar hitting accomplishments, Angrist also owns a game-used jersey or bat from virtually every major-league pitcher who has won at least 300 games in his career.

Born in Brooklyn and raised in Queens during the golden era of baseball in New York, Angrist was raised to be a baseball collector. He came of age when the game's holy trinity—the Yankees, the Dodgers, and the Giants—all played just a subway ride from his home. His father taught him the foundations of collecting with a fine assortment of Indian Head pennies and, with his undivided loyalty to the Dodgers

during the 1940s and '50s, the elder Angrist also taught his son a sense of passion and commitment. Richard played third base for the Sands Point Academy baseball team in Long Island, and he learned a hard lesson about life's capacity for heartbreak when the Dodgers left Brooklyn and his father became, gulp, a Mets fan.

Thus was the path made clear for one of baseball's most celebrated collectors, a genuine keeper of the game's articles of faith. Nearly four decades later, Angrist's odyssey is almost finished. All that remains, it seems, is to find that rose from Napoleon's uniform!

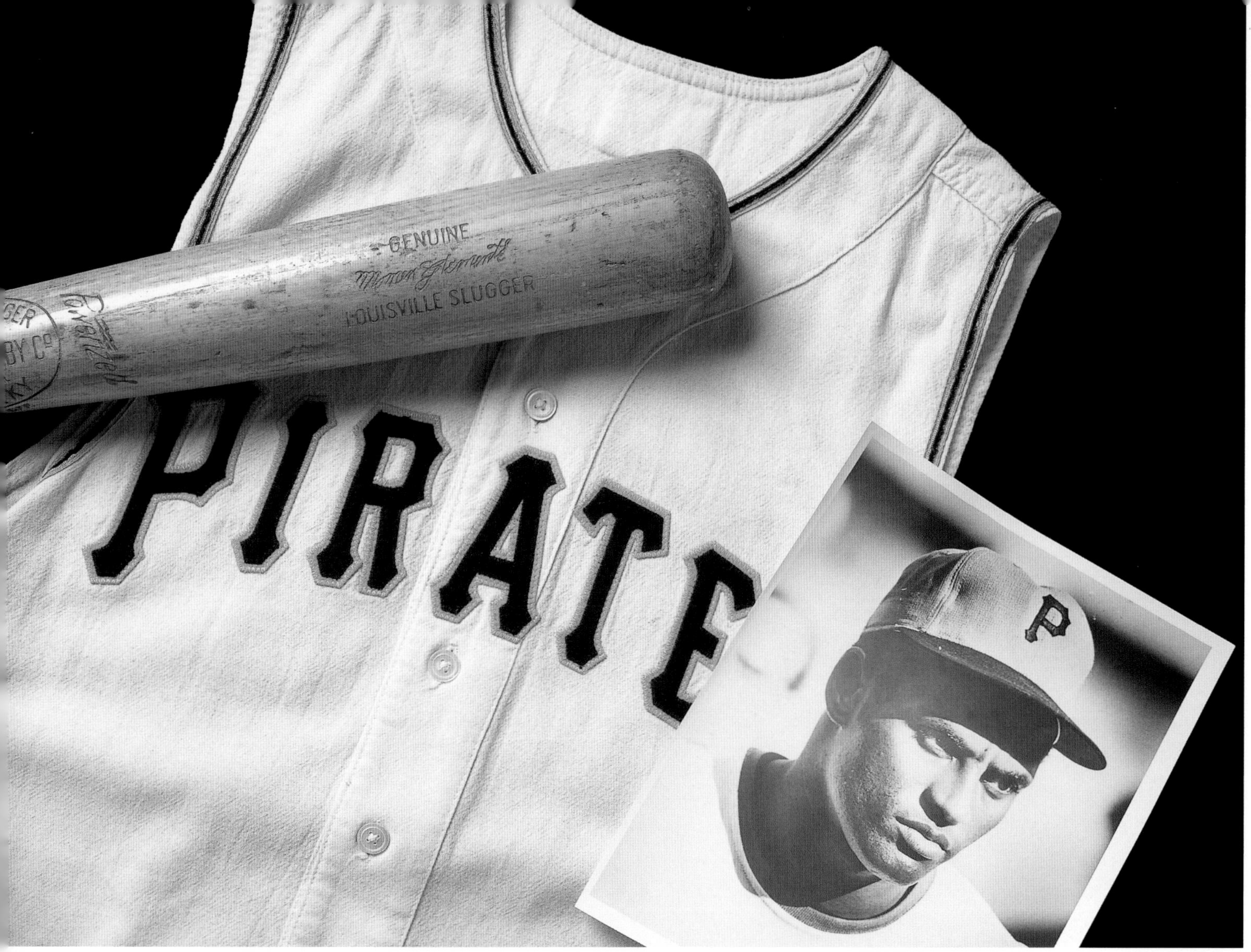

Boston Braves' pithcer Warren Spahn's game-worn jersey from 1948 (far left) and Hank Aaron's game-worn jersey from 1962 (near left, sleeve showing) reflect the reflect the transformation of the team's logo from an Indian head to a laughing brave (which took place in 1957). With 363 victories, Spahn won more games than any other left-hander in baseball history, but raw figures alone do not capture the essence of Spahn and his remarkable durability. He spent more than three seasons in the army, during which he fought in the Battle of the Bulge and received a Bronze Star and a Purple Heart for bravery in combat. Despite being injured by shrapnel, Spahn returned to baseball and led his team to three pennants and a World Series ('57). He also won the Cy Young Award in '57, and he pitched two no-hitters between the ages of 39 and 40. Spahn finally retired after the 1965 season at the age of 44.

7

THE FIRST TIME I SAW MICKEY

"So they prayed
as Ajax harnessed himself in
  burnished, gleaming bronze
and once he strapped his legs and
  chest in armor,
out he marched like the giant
  god of battle . . ."

—HOMER
translated by Robert Fagles

Venerated major-league ballparks have captured fans' imaginations for decades. For Dr. Nick Louis Depace, the spirit of no less than the literary classic *The Iliad* resonates within old Yankee Stadium, site of legendary and epic battles, home to a tragic hero (Lou Gehrig), and sanctuary to a legion of the game's deities. Depace made the connection between Homer and homers when he heard a passage from *The Iliad* during English class as a sophomore at Nutley High School in New Jersey in 1969. He was staring out the window one spring morning as his teacher read from Book VII. When she reached Homer's description of Ajax's marching out to duel Hector, Depace flashed back to his first visit to Yankee Stadium eight years earlier, when he watched Mickey Mantle walk out of the dugout and onto the field.

Now, at his office at the Jefferson Heart Center in Philadelphia, Depace fondly recalls that day. "I remember sitting out on the porch for hours waiting for my father to come home from work in his big green Chevy Bel Air so we could drive to the Bronx." He opens an old family scrapbook on his desk. A musty scent wafts up. The parchment is brittle, and the photographs are browning from decades of oxidation. Two creased ticket stubs and a scorecard from that game are glued next to a fragile newspaper clipping about Roger Maris's 41st home run of the season in the game's first inning. (He would finish the season with 61, breaking Babe Ruth's record of 60.) "The Yanks were playing the Minnesota Twins in a night game—swaybacked Bill Stafford on the mound against the devastating curve of Camilo Pascual," Depace recalls. "I was only eight years old, but I remember just about everything I saw that day. It's hard to forget your first time in old Yankee Stadium."

In the late afternoon of August 4, 1961, Depace and his father arrived at the ball-

The hallowed grounds of Yankee Stadium (above) have showcased some of baseball's greatest stars, including Mickey Mantle (below) and Lou Gehrig, whose home jersey from the landmark 1927 season (opposite) is part of Depace's collection, along with an original locker that was used in the stadium during the 1920s. The '27 Yankees went wire to wire in the American League, winning 110 games, finishing 19 games ahead of the Philadelphia Athletics, and sweeping the Pittsburgh Pirates in the World Series. Gehrig and Babe Ruth formed the heart of New York's aptly named Murderers' Row of sluggers, producing astonishing numbers: Gehrig batted .373 with 47 homers and a record 175 RBIs, while Ruth belted a record 60 home runs, hit .356 and drove in 164 runs.

Depace owns a Ty Cobb game-worn Philadelphia A's jersey (below) from the 1927 and '28 seasons, Cobb's last two years in the league—along with Cobb's game-used bat from the 1920s (with jersey). Born on December 18, 1886, in Narrows, Georgia, Cobb (left) was named after the Phoenician city of Tyre, which stubbornly resisted the onslaught of Alexander the Great. The name proved prophetic as Cobb grew up to become arguably the greatest baseball player of all time, and definitely the most stubborn and fierce competitor the game has known. Cobb's father, William, a respected schoolmaster, disapproved of his choice of vocation and sent him off to the big leagues with the freighted words,

"Don't come home a failure." Two years later, Cobb's mother, Amanda, shot his father dead, an incident that deeply disturbed Cobb for the rest of his life. Consumed with a passion to excel and prove his mettle to his father, even after the man's death, Cobb treated every baseball game as a blood fued, routinely sliding into bases with his spikes flashing. He hit .400 or better in three different seasons, led the AL in batting every year from 1907 to 1915 (as well as 1917 to '19) and finished his extraordinary career by hitting .357 in 1927 and .323 in '28 (when he was 41 years old). He retired as the leader in 90 major-league or American League offensive categories.

A four-time 20-game winner, Hall of Famer Urban Charles "Red" Faber (above) was one of the classic spitballers whose use of the pitch was grandfathered into the rules after its use was officially banned following the 1920 season. In a 1922 interview, Faber said he preferred to "load up" the baseball with tobacco juice, as he found "slippery elm too slippery and chewing gum not slippery enough." Depace's collection includes

Faber's Chicago White Sox uniform (including the socks) from the early years of his career, which began in 1914.

park about an hour and a half before game time to watch batting practice. They climbed up to the top row of seats in the third deck: the "nosebleed" section of the grandstand, overlooking the first base line, just beneath the stadium roof. Clasping his father's hand, Depace sat back in his seat with his mitt on his lap. He scanned the arcade of ornate arches along the giant, pale-green copper frieze that encircled the interior edge of the park's roof. Between each set of arches, mounts with tall steel flagpoles rose above the lip of the roof like battlements atop a castle. Splintered late-afternoon shadows fell over

Monument Park in deep center field—where plaques mounted on red granite pay tribute to Yankee avatars such as Babe Ruth, Lou Gehrig, and Miller Huggins. As a warm gentle breeze drifted through the grandstand, a great cheer went up and echoed through the park's cavernous interior: a ballplayer had emerged from the dugout.

From where Depace and his father were sitting, it was difficult to see the ballplayer's face under the brim of his cap. But Depace knew right away it was Mickey Mantle. "When I saw the number 7 on the back of his uniform, my heart started racing,"

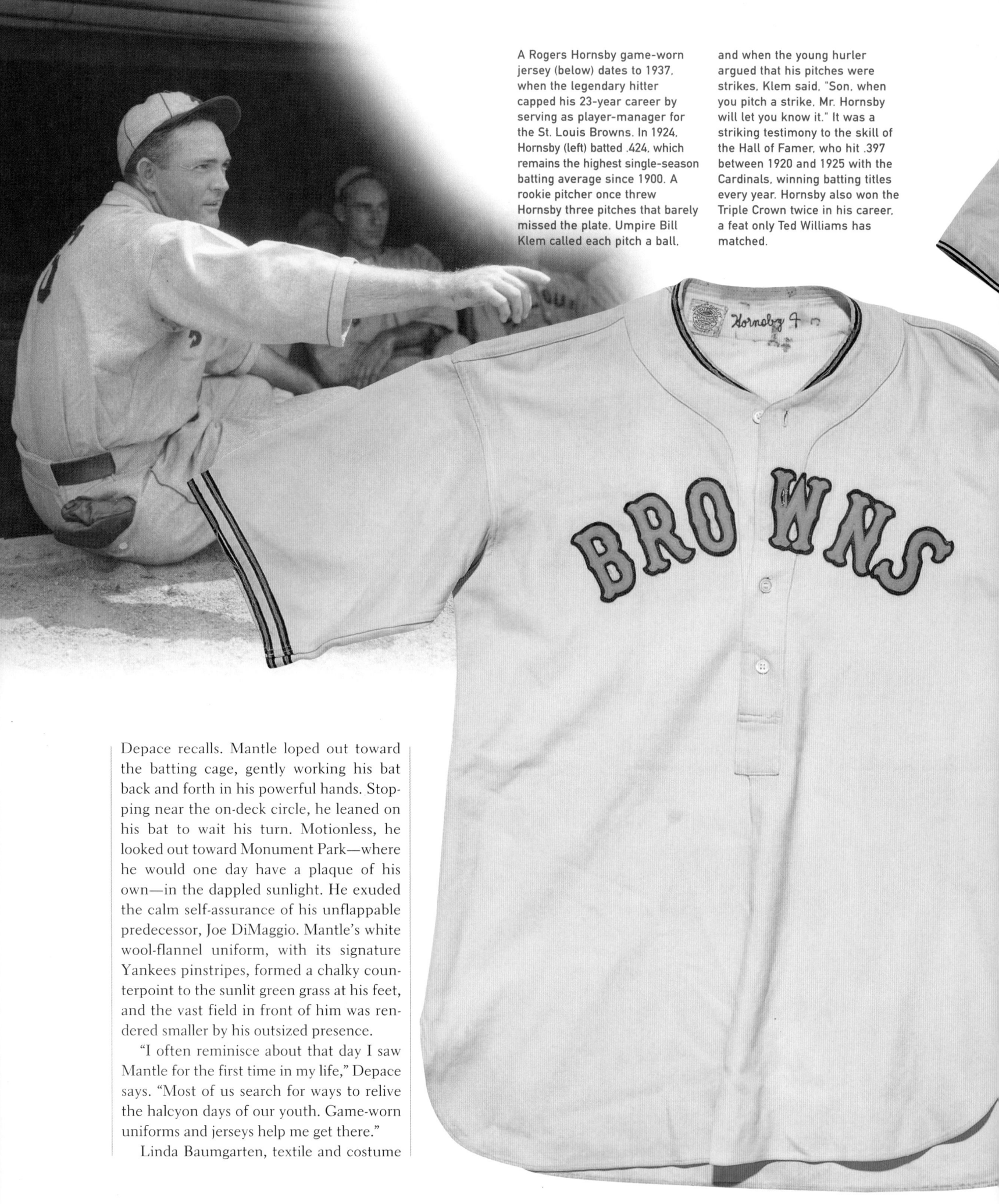

A Rogers Hornsby game-worn jersey (below) dates to 1937, when the legendary hitter capped his 23-year career by serving as player-manager for the St. Louis Browns. In 1924, Hornsby (left) batted .424, which remains the highest single-season batting average since 1900. A rookie pitcher once threw Hornsby three pitches that barely missed the plate. Umpire Bill Klem called each pitch a ball, and when the young hurler argued that his pitches were strikes, Klem said, "Son, when you pitch a strike, Mr. Hornsby will let you know it." It was a striking testimony to the skill of the Hall of Famer, who hit .397 between 1920 and 1925 with the Cardinals, winning batting titles every year. Hornsby also won the Triple Crown twice in his career, a feat only Ted Williams has matched.

Depace recalls. Mantle loped out toward the batting cage, gently working his bat back and forth in his powerful hands. Stopping near the on-deck circle, he leaned on his bat to wait his turn. Motionless, he looked out toward Monument Park—where he would one day have a plaque of his own—in the dappled sunlight. He exuded the calm self-assurance of his unflappable predecessor, Joe DiMaggio. Mantle's white wool-flannel uniform, with its signature Yankees pinstripes, formed a chalky counterpoint to the sunlit green grass at his feet, and the vast field in front of him was rendered smaller by his outsized presence.

"I often reminisce about that day I saw Mantle for the first time in my life," Depace says. "Most of us search for ways to relive the halcyon days of our youth. Game-worn uniforms and jerseys help me get there."

Linda Baumgarten, textile and costume

ted .356, set an NL record for homers (56) and a major-league record for RBIs (191). Wilson (below), who was nicknamed for his resemblance to the famous Russian wrestler George Hackenschmidt, stood only 5' 6" but weighed about 190 pounds. He had short arms, thick, stubby legs, and an 18-inch neck, all supported by tiny, size-6 feet. What he lacked in physical refinement, though, he made up for with his devastating power and skill at the plate. His NL home run record lasted until 1998, when Mark McGwire and Sammy Sosa broke it, and his RBI record still stands.

Robert Lewis "Hack" Wilson's home jersey from the 1930 season (left) constitutes a precious piece of baseball history as it was on the stocky slugger's back during a season in which he bat-

curator at The Colonial Williamsburg Foundation in Williamsburg, Virginia, understands the power of collectible clothing. "An 18th-century suit or an heirloom dress is far more than a tangible survivor," she says. "It is an event in history that continues to happen. Wrinkled by years of use, stretched and shaped by the body that wore it, clothing is the most intimately human of the surviving decorative arts. In some ways, old clothing brings the original wearers back to life." Baumgarten's observations certainly apply to game-worn baseball uniforms. Like game-used bats and gloves, game-worn uniforms— jerseys and trousers—earn their importance and mystique from their connection to a particular major-league ballplayer. But the uniform is arguably more evocative than equipment because of its unique ability to personify a ballplayer, especially famous ones—a number 7 New York Yankees jer-

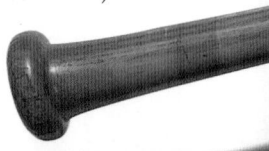

An official scorecard to the 1933 All-Star Game, which was organized by Arch Ward, sports editor for the *Chicago Tribune*, as part of the Chicago Exposition. The game, played on July 6 at Comiskey, brought back the recently retired elder statesmen of the managerial ranks, Connie Mack (above, in suit, with the AL All-Star team) and John McGraw (opposite, in the center of the NL team portrait) to lead the stars of the two circuits. The National League produced special flannel uniforms for the event, and the one worn by future Hall of Famer Chuck Klein (opposite) ended up in Depace's collection, along with the outfielder's game-used bat from the 1930s. Klein was the NL MVP in 1932, and won the Triple Crown in '33.

sey, for example, means one thing and one thing only: Mickey Mantle.

In addition to the team logo, name, or home city, game-used jerseys usually have the ballplayer's name stitched into the collar, left front tail, or back tail of the jersey. Uniform numbers became standard after 1931. Many players wore the same number throughout their careers: number 3 for Babe Ruth, 42 for Jackie Robinson, 21 for Warren Spahn, 24 for Willie Mays, and 44 for Hank Aaron. In the early 1960s, some major league teams began placing the player's name in large letters above the number on the back of the jersey.

For generations, the identities of ballplayers have been inextricably tied to their uniforms. It would be difficult, for example, to envision Ted Williams in anything but a Boston Red Sox uniform, or to separate Joe DiMaggio from Yankee pinstripes, or Stan Musial from the familiar St. Louis Cardinals colors.

According to game-used equipment experts David Bushing and Dan Knoll, from the 1910s through the 1970s, a player was typically issued two home uniforms (with a few exceptions, these were cream or white, and always worn during games at home) and two road uniforms (generally gray, worn during away games) per season. That means each

ball-player wore only four uniforms during a season that counted more than 150 games. An entire season's worth of wear and tear, of blood, sweat, and tears shows up in a game-worn uniform, imbues its fabric with a unique personal history. It's not surprising, then, that uniforms hold an uncommon power for most players. Stan Hack, third baseman for the Chicago Cubs between 1932 and 1945, remembered the first time he pulled on the Chicago colors. "My first day with the team was unforgettable—not because of my performance, but because I got to put on that uniform," he said. "I'll never forget it, the sun hitting me as I emerged from the dugout for the first time, feeling immortal in a garment so glorious. After the game, even though sweaty and soiled, I felt obliged to hang it with the same care as I found it. As I left the locker room that day, I turned to look at it once more, feeling as if I was leaving a bit of myself there."

The allure of uniforms and jerseys from the 1890s through the 1960s is deeply rooted in the fabric and the visual appeal of the garments. Until the late 1940s, uniforms were made of 100-percent wool flannel or a blend of wool and cotton. They were notoriously baggy, relatively heavy, and, quite frankly, not very comfortable, especially during the dog days of summer,

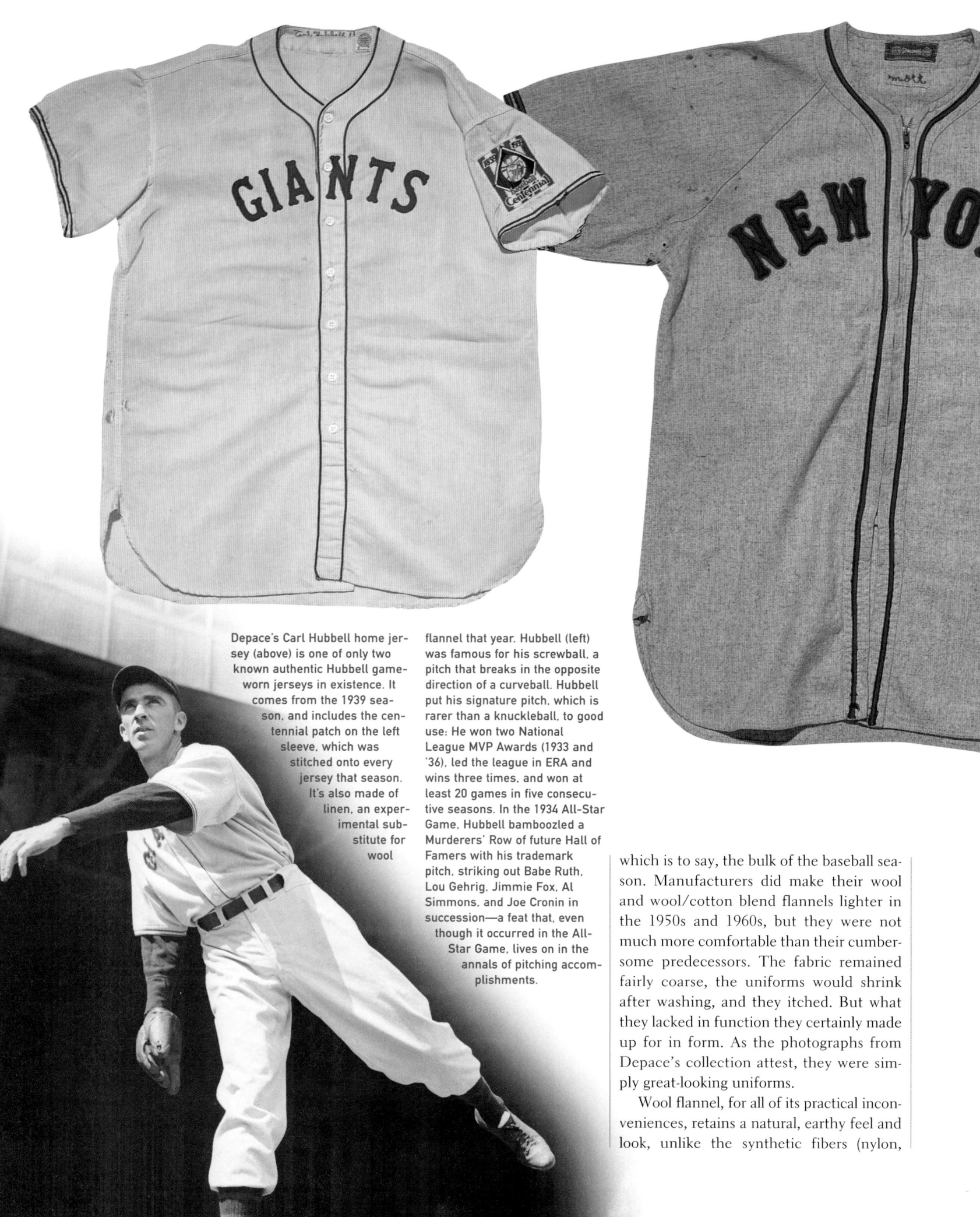

Depace's Carl Hubbell home jersey (above) is one of only two known authentic Hubbell game-worn jerseys in existence. It comes from the 1939 season, and includes the centennial patch on the left sleeve, which was stitched onto every jersey that season. It's also made of linen, an experimental substitute for wool flannel that year. Hubbell (left) was famous for his screwball, a pitch that breaks in the opposite direction of a curveball. Hubbell put his signature pitch, which is rarer than a knuckleball, to good use: He won two National League MVP Awards (1933 and '36), led the league in ERA and wins three times, and won at least 20 games in five consecutive seasons. In the 1934 All-Star Game, Hubbell bamboozled a Murderers' Row of future Hall of Famers with his trademark pitch, striking out Babe Ruth, Lou Gehrig, Jimmie Fox, Al Simmons, and Joe Cronin in succession—a feat that, even though it occurred in the All-Star Game, lives on in the annals of pitching accomplishments.

which is to say, the bulk of the baseball season. Manufacturers did make their wool and wool/cotton blend flannels lighter in the 1950s and 1960s, but they were not much more comfortable than their cumbersome predecessors. The fabric remained fairly coarse, the uniforms would shrink after washing, and they itched. But what they lacked in function they certainly made up for in form. As the photographs from Depace's collection attest, they were simply great-looking uniforms.

Wool flannel, for all of its practical inconveniences, retains a natural, earthy feel and look, unlike the synthetic fibers (nylon,

section of the ballpark "Ottville," in honor of the outielder, one of the greatest players in Giants history. Ott became the first National League player to hit 500 career home runs, and he finished his career with a .304 lifetime average.

With its HEALTH patch reminding U.S. citizens to stay healthy in support of the war effort, Jimmie Foxx's Boston Red Sox jersey (above right) dates to 1942, when the league affixed such patches to every jersey it issued. Nicknamed the Beast, Foxx (far right) succeeded Babe Ruth as baseball's preeminent slugger. Playing for Philadelphia in 1932, he smacked 58 homers, only two short of the Bambino's record, and the following season he won the Triple Crown with a beastly 48 homers, 163 RBIs, and a .356 batting average. He was traded to Boston after the 1935 season, and won a third MVP Award (and

nearly another Triple Crown) three years later, with 50 homers, 175 RBIs, and a .349 average. Yankees ace Lefty Gomez once said, "When Neil Armstrong first set foot on the moon, he and all the space scientists were puzzled by an unidentifiable white object. I knew immediately what it was. That was a home run ball hit off me in 1933 by Jimmie Foxx."

A New York Giants gray road jersey (left) comes from 1942 and once belonged to Mel Ott (above), who wore it as manager of the team with which he spent his entire 22-year career. Ott belted 511 home runs for the Giants, 323 of which landed in the rightfield porch of the Polo Grounds, which was only 257 feet from home plate. Fans who sat in the rightfield bleachers dubbed that

Dacron, and Orlon) used to make uniforms from the 1970s on. As we've said, the home uniforms were typically cream or white, while road styles are solid gray or a darker hue. Their designs were not flashy or busy, but simple, understated, and powerful. A number of teams incorporated vertical pinstripes in their uniform's fabric, a trend that started with the Chicago Cubs in 1907 but was popularized by the New York Yankees in subsequent years. Teams also experimented with a number of traditional designs and patterns, including "cross-hatch" and plaid. The team lettering, number, or logo design was made of soft felt fabric.

Vintage uniforms, particularly from the pre–World War II era, have a simple elegance, charm and craftsmanship that is utterly absent from most of today's skintight, mass-produced uniforms. Depace's stunning collection reflects some of the spirit, experiences, and emotions of ballplayers from bygone eras. The light soiling or stains in the collars, sleeves, or stomach area of some of the jerseys provide a window onto the past. Small tears or holes here and there spark the imagination: how did they get there? That stain might have come from Urban "Red" Faber wiping tobacco juice on his sleeve before delivering

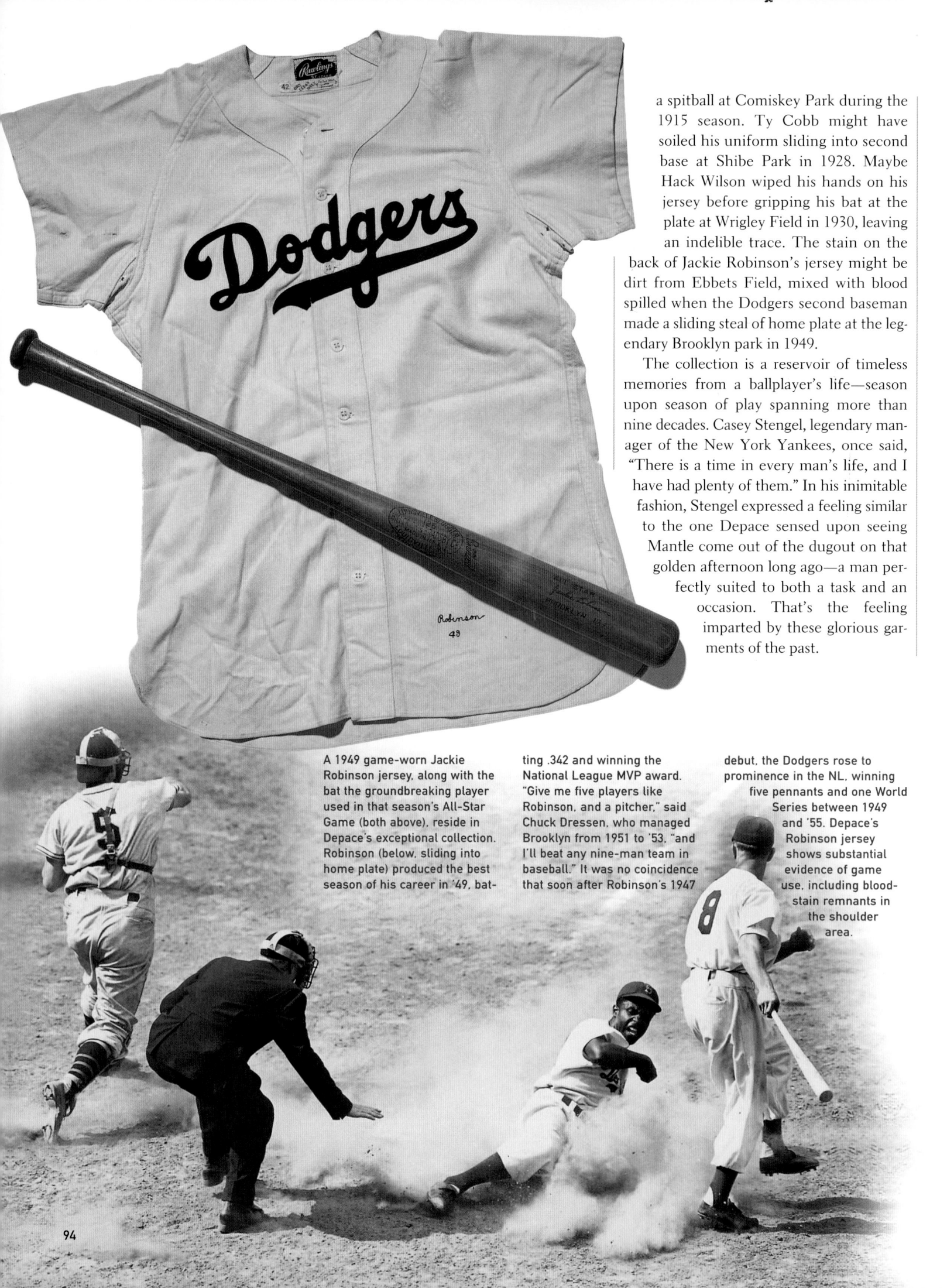

a spitball at Comiskey Park during the 1915 season. Ty Cobb might have soiled his uniform sliding into second base at Shibe Park in 1928. Maybe Hack Wilson wiped his hands on his jersey before gripping his bat at the plate at Wrigley Field in 1930, leaving an indelible trace. The stain on the back of Jackie Robinson's jersey might be dirt from Ebbets Field, mixed with blood spilled when the Dodgers second baseman made a sliding steal of home plate at the legendary Brooklyn park in 1949.

The collection is a reservoir of timeless memories from a ballplayer's life—season upon season of play spanning more than nine decades. Casey Stengel, legendary manager of the New York Yankees, once said, "There is a time in every man's life, and I have had plenty of them." In his inimitable fashion, Stengel expressed a feeling similar to the one Depace sensed upon seeing Mantle come out of the dugout on that golden afternoon long ago—a man perfectly suited to both a task and an occasion. That's the feeling imparted by these glorious garments of the past.

A 1949 game-worn Jackie Robinson jersey, along with the bat the groundbreaking player used in that season's All-Star Game (both above), reside in Depace's exceptional collection. Robinson (below, sliding into home plate) produced the best season of his career in '49, batting .342 and winning the National League MVP award. "Give me five players like Robinson, and a pitcher," said Chuck Dressen, who managed Brooklyn from 1951 to '53, "and I'll beat any nine-man team in baseball." It was no coincidence that soon after Robinson's 1947 debut, the Dodgers rose to prominence in the NL, winning five pennants and one World Series between 1949 and '55. Depace's Robinson jersey shows substantial evidence of game use, including blood-stain remnants in the shoulder area.

GAME-WORN UNIFORMS (1900–60s)

BY STEPHEN WONG WITH DAVID BUSHING AND DAN KNOLL

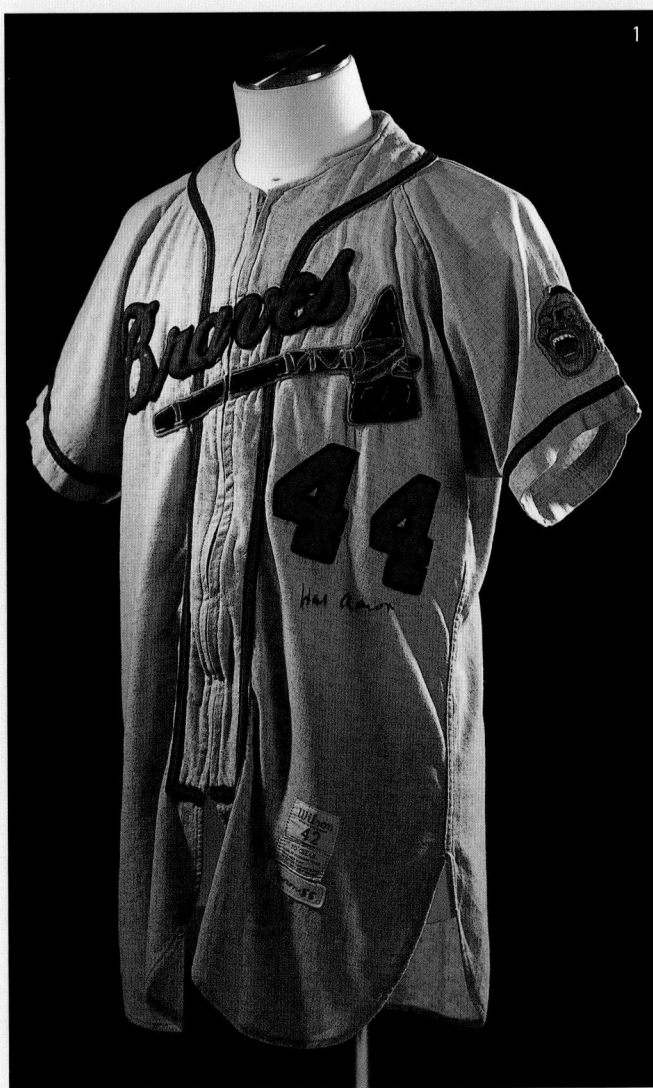

Game-worn uniforms bring collectors closer to major-league players than perhaps any other type of memorabilia. That's the primary reason col-lectors prize them, but there are other compelling reasons, including the aesthetic appeal of the uniforms, and their scarcity, which is consider-able. Game-worn uniforms are more rare than any other category of game-used/worn equipment. While game-used bats, for example, turn up regularly, pre-1960 game-worn uniforms are exceed-ingly scarce. In most cases, only one or two uniforms for an individual player are known to exist.

1. An original, unaltered Milwaukee Braves road jersey (above) that was worn by Hank Aaron (far right, with Mickey Mantle) during the 1956 and '57 seasons includes a white strip tag on the left front tail of the shirt. The tag contains Aaron's last name and the year in which he wore this jersey ("56"). It's clear that Aaron also wore this jersey during the 1957 season, in which he was named the National League's MVP, because that was the year the Braves applied a "laughing Brave" patch to the left sleeve. The Wong Family Archives Collection.

2. Ghost imaging, darkened areas, and remnants of stitching are often visible when a team name or logo has been removed from a game-worn jersey. If new lettering was subsequently applied to a jersey after the orig-inal lettering was removed, the alteration would not appear that obvious. In such cases, you should hold the jersey against a bright light to determine whether an alteration has taken place. The Nick Depace Family Collection.

3. Uniform number changes will also exhibit ghost imag-ing of the first number to have been placed on the jersey. The Nick Depace Family Collection.

Home jerseys were (and still are) cream or white in color, while road jerseys were (and are) darker, most often solid gray. In most cases, home jerseys bear the team name or logo across the chest, and road jerseys bear the name of the team's city. For example, the home jersey of the Boston Red Sox is cream and has RED SOX stitched across the chest, while the road uniform is gray with BOSTON sewn across the chest.

In the old days, a team's uniforms usually were sent to its spring-training facility, to be worn during spring training the following year. After that, a team typically sent them down to its minor-league system or donated them to semiprofessional or factory-league teams. The lower-level teams often removed the affiliate city name/initials from the front of the jerseys, (see the circa-1904 New York Giants jersey on page 95), leaving a remnant image on the shirt. Often, numbers on the backs of the jerseys were removed and replaced with the numbers of the minor-league players to whom they were issued. After being used in the majors, minors, and/or factory leagues, the uniforms were too heavily worn or soiled to

be reissued. And because it was not customary to save uniforms as keepsakes, most of them were simply discarded. Game-worn uniforms in good, unaltered condition—especially those originating from the pre-1940 era—are therefore exceptionally rare.

Game-worn uniforms consist of three pieces: the jersey (the most valuable item), the cap, and the pants. As Marc Okkonen explains in his book *Baseball Uniforms of the 20th Century* (1991), uniform design varies widely from team to team, and even from year to year within individual teams. Key jersey components, such as strip tags (players' names and/or uniform numbers embroidered onto a rectangular piece of material), manufacturers' tags, wash/dry-clean tags, and size tags, might appear on different parts of a team's jerseys from year to year (see examples above).

Given the breadth of these variations, it is very difficult to generalize about what to look for when assessing the authenticity of a game-worn uniform. Before purchasing a game-worn uniform or jersey, collectors should seek the opinions of qualified experts. But even before consulting an expert, collectors should consider a number of factors. The

following is an overview of some of these factors, which should enhance any prospective collector's understanding and enjoyment of this fascinating area of the hobby.

FABRICS AND STYLES
Up until the 1940s, baseball uniforms were made of 100% heavy wool flannel or a blend of wool and cotton. The New York Giants and Chicago Cubs had experimented in the late 1930s with a lighter weight linen material referred to as "Palm Beach style" (see Carl Hubbell's jersey on page 92), but this fabric did not last beyond the experimental stage.

During the 1940s, manufacturers began using lighter-weight wool blends to make baseball uniforms. At the same time, the Boston Braves, Brooklyn Dodgers, Chicago Cubs, and St. Louis Cardinals tried wearing uniforms made of a reflective satin fabric for night games, but the material was not durable enough, and—surprisingly, considering what they had been wearing—the players found it too heavy and warm for regular use. The advent after World War II of synthetic fibers such as nylon, Dacron, and Orlon led the way to the double-knit fabrics of the 1970s.

4. The collar of Stan Musial's road jersey from the 1949 season (above left) bears the Rawlings manufacturer's tag, the dry-clean tag, and the size tag—along with the Stan the Man's autograph The Nick Depace Family Collection.

5. In 1966, Dodgers jerseys came with the manufacturer's tag, wash tag, and size tag sewn into the front left tail, as they are on Sandy Koufax's gamer from '66 (above right), when he went 27–9 with a 1.73 ERA. The Nick Depace Family Collection.

PLAYER NAMES ON JERSEYS
On most jerseys from the Dead Ball era (1900–20), the player's name was typically stitched with black thread in one of two places—the collar below the manufacturer's tag, or the front left tail area of the jersey. During the 1920s and early 1930s, some teams, such as the Chicago Cubs, stitched the player's name and the year in which the jersey was worn on the jersey's back right tail area (see the 1930 Chicago Cubs home jersey of Hack Wilson, page 97). From the 1920s to the 1960s, this stitching was typically done in red thread, but time, oxidation, sweat, wear, and laundering tended to fade the thread color to a light salmon or pink.

By 1932, every team in major-league baseball was

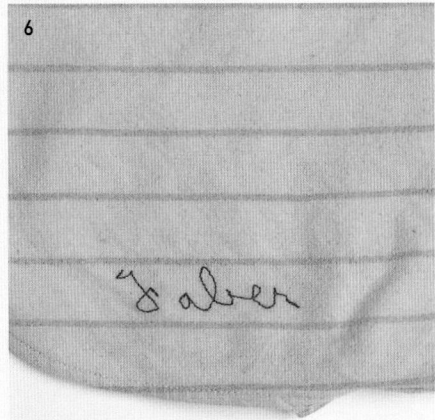

6

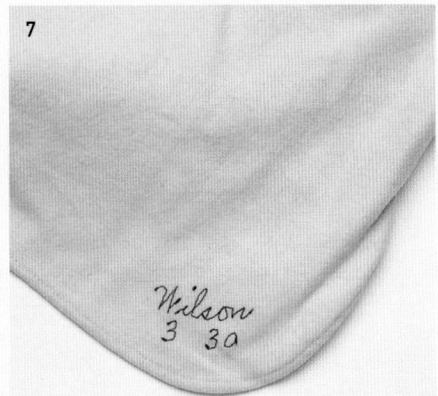

7

8

9

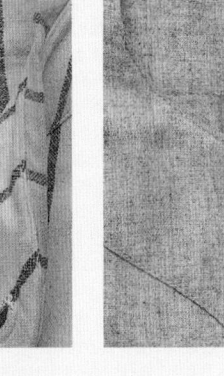

10

6. Red Faber's circa-1915 game-worn jersey (above) has his surname sewn in black thread in the front left tail area. The Nick Depace Family Collection.

7. In addition to Hack Wilson's last name and the year in which he wore the jersey (above middle), the manufacturer stitched a "3" into the back right tail area to signify that the jersey was the third of four sets (two home, two road uniforms). The Nick Depace Family Collection.

8. Red thread in the waist identifies the uniform pants (above right) of infielder Joe Cronin from the early 1930s. The Nick Depace Family Collection.

9. Though faded to a light salmon color, the identifying thread in the collar of Lou Gehrig's 1927 home jersey (near right) remains. The Nick Depace Family Collection.

10. The strip tag on Joe DiMaggio's road jersey (above right) identifies the shirt as having been issued in 1950. The Nick Depace Family Collection.

displaying uniform numbers on the backs of jerseys, but they continued to stitch the players' names into the jerseys and pants. In the 1940s and 1950s, teams commonly stitched the name—and in some cases the number of the player or the year in which the jersey originated—on a white or grey strip tag that was sewn into the collar area (see the gray strip tag on the 1950 New York Yankees road jersey of Joe DiMaggio, #10 above) or on the left front tail.

It was not until the early 1960s that major-league teams began to place the player's names—or, in the case of Charlie O. Finley's Oakland Athletics teams of the late 1960s, their nicknames—in large letters on the backs of the jerseys above the players' number. (See circa-1968 Jim "Catfish" Hunter jersey and Cal Ripken jersey on page 98). The Cincinnati Reds diverged from this custom briefly during the early 1960s, when they sewed their players' names below their numbers.

In the 1960s, some teams, such as the Chicago Cubs, used strip tags with a series of identifying numbers instead of the players' names on their jerseys. The four sets of numbers on the Ernie Banks road-style jersey, 14-1960-3-40 (see page 98), indicate that the player's number was 14, that the jersey was used in the 1960 season, that it was the third of four sets issued (two home uniforms, two road uniforms), and that it was a size 40. Different teams used different sequences, and some did not include numbers representing the size or the set.

ALTERATIONS AND RESTORATION

Ever since teams began placing numbers on the backs of their jerseys, they have modified those numbers at the end of the season and when players are released, traded, or sent down to the minor leagues while the season is in progress. As discussed, the most desirable and valuable kind of jersey is one that is just the way it was when it came off the back of a big-league player. Any alteration, such as the removal or replacement of the team name/logo, player number, player name, and/or strip tag, substantially decreases a jersey's market value. On altered jerseys, the new player's name is usually smaller in size than the original, and the number is placed lower on the back. By holding the jersey inside out against a bright light, and scrutinizing the areas around the names, numbers, and logos, collectors can usually see whether a player's name and/or number has been removed from a jersey. Ghost imaging, or darkened areas in the form of other numbers, as well as stitching holes that range from barely visible to small tears indicate that a uniform has been altered. The color and pattern of the stitching used on the numbers and team name/logos should be the same. Collectors would do well to familiarize themselves with the look of fabrics (wool flannel and wool/cotton blend) used in the numbers and lettering, and check whether all elements of the uniform feature the same style and color tone. If the fabric used on the number differs from that used on the team name/logo lettering, an alteration has probably taken place.

If a uniform number was

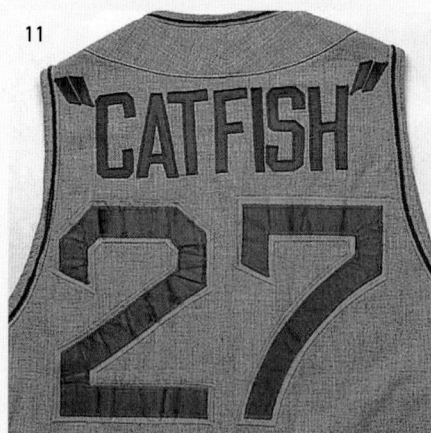

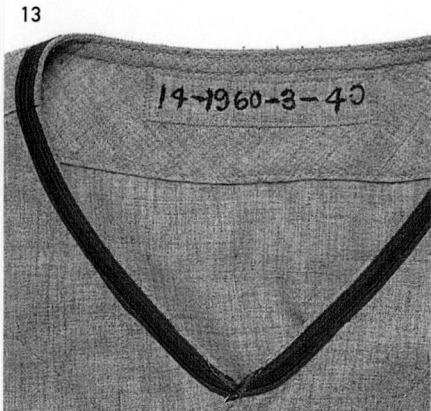

11. Jim "Catfish" Hunter's 1968 jersey (above) featured his nickname on the back. The Nick Depace Family Collection.

12. Cal Ripken's circa-1980s jersey (8) typifies the current style. The Dr. Richard C. Angrist Collection.

13. The strip tag on Ernie Banks's Cubs road jersey (above right) identifies, among other things, Banks' uniform number, and the year it was used. The Nick Depace Family Collection.

changed by a major-league team during the season in which the jersey was worn, that change may not affect the market value very much, if at all. For example, in 1939, when St. Louis Cardinal Pepper Martin's number changed from 1 to 11, the Cardinals altered Martin's jersey accordingly. This kind of "team change" is not considered to be an alteration from the "original" state of the jersey. It is merely part of the jersey's history during the time that Martin wore it. The absence of manufacturers' tags, wash/dry-clean tags, and/or size tags will not reduce a jersey's market value as much as a change in team name/logo or player number.

One alteration actually enhances the value of a jersey: the addition of commemorative patches. The HEALTH patch (see above right, as well as Mel Ott's Giants jersey and Jimmie Foxx's Red Sox jersey on page 93), for example, was applied to the left sleeve of every jersey in the majors from 1942 to 1944 to remind Americans to stay healthy in support of the war effort. The American League Golden Anniversary patch (right) was affixed to every American League jersey in 1951 to celebrate the league's 50th anniversary. In addition to dressing up a jersey, commemorative patches can sometimes help date a jersey that does not otherwise show its year of origin. Jerseys that still bear such patches are considered quite rare and valuable.

Some categories of jerseys are nearly impossible to find in unaltered condition, such as New York Mets home jerseys from the 1960s and New York Yankees home jerseys from the 1950s and 1960s. Collectors of jerseys from these two teams must accept alterations. It's important to remember that a Yogi Berra jersey with a number change but evidence of extensive game use is still, after all is said and done, a jersey that was worn by the Yankee legend. It is important, though, to verify that the purchase price reflects the fact that the jersey has undergone alterations. Removal or replacement of the team name/logo, player number, player name, and/or strip tag typically decreases a jersey's value by at least 50 percent.

HATS

Game-worn hats offer a fine opportunity to acquire game-worn items at a fraction of the cost of jerseys. They display well, take up far less room, and offer a good challenge for any collector. But with very few authentic game-worn hats of Hall of Fame ballplayers available, even the most advanced collectors have to stand in line for acquisition opportunities.

Hats are typically subject to heavy use, and it is quite rare to obtain a hat that can be attributed to a particular player. Most pre-1950s hats had the player's name chain-stitched into the leather band (see the late-1930s game-worn hat of Joe DiMaggio at the top of the opposite page). But because players generally went through several hats during a season, this practice was expensive. By 1950, most teams had abandoned it. The only way, then, to attribute most post-1950s hats to a particular player is to research the hat's provenance.

A player's name or number written under the bill or onto the sweatband is not considered proof that the player actually wore the hat. A collector interested in a specific period needs to know the type of label that a particular manufacturer used during that period as well as the style of hat worn during that period. It is crucial to know where a hat came from if it does not have a player's name stitched into the leather band. A letter or an autograph by the player who once wore the hat consti-

1942–1944 HEALTH patch.

1951 American League Golden Anniversary patch.

tutes the best form of provenance (see the Willie Mays autograph on the bill of his game-worn hat from the 1954 season on the opposite page).

Condition plays an important part in determining the value of a hat. The leather bands often deteriorate from sweat, and the hard bills typically crack from age (see the leather band inside Yogi Berra's game-worn cap from the 1953 season at the top of the opposite page). As with jerseys, if the sewn team emblem was removed and replaced or restored, the hat's value decreases by at least 50 percent. The most desirable hats are those that have the names sewn into the sweatband, are in good condition, and were worn by prominent Hall of Fame players. These are followed in value by rare styles, especially pre-1930 hats.

PANTS

Game-worn pants usually are far less valuable than game-worn jerseys and hats, and their display appeal is minimal, because a pair of uniform pants typically does not include the player's team name or logo. As a result, pants have not drawn a great deal of interest from collectors. But for that very reason,

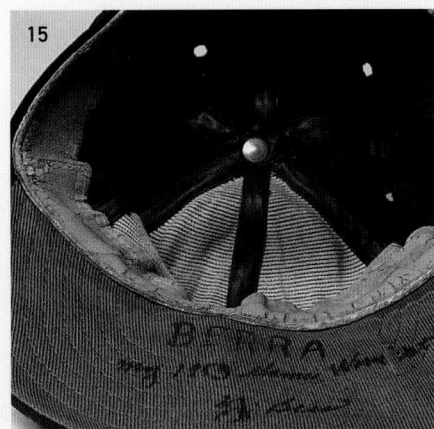

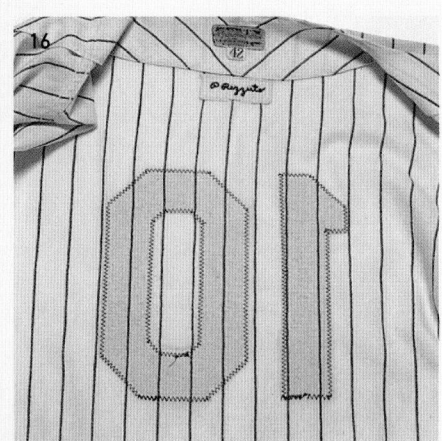

14. Joe DiMaggio's hat size (7) is stitched next to his name on the leather band inside his Yankees cap (above left). The Dr. Richard C. Angrist Collection.

15. Yogi Berra's game-worn cap from the 1953 season (above middle) took a lot of wear and tear as the Yankee backstop produced a typically excellent year, batting .296 with 27 homers and 108 RBIs. The Dr. Richard C. Angrist Collection.

16. The navy blue, zigzag-patterned stitching used to sew the number on Yankees shortstop Phil Rizzuto's home jersey from the 1952 World Series (above right) matches the stitching on the jersey's team logo. The Dr. Richard C. Angrist Collection.

17. A tribute to the Catch: A full ticket from Game 1 of the 1954 World Series (left), when Willie Mays made his famous over-the-shoulder catch of a Vic Wertz drive, lies next to the hat Mays wore during the '54 season, his game-used glove from the 1957 season, and his original, unaltered game-worn jersey from the 1959 season. The Wong Family Archives Collection.

they provide a great opportunity for someone who wishes to own a game-worn item from one of baseball's greatest players for less than five percent of the price of the same player's jersey.

Because teams often stitched the player's name onto the waistband of the pants (or into the zipper area on Dead Ball era pants), it is fairly easy to identify the player to whom a particular pair of pants belonged. Even though pants by themselves are not considered valuable, finding a full uniform—in which the pants match the jersey—is almost impossible, because the pants were often mixed up in the locker room and shipped out to the minor leagues.

CONCLUSION

Collectors should acquire jerseys only from reputable dealers and auction houses. They should also seek advice from other collectors and read past sports-auction catalogs.

Because game-worn jerseys generally constitute the most valuable segment of game-used memorabilia, collecting them requires careful attention. And there's no substitute for experience: It is best to view and handle large samples of jerseys in knowledgeable dealers' and collectors' inventories to establish a frame of reference for authenticity. Assembling a world-class collection of original jerseys that were once worn by baseball's greatest players requires the same caution and, often, the same financial commitment as assembling a collection of fine art.

With these rules of thumb as your guide, and a discerning eye, along with equal measures of both patience and caution, you can successfully navigate this wonderfully rich and rewarding segment of baseball memorabilia collecting.

THE PROOF IS IN THE PINSTRIPES

On October 1, 1961, the final day of the regular season, Roger Maris swung his way into baseball immortality, belting his 61st home run of the season. He sent a 2–0 pitch from Boston's Tracy Stallard into the rightfield stands at Yankee Stadium, breaking Babe Ruth's 34-year-old single-season home run record of 60, set in 1927. (For more on Maris's landmark achievement, see Chapter XX, "The Todd McFarlane Collection.")

The bat Maris used to hit the home run, as well as the ball, reside in the National Baseball Hall of Fame and Museum in Cooperstown. But

for years, no one knew what had happened to the jersey Maris wore on that special day. For the past few decades, collectors surmised that the Maris family had kept the jersey or that it had been sent down for use in the minor leagues, where it might have undergone so much damage and deterioration that it might have been unceremoniously discarded.

In 1998, a New York Yankees home jersey worn by Maris during the 1961 season was offered at public auction. Two years later, Maris's second home jersey from the same season was auctioned publicly. Since

ballplayers were typically issued only two home and two road jerseys per season, many observers assumed that one of the two home jerseys had to be the one Maris wore when he broke Ruth's record. A detailed comparison of the two jerseys' pinstripe alignment with numerous news-service photographs of Maris on that day only heightened the mystery—neither of the two home jerseys matched the one Maris was wearing in the photos.

On August 12, 2004, MastroNet, Inc., a leading sports and Americana memorabilia auction house, publicly auctioned a jersey that it described as the one Maris wore on that historic day in October 1961. According to MastroNet, the consignor had obtained the jersey nearly 15 years earlier from a noted collector. At that time, neither the consignor nor the collector was aware of the significance of the jersey, which was understandable since the shirt had been issued to Maris for use in the 1960 season, hence the year designation "60" that is chain-stitched into the jersey's left front tail below the Spalding manufacturer's tag.

There was no way for the consignor or the collector to have known that Maris also wore the jersey in the 1961 season. The truth came to light only after the jersey was compared to photos of Maris on that day—and it turned out the proof had always been in the pinstripes!

The pinstripe alignment on Yankees home jerseys provides collectors with an invaluable source of reference in the authentication process. Game-worn uniform experts

Dan Knoll, David Bushing, and Dave Grob of SCD Authentic explain:

"New York Yankees uniforms, in fact all pinstripe uniforms, are unique in regard to the exact alignment of their stripes. Although the body material is factory produced, there is still a human element related to their manufacture. An aspect that includes subtleties visible in the seams, stitching, buttons, and application of the 'NY' crest on the left breast. It would be impossible for two seamstresses, even if they tried to effect completely 'matching' stitch work, to position everything by hand in an identical manner. Not one, but numerous variances are often reflected from shirt to shirt. This can be substantiated by even a cursory observation of any two Yankees jerseys, especially if one focuses on the contact points of the pinstripes with the crest, buttons and seams. The crest alone has fourteen specific points of reference that can be compared. The pinstripe placement on each individual jersey is analogous to the fingerprints on human hands; no two are alike. . . . For years this has been the accepted and proven method for authenticating significant Yankees jerseys, provided of course, that a reliably dated photo is available."

The pinstripe alignment on the Maris jersey on the opposite page precisely matches the alignment of the stripes on the jersey Maris is wearing in the photos. But why would Maris have been wearing a jersey from the previous season? According to a former Yankees

When he reached the dugout after his historic clout, the unassuming Maris (left) was forced back out by his teammates to soak up the cheers from the crowd.

The alignment of the pinstripes at the "NY" crest (below, left), shoulder area (below middle), and "9" on the back of the jersey

(below, right) helped historians verify that this is the jersey Maris wore on that notable day. (below)

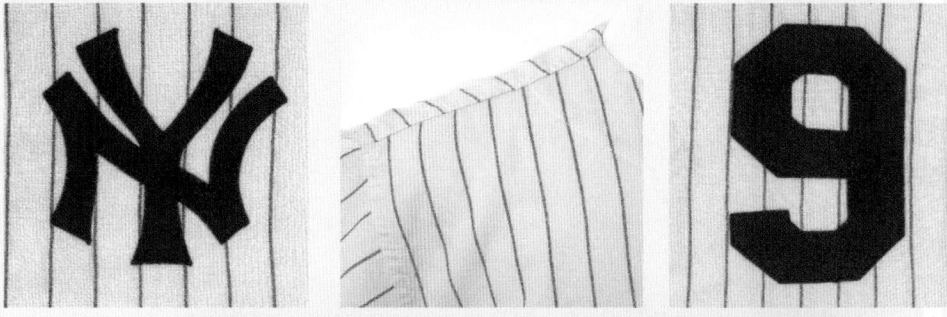

batboy, who has written a book entitled *Memories of a Yankee Batboy 1956–1961*, it was not uncommon for a Yankees ballplayer occasionally to wear last season's jersey: "During that period, Pete Sheehy, the Yankees Equipment Manager, would keep a home and road uniform and jersey for each player from the previous year as a back-up jersey in the event one of the current year jerseys was lost or damaged. Sometimes a player would wear a previous year's jersey if a clean one was not available at game time."

We may never know exactly why Maris wore his 1960 home jersey on the day he broke Ruth's record in late 1961, but we do know that it would not have been unheard of for him to do so; in fact, such a decision was consistent with Yankee custom during the time. And since the points of comparison between the pinstripe alignment on this jersey and the jersey from the photos of that historic day are numerous and match precisely, there is no doubt that Maris was wearing this very shirt when he broke one of baseball's most coveted records. The Dr. Richard C. Angrist Collection.

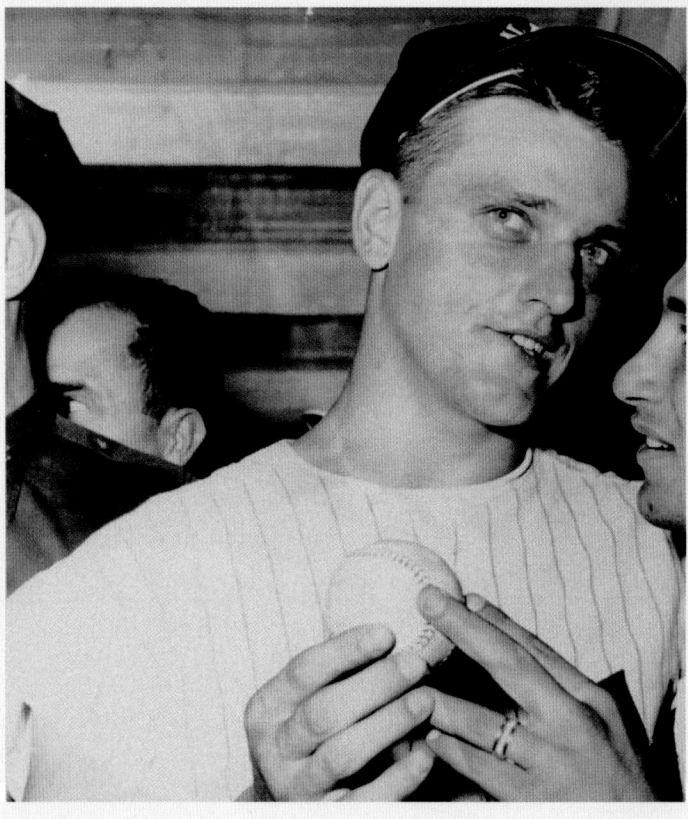

A THEATER OF MEMORIES

Baseball's Dead Ball era—when the game was played with a softer ball that didn't carry as far as the current one—ran from the turn of the 20th century until 1919. Fogel owns a number of relics from the period (opposite), including a full ticket to the 1903 World Series; an invitation to the dedication ceremony for Ebbets Field (on July 15, 1913); a 1914 Boston Royal Rooters pin; a 1908 Chicago Cubs gold medallion watch fob; an 18-karat gold pocket watch that was presented to Honus Wagner on July 17, 1908—"Honus Wagner Day" in Pittsburgh; a circa-1910 Ty Cobb mini-decal bat; an original photograph of Larry "Napoleon" Lajoie on his 10-year anniversary with the Cleveland club; a circa-1916 Chicago White Sox team pennant; and a circa-1910 store-model baseball glove.

A full ticket to Game 1 of the 1919 World Series between the Chicago White Sox and the Cincinnati Reds (top), signifies the start of one of baseball's darkest chapters: the "throwing" of the 1919 World Series by eight members of the Chicago White Sox, including the great Shoeless Joe Jackson. In the bottom of the first inning of Game 1, White Sox pitcher Eddie Cicotte plunked the Reds' first batter (second baseman Morrie Rath), signaling to gamblers that the "fix" was in. Despite being acquitted at trial, all eight conspirators were permanently banished from professional baseball by commissioner Judge Kenesaw Mountain Landis. (7" x 2")

> " Baseball, because of its continuity over the space of America and the time of America, is a place where memory gathers."
> —DONALD HALL

In his book *To Have and to Hold: An Intimate History of Collectors and Collecting*, author Philipp Blom discusses a number of themes that underlie the passion of collecting, from the Renaissance to the present. One of these themes is memory. Blom describes a peculiar Renaissance-period edifice in Paris that was known as the Theater of Memory. It was created in the 1530s by a scholar named Giulio Camillo on commission from the King of France (Francis I). According to Blom, the theater was to facilitate memory for the king, allowing him "to visualize everything on earth and put it into its appropriate place in the symbolic order of the world."

Little information about Camillo's theater remains, and it is not certain whether it was ever completed. But according to Blom, a well-known Renaissance historian named Frances Yates attempted to reconstruct the interior of the theater. She interpreted the structure as an amphitheater divided into seven segments. Each segment was decorated with allegories and symbols, and supplemented with annotations that appeared behind trapdoors. If the king wanted to ponder the arts, for example, he could look at an image of Apollo and the Muses—symbolizing the art of poetry—depicted in one of the amphitheater's seven segments. If the king wished to reminisce about glorious battles of the past, he could view two fighting serpents—signifying the art of combat—portrayed in another part of the theater. In addition to serving as an elaborate memory aid, the structure, in Blom's view, represents a unique type of collection. Blom asserts that "Giulio Camillo was the only person to try to collect the world in its entirety through allegorical representation: every element, every human quality and activity, every realm of the physical and metaphysical worlds had a place in his theatre, was localized and put into context."

Blom's observations about Camillo seamlessly apply to the baseball memorabilia collection of Marshall Fogel. Viewing his vast collection of vintage pocket-watches, photographs, periodicals, game-used equipment, baseball cards and so much more, one might conclude that Fogel is a modern-day Giulio Camillo trying to collect the world of historical baseball artifacts in its entirety. In Fogel's large display room, pennants, advertising display pieces, and ornately framed vintage photographs cover the walls. Hundreds of other objects rest on glass shelves in tall display cases or in frames atop desks, tables, and drawers. At first glance, the sheer volume of items and their astonishing diversity can be overwhelming. But on closer observation, the collection conveys a wonderful logic that embodies Fogel's own unique theater of memory. His bounteous collection graphically represents the emotions, qualities, and activities central to the various forms of baseball memorabilia from the turn of the century through the 1960s.

This chapter covers only four segments of Fogel's collection: memorabilia from the "Dead Ball" era (the first two decades of the 20th century), vintage first-generation photography, advertising displays from the 1920s to the 1940s, and baseball cards from the 1930s to the 1950s. The artifacts on the opening page of this chapter all originated in the Dead Ball era; each is aesthetically captivating and distinctive.

The Dead Ball era included many firsts in professional baseball, such as the first modern World Series, played in October 1903 between Honus Wagner's National League champion Pittsburgh Pirates and Cy Young's Boston Pilgrims (later renamed the Red Sox) of the American League. The lucky holder of the pale red ticket in that opening photograph sat in the grandstand at Boston's Huntington Avenue Base Ball Grounds to watch either Game 1, 2, 3, or 8 of the inaugural World Series, all of which were played in Boston. The eight-game series, which Boston won five games to three, reportedly drew more than 100,000 spectators. This ticket, one of only a few known to exist, is the paper key that unlocked the door to what would become one of America's great time-honored traditions, the Fall Classic.

On April 9, 1913—less than 10 years after that first World Series—Brooklyn's Ebbets Field opened its gates for the first time to host a major-league baseball game. Charles Hercules Ebbets, owner of the Brooklyn Dodgers at the time, spent $750,000 to build what ballpark historian Michael Benson has called "maybe the best ballpark ever, home to the greatest pain and greatest joy, home of the biggest family." Undoubtedly proud of Brooklyn's new shrine, Ebbets issued an ornate invitation to a few friends and dignitaries for the park's formal dedication ceremony, which took place on July 15, 1913. One of those invitations lies below the 1903 World Series ticket back on the opening page.

The Dead Ball era also included one of baseball's most celebrated comebacks. Every year from 1909 to 1912, the Boston Braves had finished the season in last place. Halfway through the 1914 season, they were there again, 15 games back. But under the innovative stewardship of team manager George Tweedy Stallings, one of the first managers to platoon players successfully, the Braves started to win. They did so in commanding fashion. With the double-play combination of Rabbit Maranville and the veteran Johnny Evers, along with brilliant pitching by Dick Rudolph and spitballer Bill James, the Braves took 52 of their last 66 games and clinched the National League pennant in early September.

The Braves then met the American League champions, Connie Mack's mighty Philadelphia Athletics, in the World Series, and knocked them off in four straight games. The Boston Royal Rooters, a rabid *Red Sox* fan club, watched the Braves' rally unfold, with no small amount of envy. Earlier in the season, the Rooters had clashed with Red Sox management over seating arrangements for the fan club, and the dispute had caused some of the Rooters to

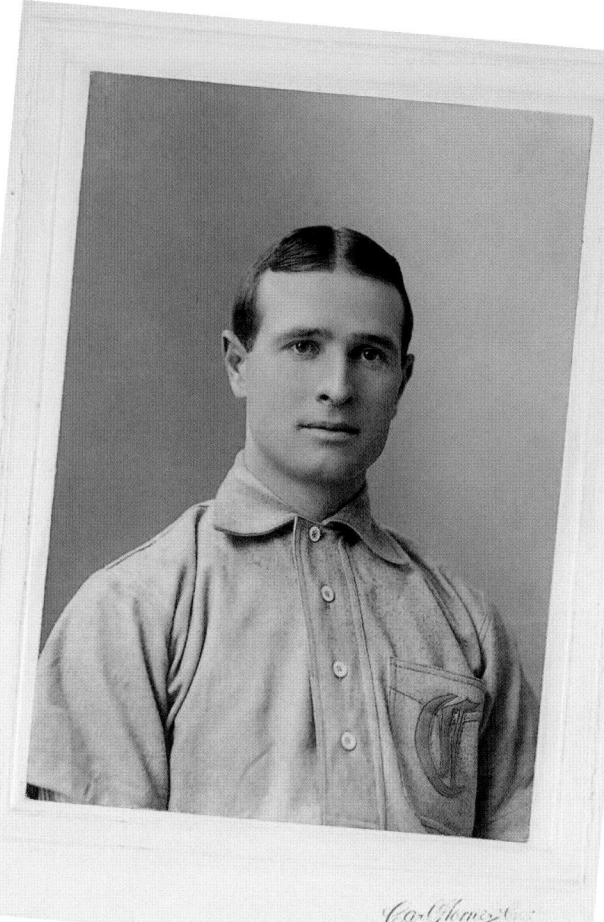

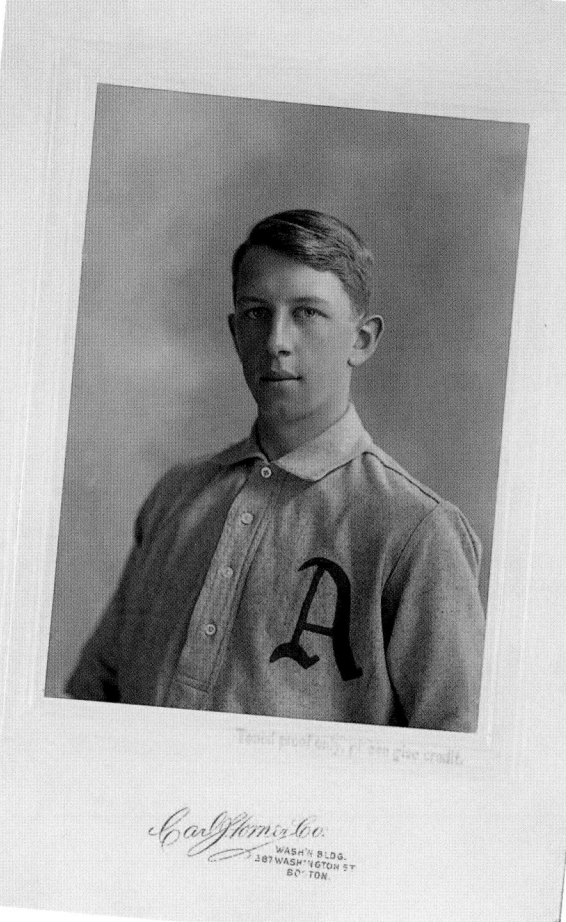

Studio-portrait master Carl Horner never failed to capture a certain gentleness and refinement in even the hardest of the ballplayers he photographed. Horner's photos (above and left) show the more vulnerable, human side of his subjects. These images were used to produce the portrait variant of each of these players in the T206 baseball card set, including the famous card of Honus Wagner (top left). The other portraits are of Hall of Famers Walter Johnson (near left), Eddie Collins (far left), Joe Tinker (top, right), and Frank Chance (top, middle). (5¼ x 7")

On July 24, 1911, major-league baseball staged a benefit game for the widow and family of Cleveland pitcher Addie Joss, who died that year after battling meningitis. Joss went 160–97 in his nine-year career, with a lifetime ERA of 1.89, which ranks him second all-time behind fellow Hall of Famer Ed Walsh. Behind Joss's

Fogel owns an original photograph from 1917 of Shoeless Joe Jackson swinging one of his trademark "Black Betsy Bats" (right), which the player darkened with tobacco juice and tar to harden the hitting surface and "give it shine." (7" x 9")

This panoramic photograph of Game 1 of the 1917 World Series between the Chicago White Sox and New York Giants at Comiskey Park (below) is a spectacular, sun-drenched image that suggests the baseball gods were looking favorably upon the hometown nine, shown on the field. The White Sox won the opener 2–1, and went on take the Series in six games. (48" x 9")

switch their allegiance to the "Miracle Braves." After the season, the remaining Rooters disbanded, but so did the Braves' magic. The organization would not win another World Series for 43 years.

The Dead Ball era had dominating teams as well, teams led by players whose names are as well known today as they were back then. In 1908, the Chicago Cubs were the best team in baseball. Consecutive World Series wins over Ty Cobb and the Detroit Tigers in 1907 and 1908 and a third straight National League pennant gave the Cubs and their president, Charles W. Murphy, good reason to swagger. The National League powerhouse averaged 107 wins a season during those three years, largely due to the talent of baseball immortals Joe Tinker, Johnny Evers, Frank Chance, and Mordecai "Three-Finger" Brown (who lost his right index finger when he accidentally put his hand into his uncle's corn grinder). Team president Murphy's gold medallion

COMISKEY PARK OCT. 6TH 1917.
1ST WORLD SERIES GAME
GIANTS 1 SOX 2
ATTENDANCE 32000

impressive statistics was a man beloved by his peers. many of whom turned up for the benefit game. and posed for this panoramic photograph (above). which includes nine Hall of Famers and is one of the most significant panoramasin the genre. (39⅞" x 8")

watch fob resides in Fogel's collection, an ornamental relic from that glorious time in Chicago baseball history.

Not even Pittsburgh's Wagner or Detroit's Cobb—whose image adorns a beautiful circa-1910 mini-decal bat in Fogel's collection—could stop the Cubs back then. But the Pirates made a good run at it in 1908, finishing second in the National League behind Chicago, a position they earned primarily through Wagner's outstanding batting and fielding. The Pirates' star finished the season with a .354 batting average, the highest in the league. On "Honus Wagner Day," July 17, 1908, a large group of Pittsburgh fans expressed their gratitude and admiration for their shortstop by presenting him with a Jules Jurgensen 18-karat-gold, minute-repeating pocket watch. The watch's inscription—To Hans Wagner From His Friends And Admirers, Pittsburgh, July 17, 1908—is a heartwarming memento of a bygone era.

Four years later, Cleveland fans presented their star second baseman, Larry "Napoleon" Lajoie, with a nine-foot floral horseshoe adorned with more than 1,000 silver dollars to celebrate his 10th anniversary with the team. Fogel owns an original first-generation print, taken by one of the most prominent early-20th-century baseball photographers, Louis Van Oeyen, that captures the moment. It's also on the opening page of this chapter.

Vintage photography comprises the second segment of Fogel's theater of baseball history. A vintage first-generation print is a photograph that was processed from the original plate or negative just after the shot was taken. By contrast, a second-generation print is a photo processed from first-generation prints (as opposed to the plate or negative), typically long after the first-generation print was produced. The photographs in this chapter illustrate the superiority of first-generation prints in terms of clarity, con-

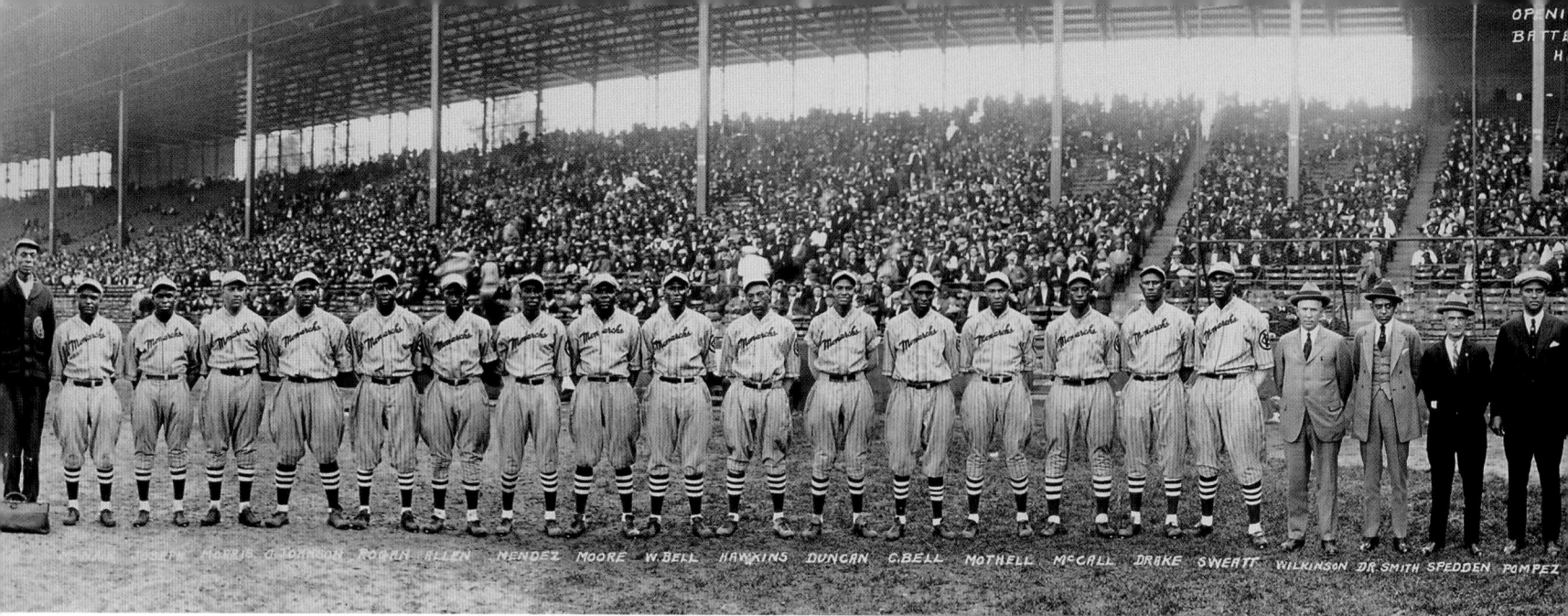

CHAMAIN JOSSELIN MORRIS O.JOHNSON ROGAN ALLEN MENDEZ MOORE W.BELL HAWKINS DUNCAN C.BELL MOTHELL McCALL DRAKE SWEATT WILKINSON DR.SMITH SPEDDEN POMPEZ

Fogel owns a glorious panoramic photograph of the inaugural Negro League World Series (above), which took place in 1924, and matched the Negro National League's Kansas City Monarchs against the Hilldale Daisies of the rival Eastern Colored League. Some historians consider this the most exciting championship series in baseball history, because in each of the last seven games, the winning team scored the decisive run in its final at-bat. (35½" x 6¾")

A sparkling original photograph shows Josh Gibson (right) whom legendary pitcher Satchel Paige described as "the greatest hitter who ever lived." Walter Johnson said that Gibson "catches so easy, he might as well be in a rocking chair." Records indicate that Gibson hit nearly 800 home runs during his career (1929–46), including 75 in a single season. Three months before Jackie Robinson's major-league debut in April 1947, Gibson died in his sleep. Major-league baseball would never get a chance to showcase the most dominating power hitter in Negro League history. (15" x 12")

trast, and tonal scheme. One of Van Oeyen's peers, Carl Horner (1864–1926), took some of the most exquisite early-20th-century baseball photographs. His studio portraits of Honus Wagner, Walter Johnson, Eddie Collins, Frank Chance, Joe Tinker, and Ed Walsh, all circa 1905, exude the purity and stateliness that helped form the public's perception of professional ballplayers during that era. Recognizing the quality and appeal of Horner's portraits, the American Lithographic Company used them to produce the famous T206 baseball card set, issued by the American Tobacco Company

between 1909 and 1911. (Examples of these cards appear in Chapter V, "The Brian Seigel Collection.")

Along with studio portraits, panoramic images of teams and major events typify early-20th-century baseball photography. Such photographs, copies of which were commonly given to team members as keepsakes, are rich in detail and sometimes provide spectacular views of ballpark grandstands and spectators. One panorama, featured on page 106, shows a grandstand full of fans in suits and straw hats attending the Addie Joss Benefit game played at Cleve-

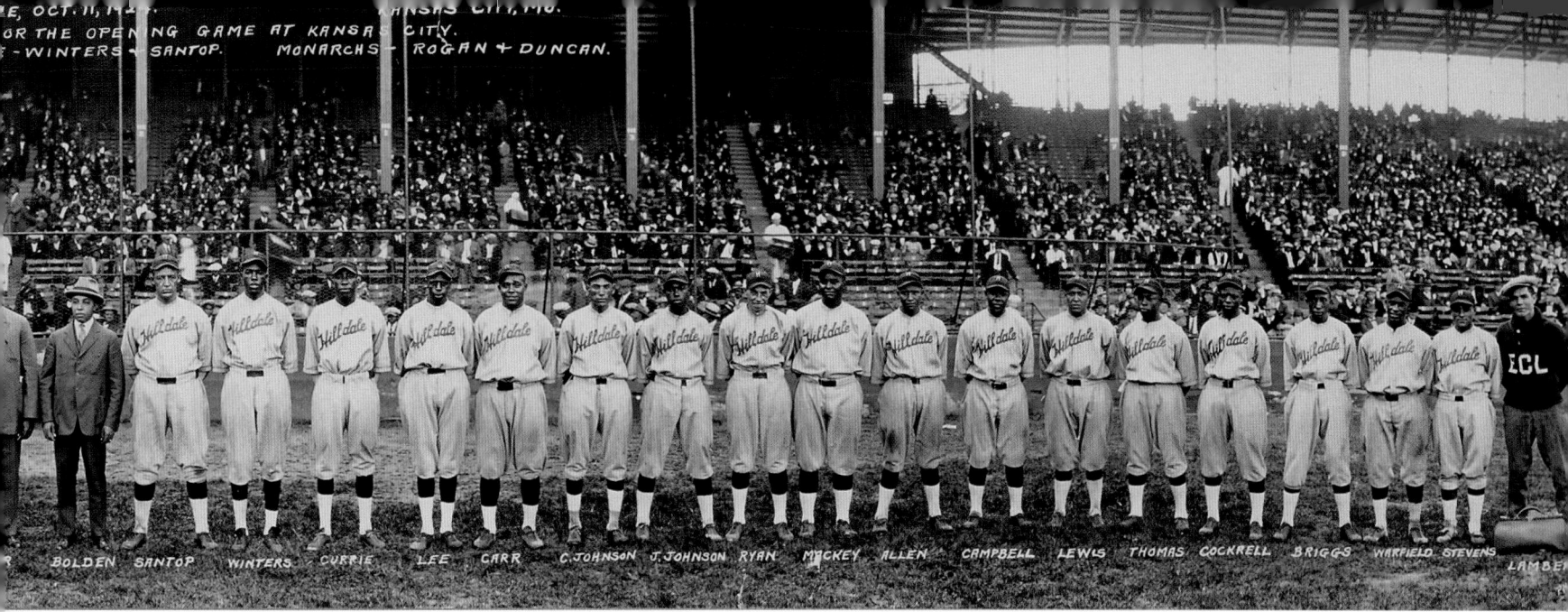

BOLDEN SANTOP WINTERS CURRIE LEE CARR C.JOHNSON J.JOHNSON RYAN MACKEY ALLEN CAMPBELL LEWIS THOMAS COCKRELL BRIGGS WARFIELD STEVENS LAMBE

land's League Park on July 24, 1911. The game, which matched an All-Star team of American League players against the Cleveland ball club, was held to raise money for the widow and family of Cleveland pitcher Addie Joss, 31, who passed away on April 14 of that year from complications related to meningitis. All league games were canceled on that date so the players could attend and pay their respects. The participants included the greatest stars of the era, from Ty Cobb, Tris Speaker, and Walter Johnson to Smokey Joe Wood, Shoeless Joe Jackson, and Cy Young. Because of this formidable lineup, many historians consider this as the antecedent to the inaugural All-Star Game, which took place at Comiskey Park in 1933.

Another panorama captures the start of the sixth game of the inaugural Negro League World Series, played on October 11, 1924, in Kansas City, between the Eastern Colored League's Hilldale Daisies and the Negro National League's Kansas City Monarchs. Andrew "Rube" Foster, black baseball's first great impresario, stands amidst a bevy of talent, including Hall of Fame third baseman Judy Johnson, pitcher Jose Mendez (John McGraw said he would have paid $50,000 for Mendez if the pitcher were white), and "Biz" Mackey, who was Roy Campanella's mentor and perhaps the best all-around catcher in Negro League history. In each of the last seven games of the nine-game series, the winning team had scored the decisive run in its final at bat, making this one of the most exciting series in baseball history.

Images of ballparks are perhaps the most visually captivating examples of early-20th-century baseball photography. Consider the large panoramic photographs in this chapter of Exposition Park, the Polo Grounds, and

Renowned Chicago photographer George R. Lawrence (1869–1938). widely regarded as the father of aerial photography. captured Pittsburgh's Exposition Park in a stunning panoramic photograph on August 23. 1904 (below). Those were the days when fans wore straw hats and three-piece suits to ball games, and ballparks were set in tranquil surroundings replete with trees. churches, and Churchill Downs–like spires. The Pirates are on the field. with Honus Wagner at shortstop and Hall of Famer Fred Clarke patrolling the outfield, while the New York Giants. with manager John McGraw lurking in the dugout and a player sprinting to first base. take their turn at bat. 35¼" x 18")

EXPOSITION PARK
PITTSBURG-NEW-YORK-BASEBALL-GAME

Fogel owns an original news service photograph of Ted Williams (above) crossing home plate after hitting his famous bottom-of-the-ninth, three-run homer that gave the American League a 7–5 victory in the 1941 All-Star Game in Detroit. The Red Sox legend considered this home run to be the biggest thrill of his major-league career. (7" x 9")

George R. Lawrence produced another photographic masterpiece with his wide-angle shot of the Old Polo Grounds (top) on May 20, 1905. Clearly, the derby was the hat of choice for the home fans, who cheered their Giants on to 105 victories and the National League pennant that season. New York beat the Pirates by nine games in the NL, then went on to defeat Connie Mack's Philadelphia Athletics in the World Series. (47" x 18")

An original news service photograph captures Yankee legend Lou Gehrig (above) selecting a bat from the dugout steps on July 7, 1934. (7" x 9")

POLO GROUNDS, NEW YORK
PITTSBURG vs NEW YORK
MAY 20, 1905. ATTENDANCE 24,520
Copyright 1905
The GEO R LAWRENCE Co.
274 Wabash Ave.
Chicago Ill.

Comiskey Park, taken in 1904, 1905, and 1917, respectively. Much of the allure of these three images lies in the angle from which they were shot. Each was taken from the outfield section of the ballpark, looking toward the infield. Huge crowds of spectators are watching the games; not one soul looks at the camera. Smoke rises from the factory smokestack in the background of Pittsburgh's Exposition Park; a banner in the outfield of the Polo Grounds flutters in the New York City breeze; sunlight pierces a section of the grandstand at Chicago's Comiskey Park. The details impart a sense of action that, combined with the camera angle, make it easy for the viewer to imagine himself back in time, in those very bleachers, watching the game with the rest of the crowd.

This emotional power also exists in several vintage color advertising-display pieces featured in the third segment of Fogel's theater of baseball history. The slogans, artwork, graphic designs, and color palette of these items transport us back to a time when it was socially acceptable for ballplayers to endorse tobacco products. From the 1920s through the 1940s, players received relatively paltry endorsement fees, enough perhaps to buy a nice dinner or two. Nevertheless, such fees were important to even the biggest stars depicted on the tobacco-related advertising pieces in this collection. Babe Ruth, whose image graces *The Sporting News* die-cut store counter display that was produced in 1927, eventually turned advertising endorsements into big money. By the 1930s, Ruth was earning as much as $5,000 from the maker of Old Gold cigarettes, more than most major-league ballplayers brought home in an entire year. Imagine what it would cost Lucky Strike or Chesterfield today to feature Roger Clemens, Derek Jeter, or Alex Rodriguez in a cigarette ad!

That these advertising display pieces have survived for more than half a century in such remarkable condition adds to their appeal. The Babe Ruth *Sporting News*

During the off-season in 1927 and 1928, Babe Ruth (above, doffing his hat) and Lou Gehrig toured the country to play in a series of exhibition games with teams comprised of local amateur ballplayers, giving fans who lived in remote areas of the country the chance to see them in action. Known as the "Bustin' Babe and Larrupin' Lou" barnstorming tour, the campaign also included entertainment like the hijinks depicted in Fogel's original photograph of the Bambino hamming it up for a capacity crowd in Brooklyn during a promotional stop touting a rodeo at Madison Square Garden.
(7" x 9½")

designed to serve as window displays to attract potential customers walking by. We don't know if these pieces were actually used for their intended purposes. But even if they were not, it seems miraculous that these relatively large objects made of fragile cardboard have survived almost unscathed for so many years.

It also seems miraculous that the baseball cards on the ensuing pages, part of the fourth segment of Fogel's theater, remain in such pristine condition. Baseball card "purists" may prefer their cardboard treasures to show the character of their age: creases, rounded corners, stains, and tack holes. But there is also something quite fascinating about a 63-year-old baseball card that appears as if it were just pulled from a new pack. Consider, for example, the Play Ball Joe DiMaggio card issued in 1941 by Gum, Inc., a Philadelphia-based bubble-gum maker. The card earned a "Mint 9" condition grade (on a scale of one to 10 with 10 being the highest grade possible) from Professional Sports Authenticator (PSA), a prominent third-party sports-card grading service. To earn such a high grade, the card must be in essentially flawless condition. The vast majority of vintage baseball cards show visible signs of the ravages of time. How did this card survive in this condition for so many years? We can only guess. Did the lucky owner tuck it safely between the cards of Bill Dickey and Lefty Gomez and leave it in a shoebox in an attic for more

piece, which includes an easel back, was designed for display on the counter of a newsstand, cigar shop, or sporting goods store that sold copies of the paper. The Lucky Strike signs of the late 1920s were affixed to the interior walls of trolley cars. The Union Leader smoking tobacco (1934) and Chesterfield (1948) pieces were

A magnificent original photograph of the 1926 New York Yankees (above) at Yankee Stadium captures the team at the dawn of its resurgence as a power in the American League. And what a resurgence it would be: the Bronx Bombers would win three pennants and two World Series between 1926 and 1928, and go on to nothing less than domination of the rest of the century. The heart of the lineup, which included Bob Meusel, Earle Combs, Babe Ruth, Lou Gehrig, and Tony Lazzeri, was so formidable sportswriters dubbed it Murderers' Row. (39" x 26")

Yankees legend Joe DiMaggio married Hollywood starlet Dorothy Arnold on November 19, 1939. Fogel owns an original photograph of the big day (far left), which took place in DiMaggio's hometown of San Francisco. (16" x 12")

Lou Gehrig (opposite) played in a record 2,130 consecutive major-league games, a milestone that stood for more than half a century, until Cal Ripken Jr. surpassed it on September 6, 1995. Suffering from the degenerative disease, amyotrophic lateral sclerosis, the Iron Horse pulled himself from the lineup on May 2, 1939, the day this original photograph was taken. Gehrig died two years later at the age of 38. He finished his career with 493 home runs and a lifetime batting average of .340. (14" x 11")

BOB *"Lefty"* GROVE
PHILADELPHIA ATHLETICS · · STAR PITCHER

"I always smoke Luckies
They never affect my
wind and they taste fine"

The Cream
of the Crop

"It's toasted"~ No Throat Irritation ~ No Cough

LLOYD WANER
PITTSBURGH PIRATES BASEBALL SENSATION · · 1927

"Luckies fine flavor is
enjoyable..and they
never cut my wind"

The Cream
of the Crop

"It's toasted"~ No Throat Irritation ~ No Cough

HA

"It's toast

Five Lucky Strike cardboard advertising signs (above and opposite) featuring major-league stars comprise a complete set. They were displayed in trolley cars in 1928, and, because very few advertising display pieces from the 1920s were in full color, are quite popular among collectors. (21" x 11")

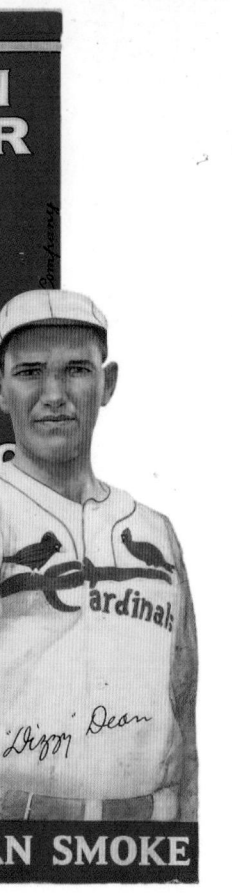

than half a century? Did the kid put the card between the pages of his Bible, thinking that Joe—with his famous 56-game hitting streak in 1941—deserved a fate better than being flipped against garage doors or clipped to bicycle spokes like his less illustrious brethren? Worn cards are indeed wonderful—they show signs of humanity. But most mint-condition cards were also deeply cherished by their youthful owners; they just may have been too precious to adorn bicycle spokes.

For many collectors today, old baseball cards in mint condition can give quite a thrill, because they look exactly as they did when they were pressed into packs of cards decades ago. Topps came out with its first major baseball card set in 1952, when Fogel

was eight years old. According to Fogel, distribution was limited primarily to retailers east of the Mississippi. No packs made it out to Denver, his hometown, that year. But Topps executives were so confident in this set that overproduction was inevitable. Indeed, in 1953, Topps shipped its excess supply to retailers, along with boxes of newly issued 1953 wax packs. One of the extra 1952 boxes crossed the Mississippi and made its way to a drugstore in downtown Denver.

The father of Fogel's childhood friend Richard owned that drugstore, so Richard and Marshall got first crack at the packs. They stood in front of the candy counter and stuffed their mouths with the pink slabs of bubble gum that came with each pack. As they were shuffling through the

Brothers-in-arms Jay Hanna "Dizzy" and Paul Dee "Daffy" Dean lent their likenesses to a splendid die-cut cardboard display (above, left) for Union Leader smoking tobacco circa 1934, the year they combined for 49 pitching victories and helped the Cardinals to the World Series title. (32" x 45")

In the late 1920s, *The Sporting News* turned to the game's biggest star, Babe Ruth, to help sell copies of its paper with a die-cut display (above), which appeared on store counters. By the 1930s, Ruth was the catalyst in turning advertising endorsements into a meaningful source of supplementary income for ballplayers. (12" x 8½")

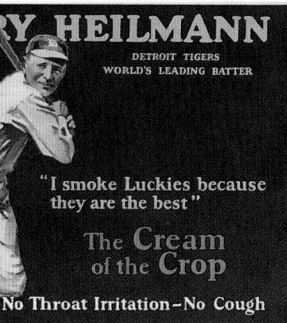

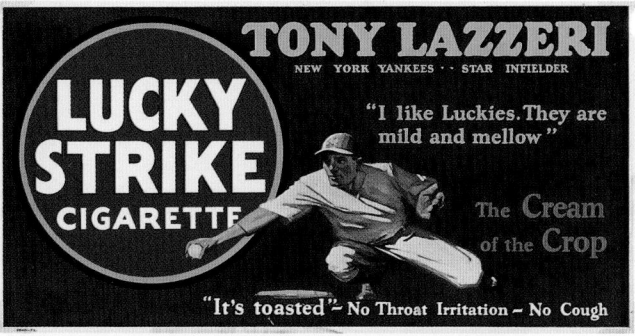

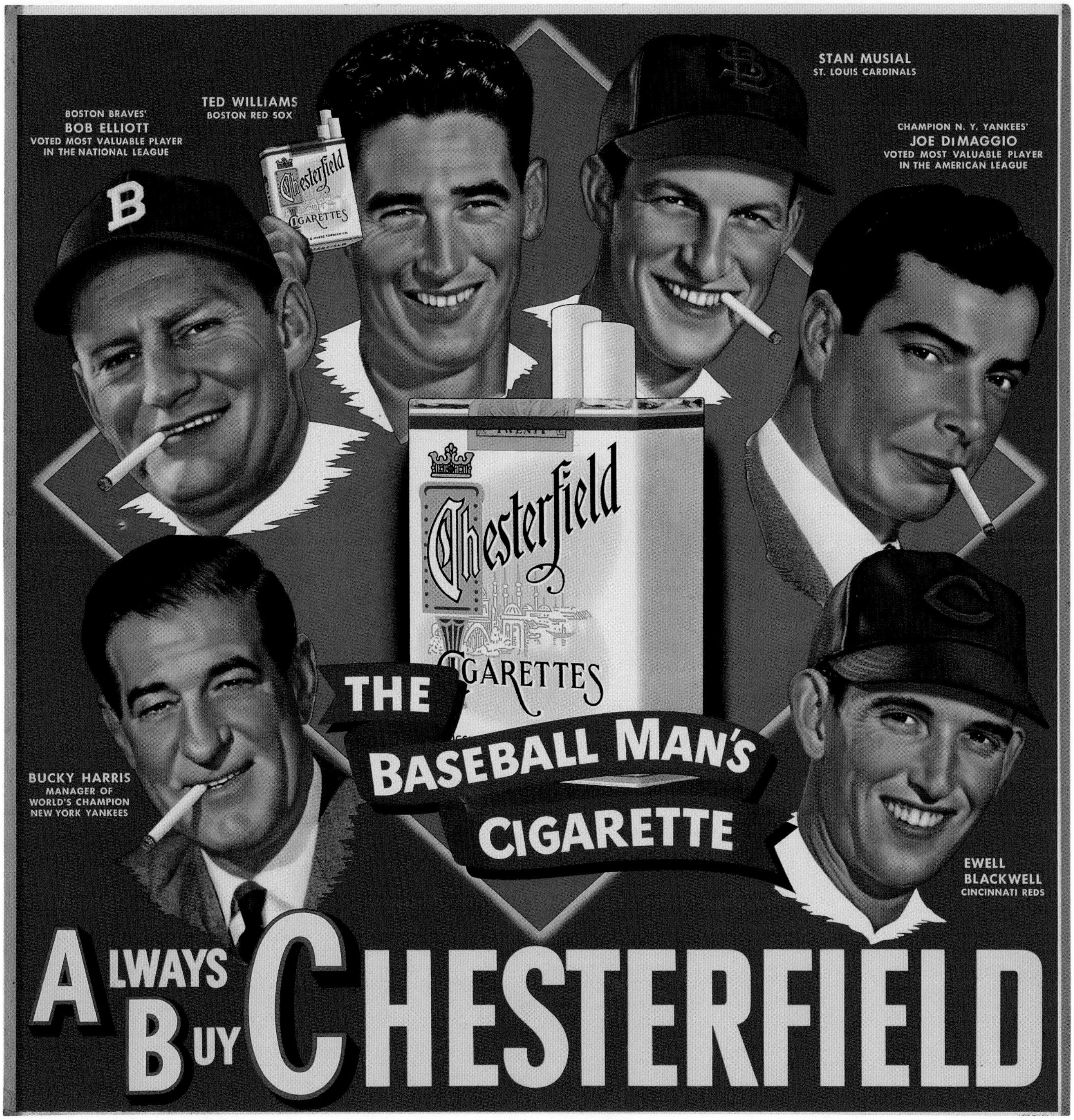

Chesterfield Cigarettes spared no expense in the promotion of their product in 1948, producing a cardboard advertising piece (above) that featured a galaxy of baseball stars, inlcuding Ted Williams, Joe DiMaggio, and Stan Musial. The display appeared in store windows to attract customers walking by. With its beautiful artwork, rarity, and the fame of the players featured on it, this piece is widely considered to be the most significant advertising display of the postwar era. (21¾" x 21")

Baseball cards that have been professionally graded by third-party sports-card grading services constitute a major segment of sports-memorabilia collecting. (See "Collecting Vintage Baseball Cards (1915-70)" by Kevin Struss and Stephen Wong in Chapter XIII.) The ten cards on this page and the next one represent a card-collecting pantheon of sorts: They are among the most popular issues in the history of the hobby, and each one is among the highest (if not the highest) graded examples known.

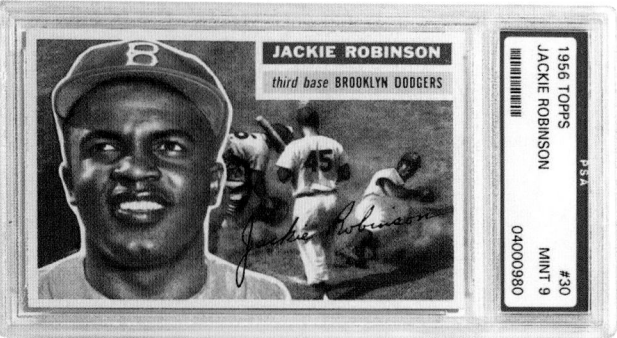

The Topps baseball card of Jackie Robinson (right) from 1956, the last year of Robinson's remarkable career, shows the Dodgers' star performing one if his legendary feats: stealing home.

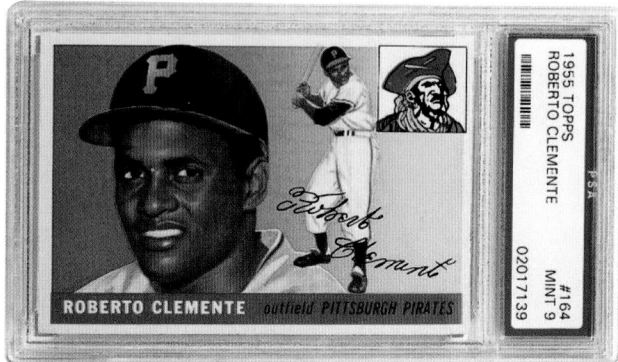

Roberto Clemente's rookie card (right) came from Topps in 1955, the year scout Clyde Sukeforth told Pirates general manager Branch Rickey, "You will never live long enough to draft a boy with this kind of ability for $4,000 again." Sukeforth proved prophetic, as Clemente went on to win four batting titles, 12 Gold Gloves, and the 1971 World Series MVP.

A Play Ball baseball card of Joe DiMaggio (above), from Gum, Inc. of Philadelphia, came out in 1941, the year the Yankee Clipper produced his famous 56-game hitting streak.

The 1953 Topps baseball card of Mickey Mantle (right) is nothing short of astounding because it features one of the most popular players in the history of the game and has been designated the highest grade possible from PSA, "Gem Mint 10": The reason this grade is so impressive is that cards from the 1953 Topps set were especially susceptible to condition problems because the edges of the red box (black for some cards) in the lower-left area of the card that listed the player's name, team, and position were highly prone to chipping. This one survived the years unscathed, hence its top rating.

The 1953 Bowman baseball card of Pee Wee Reese (right) is the first card to depict a ballplayer in action. By 1953, Topps posed a threat to Bowman's reign as the baseball card of choice among America's youth, prompting Bowman to break new ground with this issue, which was also the first to feature color photographic images of ballplayers.

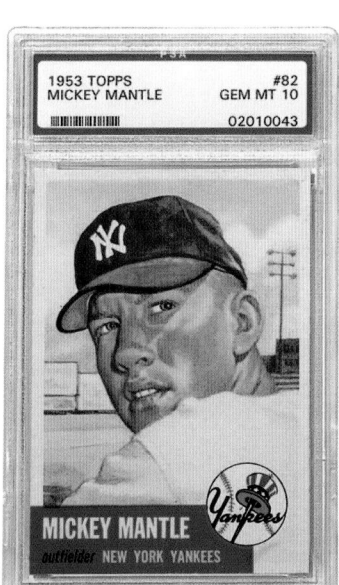

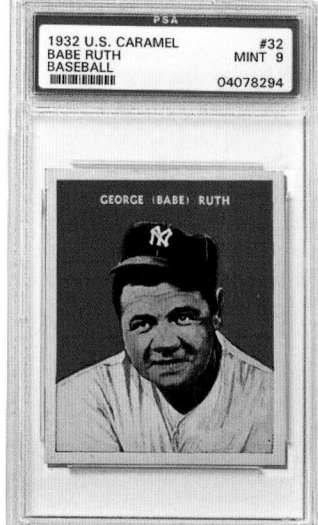

The Boston-based confectionary United States Caramel issued a Babe Ruth card (above) as part of its 32-card set featuring athletes from several sports, including baseball, boxing, golf, pool, and tennis.

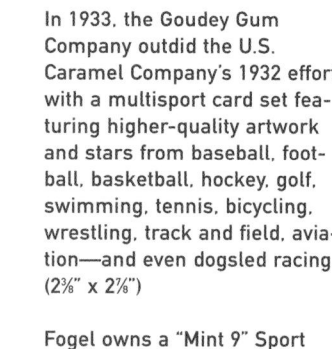

In 1933, the Goudey Gum Company outdid the U.S. Caramel Company's 1932 effort with a multisport card set featuring higher-quality artwork and stars from baseball, football, basketball, hockey, golf, swimming, tennis, bicycling, wrestling, track and field, aviation—and even dogsled racing. (2⅜" x 2⅞")

Fogel owns a "Mint 9" Sport Kings baseball card of Carl Hubbell, the era's master of the screwball. Joining Hubbell as the "Sport Kings" representing baseball in the Goudey set were Ty Cobb and Babe Ruth.

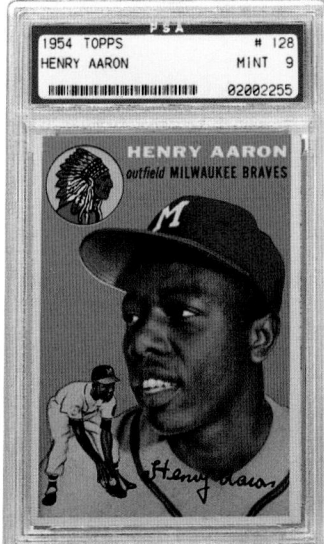

Some of the most treasured baseball cards in the hobby are those that depict famous players in their rookie season, making the rookie card of home run king Henry Aaron (above) among the most precious to collectors.

Fogel's Leaf baseball card of Ted Williams (above) was issued in 1948, a year after the Splendid Splinter won the Triple Crown.

Mickey Mantle's home uniform from the 1968 season (above, right) once resided in Mantle's restaurant on Central Park South in Manhattan. Today, it is part of Fogel's collection, along with an autographed bat used by Mantle in 1961, and a 1952 Topps baseball card of Mantle graded "Gem Mint 10" by PSA—perhaps the most popular baseball card ever issued, and one of only three to be awarded this lofty grade.

cards, Marshall kept glancing at Richard to see the expression on his face. Richard did the same to Marshall. After the third card in his third pack, Marshall stopped shuffling. His face went slack, and Richard knew Marshall had him beat. "The Mantle card pictured with his game-worn uniform and game-used bat (above) looks as fresh as the one I held in my hand 51 years ago in that drugstore," Fogel says. "I used to put myself to sleep every night dreaming about being the Mick, Yogi, or Scooter. My 1952 Topps cards were instrumental in procuring this childhood fantasy. . . and when I look at the three items together, I can imagine myself suiting up in Mantle's uniform, grab-bing his bat, and walking to the plate. I guess that's what my theater is all about."

Indeed, that is the essence of Fogel's theater. In the words of Philipp Blom:

Every collection is a theatre of memories, a dramatization and a mise-en-scene of personal and collective pasts, of a remembered childhood and of remembrance after death. It guarantees the presence of these memories through the objects evoking them. It is more even than a symbolic presence: a transubstantiation. The world beyond what we can touch is with us in and through them, and through communion with them it is possible to commune with it and become part of it.

COLLECTING RARE AND IMPORTANT BASEBALL PHOTOGRAPHS

BY DAN KNOLL WITH STEPHEN WONG

Very Best Regards.
Chas. M. Conlon

Ty Cobb stealing third, one of the 76 bases he stole in 1909.
Jimmy Austin, Yankee third baseman

CHARLES M. CONLON'S visceral action shot of Ty Cobb from 1909 remains one of baseball's iconic images. Dan Knoll owns a vintage print of the photo (above) that is special because the photographer provided, in his own hand, a notation, inscription, and signature on the back of the photograph (left). These markings suggest that Conlon printed it himself from the original glass plate. (8" x 10") The Dan Knoll Collection.

My fascination with photography began at age 10. During a fifth-grade unit about United States presidents, I was assigned to write an essay on John Quincy Adams, the sixth man to hold the country's highest office. Equipped with several comprehensive biographies from the local public library, I dutifully immersed myself in the project, absorbing whatever important facts and compelling tidbits I could find

about Adams. The further I probed into Adams's life and spirit, the more I realized, even as a fifth grader, that this son of the second U.S. president did not come into office by riding his father's coattails. Adams was a strong individual who tirelessly fought for what he considered right.

While doing my research, I came across a photograph of the man. It was the first photographic image of a U.S. president. I was immediately struck by its power. It revealed a strength in Adams's eyes that was consistent with what I had come to know about him. I had not seen this quality in any of the portraits painted by the accomplished artists of Adams's lifetime. What I saw in the image was stark, true, and telling. I felt as though I was peering through a window into the past.

That summer, while attending a local

Conlon captured the characteristically grumpy visage of Samuel Earl "Wahoo Sam" Crawford in a circa-1913 portrait (above). Nicknamed for his hometown of Wahoo, Nebraska, Crawford played for the Detroit Tigers and still holds the record for career triples (309). Perhaps his gloomy demeanor came from sharing the dugout and outfield with the irascible Ty Cobb for eight seasons. Crawford once said that Cobb "was still fighting the Civil War, and as far as he was concerned, we were all damn Yankees. But who knows? If he hadn't had that terrible persecution complex, he never would have been about the best ballplayer who ever lived." (5" x 7") The Marshall Fogel Collection.

The knuckle ball grip of infamous "Black Sox" pitcher Eddie Cicotte received close scrutiny from Conlon's lens in a circa-1913 photograph (above). According to authors Neal McCabe and Constance McCabe, Conlon found "unexpected beauty in ordinary places." Conlon shot a wide variety of subjects, and some of his most unique images are detailed close-up shots of hands like this one. (5" x 7") The Bill Mastro Collection.

Ted Williams (above) posed for Conlon before his big-league debut at Yankee Stadium on April 20, 1939. "The Kid"—as sportswriters dubbed Williams because he was only 17 when he became a professional ballplayer—finished his rookie season with a .327 average, 31 home runs, and 145 RBIs—a harbinger of things to come and perhaps the greatest rookie batting performance in baseball history. (8" x 10") The Bill Mastro Collection.

baseball banquet, I saw an elderly ex-major leaguer looking at a photograph of himself taken 50 years earlier. His gaze lightened, his eyes twinkled, and a soft smile came to his face. He was young again. The image had captured and preserved, even immortalized, a moment from his youth when his hands were strong, his feet were swift, and the world and its opportunities were his for the taking. He looked up and saw my eyes upon him. With a kind smile and a wink, he hinted to me that he knew I somehow understood. What I witnessed opened my 10-year-old mind to the power of photography, its connection to the past, and its potential to evoke human emotion.

When I returned home that evening, I pulled out a book of sports stories that my father used to read to me at bedtime. Then I consulted an encyclopedia to find better photographs of the players featured in the book. My favorite was Ty Cobb. In a 1907 photograph, he appeared almost boyish, while a photo from 1926 showed the effect of 19 years on his appearance. Those years had not been kind to Cobb, just as he had not been kind to those who shared his world. The photographs led me to think that perhaps the burden of carrying around so much hatred had actually changed Cobb's physical demeanor.

A visit to my school library turned up an armful of picture books about baseball and

the Civil War. I was immediately drawn to the work of renowned Civil War photographer Mathew Brady. The realization that not all images were created equal raised my awareness and appreciation of the skill required to consistently produce great pictures. In addition to understanding subject, light, focus, angle, contrast, and exposure, the photographer needs the vision to anticipate a compelling image. He must recognize the moment when it presents itself, and react. Sometimes he has only a split second to capture an image or lose it forever.

EARLY-20TH-CENTURY MASTER PHOTOGRAPHERS

With most great photographers, the clicking of the shutter is instinctive. Baseball's consummate photographer, Charles Martin Conlon (1868–1945), vividly illustrated this point when he snapped a shot of Ty Cobb that turned out to be arguably the greatest baseball action photo ever taken (see the vintage print on the opposite page). In 1909, Conlon was photographing a game between the New York Highlanders and Cobb's Detroit Tigers. Cobb was on second base with one out; a Tigers batter was attempting to bunt him to third. Conlon was standing off third base chatting with New York third baseman Jimmy Austin, who, in anticipation of the sacrifice bunt, had taken several steps toward home plate and was standing in the base path. Suddenly, Cobb

broke for third, catching Austin and the Highlanders off guard. Austin dashed to the bag to receive the throw as Cobb flew in, spikes up. The fury and force of Cobb's slide knocked Austin to the ground.

Later, Conlon recalled Cobb's determined look, his clenched teeth, his flashing spikes, and the spray of dirt as he hurled himself into Austin. But at the moment, Conlon's only concern was for his friend Jimmy Austin, who had fallen hard after the collision. After making sure that Austin was unhurt, Conlon then began to wonder if he had captured the moment on camera. Though much in doubt, he removed the glass plate just in case, replacing it with a new one. For the next several hours, Conlon chastised himself for missing such a remarkable opportunity, only to find out the next day, when developing the plates from the game that, in his excitement, he indeed had snapped the camera instinctively. The result is an indelible image of the game: In a single frame, Conlon had captured the essence of Ty Cobb as well as the essence of baseball during that golden age.

It is hard to believe that for Conlon photography was only a spare-time hobby, not a profession. While working as a proof-reader for the *New York Telegram* at the turn of the century, he had befriended John B. Foster, the *Telegram*'s sports-page editor who later succeeded Henry Chadwick as editor of the *Spalding Base Ball Guide* in

WALSH, CHICAGO AMER.

Carl Horner's circa-1905 original photograph of "Big Ed" Walsh (above, left) served as the basis for Walsh's T206 baseball card (above, right). A righthander for the White

Sox, Walsh relied on a devastating spitball to win 40 games in one season (1908) and set the major league record for career earned- run average (1.82)—a standard that remains to this day. (5¼" x 7"). The Marshall Fogel Collection.

Horner was renowned for his beautiful team composite photographs, including his portraits of the 1903 New York Highlanders (below), the team that would be renamed the Yankees. Included in the composition are the stoic images of Hall of Famers Wee Willie Keeler (bottom left), Clark Griffith (center), and Jack Chesbro (top row, third from the right). (28¾" x 26½") The Corey R. Shanus Collection.

George Grantham Bain captured Christy Mathewson's famous "body swing" (windup) in a photograph (opposite, top left) taken at the Polo Grounds carriage park (the turn-of-the-century equivalent of the parking lot) at the dawn of Matty's illustrious career, circa 1902. In 1904, Matty struck the same pose for Charles M. Conlon's first baseball photograph. (4½" x 3") The Wong Family Archives Collection.

In 1910, Bain snapped an image of Christy Mathewson's graceful follow-through at the Polo Grounds (opposite, top right). By that point in his career, the Giants' ace had won 30 or more games in a season four times and pitched three consecutive shutouts in a World Series (1905). Writer John Kieran called Mathewson "the greatest pitcher I ever saw. He was the greatest anybody ever saw. Let them name all the others. I don't care how good they were. Matty was better." (4½" x 6½") The Bill Mastro Collection.

Ty Cobb (opposite, top middle) demonstrated his batting style for Bain in 1916. According to sportswriter Jimmy Cannon, "The cruelty of Cobb's style fascinated the multitudes, but it also alienated them. He played in a climate of hostility, friendless by choice, in a violent world he populated with enemies . . . but not even his disagreeable character could destroy the image of his greatness as a ballplayer. Ty Cobb was the best. That seemed to be all he wanted." (5" x 7") The Bill Mastro Collection.

Bain photographed Babe Ruth (opposite, bottom left) in 1919, his final season with the Boston Red Sox and the one in which the team recognized his burgeoning prowess with the bat and made him a regular outfielder on his off days from pitching. The back of Bain's photograph is dated August 26, 1919, and inscribed with a notation that Ruth had just hit his 22nd home run of the season. He would finish the year with a major-league record 29. (5" x 6½") The Wong Family Archives Collection.

As with great painters, each of the early-20th-century photographic masters possessed a certain style that became his trademark. At the beginning of the 20th century, Boston-based photographer Carl Horner created wonderful studio portraits of players in uniform. To Horner, the uniform was as integral to the image as the player wearing it. He produced surprisingly gentle and refined portrayals, such as his cabinet portrait of legendary spitballer Ed Walsh. Horner's portrait photos appeared in newspapers and magazines, on board games, and on trading cards, including the 1909 Colgan's chips and the 1914–1915 Cracker Jack baseball card sets, and the landmark T206 tobacco card set produced between 1909 and 1911 by the American Tobacco Company. In addition to its artistry, Horner's work provides an accurate and comprehensive reference for

1908. "I came to know Foster very well," recalled Conlon. "He came to know about my hobby—taking pictures. He said to me one day, 'Charley, they need pictures of ball players for the *Guide*, and there is no reason why you can't take pictures of the players, as well as landscapes. It will be a good pickup for you, and it will be something for a day off.'" Conlon kept his proofreading job, but he also became the *Guide*'s chief photographer. His photos appeared in the *The Sporting News*, the *New York Telegram*, and the Reach *Base Ball Guide* (a subsidiary of the *Spalding Guide*), as

well. By 1920, Conlon had become the staff photographer for *Baseball Magazine*, and his work appeared on posters, textbooks, baseball cards, baseball manuals, and World Series souvenir programs.

From 1904 to 1942, Conlon's vision and innate sense of the moment enabled him consistently to capture the essence of his subject matter, be it the ferocity of Cobb's slide, the peevishness on the face of "Wahoo Sam" Crawford, or the self-assurance in rookie Ted Williams's eyes. This ability to communicate emotions distinguishes a great image from a good one.

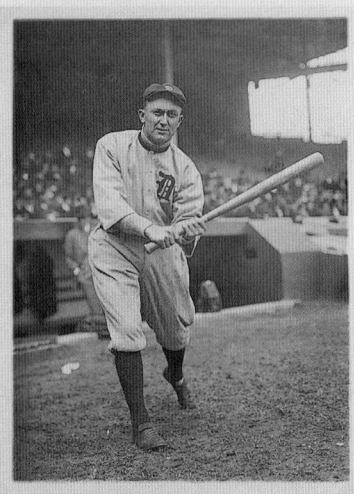

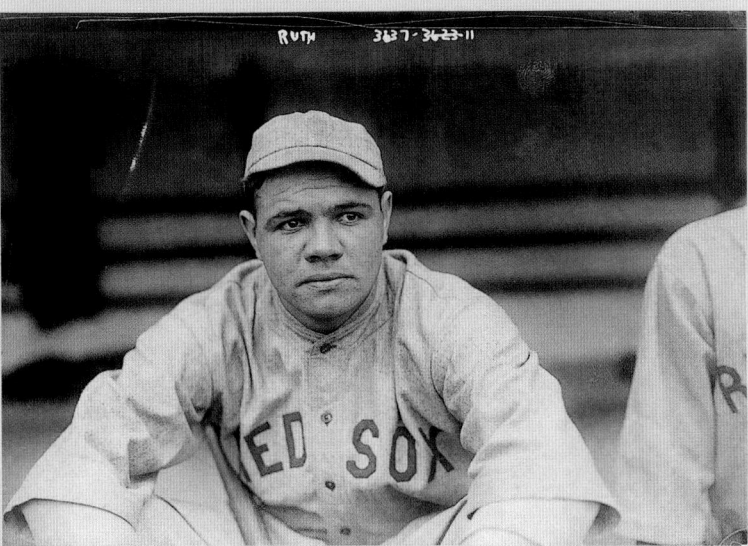

Ever resourceful, Bain sometimes ventured outside the ballpark to document the pageantry and culture of baseball. There wasn't room enough in Philadelphia's Shibe Park to accommodate every fan who wanted to watch the 1913 World Series in person, so residents of 20th Street, whose homes (above right) overlooked the 12-foot rightfield fence of the ballpark, rented roof space during the Series between the Athletics and the New York Giants. After Philadelphia manager Connie Mack failed to prevent this bustling business with a lawsuit, he arranged for the construction of a new fence in rightfield—one that would be tall enough to obstruct the view from the 20th Street rooftops. (5" x 7") The Wong Family Archives Collection.

early-20th-century baseball uniforms and player images.

While Horner was creating his memorable studio portraits, New York–based photographer George Grantham Bain was also making his mark in baseball photography. Hailed today as "The Father of News Photography," Bain began his career as a photojournalist for United Press in the late 1800s. He captured profound images of cultural America and newsworthy events. Having quickly established his credentials, he left United Press and formed the Bain News Service in 1898. In the subsequent decades, Bain amassed a library of photographs that included a number of outstanding baseball images, a select few of which appear on these pages.

Bain recognized the importance of baseball in our culture, and he seized the opportunities offered by his hometown New York Giants, and their spacious ballpark, the Polo Grounds, which featured magnificent wooden architecture and was set against the sprawling backdrop of New York shortly after the start of the Industrial Revolution.

One of Bain's favorite subjects was Giants pitcher Christy Mathewson, a tall, handsome, and refined young athlete whose prowess on the mound made him baseball's first superstar of the 20th century. Before signing with the Giants in 1900, "Matty," as he was fondly called, was the class president at Bucknell College and was named to the All-America football team. America's youngsters admired other ballplayers, but they worshipped Mathewson. Sportswriters referred to him as "the Christian gentleman" because of his high moral convictions and record of clean play. During an era in which rowdiness, profanity, and fistfights plagued professional baseball games, Mathewson's noble demeanor inspired a generation of fans. Bain's photographs consistently captured the pitcher's unique character and commanding presence. The photographer's cool, steely-toned images were always direct, candid, and compelling, and they reinforced the heroic quality of the game's greatest stars.

Like Conlon, Bain bridged the gap between photojournalism and art. He illuminated the pageantry of baseball. From shots of spectators watching a World Series game at the Polo Grounds (see page 4), to a rooftop overlooking Shibe Park, Bain understood the moments that make baseball an American spectacle. His thoughtful, inclusive approach to the game is believed to have influenced a number of other notable photographers, among them Conlon, Paul Thompson, Louis Van Oeyen,

CLEVELAND AMERICAN LEAGUE BALL CLUB, 1910

Philadelphia Athletics Champions 1911

A panoramic photograph (top) shows the 1910 Cleveland ball club, known as the "Naps" in honor of player/manager Larry "Napoleon" Lajoie. Addie Joss and Cy Young stand to Lajoie's left. (37½" x 9½") The Wong Family Archives Collection.

Connie Mack and his Philadelphia Athletics (above) posed for a panoramic team photo in 1911, after defeating John McGraw's Giants in the World Series. (38¼" x 13") The Wong Family Archives Collection.

Early-20th-century news photographer Paul Thompson snapped this shot of the 1917 World Series champion Chicago White Sox (right), essentially the same team that threw the Series in 1919. All eight conspirators are in the photograph, including Shoeless Joe Jackson, who is seated in the second row, third from the right. First baseman Chick Gandil stares out from the center of the back row with a big wad of tobacco in his mouth. Two years later, he would be at the center of the scandal, as its chief instigator. (8" x 10") The Wong Family Archives Collection.

and George Burke.

Chicago native George Burke, who began photographing baseball in 1929, took the torch from Bain and Conlon, introducing a new style that became popular with fans and players alike. Although influenced by Conlon, Burke presented baseball in a much less formal manner than his predecessor. He photographed his subjects in warm, relaxed poses, encouraging them to smile or even clown for the camera. Like Horner, Burke looked for other creative

ways to present his work, and he sometimes designed striking composite photographic displays (including a composite photograph of the 1932 New York Yankees). Burke often presented the lighter side of celebrated ballplayers.

Conlon, Horner, Bain, and Burke are among the select few early-20th-century photographic masters who deeply understood their subjects and possessed the talent to create poignant and timeless images with a camera. Because these photographs

appeared in numerous publications, people who had never set foot in a major-league ballpark could experience baseball's magic and enchantment. While each of these men created a singular style of photography, they shared the same passion for the splendor of baseball and baseball culture, which they enriched immeasurably.

KEY PHOTOGRAPHIC FORMATS
Collecting vintage baseball photographs can be a fascinating and rewarding lifetime

GEORGE BURKE had a knack for capturing the lighter side of a ballplayer, as exemplified by his early 1930s original photograph of Lou Gehrig (left). (4" x 6") The Wong Family Archives Collection.

A unique piece (below) produced by Burke features 26 portraits of the 1932 Bronx Bombers super-imposed over a panoramic view of Wrigley Field, home of the Chicago Cubs, whom the Yanks swept in the '32 World Series. (13" x 10¼") The Marshall Fogel Collection.

During the 1919 World Series, throngs of fans from the city gathered at Times Square (right) to follow the action between the White Sox and the Cincinnati Reds on an automated scoreboard linked to Comiskey Park by telegraph. Thompson was there to capture the memorable scene on film. The gathering occurred before the advent of radio-broadcast games, so the fans clamoring for information about the Series had to make do with the bare-bones updates provided by the changing numbers on the Comiskey score-board. Little did they know that the Series—and the game of baseball—were being dishonored by great scandal in Chicago, where eight members of the White Sox conspired with gamblers to throw the Series. (7" x 8¼") The Wong Family Archives Collection.

As the first newspaper staff photographer in Cleveland, Louis Van Oeyen (1865-1946) shot portraiture, politics, disaster, crime, scandal, and sports with con-summate skill. Van Oeyen's favorite subject, however, was baseball, and he was named the official photographer of the American League in 1908. On July 24, 1911, at Cleveland's League Park, he photographed the American League All-Star team (above) which was handpicked to play against Cleveland in the Addie Joss Benefit Game. Among the notables in this one-of-a-kind photograph are Frank "Home Run" Baker, Smokey Joe Wood, Walter Johnson, Hal Chase, Eddie Collins, Tris Speaker, and Ty Cobb, who wears a Cleveland uniform because he left his Tigers uniform at home. (9½" x 11") The Corey R. Shanus Collection.

endeavor. But prospective collectors should consider a number of factors before embarking on this wonderful journey down memory lane. These factors significantly affect a photograph's market value. First and foremost are the various formats in which vintage baseball photographs are presented.

ORIGINAL AND VINTAGE PRINTS
Original and vintage prints are the most desirable and usually the most expensive photographs. Original prints were produced by the photographer from the original negative or transparency soon after the photographic image was shot. Many originals bear the photographer's personal stamp, signature, captions, and/or notes. An image that was made from the original negative or transparency during the period of its subject matter, but lacks the markings of an

1118820

MICKEY MANTLE BATTING DURING

Game

MAY 1956 ALT #2
CH. X

PLEASE CREDIT
United Press Photo
UNITED PRESS ASSOCIATIONS
461 EIGHTH AVENUE, NEW YORK

An original news service photo of Satchel Paige (top left) shows the legendary Negro League pitcher at age 39 in the Cleveland Stadium dressing room, preparing to make his debut with the Cleveland Indians.
(8¼" x 6½") The Bill Mastro Collection.

Original and vintage news service photographs show the future home-run king Hank Aaron (top right, 8" x 10"), a retired Honus Wagner, wielding two pistols (7" x 9"), and the iconic Mickey Mantle, striking the batting stance that produced 536 home runs in his 18-year career with the Yankees (above, 8" x 10"). The Marshall Fogel Collection and The Bill Mastro Collection.

original, is typically described as "vintage." Original and vintage prints provide the best clarity, contrast, and tonal scheme. All of the prints by Conlon, Horner, George Bain, George Burke, Paul Thompson, and Louis Van Oeyen in this chapter are original or vintage prints.

CONTEMPORARY PRINT MADE FROM ORIGINAL
A contemporary print is one that is made from the original negative or transparen-

cy but at a much later date than when the photographic image was shot. An example of this would be an image that was shot in 1933 but not printed from the original negative or transparency until decades later. Although these prints can yield beautiful images, they are substantially less desirable and valuable than original and vintage prints because they usually have been mass-produced.

SECOND-GENERATION PRINTS
A photograph that was made from a copy of a negative, or a photograph of a photograph is considered a second-generation print. The overall quality of second-generation prints is considerably inferior to originals. Second-generation prints are inexpensive, but not especially desirable.

Far left is a large-border variant of a Burke original print of Detroit Tiger legend Hank Greenberg. The original photograph was taken in the early 1930s, when Greenberg—a .313 lifetime hitter who hit 331 career homers—began terrorizing American League pitchers. (8" x 6") The Wong Family Archives Collection.

Agency and photographers' stamps, such as George Grantham Bain's, Culver Pictures', and George Burke's (left) can be instrumental in identifying the provenance of photographs.

NEWS SERVICE PHOTOGRAPHS

Perhaps the most widely collected rare and important baseball photographs are those produced and/or distributed by large news services like Associated Press (AP), United Press (UP), International News Service (INS), Underwood & Underwood (UU), World Wide Photos (WWP), and ACME. These agencies compiled hoards of photographs for distribution to subscribing newspapers and magazines. The backs of these photographs usually contain a typed or teletyped paper caption tag that includes the date of the photograph, the name of the news service, and an explanation of the image's content. On most news service photos that originated from the first half of the 20th century, the caption tag is grocery-bag brown in color.

A news service usually stamped its name and address in ink, along with the terms of use on the back of the photograph. Although such a stamp does not reveal the exact date of a photo, it can help assign a photograph to a general era. For example, if a photograph has a United Press stamp on the back, you can be sure it comes from before May 1958, when the UP merged with INS to become the United Press International (UPI).

WIREPHOTOS

News service photographs are often mistaken for Wirephotos. They are, in fact, quite different. A Wirephoto is the photograph created by the Wirephoto process. If the United Press, for example, sent a copy of an original photograph via wire to the *New York Times*, only the copy is a Wirephoto. The image quality of Wirephotos is typically inferior to that of original/vintage news service photographs.

PANORAMIC PHOTOGRAPHS

One of the most popular and impressive formats of early-20th-century baseball photography is the panorama, which provided sweeping views of professional teams and major-league ballpark interiors. The wide views were achieved with a special camera that rotated while the shutter was open. These photographs are relatively scarce, and come in black-and-white or sepia tones.

Identifying Original and Vintage Prints
Charles M. Conlon Prints: Original or vintage Conlon photographs dating from 1904 to 1915 typically have a 5" x 7" format, while those from 1916 to 1934 typically have a 4" x 5" format. A number of Conlon originals were also produced with an 8" x 10" format. Conlon was inconsistent in marking his photographs on the reverse. He sometimes hastily penciled in the name of the ballplayer in the photo, with captions or notes. Sometimes he signed or stamped the back of his pictures. His signature usually appears at the top or bottom of the back. The stamp usually appears in purple ink in the middle of the back and states: CHARLES M. CONLON / EVENING TELEGRAM / NEW YORK, or CHARLES M. CONLON / 216 WEST 111TH STREET / NEW YORK, or CHARLES M. CONLON / 189 ALDEN PLACE / ENGLEWOOD, NEW JERSEY. Conlon original and vintage prints are scarce.

Carl Horner Prints: Original T206 cabinet photographs by Carl Horner are very rare. These photos are usually on light-colored, ornately embossed mounts with Horner's name printed on the bottom right.

George Grantham Bain Prints: Original or vintage Bain prints are not mounted and typically come in a 5" x 7" or smaller format, with his name or BAIN NEWS SERVICE stamped on the back. Many Bain originals are found with CULVER PICTURES, INC. or CULVER PICTURE ARCHIVES stamped on the reverse, because this company purchased a number of Bain's originals during the first half of the 20th century. Bain original and vintage prints are scarce.

George Burke Prints: The backs of Burke photos typically have a purple-ink stamp stating GEO. BURKE / 847 BELMONT AVE. /CHICAGO, as well as a cataloging number and player's name in type at the top. They usually measure about postcard size, or 8" x 6" with large borders. While Burke images are of the highest quality, with sharp clarity and contrast, they remain affordable because they are not as rare as those of Conlon, Horner, Bain, Thompson, or Van Oeyen.

The caption tag on the reverse side of an original news service photograph of Babe Ruth from February 12, 1920 (left), reads: BABE RUTH, HOME RUN KING AND YANKEE OUTFIELDER IS NOW IN BOSTON PUSHING THE SALE OF "BABE RUTH" CIGARS OF HIS OWN MANUFACTURE. BABE WAS A CIGAR MAKER BEFORE HE ENTERED BASEBALL AND DURING THE WINTER OFTEN GOES BACK TO HIS OLD TRADE. THE PHOTO SHOWS RUTH IN A BOSTON SHOP SELLING SOME OF HIS PERFECTOS. WONDER IF THEY ARE AS STRONG AS THEIR NAMESAKE. (9" x 6½") The Wong Family Archives Collection

The Bambino proudly exhibits three of his favorite "Indian Clubs," as Paul Thompson noted on the back of his original photograph of the slugger (opposite, top left), taken during the 1920 season. That year was Ruth's first with the Yankees, and one in which he shattered the record for home runs with 54, while the Yanks set a new record for attendance, drawing 1,289,422 fans to Yankee Stadium and becoming the first ball club to crest a million in attendance. "They all flock to him," Yankee manager Miller Huggins said, because the American fan "likes the fellow who carries the wallop." (8¼" x 6¼") The Wong Family Archives Collection.

The Babe applies pen to horsehide for a lucky fan in a straw boater in an original news service photo (opposite, top right), thereby creating one of the most coveted artifacts in the realm of baseball memorabilia: a baseball autographed by Babe Ruth.(9½" x 7½") The Bill Mastro Collection.

"Bustin' Babe" Ruth and "Larrupin' Lou" Gehrig (opposite, bottom left) pose for the camera during a stop on their famous 1927 postseason barnstorming tour. An original news service photograph, this image has been reproduced and published many times. It is one of the most popular images of the two Yankee avatars in existence. (8" x 10") The Bill Mastro Collection.

A haunting original news service photo from May 12, 1925 (opposite, bottom right) captures Ruth sitting in a wheelchair on the balcony of St. Vincent's Hospital, with his daughter on his lap. Excessive drinking, eating, and womanizing had caught up with the Babe, who showed up to spring training that year 30 pounds overweight, feverish, and weak. Some wags called it "the bellyache heard round the world." (8" x 10") The Wong Family Archives Collection.

The Babe

Babe Ruth once said, "I swing big, with everything I've got. I hit big or I miss big. I like to live as big as I can." By far the most charismatic and famous player in baseball history, Ruth is a Bunyan-esque figure who transcended the game. In his definitive biography, *Babe: The Legend Comes to Life*, sportswriter Robert W. Creamer writes that Ruth "moved far beyond the artificial limits of baselines and outfield fences and sports pages. As I write this, he is dead and buried for more than 25 years, and it is nearly 40 years since he played his last major-league game. Yet almost every day, certainly several times a week, you read and hear about him."

Creamer's book was published in 1974, the year Henry Aaron broke Ruth's career record for home runs, but his point remains valid today: Ruth is an American icon, and many of the early-20th-century photographic masters helped make him one. They roamed the diamond with their large box cameras trying to capture that special shot of baseball's biggest star. And while the slugger's home runs caught the attention of sportswriters and fans, it was Ruth's larger-than-life persona that catapulted him to stardom outside the game. His round belly, spindly legs, twinkling eyes and broad, impish grin gave him an almost cartoonlike appearance. His life-of-the-party personality and penchant for shenanigans endeared him to fans and media alike.

Ruth was a pitcher's nightmare and a nation's dream. He brought fans back to the ballparks after the 1919 Black Sox scandal; was voted the most popular American of the Roaring '20s; and helped average Americans forget their troubles, if only for a moment, during the Great Depression. Seventy-five years later, Ruth's legend is as grand as it was during his playing days. Although few Americans who witnessed Ruth's feats are still alive, we can experience the man and his legend through photographs that have endured for decades. The ones on these pages reveal the essence of Babe Ruth, giving us a glimpse of his unique appeal and enduring legend.

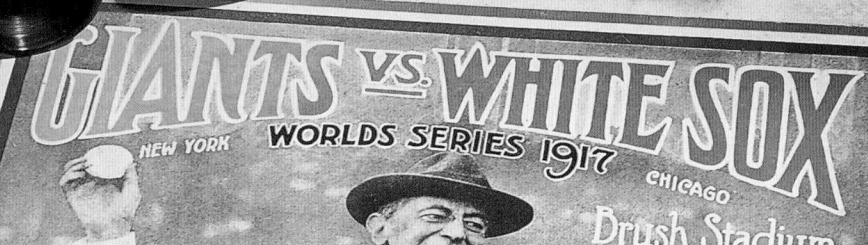

GIANTS VS. WHITE SOX

NEW YORK — WORLDS SERIES 1917 — CHICAGO

Brush Stadium Polo Grounds

PRESIDENT WILSON THROWING OUT BALL AT THE OPENING OF THE AMERICAN LEAGUE SEASON AT WASHINGTON.

A BIG ENOUGH BOY TO ENJOY THE NATIONAL GAME — AND — A MAN BIG ENOUGH TO GUIDE OUR COUNTRY THROUGH ITS GREATEST CRISIS.

PRICE 25 CENTS

HARRY M. STEVENS, Publisher

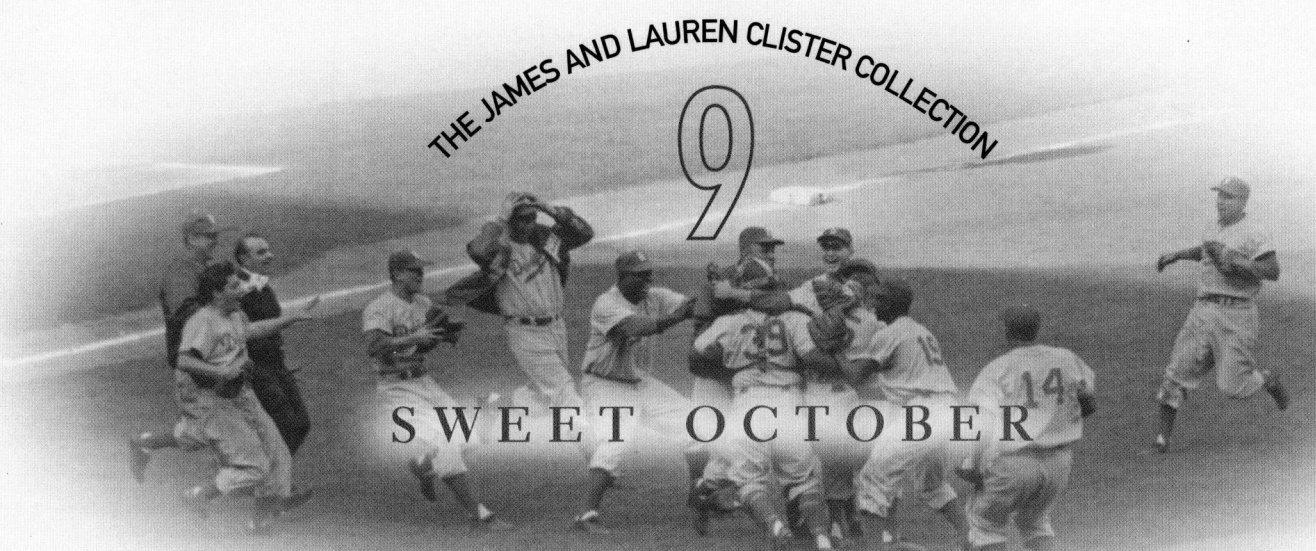

THE JAMES AND LAUREN CLISTER COLLECTION

9

SWEET OCTOBER

"World Series meant you had to wear a sweater, it was always cool out and great and the leaves were already changing. We use to call it World Series weather. And before the playoffs and when they added all these other divisions and everything, there were eight teams in both leagues. So there was less time so it came earlier. So it meant it was a Jewish holiday, so there would be no school or they would be taking the Census. Now the Census was somebody would come to your house and go, 'How many you got here? Four? Ok!' You had to stay home, somebody was counting heads. It was absolutely hysterical. But you got to see a couple of games. The Yankees and the Dodgers—there was nothing like it. It was like watching Ali fight every day. You know it was that excitement that you could just remember and sitting there like this [*makes mesmerized face*]. You took the phone off the hook, you didn't do anything else, you just sat there and you screamed at people you loved and you ate things you would never eat before. But you made your whole day around it. It was the World Series. . . ."

—*BILLY CRYSTAL,*
filmed interview with Ken Burns in
Baseball: An Illustrated History

After covering baseball as a sportswriter for the Cincinnati *Commercial Gazette* for several years, Byron Bancroft "Ban" Johnson became president of the Western League, a struggling minor-league franchise, in 1894. He eventually turned the league into a finan-

cially successful enterprise and, in October 1899, renamed it the American League to impart a more patriotic tone. He also positioned the circuit to challenge the well-established National League, which had been formed in 1876. Johnson's objective was to introduce a "cleaner" form of baseball that would combat the rampant profanity and rowdiness that people associated with many National League games at the time. Little did Johnson know that his efforts would give rise to one of America's most time-honored sports traditions, the World Series.

When Johnson asked to present his ideas at the National League's annual meeting in Philadelphia in 1900, the National League team owners kept him waiting, only to adjourn without granting him a hearing. Nevertheless, Johnson pursued his agenda. He established new baseball clubs in Philadelphia, Boston, Washington, and Baltimore, and he lured players from the National League with offers averaging $500 more per season than those players were earning in the established circuit. More than 100 National Leaguers jumped to Johnson's new American League.

In February 1901, Johnson declared that his upstart circuit had achieved a major-league level, equal to that of the National League. His announcement, which National League ballclub owners refused to acknowledge, ignited a two-year war between the leagues that resulted in threats, lawsuits, contract disputes, and rampant piracy of ballplayers. In January 1903, the National League relented and signed a peace agreement with Johnson that permitted the leagues to carry on separately, while binding them to common play-

The cover of the 1917 World Series program, issued by the New York Giants (opposite), features President Woodrow Wilson throwing out the first ball at the Washington Senators' opening-day game at National Park on April 10, 1913. That opener was the first of 11 baseball games Wilson attended while in office. He never used his Presidential Pass, opting instead to pay for each game he attended. In 1915, Wilson became the first sitting President to attend a World Series when he brought his fiancée, Edith Gault, to Philadelphia to watch Game 2 between the Phillies and the Red Sox. The President witnessed a 2–1 victory for Boston, which went on to win the Series four games to one. (11" x 9¼")

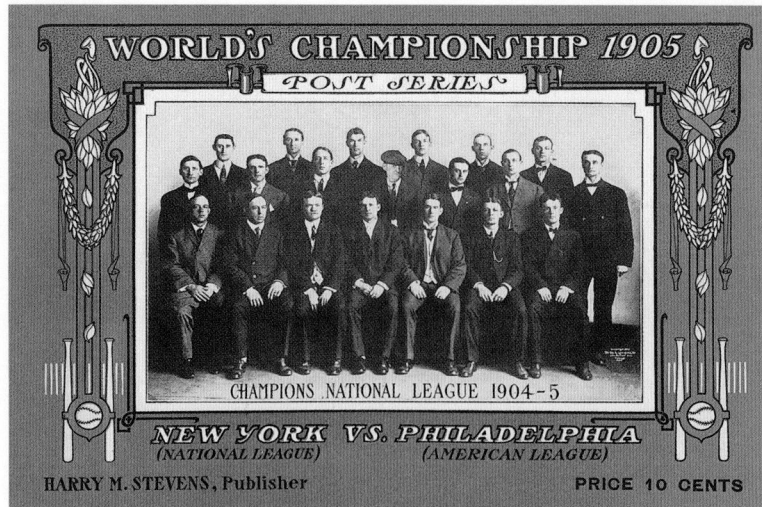

WORLD'S CHAMPIONSHIP 1905

POST SERIES

CHAMPIONS NATIONAL LEAGUE 1904-5

NEW YORK VS. PHILADELPHIA
(NATIONAL LEAGUE) (AMERICAN LEAGUE)

HARRY M. STEVENS, Publisher PRICE 10 CENTS

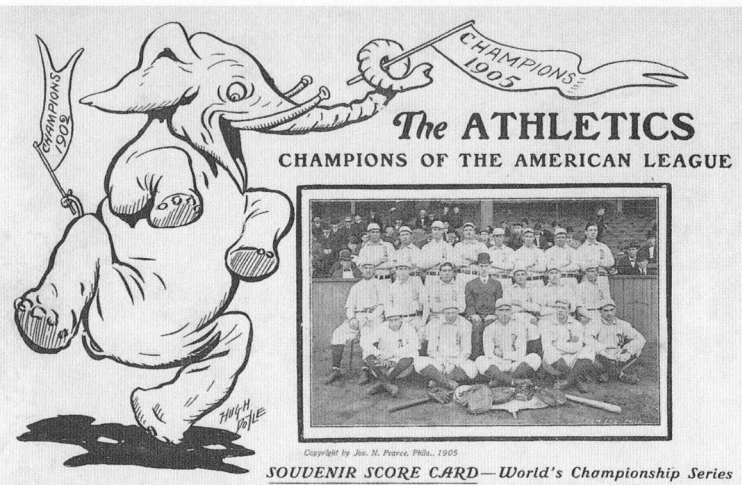

CHAMPIONS 1905

CHAMPIONS 1902

The ATHLETICS
CHAMPIONS OF THE AMERICAN LEAGUE

HUGH DOYLE

Copyright by Jos. N. Pearce, Phila., 1905

SOUVENIR SCORE CARD — World's Championship Series

The Clisters' collection includes souvenir scorecards issued by both teams in the 1905 World Series, the Giants and the Athletics. The one from the Giants (top) was produced by none other than Harry Moseley Stevens, the inventor of the modern scorecard. (9" x 6")

The scorecard from Game 3 of the 1905 World Series (above), was issued by the home team, the Philadelphia Athletics. Played at Philadelphia's Columbia Park, the game featured a pitching gem by the New York's Christy Mathewson, who threw the second of his three straight shutouts in the Series, a feat widely considered to be the greatest pitching performance in World Series history. (9" x 6")

White, who practiced dentistry in Washington, D.C., while also playing for the White Sox, went 18–6 that season and had the lowest ERA in the American League (1.52). The multi-talented southpaw clinched the final game of the 1906 Series, completing the Hitless Wonders' upset victory over the heavily favored Cubs. The following season, White topped the American League in wins, going 27–13 with a 2.26 ERA. (9" x 6") In an original sepia-toned panoramic photograph from Game 6 at South Side Park in Chicago (below), the Cubs are in the field behind their ace Mordecai "Three Finger" Brown during the bottom of the second inning. The White Sox lead 3–1 and will go on to an 8-3 victory and the World Series title. (29¾" x 11½")

When Don Drysdale pitched five consecutive shutouts in 1968, he tied a record set 64 years earlier by Harry "Doc" White, who appeared on the cover of the scorecard from Game 4 of the 1906 World Series (top, right).

The 1909 World Series scorecard (right) heralds the Pirates' new home, Forbes Field, which opened on June 30, 1909. The new ballpark marked the beginning of an auspicious year for Pirates fans as their team would win its first World Series. In 1910, the Reach Guide wrote, "The formal opening of Forbes Field was an historic event. . . . a tribute to the national game, a beneficence to Pittsburgh and an enduring monument to [team owner Dreyfuss]. For architectural beauty, imposing size, solid construction and public comfort and convenience, it has not its superior in the world." (9" x 7")

OFFICIAL SCORE BOOK
CHICAGO WHITE STOCKINGS PRICE 5¢

1906

CHICAGO

DR. HARRY WHITE

READ THE DAILY NEWS ILLUSTRATED SPORTING EXTRA EVERY EVENING.

OFFICIAL SCORE CARD PRICE 5 CENTS
PITTSBURG BASE BALL CLUB HARRIS & SON PUBLISHERS PITTSBURG PA.

Forbes Field THE PIRATES NEW BALL PARK
THIS IS THE MOST MAGNIFICENT BASE BALL PARK IN THE WORLD

ERECTED BY
THE NICOLA BUILDING COMPANY
OF PITTSBURGH

ing rules, schedules, and mutually recognized contracts.

Johnson's American League was now an officially recognized major-league entity, and the way to the first interleague postseason series was clear. On September 16, 1903, Barney Dreyfuss (owner of the National League's Pittsburgh Pirates) and Henry Killilea (owner of the AL's Boston Pilgrims) signed an agreement to play in a best-of-nine "World Series" competition.

Boston won that inaugural Series five games to three, and in almost every year since, the Fall Classic, as the World Series came to be nicknamed, has captured the imagination of fans. Generations of baseball followers have embraced the event as the sport's sacred crucible, in which legends, dynasties, and even tragedies have been forged and immortalized; where the unex-

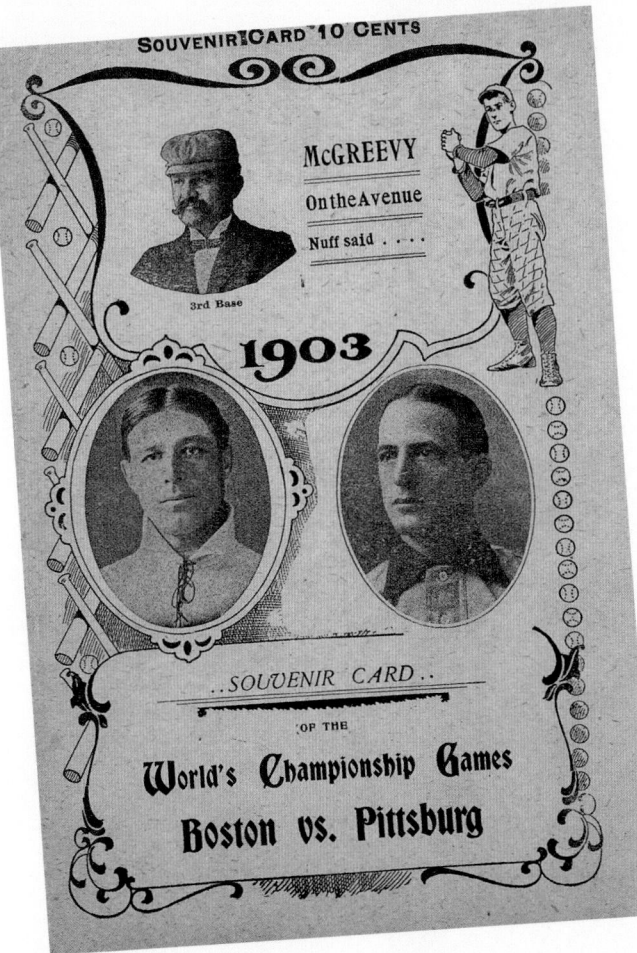

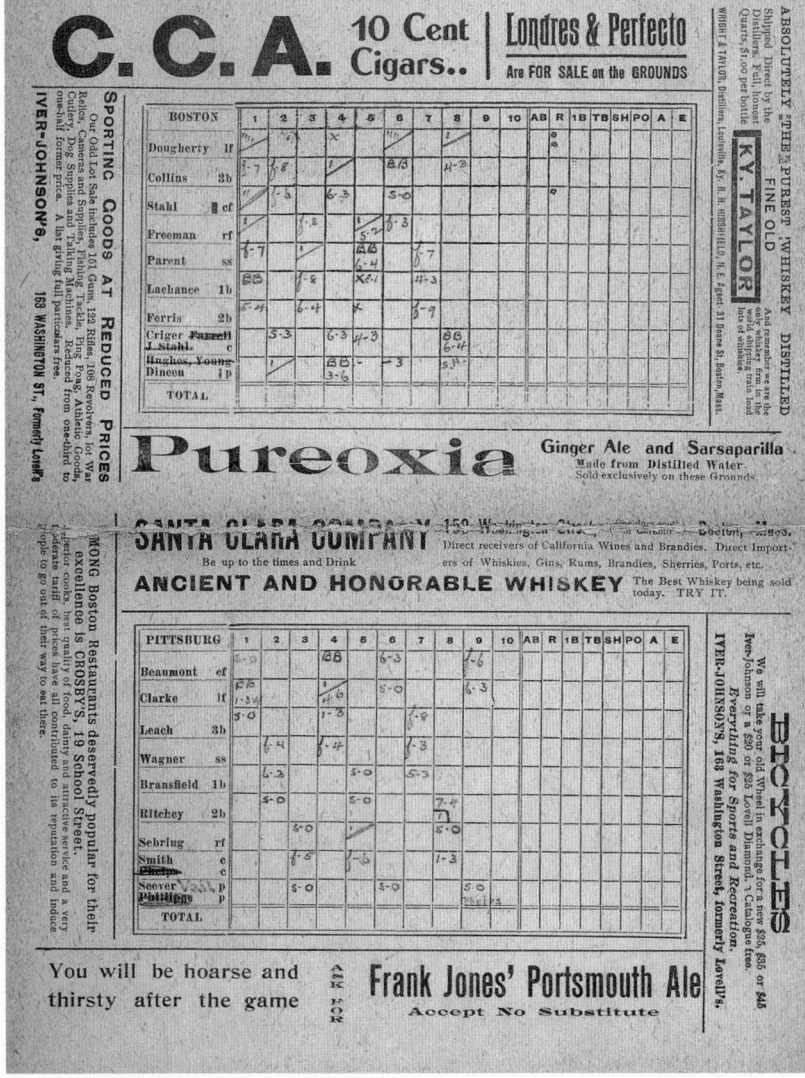

Though the scorecard from Game 2 of the 1903 World Series (above and right) features future Hall of Famers Jimmy Collins and Fred Clarke, the biggest star pictured on its cover is the mustachioed fellow above the two players. That's Mike McGreevy (the souvenir card uses a variant spelling of his name), the ringleader of Boston's Royal Rooters and the owner of a bar near Huntington Avenue Grounds. Known as the Third Base Saloon because it was the fans' last stop on their way home, McGreevey's bar was the site of many a baseball argument, and its owner's word was final on all such disputes. He would end his authoritative baseball sermons with, "Enough said!" (hence the

tagline next to his photo). McGreevey led the Royal Rooters in variations of the popular song "Tessie," which apparently drove the Pirates to distraction while the Pilgrims won Game 5 and ultimately the Series. (8" x 5⅜")

This 1906 Fall Classic memento was sold at Chicago's West Side Grounds, the Cubbies' home before Wrigley. The team won a record 116 games during the regular season, but they were no match for White Sox pitchers "Big" Ed Walsh, Nick Altrock, Frank Owen, and Harry "Doc" White, who produced a combined ERA of 1.50 during the Series.

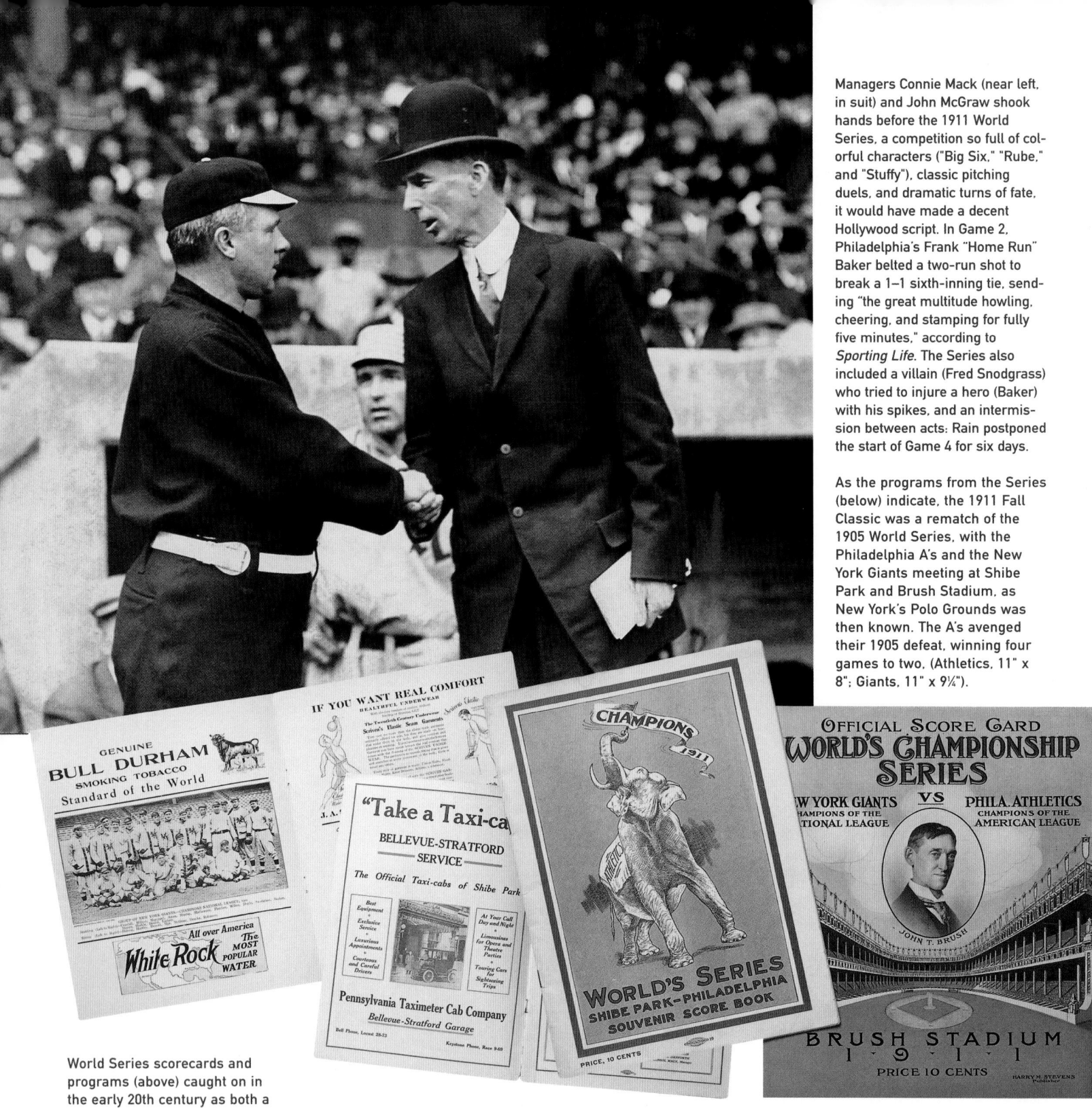

Managers Connie Mack (near left, in suit) and John McGraw shook hands before the 1911 World Series, a competition so full of colorful characters ("Big Six," "Rube," and "Stuffy"), classic pitching duels, and dramatic turns of fate, it would have made a decent Hollywood script. In Game 2, Philadelphia's Frank "Home Run" Baker belted a two-run shot to break a 1–1 sixth-inning tie, sending "the great multitude howling, cheering, and stamping for fully five minutes," according to *Sporting Life*. The Series also included a villain (Fred Snodgrass) who tried to injure a hero (Baker) with his spikes, and an intermission between acts: Rain postponed the start of Game 4 for six days.

As the programs from the Series (below) indicate, the 1911 Fall Classic was a rematch of the 1905 World Series, with the Philadelphia A's and the New York Giants meeting at Shibe Park and Brush Stadium, as New York's Polo Grounds was then known. The A's avenged their 1905 defeat, winning four games to two. (Athletics, 11" x 8"; Giants, 11" x 9¼").

World Series scorecards and programs (above) caught on in the early 20th century as both a way to document a game and an effective advertising medium for a variety of merchants, products, and services.

pected has turned hope into despair; and where miracles have turned despondency into jubilation.

The World Series—one of sport's grandiose theaters—has provided all the exhilaration and drama of the most powerful Greek myths. Consider, for example, Game 3 of the 1932 Series, when Babe Ruth pointed to the centerfield bleachers and, on an 0–2 pitch from Charlie Root of the Cubs, hit his legendary "called shot" home run to

the exact spot he had indicated—or so the story goes. That anecdote has as much myth in it as reality, but it suits the legend of the Bambino perfectly. Then there was Game 1 of the 1954 World Series, when the New York Giants' Willie Mays dashed out to right centerfield at the Polo Grounds, the deepest part of the park, to make an astonishing over-the-shoulder catch, his back to the infield, of a tremendous drive by Cleveland's Vic Wertz. Many fans know the play simply as

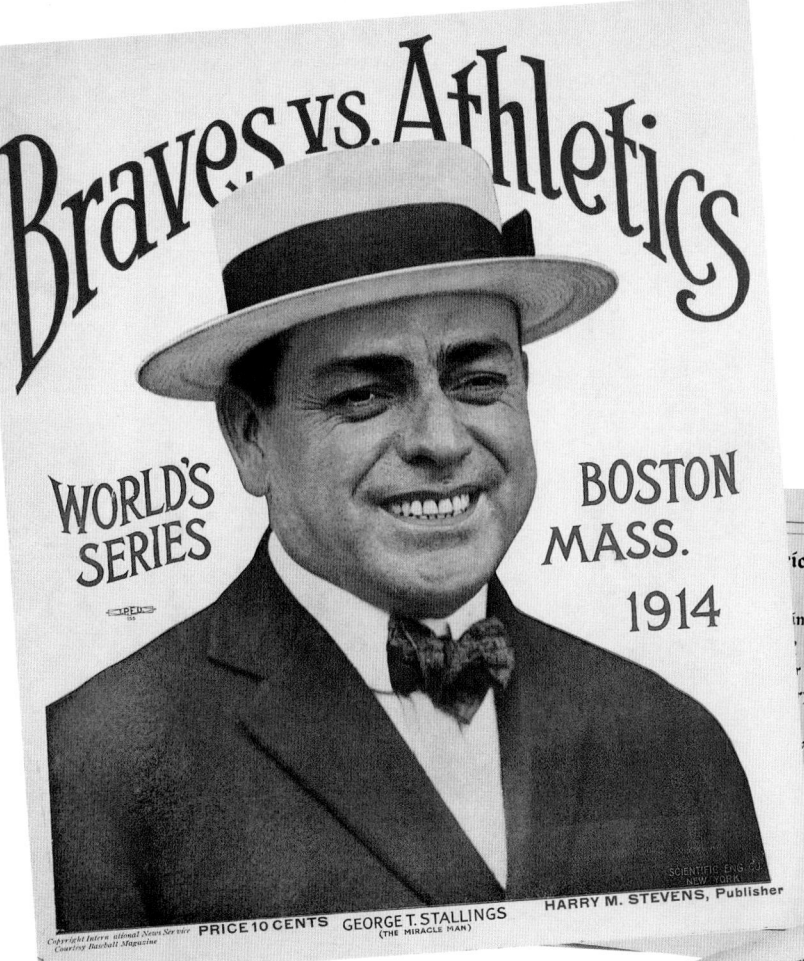

Boston manager George Tweedy Stallings, "the Miracle Man," graced the cover of the Braves' program for the 1914 World Series (above). Stallings, who led "the Miracle Braves" from last place in the middle of that season to a victory in the Fall Classic over the Philadelphia Athletics, relied on some peculiar superstitions to help achieve the miracle. When something good happened for the Braves, Stallings froze his position until his luck changed. He believed that by doing this he could prolong the good luck. One day, he leaned over to pick up a piece of paper when one of his players got a hit. According to writers David Pietrusza, Matthew Silverman, and Michael Gershman, Stallings "held that position through a 10-hit rally and then was carried off from the field." (11" x 9¼")

For the second time in four years, a team that built a new ballpark won a championship the year the park opened. First it was the Pirates with Forbes Field in 1909, then it was the Red Sox with Fenway Park in 1912. The souvenir

program Boston issued for that Series (top right and open-page inset) included short biographies of Red Sox stars like Tris Speaker, Harry Hooper, and Smokey Joe Wood, who went 34–5 as a pitcher during the regular season then won Games 1 and 4 of the Series. (9" x 7")

If Cubs fan Steve Bartman had not reached out and deflected a catchable foul ball in the eighth inning of Game 6 of the 2003 NLCS, and if the Yankees' Aaron Boone had not hit the home run of his life in the 11th inning of Game 7 of the 2003 ALCS, baseball fans might have had the chance to see something that hasn't happened since 1918—a Cubs–Red Sox World Series. The Clisters own two scorecards (above right) from the last time the matchup occurred. Due to paper drives during World War I, the artifacts were made of brittle paper stock and are quite fragile; very few of them made it out of the ballpark without sustaining significant damage. These two are examples of an exceedingly rare breed. (9" x 6")

The Catch. In Game 7 of the 1960 World Series between the unheralded Pirates (who hadn't won a title since 1925) and the mighty Yankees (who were playing in their 10th Series in 12 years), Pittsburgh second baseman Bill Mazeroski stepped to the plate in the bottom of the ninth with the score tied at 9–9. The term "walkoff home run" was not yet in vogue, but that's what the normally light-hitting Mazeroski belted off Yankee reliever Ralph Terry to win the Series for the

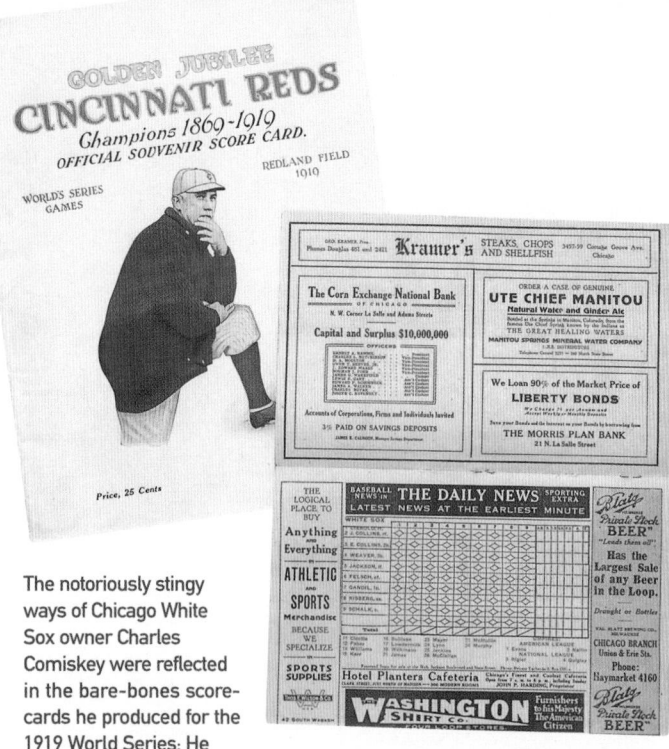

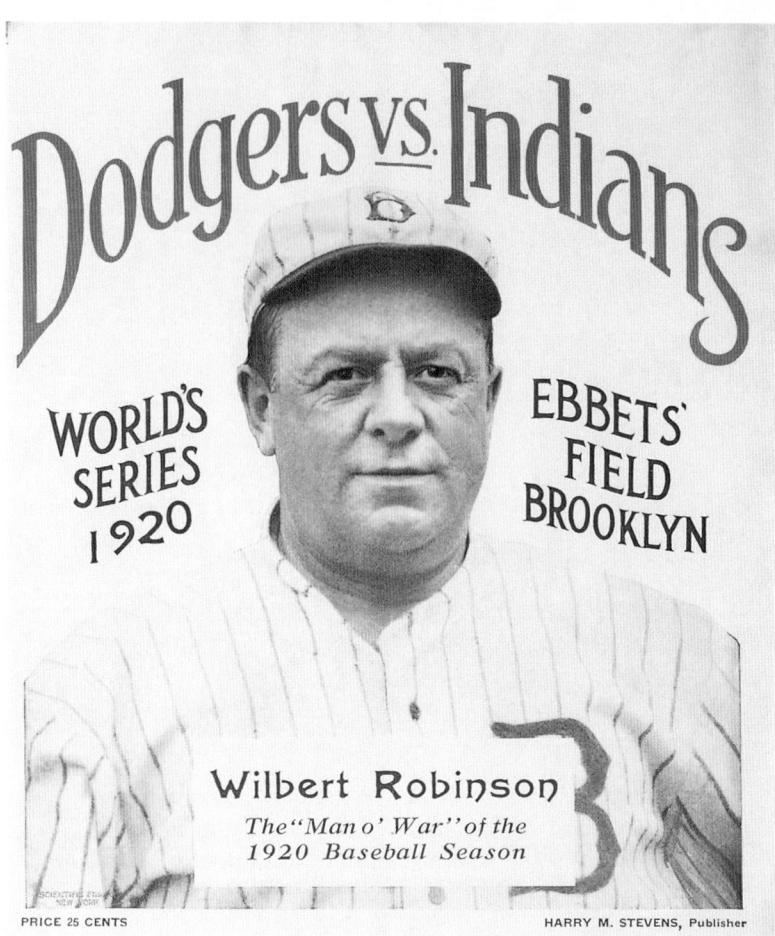

Wilbert Robinson
The "Man o' War" of the
1920 Baseball Season

PRICE 25 CENTS

HARRY M. STEVENS, Publisher

The notoriously stingy ways of Chicago White Sox owner Charles Comiskey were reflected in the bare-bones score-cards he produced for the 1919 World Series: He simply had the names of the White Sox's and Reds' roster typed onto the regular-season scorecards (above, right). They were a far cry from the large, high-quality pro-grams produced by the Cincinnati Reds (top), Chicago's opponent in the Series. Comiskey, who paid the lowest wages in baseball and deducted petty expenses like laun-dry fees from his players' pay-checks, would ultimately pay for his tightfistedness as eight of his play-ers conspired with gambling syn-dicates to throw the 1919 Series and earn what they believed they were worth. Known as the Black Sox Scandal, the episode put major-league baseball on the brink of dis-aster. (Reds, 11¼" x 9¼"; White Sox, 9" x 6")

The jolly, rubicund Wilbert Robinson adorned the cover of the Brooklyn Dodgers' program for the 1920 World Series against Cleveland (top right). During his 18 years as manager of the Dodgers, Robinson was so beloved that the team became known as the "Robins" in his honor. Alas, his charges fell short against Cleveland, losing the nine-game Series 5–2. (11" x 9¼")

Pirates. It was the first time a World Series ended with a home run, a feat that would not be repeated until 1993. An even more famous World Series home run—thanks to the power of television—came in Game 6 of the 1975 Fall Classic, when 35,205 ecstatic Red Sox fans joined Boston catcher Carlton Fisk in waving his bottom-of-the-twelfth home run blast into fair territory at Fenway Park. These are just a few of the many gilt-edged memories from the Fall Classic, which celebrated its centennial in 2003.

Since 1992, Pittsburgh natives James David Clister and his daughter Lauren Alexandra have been creating their own unique celebration of the Fall Classic, assem-bling the world's most impressive collection of World Series scorecards and programs. The breadth of the Clisters' collection and the generally immaculate condition of its artifacts comprise an extraordinary tribute to baseball's most celebrated annual event and speak volumes about the collectors' shared passion.

The items in the Clisters' collection were originally sold to fans at the ballpark of each team playing in a World Series. In some years, teams issued scorecards made of heavy paper stock that was folded in half. The inte-rior of this scorecard featured two rectangu-

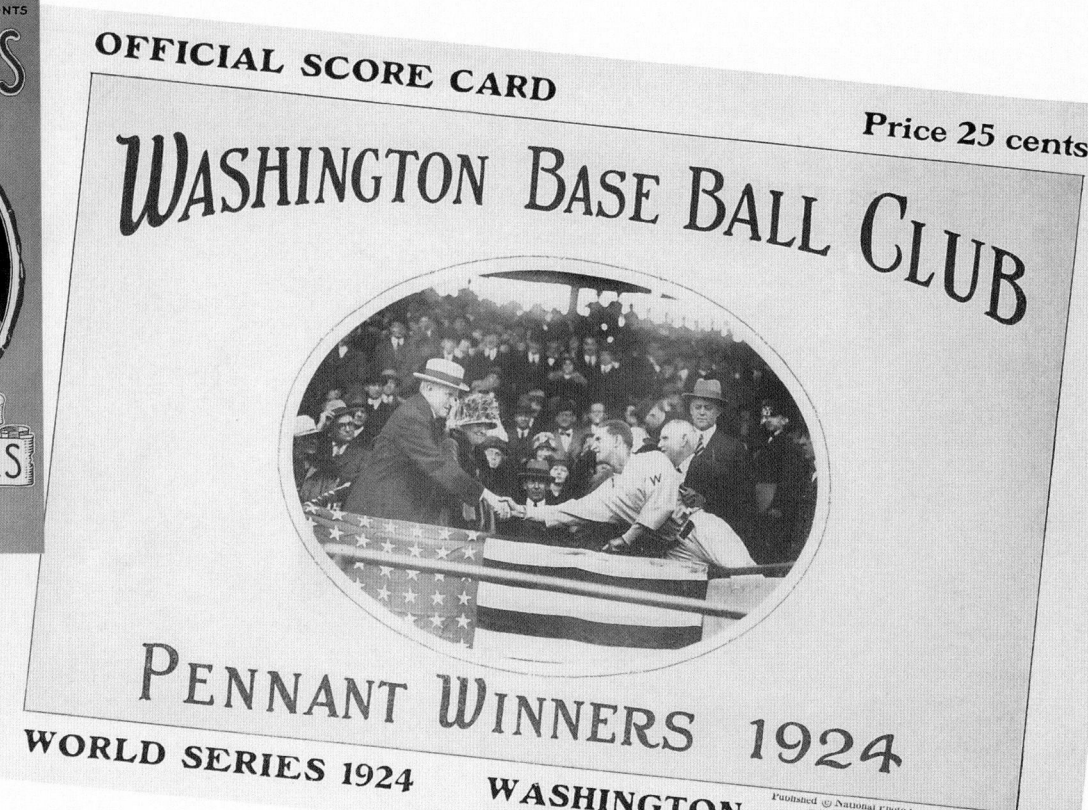

The Clisters' program from the 1923 World Series (above) was issued by the Yankees, who faced their city rivals the Giants in the Fall Classic for the third straight year, finally winning after two straight Series defeats. To minimize production costs, program publisher Harry M. Stevens used one design for both teams, placing a portrait of the manager of the home team on the left side of the cover. (11" x 9¼")

lar grids, each of which was used to record a team's batting results, inning by inning. Henry Chadwick, one of baseball's founding fathers, invented this ingenious scoring system during the late 1850s and 1860s. Chadwick believed it was important to establish statistical means by which one player's performance could be measured fairly against another's. According to baseball historian Jules Tygiel, "Chadwick developed a scoring system to document all plays on offense and defense. . . . He assigned a letter to each possible play for easy recording. Thus, a "K" came to stand for a strikeout. Chadwick constructed and distributed scoring forms to

facilitate this practice. These innovations allowed people to transfer a contest from the field onto paper, creating a historical record of each game."

Mass-produced scorecards for spectators at the ballpark first appeared around 1870 (see the June 14, 1870, scorecard from the match game between the Brooklyn Atlantics and Cincinnati Red Stockings on page 9, "The Corey R. Shanus Collection"). Relatively bland in appearance, they typically consisted of a single sheet with a scoring grid on one side and some advertising on the other. In 1871, former player and entrepreneur Mort Rogers introduced the notion of scorecards as

The cover of the 1924 World Series program (above) features a photo of Washington Senators player-manager Bucky Harris stretching to shake the hand of President Calvin Coolidge. Unlike Woodrow Wilson, though, Coolidge was not a baseball fan; his appearances at games were strictly political in nature. (9" x 6")

A telegram from a supporter once urged President Calvin Coolidge to attend the 1924 Series as it "would be one of the finest political strokes in history." Coolidge did just that, posing for a photograph (below) during Game 7 between the Washington Senators and the New York Giants.

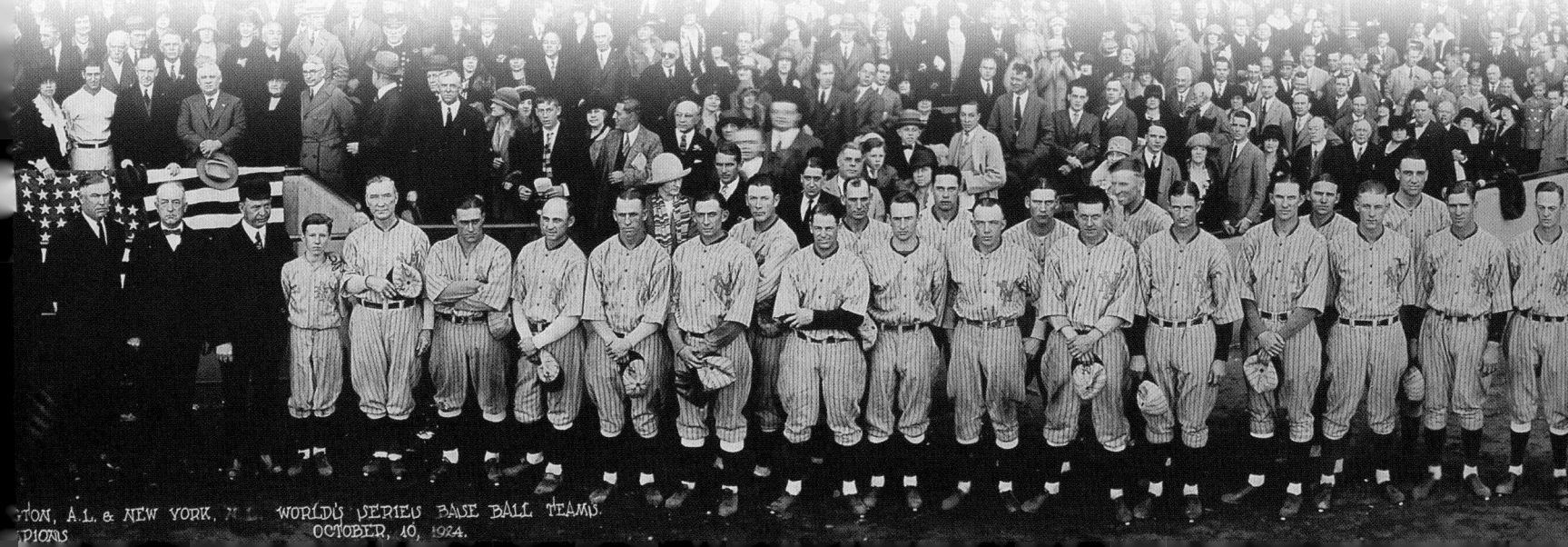

The Pittsburgh Pirates scorecard from 1925 (above) touts the Golden Jubilee Year of the National League, which staged its first season in 1876. The Pirates celebrated the occasion by winning their first World Series since 1909, rallying from from a three-games-to-one deficit to take the Series in seven over Washington. Senators shortstop Roger Peckinpaugh, the 1925 AL MVP, made two pivotal errors in the deciding game. (9" x 7")

The St. Louis Cardinals' score-card from the 1926 World Series (above) heralds the team's matchup with the New York Yankees, who had been to three straight Series from 1921 to '23 (winning one) while St. Louis was making its first appearance in the Fall Classic. The Cards won this one in seven games, but the Yankees bounced back to win the next two Fall Classics en route to establishing themselves as baseball's most dominant franchise, with 26 champi-onships. The Redbirds, however, are no slouches in the title department: they've won nine, tied with the Athletics for second-most all-time. (9" x 6¼")

souvenir items by producing a scorecard with a player's photograph on the front cover. It was not until the 1880s, however, that score-cards started to appear in full color and become a more popular advertising medium.

English immigrant Harry Moseley Stevens, who would eventually build a ballpark-concessions empire, helped trans-form the scorecard into the more attractive format of the many World Series scorecards and programs in the Clisters' collection. The impetus for his innovations came at a game at Recreation Park in Columbus, Ohio, in 1887. Perusing his scorecard, Stevens could not tell which roster was for the home team and which one was for the visitors. Appar-ently, the scorecard simply listed the players' names. Stevens set out to make a more informative and aesthetically appealing scorecard. He would increase the number and quality of ads appearing in scorecards and revive Rogers's idea of using ballplayer images on the covers. According to baseball historian Michael Gershman, Stevens's inno-vations allowed advertisers "to reach con-sumers who might not read newspapers or church journals, exhibit some community spirit by 'supporting our lads,' and benefit from baseball's growing popularity." To help finance the printing of his scorecards, Stevens sold advertising rights to companies. He eventually acquired permission to sell his enhanced scorecards at Recreation Park and other parks in Pittsburgh, Milwaukee, Toledo, and Wheeling, Illinois. By 1894, Stevens was selling scorecards at the Polo Grounds in New York. He became known as "Scorecard Harry."

For the World Series, teams sometimes issued programs instead of scorecards. In addition to the scoring grids, programs included pages for advertisements, as well as player photographs and biographies. Each team playing in a World Series issued

The program for the 1929 World Series between the Athletics and the Cubs (right) featured managers Connie Mack and Joe McCarthy on its cover, but it could have spotlighted one of seven future Hall of Famers who were playing in the Series—some of whom rank with the greatest players of all time. Rogers Hornsby, Hack Wilson, and .321 lifetime hitter Kiki Cuyler all suited up for Chicago, while Jimmie Foxx, Al Simmons, Mickey Cochrane, and Lefty Grove turned out for Philadelphia. Still, this galaxy of stars was outshined by a little-known side-armer, Howard Ehmke, in Game 1. Two months earlier, Ehmke, who was at the tail end of his marginal career, had to convince Mack not to release him. He repaid his manager's faith handsomely, striking out 13 Cubs in the opener to break a 23-year-old Series record, and lead the Athletics to a 3–1 win. They would take the Series in five games. (9" x 6")

The cover of the 1932 Series program issued by

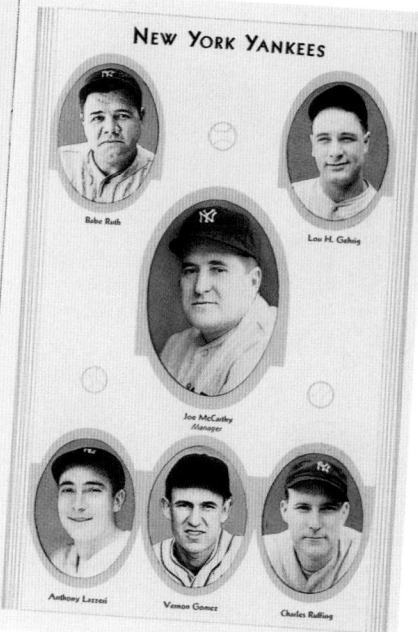

Chicago National League
BALL CLUB
WRIGLEY FIELD
WORLD SERIES
1929
CHICAGO CUBS
vs.
PHILADELPHIA ATHLETICS

SOUVENIR SCORE CARD
PRICE **25¢**

its own version of the score-card or program (see the two publications from the 1911 Series on page 132). Advertisements were an integral part of these keepsakes. They covered a wide range of products and services from banking, taxicabs, and steak houses to ice cream, tobacco, and "Pneumatic Cushion" rubber heels.

Compared with today, the range of ballpark souvenirs in the first half of the 20th century is fairly limited (see Chapter X, "The Robert Edward Lifson Collection"). Scorecards and programs were among the few mementos fans could take home from the ballpark; the World Series scorecards and programs in the Clisters' collection thereby represent bookmarks in the annals of the Fall Classic—or, to use historian John Thorn's phrase, "stones in the river of time." Most of the covers of these treasured mementos feature the names of the contestants, the year in which the Series took place, and striking images of ballparks, managers, players, team mascots, and/or team logos. Programs issued for the 1942 and 1943 Series have patriotic themes to honor the U.S.

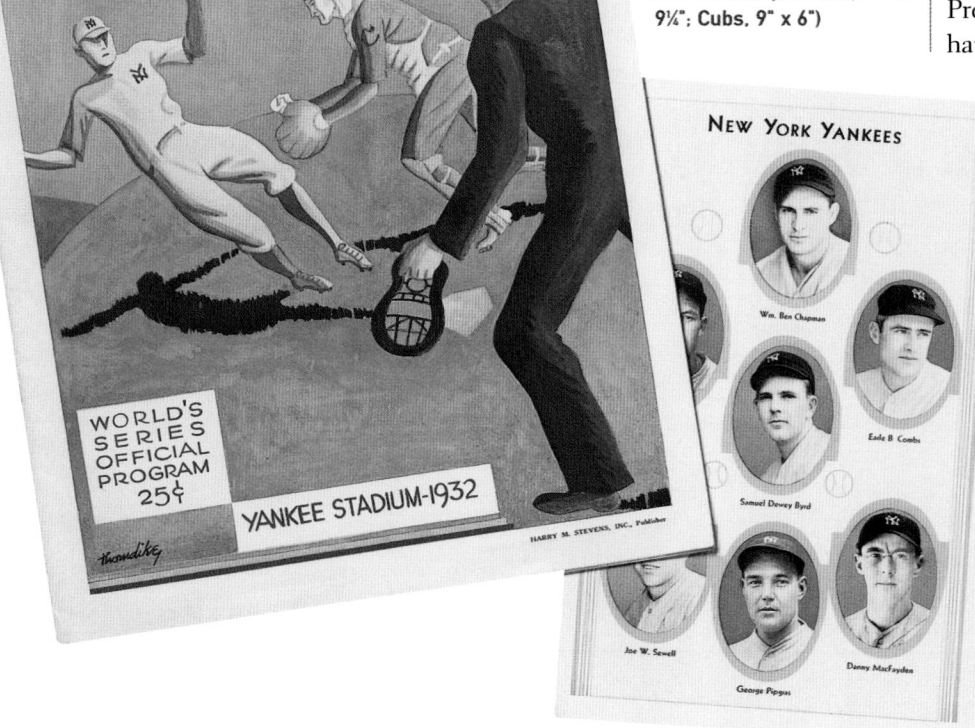

the Yankees (left) features art-deco artwork and is regarded as one of the most beautiful designs from the 1930s. The interior of the Cubs' program for the same Series (bottom) featured player portraits of both teams. (Yankees, 11" x 9¼"; Cubs, 9" x 6")

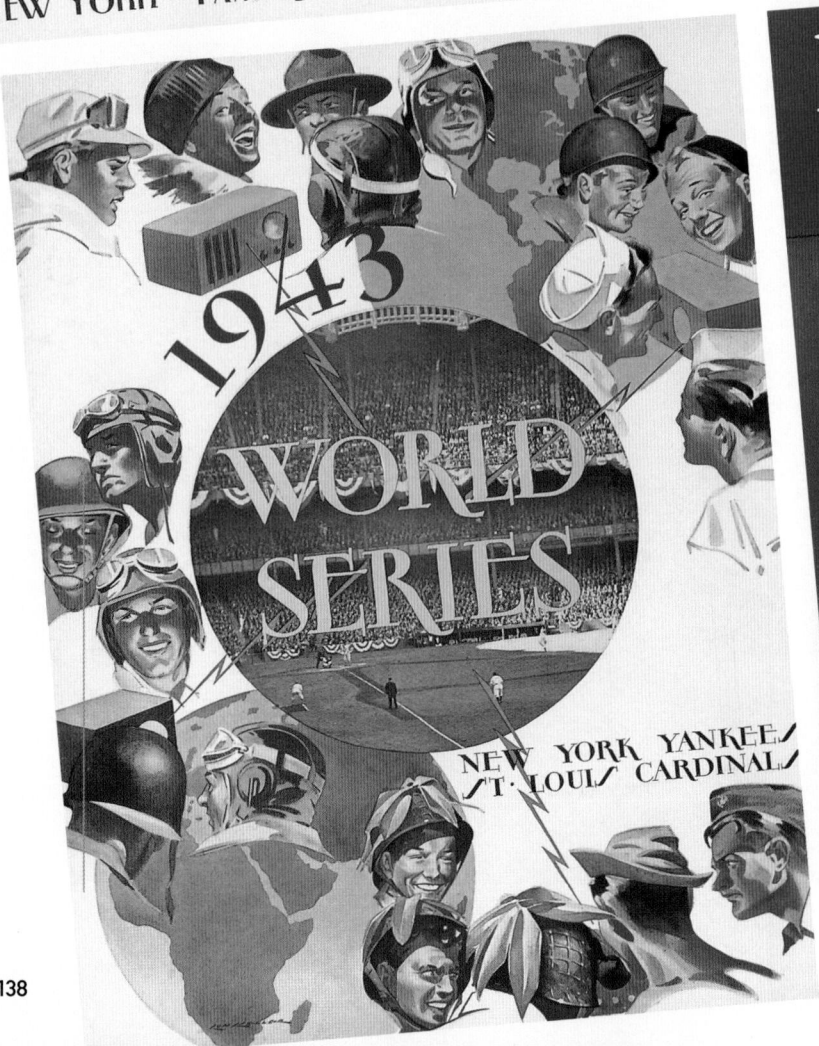

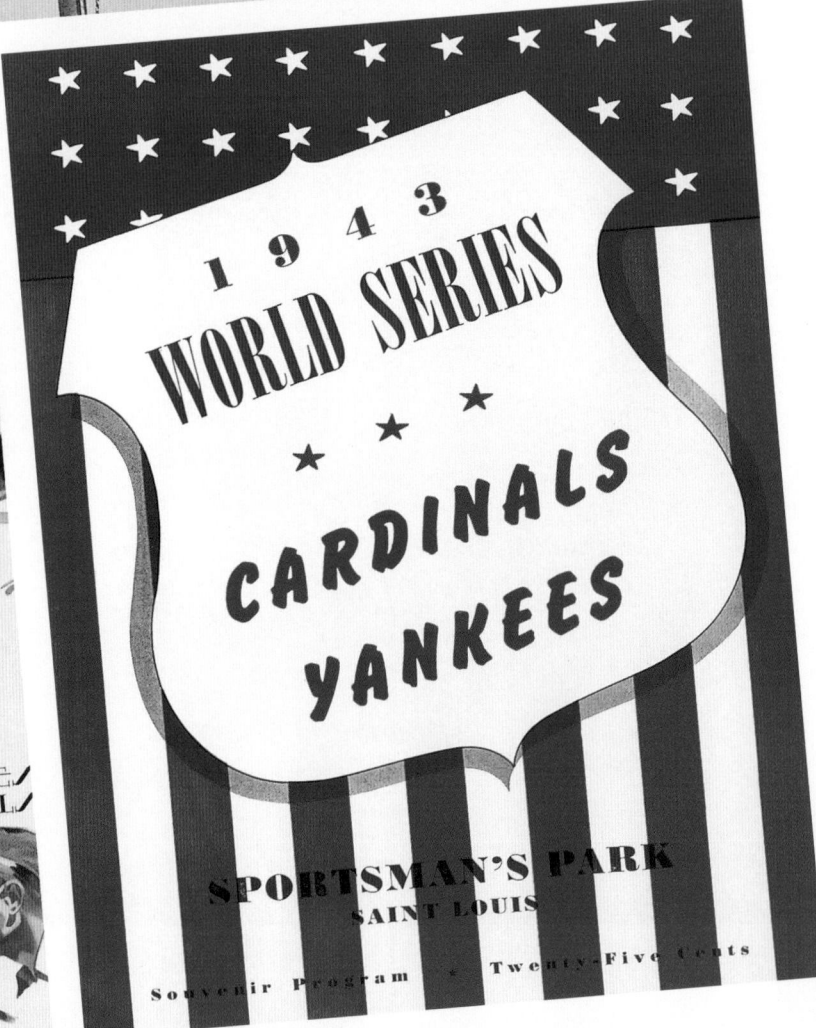

138

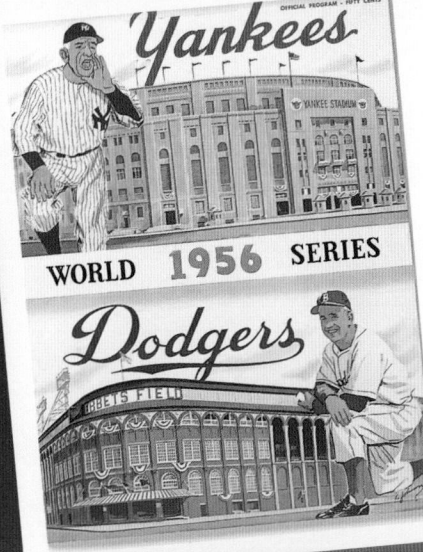

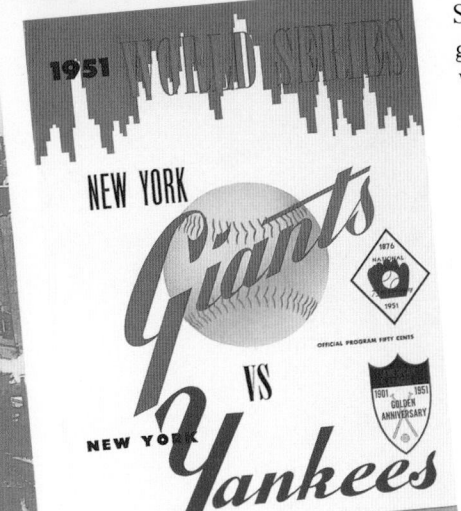

troops serving in World War II. Some of the players featured in the biographies and photographs in the interior pages are legendary; some are long forgotten. But whatever their legacy, they all experienced the rarefied air of October baseball, when champions are crowned.

Perhaps the most intriguing aspect of the Clisters' collection is that some of the scorecards and programs have been neatly dated, marked, and in some cases scored by the lucky fans who first held them. Unlike World Series tickets, each of which identifies the game that the holder is entitled to attend, World Series scorecards and programs are not issued for a particular game in a Series. Generally speaking, Games 1 and 6 of a particular Series are played at the same park. Therefore, the scorecard or program sold at Game 1 would be the same one sold at Game 6, so unless a scorecard or program has been dated, marked, or scored, it is difficult to pin it to a specific Series game.

Fans crowded the box office at Chicago's Wrigley Field (below) before the start of Game 7 of the 1945 World Series between the Cubs and the Detroit Tigers. The hometown fans went home disappointed, though, as the Tigers scored five runs in the first inning and held on for a 9–3 victory.

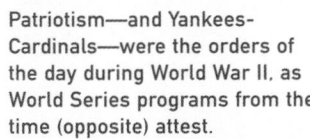

Patriotism—and Yankees-Cardinals—were the orders of the day during World War II, as World Series programs from the time (opposite) attest.

The Clisters' programs from the 1947, '51, '55, and '56 World Series (above) reflect the mid-century dominance of New York baseball teams. From 1947 to '58, a New York franchise, and often two of them, played in the Fall Classic every year but one (1948). (11½" x 9¼", all)

WORLD SERIES 1963
YANKEE STADIUM · HOME OF CHAMPIONS · OFFICIAL PROGRAM 50 CENTS

NEW YORK YANKEES LOS ANGELES DODGERS

The Clisters are fortunate enough to own a number of marked and/or scored scorecards and programs from some of the most exciting World Series games in history—documented links to the Fall Classic's great home runs, sparkling defensive plays, and extraordinary pitching performances. One such artifact comes from Game 2 of the 1903 Series, in which the Boston Pilgrims' Bill Dineen shut out the Pittsburgh Pirates 3–0. We can attribute the scorecard to that game because it was sold at Boston's Huntington Avenue Grounds, and its original owner's notations indicate that Dineen was pitching against Pittsburgh's Sam Leever. Game 2 was the only game in the 1903 Series in which Dineen pitched against Leever at Huntington Avenue Grounds. The Clisters also own completed scorecards from Game 3 of the 1905 Series, when Christy Mathewson pitched one of his three consecutive shutouts; Game 2 of the 1911 Series, when Frank "Home Run" Baker hit a homer off Richard "Rube" Marquard in the sixth inning; and Game 6 of the 1947 Series, when Al Gionfriddo made a remarkable catch to rob Joe DiMaggio of an extra base hit in the sixth inning. The extraordinary collection also includes a scorecard that can be definitively tied to Game 4 of the 1957 Series, when Elston Howard hit a three-run homer in the ninth inning to send the game into extra innings; and one from Game 1 of the 1967 Series, when Lou Brock led the Cardinals offense with a record-tying four hits, two stolen bases, and both of his team's runs in a 2–1 win.

Some fans believe that with the advent of artificial turf, Diamond Vision, loud between-innings music and commercials, the game of baseball has changed substantially from the "good old days." But as W. P. Kinsella has written, "[Baseball] is the same game that Moonlight Graham played in 1905. It is a living part of history, like calico dresses, stone crockery, and threshing crews eating at outdoor tables. It continually reminds us of what it once was, like an Indian-head penny in a handful of new coins." Kinsella's words capture the spirit of the Clisters' outstanding collection. Like "stones in the river of time," these World Series artifacts remind us that not even the distractions of Diamond Vision and shrill pop music can sour the sweet bliss of October baseball.

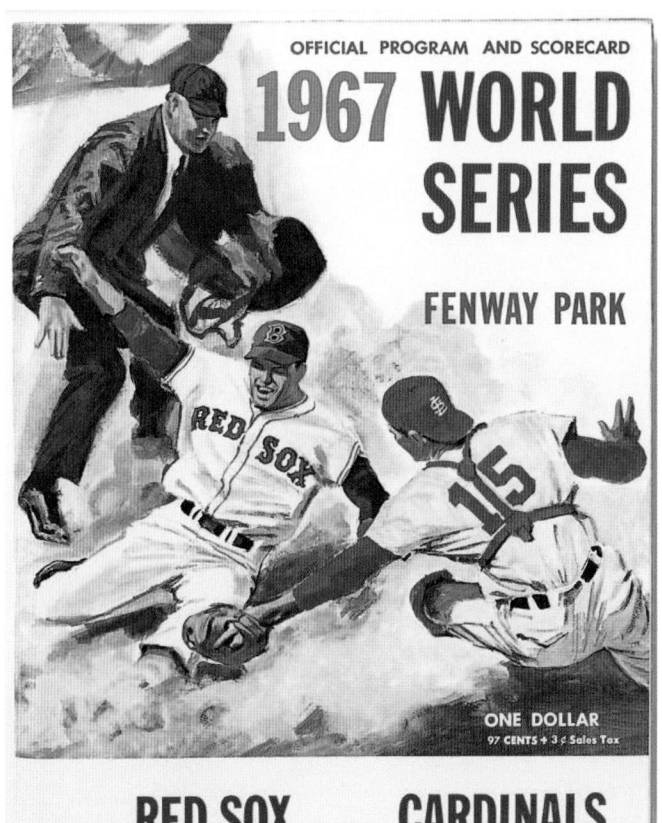

With the proclamation YAZ FOR GOVERNOR scrawled by the original owner on the completed scoresheet, the Clisters' copy of the 1967 World Series program (above) is a unique artifact. The slogan, which was printed on a pin-back button and sold at Fenway Park during the Series, celebrated Boston leftfielder Carl Yastrzemski, the '67 Triple Crown winner who belted two home runs to spark a 5–0 Sox victory in Game 2 of the Series. Alas, Yaz and the Sox fell in seven games. (11½" x 9¼")

The "Miracle Braves" of 1914 found a descendant in the 1969 New York Mets, who staged a furious late-season rally to overtake the Cubs and win the NL East. By October, the Mets were world champions—and light-years removed from their inept debut season in 1962, as the Clisters' 1969 World Series program (top right) illustrates. After the Series, outfielder Ron Swoboda said, "Nothing else will ever be as good as this. The only thing left for us to do is to go to the moon." That miracle, however, had been achieved three months earlier. (11½" x 9¼")

Harry M. Stevens would have been proud to know that programs (right) remain an intergral part of baseball today, more than 120 years after he transformed them.

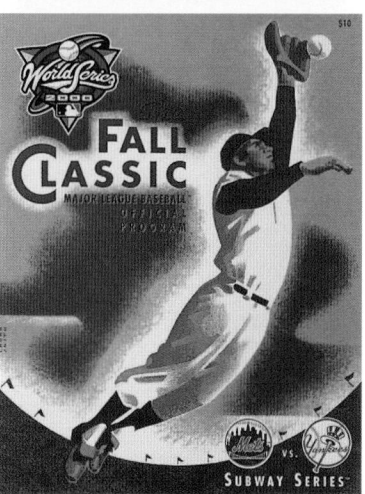

A POTPOURRI OF PIN-BACKS

> "Pin-back buttons represent an American diary. From their 1896 advent to the present day, they document, commemorate and promote people, places, products, events, and ideas. For everyone with an interest in the past century of American life, pinbacks are miniature graphic time capsules—historical artifacts that reflect our culture in all its forms."
>
> —*TED HAKE*
> *Author and renowned expert*
> *on pin-back buttons*

Some of the pin-back buttons from Robert Lifson's collection pictured on the opposite page may seem strangely familiar. Perhaps one of them adorned your elementary school knapsack, suspenders, or lapel. Or maybe you pinned one to your hat, scarf, or coat while sitting in a ballpark on a cool spring day waiting for a game to begin. If so, you were part of a time-honored custom among baseball fans during the first half of the 20th century. At the heart and soul of any devout baseball fan lies a fierce loyalty to a particular team. Sportswriter Mike Barnicle summed up this emotional attachment when he said, "Baseball isn't a life-and-death matter, but the Red Sox are." The opportunity to share and express this allegiance with others is the essence of being a sports fan. In their day, pin-back baseball buttons were an integral part of this experience.

Today's baseball fan has access to a plethora of souvenir merchandise sold at major-league ballparks and shopping centers across the country. Team names and logos, and the names and uniform numbers of ballplayers, adorn a host of items, including T-shirts, sweatshirts, jackets, caps, and literally dozens of other objects and apparel. Turner Field in Atlanta sells foam tomahawks to Braves fans, while Safeco Field in Seattle sells Mariners Palm Pilot cases and Ichiro Suzuki teddy bears. But during the first half of the 20th century, fans could choose from only a handful of souvenir items. Furthermore, the dress code customary for attending ball games during the period precluded the sale of team-sponsored apparel: Most of the male fans wore suits, and women wore dresses or blouses and skirts. These circumstances conspired to make the pin-back button the ideal way to show your allegiance at the ballpark.

Designed to be worn on an article of

Pin-backs (opposite) are a many-splendored category of baseball memorabilia, as they came in an almost infinite variety of styles and subjects, from the straight-forward (SANDY KOUFAX) to the cryptic (the Babe Ruth ASK ME pin-back) to the competitive (BEAT! DEM BUMS New York Yankees pin-back) and beyond. The Ruth ASK ME pin-back was produced by Texaco, to be displayed on the uniforms of its gas station attendants during the 1930s. What question the slogan was to have prompted, however, seems to have been lost in the sands of time.

Before the pin-back button was patented in 1896, baseball fans and players wore celluloid pendants with ribbons attached (right, front and back of pendant). The dignified style of the pendant contradicted the brutal style of the team it commemorated, the 1894 National League champion Baltimore Orioles, who stood out as particularly rough in an era characterized by rugged play. "They were mean, vicious, ready at any time to maim a rival player or an umpire if it helped their cause," recalled a sportswriter of the time. The Orioles' behavior became so atrocious that National League owners felt compelled to issue a ruling called "A Measure for the Suppression of Obscene, Indecent and Vulgar Language upon the Ball Field." (1¾" diameter)

BASE BALL SCHEDULE
NATIONAL LEAGUE

1904
PITTSBURG CLUB
AT HOME

WITH	APR.	MAY	JUNE	JULY	AUG.	SEP.	OCT.
PHILADELPHIA		6 7 9 10		12 13 14 15	24 25 26		
BROOKLYN		11 12 13 14		21 22 23 25	27 29	2	
NEW YORK		16 17 18 19		16 18 19 20	20 22 23		
BOSTON		20 21 23 24		8 9 11 11	30 31	1	
CINCINNATI	21 22 23	26 27 28		1 2		3 3 5	
ST. LOUIS		25 26 27	30 30	17 18	27 28 29 30		
CHICAGO		28 29 30		25	4 4 5	9 10	7 8

COMPLIMENTS OF THE
Pittsburg Leader.

THE BEST BASE BALL
NEWSPAPER

F. F. PULVER CO. ROCHESTER N. Y.

The Hyatt brothers new "miracle substance," celluloid, was used in all sorts of products, including a complimentary 1904 home schedule for the Pittsburgh Pirates (above and left, front and back) issued by the *Pittsburgh Leader* newspaper, and featuring the Pirates' star shortstop, Honus Wagner, on the front.

In 1904, after leading the National League in batting for the third time, Honus Wagner probably could have sold anything, including insurance, as he proved by appearing on a pin-back (right) for the Commercial Oldest Accident Company. (1" diameter)

In 1897, the American Pepsin Gum Co., makers of Cameo Pepsin Gum, commissioned Whitehead & Hoag to produce a set of pin-backs as a premium for its customers. It was the first major baseball pin-back set, and it featured sepia-toned photographic images of the biggest stars from the 1890s (opposite), including Louis "Chief" Sockalexis (top row, second from right) for whom the Cleveland Indians team was named. (1¼" diameter)

clothing but small enough not to impinge on fashion, pin-backs became one of the first baseball souvenirs that allowed fans to express their feelings about not only a team but also a specific ballplayer or event. For example, by wearing the I'M ROOTING FOR JACKIE ROBINSON pin-back, which commemorated Robinson's major-league debut in 1947, a fan could express support, pride, and hope for the Brooklyn infielder's historic breaking of the game's color barrier. Fans could show their allegiances, and celebrate their team's past glories, with pin-backs reading RED SOX AL 1915 CHAMPIONS or NATIONAL LEAGUE CHAMPION PHILLIES. There was no doubt what team a fan supported if he or she wore a pin-back emblazoned BEAT! DEM BUMS or GO TO BAT FOR THE DODGERS. (Dem Bums was a Brooklyn Dodgers' nickname.) Other pins touted the MICKEY MANTLE FAN CLUB,

ROBERTO CLEMENTE ELEMENTARY SCHOOL, NELSON FOX, WHITEY FORD, or SANDY KOUFAX. The Lou Gehrig NEVER FORGOTTEN button conveyed sadness for the untimely death of the Iron Horse, as well as reverence for his legacy.

Many fans today treasure their Red Sox or Yankees baseball caps, their Cardinals or Tigers crew-neck sweatshirts, or their replica jerseys bearing the name and number of their favorite player. Modern fans wear these articles of clothing with great pride. In the old days, fans were just as proud of their idols and teams, but they expressed their feelings through pin-backs, which, while subtle, spoke directly and succinctly to the point.

That so many pin-backs have survived is a tribute to their significance as keepsakes, says Lifson, who has collected pin-back buttons for 35 years. He runs Robert Edward

Baseball-related pin-backs (right) came from dozens of sources during the artifact's heyday, including newspapers, sporting goods stores, and book stores.

MART McHALE
1ST TENOR

TOM (BUCK) O'BRIEN
2ND TENOR

Red Sox Quartette

MEMBERS OF

BOSTON AMERICAN LEAGUE

BASEBALL TEAM

HUGH BRADLEY
BARITONE

RED SOX
QUARTETTE

BILL LYONS
BASSO

AUDITORIUM
DEC. 25

A pin-back and a business card (above) touted the Red Sox Quartette, a singing group composed of Boston ballplayers that toured parts of New England on the vaudeville circuit, starting in 1910. Formed by Red Sox pitcher Marty McHale, whom *Variety* magazine dubbed "the Caruso of Baseball," the group consisted of Red Sox pitcher Tom "Buck" O'Brien, outfielder Hugh Bradley, and Bill Lyons, who replaced second baseman Larry Gardner at basso in 1911. The rare pin-back advertised the group's

Christmas Day show in 1911. The Quartette quietly disbanded in 1913, when McHale went to the Yankees. (3/4" diameter)

The Boston Royal Rooters, rabid fans of the Boston Pilgrims, had their own pin-back button (far left, middle). The Rooters are said to have contributed greatly to the 1903 World Series triumph for the Boston Pilgrims over the Pittsburgh Pirates. With the Pilgrims down three games to one, the Rooters traveled to Pittsburgh for Game 5 and cheered as loudly as they could. But what really unnerved the Pirates was the way the Rooters altered the words to a popular song called "*Tessie*". Instead of singing "Tessie, you make me feel so badly," they bellowed, "Honus, why do you hit so badly?" When asked, more than 60 years later, about the outcome of that Series, Pirate third baseman Tommy Leach recalled, "that damn '*Tessie*' song . . . sort of got on your nerves after a while. And before we knew what happened, we'd lost the World Series." (1¾" diameter)

A unique pin-back set (bottom) issued in 1910 by Schmelzer's Sporting Goods of Kansas City, was the first to combine photographs of famous ballplayers with color lithographic artwork. Distributed only regionally, this is one of the rarest of all early-20th-century pin-back sets. (1¼" diameter)

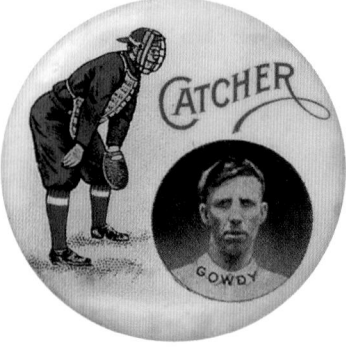

A pin-back from the *Chicago Daily News* (above) advertised the fact that excerpts from *Won in the Ninth*—the first book in a series of ghostwritten baseball tomes with Christy Mathewson's name attached to them—would be appearing in the newspaper. *Won in the Ninth* was published in 1910 and included in its cast of fictional characters an odd-looking shortstop named Hans Hagner and a double-play specialist called Johnny Everson. (1¾" diameter)

Lifson owns a pin-back (top right) from 1905 that advertised the weekly *Sporting Life*, founded in 1883 by Francis C. Richter and "Devoted to Base Ball, Trap Shooting, and General Sports." A former writer for Philadelphia's *Public Ledger*, Richter was the first newspaper scribe to include feature articles on baseball, in addition to box scores and game reports. The coverage proved so popular it inspired Richter to launch *Sporting Life*, which became one of the most successful baseball publications of its era. (1" diameter)

Walter Johnson appeared on the pin-back commemorating the Washington Senators' 1924 NL pennant (above, inset). Until that year, Johnson was considered the greatest pitcher never to have won a World Series, but the Senators went on to win the '24 Series 4–3 over the New York Giants. Giants pitcher Jack

Bentley said afterward, "The good Lord just couldn't bear to see a fine fellow like Walter Johnson lose again." (1" diameter)

A tiny pin-back from late 1941 (far right) heralded Honus Wagner for deputy sheriff of Allegheny County, an office to which he was elected on January 15, 1942. He served without giving up his position as a coach with the Pittsburgh Pirates. (¾" diameter)

Auctions, a prominent New Jersey–based sports and Americana memorabilia auction firm. Fans and collectors have preserved buttons, Lifson explains, because of their sentimental value as an important medium of human expression and because of their aesthetic appeal. Amazingly bright colors and remarkably intricate detail come together within a tiny area of space to give each button its distinctive charm. Celluloid, the "miracle substance," made such design possible. Without celluloid, we would not have these striking keepsakes today. The history of celluloid and its use in pin-back buttons provides insight into the enduring appeal of pin-back buttons.

In 1863, a prolific American inventor

named John Wesley Hyatt began experimenting with cellulose nitrate to find a way to produce billiard balls from materials other than ivory. His work led to the creation of a short-lived collodion-coated billiard ball that sometimes broke apart—some said explosively—during play.

Hyatt and his brother Isaiah quickly refined the formula, and, in 1870, they obtained a patent for celluloid, a tough, thermoplastic compound that became America's first commercially profitable synthetic material. Celluloid was well suited to pin-back buttons as well as billiard balls and a host of other products because of its pliability, its low cost, and its ability to accommodate a wide range of printing ink

When the Philadelphia Athletics won their first World Series in 1910, it was a source of great pride to the City of Brotherly Love and its baseball fans. Apparently, the Leeds Base Ball Club of Philadelphia felt that its stature was somehow enhanced by the success of its major-league cousin, producing an elaborate pin (above middle) that used celluloid in three separate sections (ATHLETICS, 1910, and the image of Connie Mack), and—on a cursory glance, at least—gave the impression that it was the *Leeds* club, and not the A's, that had won the world title.

Artists created a variety of ingenious designs to commemorate the World Series champions in pin-backs (above). Some designs incorporated American flags made of cloth and attached to the pin. A celluloid pocket mirror (above, far left), celebrated the hero of the 1911 World Series, Frank Baker, who became the first player to hit home runs in two consecutive Series games. (Leeds pin. 8½" x 2¼"; pins with flags and pocket mirrors. 2" diameter; small pin with flag. ¾" diameter)

Some of the hobby's most striking trinkets are associated with Connie Mack's Philadelphia Athletics teams between 1905 and 1914. A 6½" x 4", oval stand-up pin featuring the 1905 American League champions (right) was designed to stand on a desk, and is among the largest baseball-related pins known to exist.

colors. Political campaigns immediately caught on to celluloid's usefulness. In the 1888 presidential race, for example, all three candidates (Benjamin Harrison, Grover Cleveland, and Clinton B. Fisk) had their images on widely distributed celluloid lapel studs. Duly inspired, makers of American consumer goods began producing a number of advertising-related celluloid objects, including, eventually, the pin-back button.

Whitehead & Hoag Company (W&H) of Newark, New Jersey, the country's largest manufacturer of advertising novelties at the time, patented the pin-back button in 1896. Manufacturers and retailers could print almost any image on its surface—photographs, slogans, emblems, or any combination of these. The pin-back button was more durable and less expensive to produce than other advertising media, such as trade cards, prints, and cardboard posters. The J. E. Lynch Company of Chicago later introduced the lithographed button (tin with color printed on it) as a less expensive alternative to celluloid for the World War I Liberty Loan and War Savings campaigns. Yet celluloid still prevailed beyond the early 1920s, because colors on lithographed buttons did not blend well and therefore offered only a limited range.

From the late 1890s to the early 1920s, many baseball pin-backs were distributed as premiums with tobacco, chewing gum, and various food products. The relatively tiny surface area of most buttons—typically less than one inch and no greater than two inches in diameter—challenged artists to produce eye-catching images, slogans, and designs. To accomplish this, artists sometimes applied spectacular photographic images to the button's surface area (see the EBBETS FIELD, BOSTON ROOTERS, and HEADIN' HOME BABE RUTH pin-backs, as well as examples of buttons issued by Sweet Caporal and Cameo pepsin gum). Buttons that did not depict famous ballplayers, teams, or events demanded even greater creativity to make their images catch the eye. In these cases, artists often turned to color lithography, as featured on pin-backs for the *Chicago Daily News*, *Pittsburgh Sunday Dispatch*, and *Atlantic City Press Union*. Buttons depicting prominent teams of the era employed slightly more elegant and unique designs. Two examples are the 1909 Golden's Café pin-back (see page 150, top left), which features oval composite photographs of members of the World Series champion Pittsburgh Pirates, and the 1911 Philadelphia Athletics pin, which pres-

The Chicago Cubs issued pinbacks (above) celebrating their teams from 1907 to 1910, which went to three World Series and won two. Fans of the era often affixed pin-backs to their derby hats as well as their lapels. Celluloid was also a component in matchstick holders (above left). (Composite button, 2½" in diameter; Cubs Champion Base Ball Club of the World button and 1910 button, 1½" diameter)

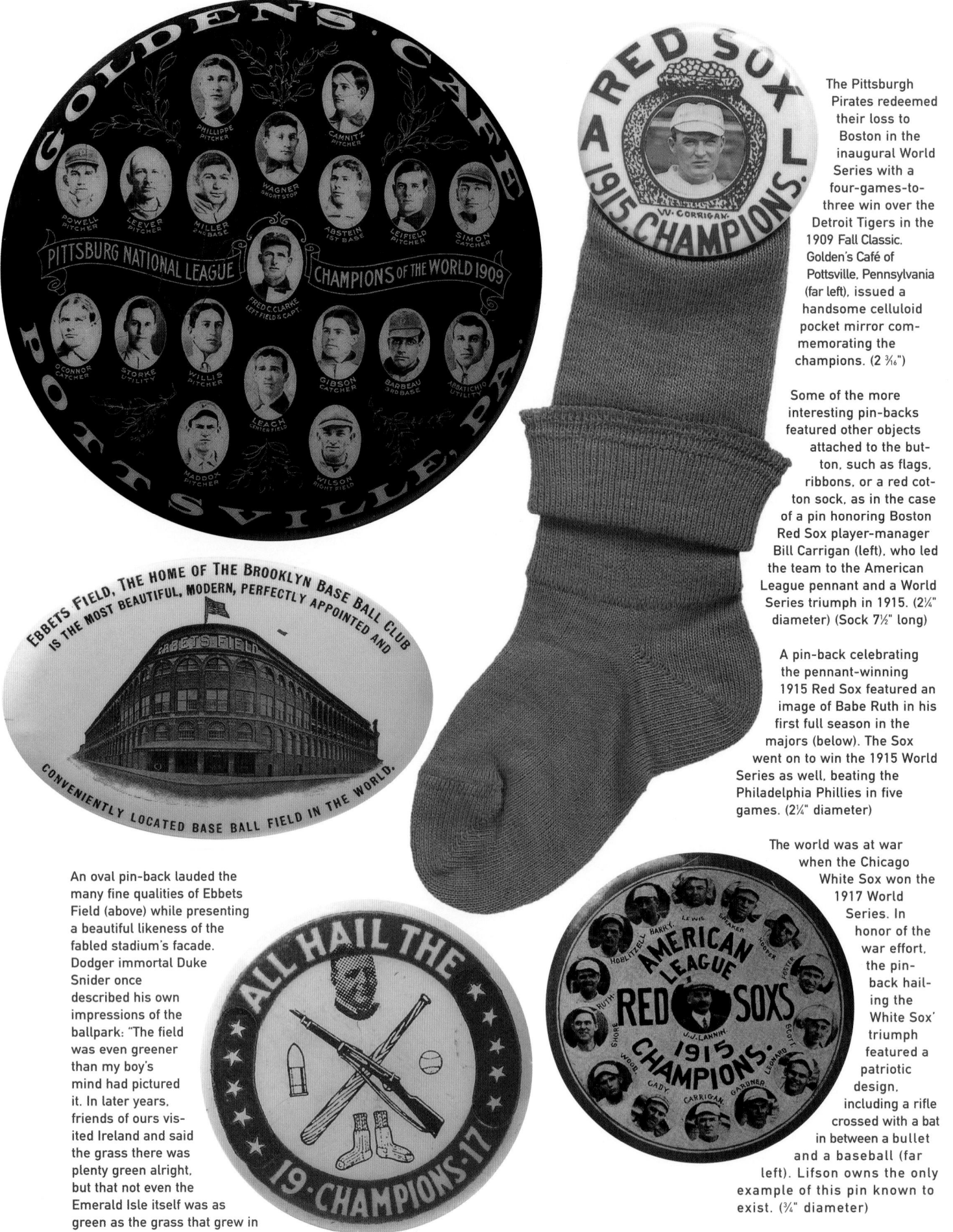

The Pittsburgh Pirates redeemed their loss to Boston in the inaugural World Series with a four-games-to-three win over the Detroit Tigers in the 1909 Fall Classic. Golden's Café of Pottsville, Pennsylvania (far left), issued a handsome celluloid pocket mirror commemorating the champions. (2 ³⁄₁₆")

Some of the more interesting pin-backs featured other objects attached to the button, such as flags, ribbons, or a red cotton sock, as in the case of a pin honoring Boston Red Sox player-manager Bill Carrigan (left), who led the team to the American League pennant and a World Series triumph in 1915. (2¼" diameter) (Sock 7½" long)

A pin-back celebrating the pennant-winning 1915 Red Sox featured an image of Babe Ruth in his first full season in the majors (below). The Sox went on to win the 1915 World Series as well, beating the Philadelphia Phillies in five games. (2¼" diameter)

An oval pin-back lauded the many fine qualities of Ebbets Field (above) while presenting a beautiful likeness of the fabled stadium's facade. Dodger immortal Duke Snider once described his own impressions of the ballpark: "The field was even greener than my boy's mind had pictured it. In later years, friends of ours visited Ireland and said the grass there was plenty green alright, but that not even the Emerald Isle itself was as green as the grass that grew in Ebbets Field." (2¾" x 1½")

The world was at war when the Chicago White Sox won the 1917 World Series. In honor of the war effort, the pin-back hailing the White Sox' triumph featured a patriotic design, including a rifle crossed with a bat in between a bullet and a baseball (far left). Lifson owns the only example of this pin known to exist. (¾" diameter)

The New York Yankees sold a mournful pin-back in remembrance of Lou Gehrig (above) after the Hall of Fame first baseman died of amyotrophic lateral sclerosis on June 2, 1941, at the tender age of 38. (1¼ diameter)

On July 4, 1939, a terminally ill Lou Gehrig addressed the baseball world for the last time. His words reverberating off the Yankee Stadium facade, he began a speech that instantly passed into legend. "Fans, for the past two weeks you have been reading about a bad break I got. Yet today I consider myself the luckiest man on the face of the earth. . . ."

ents portraits of the team members superimposed on an elephant—the team's mascot.

According to Lifson, collecting buttons, unlike collecting many other kinds of baseball artifacts, remains as rewarding today as it was four decades ago. For now, at least, buttons have escaped the high-stakes frenzy that overtook baseball collecting in the 1990s. In September 1999, Sotheby's generated more than $27 million in revenue from the sale of the famous Barry Halper collection of baseball memorabilia. In July 2000, the legendary T206 baseball card of Honus Wagner sold in public auction for $1.265 million, and in 2002, a handful of major sports memorabilia auction companies generated, in aggregate, more than $40 million of revenue from baseball memorabilia alone. Whether through private sale or auction, most types of vintage baseball artifacts related to Hall of Fame ballplayers continue to command impressive prices. But most of the significant items have already been discovered

and are buried in advanced collections, not soon to surface for public sale. Any seasoned baseball collector will admit that nowadays the traditional sources (an attic, basement, sports memorabilia show, garage sale, or flea market) of important memorabilia pieces are all but exhausted.

Baseball pin-back buttons, on the other hand, were mass-produced, were inexpensive, and could be purchased at a number of venues, including ballparks, newsstands, and a variety of shops. Often, pin-backs were distributed to customers for free, as promotional items or giveaways. Thanks to sheer production volume, many pin-backs remain in circulation. In addition, button collecting is highly unstructured, compared to other kinds of baseball memorabilia collecting. Whereas baseball cards and game-used bats, for example, provide collectors with opportunities to build sets and/or themes oriented toward eras, teams, Hall of Fame players, or specific benchmarks (e.g., a bat from every player who has hit at least 500 career home runs), many pin-back buttons are unique, stand-alone items that are

HEADIN' HOME
"BABE" RUTH

A rare button from 1920 promoted Babe Ruth's silver-screen debut, a 56-minute silent feature children's film called *Headin' Home*. The movie paints The Babe as a lazy good-for-nothing washout until he goes to a ball game and clouts a mammoth homer. He also saves a banker's daughter from a swindler, reaches the big time, then saves the banker's son from a vamp, before finally "headin' home" to stardom. (1" diameter)

I'M FOR MARIS
60 IN '61

I'M FOR MANTLE
60 IN '61

HONORARY
ROGER MARIS
Gold Mine. BOOSTER

ROGER MARIS
61 IN '61
HOMERS

61 IN '61 OR BUST
MANTLE
MARIS

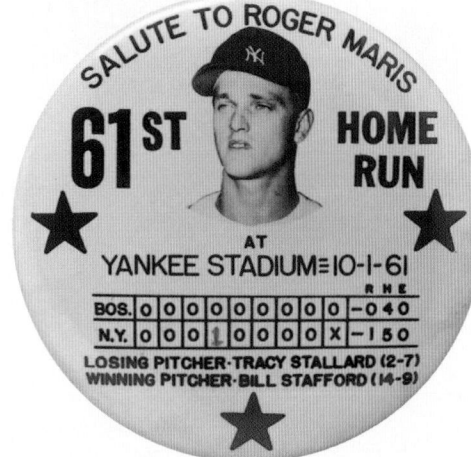

SALUTE TO ROGER MARIS
61ST HOME RUN
AT YANKEE STADIUM≡10-1-61
	R	H	E
BOS. 0 0 0 0 0 0 0 0 0	0	4	0
N.Y. 0 0 0 1 0 0 0 0 X	1	5	0
LOSING PITCHER·TRACY STALLARD (2-7)
WINNING PITCHER·BILL STAFFORD (14-9)

A series of pins (above) saluted Roger Maris and Mickey Mantle for their pursuit of Babe Ruth's single-season home-run record in 1961. Thirty-seven years before Sammy Sosa and Mark McGwire captured the nation's imagination with their home-run derby, the "M&M" boys staged one of their own. But, sadly, the attention focused on Maris was not all positive, and it took its toll. Some fans and reporters deemed him unworthy of dethroning the legendary Ruth, and openly rooted for Mantle, an established star, to break the record—if it had to be broken at all. "Maybe I'm not a great man, but I damn well want to break the record," Maris said. He did just that on the last day of the season, sending home run No. 61 into Yankee Stadium's right-field seats. (Large pins, 2½" diameter; small pins, 1" diameter)

not affiliated with any particular set or broader themes. For this reason, and because there is little meaningful literature available on buttons, there are relatively few advanced collections of pin-backs. As a result, the public supply of pin-backs remains high enough to engender what most passionate collectors like Lifson live for—the thrill of the hunt. Nothing jolts collectors like the thrill of finding previously undiscovered rarities in attics, basements, or shoeboxes in old houses, at yard sales, antique bazaars, flea markets, or sports memorabilia shows. "Collecting buttons is a boundless treasure hunt," Lifson says. "The hunt literally never ends, as it would be virtually impossible to collect them all. . . . Just when one thinks he has seen every button, another incredible design turns up."

In a sense, unlike most of the other collections in this book, Lifson's is more about the people who collected pin-backs than it is about the people and events depicted on the pin-backs. The collection evokes the generations of ordinary men, women, and children who sat in the bleachers and bestowed all manner of cheers, boos, affection, and ridicule upon baseball teams from Maine to California. These are the fans who spilled hot-dog mustard on their shirt sleeves as they stood up for the seventh-inning stretch, the ones who closed their eyes and prayed for a home run in the bottom of the ninth, who cavorted in the streets after a victory, and who ate cold suppers at home after a defeat.

This collection, in other words, is about all of us, the baseball fans. If you have not begun looking for the perfect souvenir to complement your baseball cap on the next Turn Back the Clock Day at Fenway Park, Wrigley Field, or Camden Yards, perhaps it is time to go through some of those old shoeboxes in the closet. You just might find a unique baseball pin-back.

Jackie Robinson's historic debut in major-league baseball generated a number of pin-backs (above). Yankees legend Mickey Mantle described a meeting with Robinson after the 1952 World Series: "After the game, Jackie Robinson came into our clubhouse and shook my hand. He said, 'You're a helluva ballplayer and you've got a great future.' I thought that was a classy gesture, one I wasn't then capable of making. I was a bad loser. What meant even more was what Jackie told the press, 'Mantle beat us. . . . They didn't miss DiMaggio.' I have to admit, I became a Jackie Robinson fan on the spot. And when I think of that World Series, his gesture is what comes to mind. Here was a player who had without doubt suffered more abuse and more taunts and more hatred than any player in the history of the game. And he had made a special effort to compliment and encourage a young white kid from Oklahoma."

GATES
19&20

TAKE ME OUT TO THE BALLPARK

"Doubtless, there are better places to spend summer days, summer nights, than in ballparks. Doubtless. Nevertheless, decades after a person has stopped collecting bubble-gum cards, he can still discover himself collecting ballparks ... their smells, their special seasons, their moods."
—THOMAS BOSWELL *from* *How Life Imitates the World Series*

Bruce Spencer Hellerstein's fascination with baseball and its ballparks started when he was in the second grade, back in 1955. For Show and Tell one day, a classmate named Carol shared her experience of going to a Denver Bears baseball game at Bears

Stadium, which had been built in 1948 (and later became Mile High Stadium, the former home of the Colorado Rockies). Young Bruce went home and told his parents about Bears Stadium. They took him there the next day, and it was love at first sight.

The Denver Bears were not a major-league baseball team, but no matter: Hellerstein was more curious about seeing where ballplayers played than about who was playing. This bent of Hellerstein's was even more pronounced two years later, when he traded his 1957 Topps baseball card of legendary New York Yankees catcher Yogi Berra for the card of lesser-known second baseman Charley Neal of the Brooklyn Dodgers. The Berra card, Hellerstein

Hellerstein's collection of ballpark artifacts includes bricks and pieces of concrete (above) from baseball's most fabled ballparks of the past.

Fans queued up outside Ebbets Field (opposite) on October 5, 1920, for a World Series game between the Cleveland Indians and the Brooklyn Robins, as the Dodgers were then known.

Shibe Park, Philadelphia, Pa.
The Home of the Athletics.

A "straight-back" seat (left), from Philadelphia's Shibe Park—either at its opening in 1909, or from the addition of an upper deck in 1925—features the heart-shaped design under the armrest that was characteristic of all early Shibe Park straight-back seats. Major league ballparks did not start using today's more comfortable curved-back seats until the 1930s. (34" tall, 22" wide,16" deep, opened)

Hellerstein owns a marble figural piece (above) from the Lehigh Avenue side of Philadelphia's Shibe Park. Opened on April 12, 1909, Shibe Park was the first major-league ballpark constructed out of concrete and steel. (9½" tall, 7½" wide base)

As an original postcard from 1910 shows (top), the stadium featured a French Renaissance facade with columns, arched windows, and a domed tower, inside of which was A's manager Connie Mack's office. The stadium walls were made of brick with terra cotta and marble ornamentation. The beauty and grandeur of Shibe spurred other club owners to try to match it, resulting in the construction of Forbes Field, Comiskey Park, Fenway Park, Ebbets Field, Wrigley Field, and Braves Field in the next five years. (5¾" x 4")

explains, featured only an image of the Hall of Fame catcher's face, while the Neal card included a glimpse of Ebbets Field's famous red-and-white Schaefer beer billboard, its imposing scoreboard, and, right below that, the HIT SIGN, WIN SUIT advertising sign for Abe Stark clothier of 1514 Pitkin Avenue.

So Hellerstein's trade wasn't Berra-for-Neal so much as Berra-for-a-slice-of-Ebbets-Field-history. His interest in ballparks blossomed from there. As a teenager, he attended garage sales, flea markets, and antique shows in search of postcards and photographs featuring images of minor- and major- league ballparks. Indeed, his pursuit almost ruined his honeymoon. On May 31, 1976, while newlyweds Bruce and Lynn Hellerstein vacationed on the beaches of

B16 :—EBBET'S FIELD, BROOKLYN, N. Y.

47795

Southern California, Bruce convinced Lynn, who did not care much for baseball, to go to Dodger Stadium, where the Los Angeles Dodgers were playing the New York Mets. After parking their rental car in the stadium's parking lot, the largest stadium parking lot in the world, Bruce and Lynn joined a capacity crowd to watch Dave "King Kong" Kingman belt three home runs and Tom Seaver pitch a complete-game victory for the Mets. It was a night to remember. The air was crisp and clear, the stadium lights burned like stars against a pitch-black sky, and some of the game's top players were performing at their best. Lynn will love attending baseball games after this one, Bruce thought as he put his arm around her following the game. Everything was perfect . . . until they began looking for their car. Bruce had been in such a state of excitement that he hadn't paid attention to where he was parking before the game. They had to wait more than two hours for the parking lot to empty out before Bruce finally found the car. Their mood had dimmed considerably by the time they left Dodger Stadium, and

An original postcard (above) shows Brooklyn's Ebbets Field in the 1930s. (5¾" x 4")

Hellerstein owns a turnstile (far left) that was used at Ebbets Field in the 1950s. Writer Pete Hamill describes childhood visits to the famous park: "As kids, we used free tickets from the Police Athletic League to get in, or brought one of our friends who had been crippled by polio and played on the sympathies of the special cops, who always let us in, with a growl and a wink. Then we climbed dark ramps, higher and higher, climbing to the distant reaches and the cheapest seats in the ball park. Finally we were at the top level, and walked through a gate, out of the darkness, and there before us was the field. No grass has ever been greener. Each time I went back to Ebbets Field, and made that climb, and saw that field, my skin pebbled once more, at the sight of all that beauty." (41" tall, 26" deep)

Comiskey Park (above, in an original postcard from the 1950s) was home to the White Sox from 1910 to 1990. (5¾" x 4")

A straight-back, figural-end seat from Comiskey Park (left inset) supported fans who bore witness to baseball's darkest days, when Chick Gandil, Eddie Cicotte, Shoeless Joe Jackson, and the rest of the "Black Sox" conspirators threw the 1919 World Series. But better times were ahead for Comiskey Park denizens: the stadium hosted the first All-Star Game, in 1933, and was the site of Larry Doby's first major-league game, on July 5, 1947, which broke the color barrier in the American League. (34" tall, 22" wide, 16" deep, opened)

Lynn, to borrow a phrase from "Take Me Out to the Ballgame," didn't care if she ever got back to a baseball stadium.

But Bruce could not stay away from ballparks. What started as childhood fascination was turning into an adulthood obsession. In 1984, Hellerstein attended a personal development and growth seminar in Denver. On the first day of the seminar, the instructor told the participants to close their eyes and visualize the perfect paradise. While everyone in the class envisioned mountains, waterfalls, and wild orchids, Hellerstein immediately pictured the leftfield wall at Fenway Park in Boston. Known by several nicknames in its storied history (including the Cliff, and most famously, the Green Monster) the leftfield fence at Fenway is considered, in the words of writer Michael

A Baseball Game at the Polo Grounds as seen from an airship, New York

Gershman, "baseball's most famous architectural feature, as fabled as barriers in Jericho, Jerusalem, China, and Berlin."

For his perfect paradise, Hellerstein imagined sitting alone in one of Fenway's red-and-blue curved-back seats behind home plate, eating a hot dog, and admiring the Green Monster and the contours of the park's unique interior. John Updike once described Fenway Park as a "lyric little band-box of a ballpark. . . . Everything is painted green and seems in curiously sharp focus like the inside of an old-fashioned peeping-type Easter egg." Lost in his Fenway reverie, Hellerstein drifted through generations of fabled Red Sox memories, from the glory days of the Golden Outfield (Harry Hooper in right, Tris Speaker in center, and George "Duffy" Lewis in left) that helped Boston win the first World Series played at Fenway, in 1912, to the disappointment of the 1946 Series loss to the St. Louis Cardinals to Ted Williams's last at bat on September 28, 1960.

When he emerged from his daydream, Hellerstein had no doubt that a classic major-league ballpark like Fenway was, in fact, his perfect paradise. But Denver did not have a major-league baseball team at the time, and the city was relatively far from any place that did. Further, attending the occasional ballgame while on vacation would be a touchy topic with his wife, and it would not

An original postcard of the Polo Grounds from the 1930s (top) shows the park's distinct horseshoe-shaped grandstand rooftop. (5¾" x 4")

A curved-back, figural-end seat that was in the fabled Polo Grounds from the 1930s onward (right inset) features the New York Giants logo beneath its armrest. In the spring of 1963, *New Yorker* writer Roger Angell composed a eulogy for the Polo Grounds, which housed the Giants, Yankees and Mets from 1911 to '63. At the end of the piece, Angell envisaged a conversation among fans of the park: "Funny, I was thinking of the old place today. Remember how jammed we used to be back there? Remember how hot and noisy it was? I wouldn't move back there for anything, and anyway it's all torn down now, but, you know, we sure were happy in those days." The park was the site of some of baseball's biggest thrills, including Bobby Thompson's pennant-winning homer in 1951, and Willie Mays's famous catch in the 1954 World Series. (31" tall, 22" wide, 16" deep, opened)

Entrance to Braves Field, Boston, Mass.

An original postcard of Braves Field from 1915 (above) offers a view of the ballpark's particularly attractive entrance. The gold sign hanging from the ticket booth shows an image of Tamenund, an Indian chief from Bucks County, Pennsylvania, who was known for his honesty. In 1789, a New York–based political group that opposed the Federalists, named itself after Tamenund. The group's headquarters eventually became known as Tammany Hall. One of its members, James Gaffney, was the owner of the Braves. (5¾"x 4")

Hellerstein owns figural-end stadium seats from Briggs Stadium (near right), which was renamed Tiger Stadium in 1961 and housed the Detroit ballclub from 1912 to 1999, and from Braves Field (right inset). The last major-league game played at Braves Field, home of the Boston Braves since 1915, took place on September 21, 1952. The property was purchased by Boston University and converted into a football field; Hellerstein's seat is one of only a few Braves Field figural-end seats in original condition known to exist. (31" tall, 22" wide, 16" deep, opened)

107:-NIGHT GAME AT CROSLEY FIELD: CINCINNATI, OHIO.

The first night game at Cincinnati's Crosley Field was captured on an original postcard (above) from 1935. (5¾" x 4")

The fan who sat in Hellerstein's Crosley Field seat from 1935 (right)

witnessed the first night game in major-league history, which took place on May 24 of that year at the Reds' home stadium. The move to night baseball was designed to boost attendance levels, which had been severely affected by the Depression. (31" tall, 22" wide, 16" deep, opened)

be enough to satisfy his passion anyway. It was time for Hellerstein to recapture the excitement he had experienced as a child when he saw Bears Stadium for the first time, and to transform his daydream into reality. If he could not go to a major-league ballpark as often as he wished, he would have to create a major-league ballpark at home.

In December 1985, Hellerstein cleared out his basement to make room for what would become B's Ballpark Museum, a collection dedicated to the preservation and display of stadium artifacts mostly from major-league baseball's classic ballparks. As president of the museum and a member of its board of directors, Bruce has spent the past 18 years acquiring and caring for every item in its collection. The museum includes original stadium seats from the Palace of the Fans (Cincinnati, 1902–11), Shibe Park (Philadelphia, 1909–70),

Forbes Field (Pittsburgh, 1909–70), the Polo Grounds (New York, 1911–64), Ebbets Field (Brooklyn, 1913–60), and many other beloved parks.

In addition to these remarkable relics, Hellerstein's museum houses bricks from classic ballparks, a marble cornerstone figural piece from Shibe Park, and a turnstile used at Ebbets Field during the 1950s. He also owns a copper facade piece from "Old" Yankee Stadium, a home plate used at Fenway Park, and an extensive collection of stadium postcards and photographs. To top it all off, the entrance to the room that houses most of these artifacts is a replica of the grand marble rotunda entrance to Ebbets Field. It includes a ticket window carved into the marble wall, and the original brass light fixtures that hung at the legendary Brooklyn park.

On February 23, 1960, a soprano named

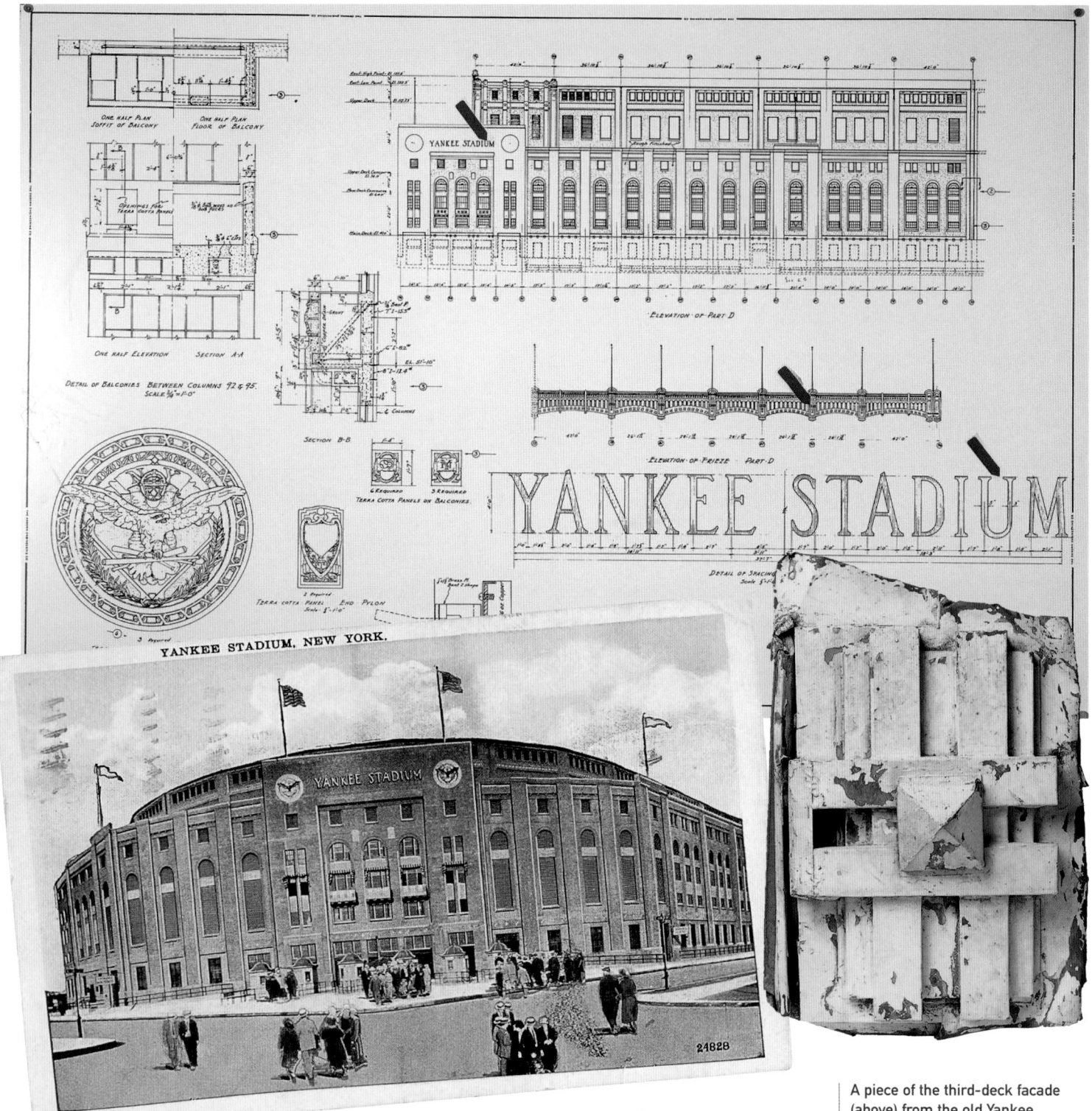

YANKEE STADIUM, NEW YORK.

Lucy Monroe sang the national anthem for the last time at Ebbets Field. When she finished, 200 mournful fans and several former Brooklyn Dodgers watched as a two-ton iron ball, painted to resemble a baseball, demolished the borough's beloved ballpark. Four years later, the same wrecking ball would take down the Polo Grounds, home of the Dodgers' crosstown rival, the New York Giants, since 1891. The Washington Sena-

tors' Griffith Stadium was next, followed by the St. Louis Cardinals' and Browns' Sportsman's Park, the Cincinnati Reds' Crosley Field, and the Philadelphia Athletics' and Phillies' Shibe Park.

Only Fenway Park in Boston and Wrigley Field in Chicago remain—they are the last two surviving classic ballparks. Each is a sacred repository of more than eight decades of memories shared among club

A piece of the third-deck facade (above) from the old Yankee Stadium (1923–73), along with blueprints (top) from the Osborn Engineering Company of Ohio, which built the stadium, reside in Hellerstein's collection. The middle red arrow on the blueprints shows precisely where Hellerstein's chunk of the stadium came from. (Stadium piece, 14½" x 11½"; Blueprint, 48" x 36")

An original postcard from the 1930s (above left) depicts the House that Ruth Built. (5¾" x 3")

Fenway Park, Boston, Mass.

An original postcard (above), postmarked 1913 on the reverse, shows Fenway Park, a stadium that has, according to baseball historian Michael Gershman, "led writers to soar on wings of rhetoric in describing it." Witness the words of *Boston Globe* sportswriter Dan Shaughnessy: "Fenway is only a ballpark the way the Sistine Chapel is only a church." Today, Fenway is the oldest surviving major league ballpark. (5¾" x 4")

A Fenway Park straight-back double seat (right) in Hellerstein's collection came from before 1934, when the stadium underwent a significant renovation and had all of its seats uprooted. Fans witnessed the first major-league game played at Fenway, on April 20, 1912, from these seats, which were part of the glory days of the Red Sox, when the team won four World Series between 1912 and 1918. (34" tall, 43" wide, 16" deep, opened)

owners, coaches, ballplayers, families, and friends. One can only hope that Fenway and Wrigley will be spared the same fate, but one also has to prepare for the worst. Fortunately, devoted fans like Hellerstein are committed to preserving the memories associated with the treasured ballparks of the past. Hellerstein is still, as Thomas Boswell wrote, "collecting ballparks . . . their smells, their special seasons, their moods.

Boston legends such as Carl Yastrzemski, Fred Lynn, Jim Rice, and Dwight Evans helped crack and weather the home plate (left) used at Fenway Park during the early 1980s. Other notables to have put spikes to Hellerstein's relic include Rich Gedman, Carney Lansford (who hit .336 for the Sox in 1981), Dave Stapleton, Tony Armas, and all of their American League foes. (17" x 8½" x 12")

"A WORLD IN A GRAIN OF SAND"

> To see a world in a grain of sand
> And a heaven in a wild flower,
> Hold infinity in the palm of your hand
> And eternity in an hour."
>
> —*WILLIAM BLAKE*
> *Auguries of Innocence*

"A few years ago, I was flipping through an auction catalog full of baseball stuff," recalls Penny Marshall, director of the baseball movie *A League of Their Own*. "I went past the things that most collectors typically have to have—Mickey Mantle's baseball card, Hank Aaron's game-used bat, an autographed Babe Ruth ball—and settled on a brown card with the words BITTE NICHT STÖREN/DO NOT DISTURB printed on it. [above, bottom left.] The card was issued by a hotel in Frankfurt, Germany, and it still had the red string from which it hung on the door knobs of each guest room. What appeared at the bottom of the card made it a must-have for me: an old fountain-pen signature of Ty Cobb. I knew that Cobb was a grumpy guy, so a 'Do not disturb' sign seemed to fit him." Much as the sign's inclu-

A range of items from Marshall's offbeat collection (above) demonstrates how baseball has been incorporated into almost every imaginable medium, from thermometers, razors and fans to leather coin pouches, ashtrays, and pocket watches.

Marshall owns a commemorative quilted blanket (opposite) that an unknown folk artist presented to Rogers Hornsby after the St. Louis Cardinals' 1926 World Series victory, the franchise's first world championship. (76" x 72")

Since its beginning, baseball has inspired a multitude of songs celebrating championship teams, famous players, and the joy of attending a game. With its aesthetically pleasing covers, and lyrics that shed light on the history of the game and America itself, the sheet music for these baseball-themed compositions forms a delightful segment of baseball memorabilia. Marshall owns numerous examples of early-20th-century baseball sheet music (left) including an original copy of "Take Me Out to the Ballgame," which was composed in 1908 by Jack Norworth (lyrics) and Albert von Tilzer (music), and quickly became baseball's anthem.

sion in Marshall's collection fits her and her idiosyncratic approach to the hobby.

The artifacts in Marshall's collection are wonderfully eclectic, and they demonstrate an appealingly offbeat side of baseball commemoration. For example, in the top left of the collage on the previous page is a James M. Delp Meat Market thermometer featuring a picture of Lou Gehrig swinging away. Marshall also has an old-fashioned barber's shaver from the 1910s that commemorates the Red Sox, a Joe DiMaggio leather coin pouch, Yankees ashtrays, early-20th-century Pittsburgh Pirates collapsible handheld fans, and Babe Ruth pocket watches.

The list goes on: Marshall's collection is full of curious objects that provide delightful surprises. She owns a multicolored marble checkerboard in a wooden casing, which sits atop four baseball bats that serve as legs. On the reverse side of the board, Christy Mathewson etched his signature and the date of May 24, 1924. This checker-

board once belonged to Mathewson, who, besides being a top pitcher of his day, was known to be an avid checkers player (as the original photograph on the opposite page suggests; that's the Hall of Fame twirler playing checkers with his father in 1922).

Other items in Marshall's collection are noteworthy for their unusual appearance or sheer obscurity. An original cast-iron mutoscope machine from the 1930s fits both categories. With its narrow stand, protruding red eyepiece, and brass hand-crank, the mutoscope looks like some ill-conceived hybrid of a telephone and a mailbox. It is actually one of the earliest motion-picture devices, housing a sequence of images mounted on a rotating drum. Each image was

An odd contraption to modern eyes, Marshall's 1930s mutoscope machine (above) contains a "flip-book" of Bobby Thomson's famous home run. (height, 64")

slightly different from the preceding one, and when the series passed before the viewer's eyes in rapid succession, it looked as though the figures were actually moving. From the late 19th century through the 1940s, mutoscopes were popular forms of entertainment at nickelodeons and amusement parks. By dropping a penny in the slot and moving the crank of Marshall's mutoscope, a viewer can watch Bobby Thompson's famous Shot Heard 'Round the World home run that won the pennant for the New York Giants in 1951.

Marshall's finds come from every nook and cranny of the baseball world. She owns, for example, a broadsheet from the Israelite House of David colony of Benton Harbor, Michigan, which embraced baseball in the first half of the 20th century. A religious community founded in 1903 by Benjamin Purnell, the House of David colony started a baseball team in 1920. The long-haired, bushy-bearded players barnstormed the country to raise money for the colony and preach to potential members. They dazzled crowds with their pepper-game routine and played local clubs in exhibition games that sometimes included big-league stars like Grover Cleveland Alexander and Babe Ruth. The NITE BASEBALL UNDER FLOODLIGHTS broadside on the next page was issued to advertise one of the games on the House of David tour in the early 1930s. Faintly written in pencil on the bottom half of the broadside is a notice that the team will play against a local town club called the Damascus Beavers at Backer Park in Damascus Township, Pennsylvania.

After filming *Riding in Cars with Boys*

In the photo above, Hall of Fame pitcher and avid checkers player Christy Mathewson (top left in photo) plays the game with his father. (6½" x 8½") Mathewson autographed and dated the reverse side of a custom-made checkerboard table (above) that now resides in Marshall's collection. (22" tall, 15" square)

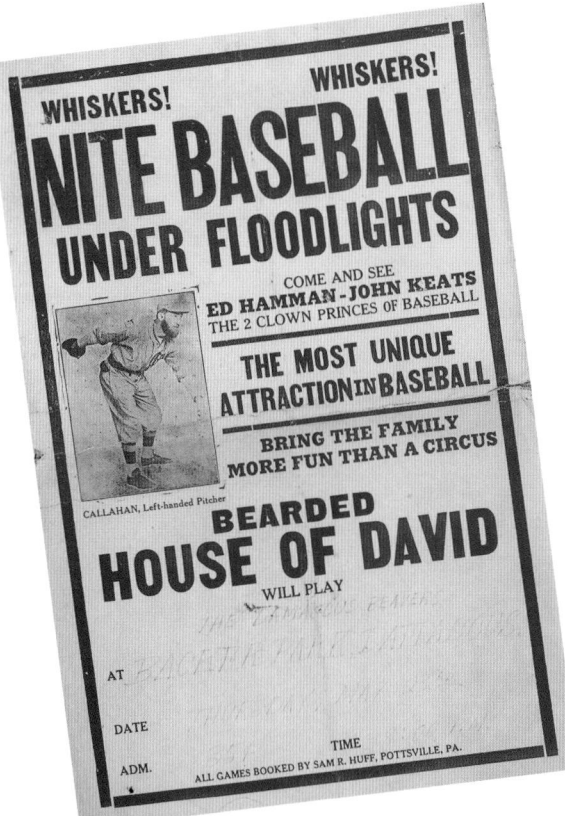

in 2001, Marshall visited Cuba, where word spread that she was looking for baseball photographs. Four mornings each week, merchants from local book fairs assembled outside Marshall's hotel with old baseball photos. Although she knew that baseball has an extensive heritage in Cuba, Marshall did not expect to find many baseball-related artifacts, especially not any depicting ballplayers from the United States. Surprisingly, one merchant had a photograph of Ted Williams sitting on a barstool next to a giant novelty bottle of Cuban rum. The photo was probably taken in a Havana pub during the 1950s.

During her trip, Marshall met a photographer named Roberto Salas, whose father was the personal photographer of Fidel Castro. Salas brought Marshall some photos, one of which shows Castro standing next to members of the Minneapolis Millers, a Boston Red Sox farm team that played the Havana Sugar Kings in the 1959 Junior World Series. From the early 20th century up until the 1970s, the postseason Junior World Series pitted the champions of the American Association against those of the International League. In early 1959, Castro had overthrown dictator Fulgencio Batista, so the political climate in Cuba was still unstable at the time of the photograph. Indeed, on July

Touting WHISKERS! WHISKERS!, a broadside (top left) announced the famously hirsute House of David baseball team's game against a local team called the Damascus Beavers, at Backer Park in Damascus Township, Pennsylvania, in the early 1930s. (The game information is printed, in very faint pencil, on the bottom half of the broadside.) (22" x 14")

Photographer Roberto Salas captured Fidel Castro (above) demonstrating his windup in 1965. A great fan of baseball and reportedly a passable pitcher, Castro attended all of the 1959 Junior World Series games between the Havana Sugar Kings and the Minneapolis Millers at Gran Stadium in Havana. Before the start of the first game there, he told the 25,000 fans in attendance, "I came here to see our team beat Minneapolis, not as premier but as just a baseball fan. I want to see our club win the Little World Series. After the triumph of the revolution, we should also win the Little World Series." The Sugar Kings came through for the dictator, downing the Millers in seven games. (9" x 11")

26, 1959, during a game between the Sugar Kings and the Rochester Red Wings, Havana shortstop Leo Cardenas and Rochester third base coach Frank Verdi were struck by bullets after shots rang out in the stadium. Fortunately, neither man was seriously hurt. Although the Millers lost that 1959 Junior World Series to the Sugar Kings in seven

games, none of the players was overly distraught, given the events in that stadium earlier in the year. As Millers pitcher Ted Bowsfield said, "Nobody minded losing the game in that country and under those conditions. We were just happy to get it over and to get out of town with our hides."

One of Marshall's favorite areas of base-

Marshall acquired a number of original baseball-related photographs during a visit to Cuba in 2001, including one of Ted Williams in Havana (above) and one of Fidel Castro with members of the Minneapolis Millers (top left) (montage. 16" x 20")

A circa 1900 hand-made pillow (top) from Marshall's collection commemorates the 1869 Cincinnati Red Stockings, baseball's first professional team, which included Hall of Famers Harry and George Wright. (11" x 16½")

Marshall's Rival Base-Ball Club equipment trunk (above) is from the 1870s, while her Albany Base-Ball Club presentation bat is from an 1888 game. (trunk: 13 ¾" tall, 49" x 20" base) (bat height, 60")

ball collecting is folk art. Loosely defined, folk art is any object that reflects the values, characteristics, and traditions of a particular culture. Though folk art objects often are created for utilitarian purposes, they are regarded as art because they are designed to be visually appealing. According to Gerard C. Wertkin, the director of the American Folk Art Museum in New York, "Folk artists almost invariably draw deeply from the wellsprings of vernacular culture, recording, interpreting, and often celebrating everyday life in its rich and colorful diversity." The combination of idealized aesthetics and functionality results in one-

of-a-kind objects that are both useful and culturally meaningful.

Marshall's collection includes a number of baseball-related folk art pieces that were created for use within the sport itself, such as the circa 1870s Rival Base-Ball Club equipment trunk. The word "Eckley" painted on the side of the trunk may refer to the 19th-century coal-mining village of Eckley, which was established in Pennsylvania's anthracite region in 1854 by the mining firm of Sharpe, Leisenring, and Company. The village provided housing, schools, stores, and churches for the miners and their families. In the latter part of the 19th century, many towns and villages throughout Pennsylvania had minor-league ball clubs. Other folk art items served as commemorative, presentational pieces given to teams from small-town professional associations and clubs. Winners of baseball competitions often received ornate figural pieces or hand-crafted trophy baseball bats, such as the 60-inch black trophy bat on this page.

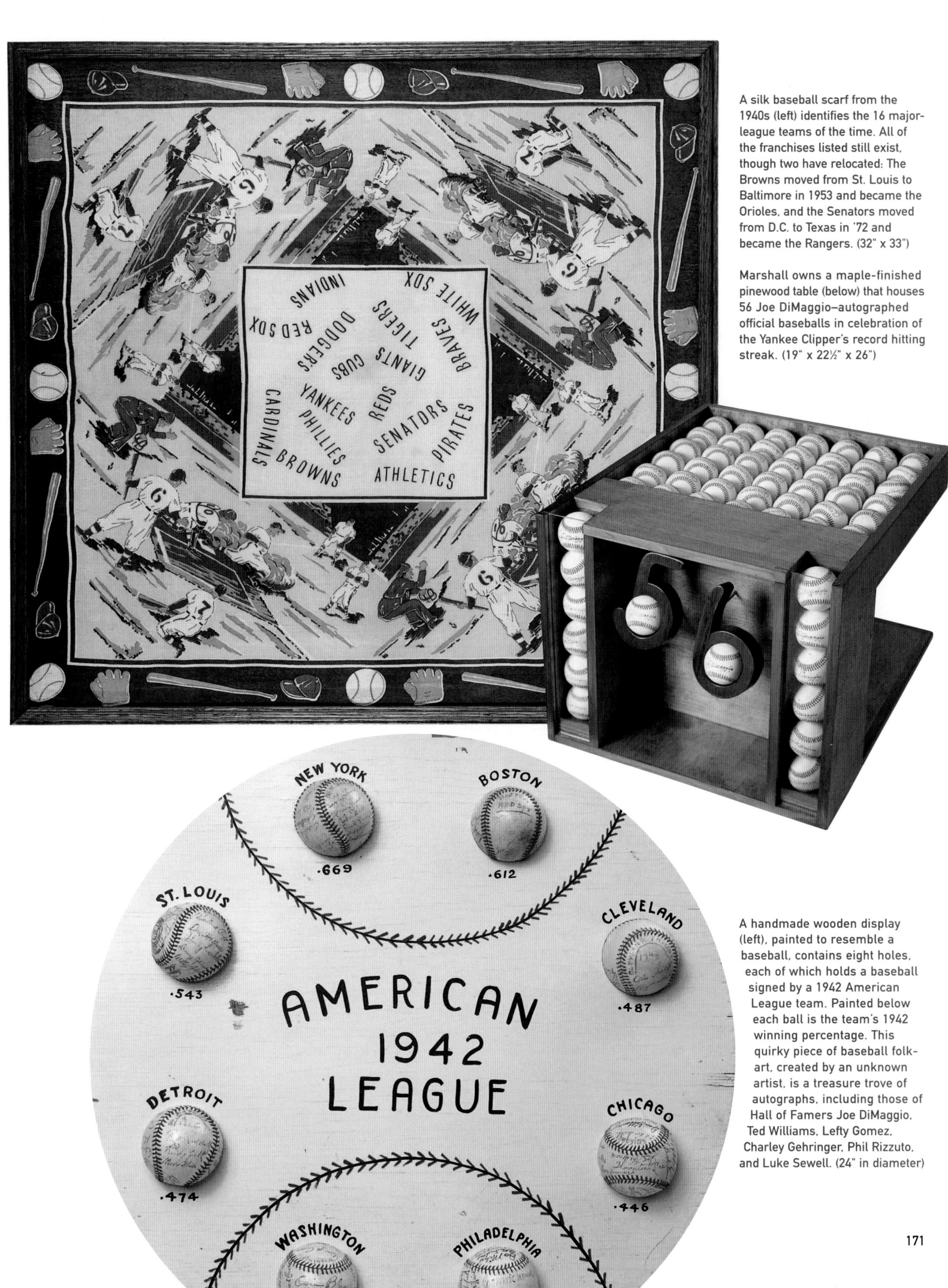

A silk baseball scarf from the 1940s (left) identifies the 16 major-league teams of the time. All of the franchises listed still exist, though two have relocated: The Browns moved from St. Louis to Baltimore in 1953 and became the Orioles, and the Senators moved from D.C. to Texas in '72 and became the Rangers. (32" x 33")

Marshall owns a maple-finished pinewood table (below) that houses 56 Joe DiMaggio–autographed official baseballs in celebration of the Yankee Clipper's record hitting streak. (19" x 22½" x 26")

A handmade wooden display (left), painted to resemble a baseball, contains eight holes, each of which holds a baseball signed by a 1942 American League team. Painted below each ball is the team's 1942 winning percentage. This quirky piece of baseball folk-art, created by an unknown artist, is a treasure trove of autographs, including those of Hall of Famers Joe DiMaggio, Ted Williams, Lefty Gomez, Charley Gehringer, Phil Rizzuto, and Luke Sewell. (24" in diameter)

171

Inscribed on the bat in gold lettering is the legend, PRESENTED TO THE ALBANY BASE-BALL CLUB, WINNERS OF THE FIRST CHAMPIONSHIP GAME, 1888, BY GARSONS. This event was most likely a minor-league series competition; Garsons may have been a local social organization in Albany. Another folk art trophy bat was given to the Tri-Mountain Base Ball Club of Boston in 1867. (See Chapter I, "Collecting 19th - Century Memorabilia.")

Perhaps the richest sources of baseball-related folk art are the household and commercial items that were used in everyday life, such as hand-painted mugs, carved ticket-window signs, baseball-themed hairpins, blown-glass perfume bottles, and carved wooden baseball-player figures. The 76" x 72" hand-sewn quilted blanket by an unknown artist, pictured on the opening page of this chapter, demonstrates how certain ballplayers or teams inspired commemoration by artists. The quilt's design and detail are extraordinary. Intricately cross-stitched patterns in red thread frame a large oval portrait of St. Louis Cardinals manager Rogers Hornsby. Above Hornsby's portrait is one of the 1885 St. Louis Browns (the franchise's first championship team), embroidered in brown thread. Browns

A Negro League broadside from 1955 (above left) invited fans to see the legendary Satchel Paige pitch in an exhibition game in Indianapolis against the Harlem Stars, a team featuring Harlem Globetrotters basketball legend and former Negro League baseball star Reece "Goose" Tatum. The loose-limbed Tatum was famous for his clowning, even as a baseball player, and he created and developed most of the Globetrotters' classic comedy routines. (22" x 14")

A baseball "crying towel" (above right) commemorates a classic line from Marshall's film *A League of Their Own*: "There's no crying in baseball!" (18" x 10")

Fans from the 1940s could listen to major-league games on an Official League baseball radio (left). (10" in diameter)

In 1992, Penny Marshall directed *A League of Their Own*, a film based on the All-American Girls Professional Baseball League (AAGPBL), which was established in 1943 by chewing-gum magnate Philip Wrigley, who wanted to maintain interest in baseball during World War II. After Marshall's film debuted, the members of six AAGPBL teams—the Rockford Peaches, the Racine Belles, the Kenosha Comets, the South Bend Blue Sox, the Minneapolis Millerettes and the Fort Wayne Daisies—signed the matte of an original photograph (above) and presented it to the director. The league lasted from 1943 to '54, and its players, whom sportswriters dubbed "the Queens of Swat" and "the Belles of the Ball Game," attracted large crowds, including more than a million in their most successful year. (19½" x 15½")

owner Chris von der Ahe and manager Charles Comiskey are depicted in small oval portraits in the upper left and right, respectively. Below Hornsby's portrait are 25 full-length figures of each member of the 1926 St. Louis Cardinals in various batting and fielding poses. The blanket was presented to Hornsby following the Cardinals victory in the 1926 World Series, the franchise's first world championship.

Marshall owns a handmade pillow, which probably dates from the early part of the 20th century, commemorating the 1869 Cincinnati Red Stockings team, baseball's first professional team and the most recognized club of its day. Devoted fans sometimes took note of players, managers, and teams in familiar poses, then reproduced them in their chosen medium. The image on this pillow was based on a trade card issued in 1869 by famous sporting goods

merchant Peck & Snyder (see Chapter I, "The Corey R. Shanus Collection").

All of these objects, however small or obscure they may be, invite contemplation. What type of artist stitched the Rogers Hornsby quilt blanket? How did a German "Do not disturb" card autographed by Ty Cobb make its way to the United States more than half a century later? How did the photos of minor-league American baseball players in Cuba survive the decades, and where did the Cuban book fair merchants get them? For Marshall, such unanswered questions are part of the allure of each object, and of collecting baseball memorabilia in general. She tries to imagine the artistic motivation behind each piece of baseball folk art; or the provenance behind promotional and other commemorative items. Every object has meaning and a story behind it, which allows Marhsall, in the words of the poet Blake,

BASEBALL FOLK ART

BY DAVID HUNT

Like 18th-century American silversmiths or early-20th-century itinerant painters, the creators of baseball folk art are judged on standards of quality and craftsmanship. Some pieces are as basic as a baseball bat painted in one color by a player. Other examples, such as a period painting of a baseball player, or the 1870s hand-sewn decorative belt (below, 36" long) once worn by a semiprofessional ballplayer, might compare to a Tiffany bracelet in terms of the technical skill they exhibit. Although technical proficiency

cards from the early 20th century. I eventually made my way from selling baseball cards at antique shows on a part-time basis to a full-time career in the sports memorabilia auction business. Although my business covers all areas of sports, my personal focus remains on baseball. As I have come across more and more material over the years, I've gravitated to those items that were fashioned by so-called folk artists, untrained individuals expressing their personal feelings about people or events in baseball, or about

the satisfaction of possessing it. Once, I found a wonderful pair of 19th-century high-top baseball shoes accompanied by an original cabinet photograph of a player wearing the shoes. This combination was impressive on its own, but it became even more special when, to my surprise, I discovered the original 1870s lemon-peel style baseball the player had used, tucked inside of one of the shoes. (Lemon-peel style baseballs are discussed in Chapter III, "The Greg Gallacher Collection.") Knowing that these pieces had stayed together for more than 100 years means more to me than the ensemble's dollar value (though the value is considerable).

can significantly affect the value of a piece of folk art, more often than not it is the "intangible" attributes that determine the desirability of baseball folk art. Indeed, the allure of collecting baseball folk art lies in the innately interpretive nature of the genre. Each collector uses his or her own reference points to assess an item and determine its value. The piece must speak to you, and you must connect with the piece. In this context, beauty truly is in the eye of the beholder. My passion for collecting baseball-related folk art lies not only in the historical intricacies, but also in the unique origin of each individual piece.

I was introduced to this hobby while helping my father with his American antiques business. During our travels to find new items, we often came upon baseball artifacts, ranging from cast-iron, baseball-themed mechanical banks from the 1880s to the proverbial "shoe boxes" of baseball tobacco

the sport itself. Primarily, my focus has been on painted objects such as baseball bats, wooden and metal figural pieces, and paintings of baseball scenes.

Sometimes you seize on a piece because it will complement another piece in your collection. Attending an outdoor antique market one summer, I was walking down an aisle when my eye locked on an occupational shaving mug (top right, 3" tall) with a beautiful color image of a bat, an American flag, and a 19th-century workman's-style baseball glove painted on the front. I immediately reached for the item and asked the price. My money was on the table before the price quotation was complete, and the mug now sits in my living room on a shelf next to a 19th-century straight razor with a baseball-motif celluloid handle.

When you are fortunate enough to discover a piece in the very spot it has occupied since its creation, the intrigue and feeling of discovery add to

Although I have bought and sold many memorable items, like all collectors, I have my favorite pieces. The first is a light-blue-painted baseball bat, made around the 1860s, with a small red-painted termination knob and the original twine-wrapped handle grip visible under the period paint (above, 34" long). Most likely, this bat had been used and was subsequently painted for presentation purposes. I particularly enjoy this piece because of its simplicity and visual appeal. Such characteristics are inherent in most forms of baseball folk art. The circa-1910 hand-carved wooden baseball figure (right, 12½" tall), for example, is almost primitive in appearance. This piece may have been displayed on a chest of drawers at home or on a countertop at a

tobacco shop or sporting goods store. Another personal favorite is an oil-on-board painting (opposite, 12" x 15") of a late-19th-century baseball player in an "Oriole" uniform standing on a hillside, with a game in progress below. The painting transports me to that hilltop setting that evokes a small rural American town at a time when the sport was exploding in popularity across the country. Whenever I look at this painting, my eye is first drawn to the American flag in the background that illustrates the deep ties between this country and baseball. This particular painting came with an extensive collection of papers and related ephemera documenting the history of the player and the artwork, and citing the artist's affiliation with a Boston school of painting. But the name of the player and team, or lack thereof, in a given piece of

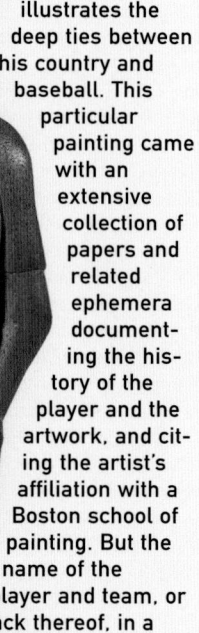

in which the artist worked, and what style of uniforms and/or equipment, if any, are depicted in the piece.

2) Has the piece undergone any restoration? When possible, examine the item in either natural daylight or under a black light to expose restored areas. Does the object retain its original surface (i.e., paint)? Look for surface cracking. Is the surface uniform, or does it exhibit areas of unevenness that may indicate restoration has taken place? As with other types of memorabilia, restoration can decrease the market value of the item by at least 50 percent.

3) Does the piece resemble comparable items that you have encountered in the past and in what manner? If you can identify certain similarities between an object and other known examples, you at least have some basis for comparison with respect to price.

4) Does the price of the piece accurately reflect its importance and desirability? Have you seen similar items sell for more or less than the asking price?

All of these questions are part of the process of assessing the market value of baseball folk art. Because each piece is unique, standard valuation benchmarks are not available, as they are for baseball cards and other mass-produced items. A painted baseball bat from the 1880s with its original surface in an attractive color, such as blue with a red ring decoration, could sell for as much as $5,000. But a bat from the same period with a mottled mixture of primary-color paints that has been cleaned and lacquered in the 1920s might fetch only $400. The discriminating collector must focus on rarity, originality, visual appeal, and provenance.

Collectors, dealers, and auction houses overuse the phrase "folk art." In the end, the definition of this broad category lies in individual interpretation. This aspect lends a unique element of intrigue to this wonderful segment of collecting.

baseball folk art is often not as significant as the execution of the work or the details inherent in the piece.

Building a collection of baseball-related folk art has become challenging in recent times. Even though these items are largely underappreciated in sports-collecting circles, pieces are not readily available. Folk-art items are by definition one-of-a-kind pieces, and many of them remain in museums or private collections. The scarcity, of course, adds to the attraction and enhances the thrill of the hunt. Among the best venues to find baseball folk-art pieces are American antique shows and outdoor markets. You can

also find a sizeable number of baseball-related folk art pieces at exhibition shows, though the high-quality items are typically reserved for auction houses. When visiting an antique show, you should learn about the theme of the show itself and its dealers' specialties. Is the show focused on a specific genre or type of art (i.e., paintings, sculptures, or woodworks)? If a show is focused on 17th-century Orientalia, for example, then you probably will not find any baseball-related items. To narrow your targets, find out which dealers might have a piece at the next show. Look for dealers with related collectibles such as Americana or

sports memorabilia. Arrive as early as the show promoters allow. There are always other buyers looking for the same items as you are. Who walks away with a particular piece often comes down to who saw it first.

ASSESSING VALUE OF BASEBALL FOLK ART

Before you start looking for baseball folk art, acquire and study past auction catalogs and other reference materials. When you discover a piece that interests you, consider the following:

1) What is the date of the piece? If a piece is undated, then look for clues. Good places to begin are the period

A KID AT HEART

In the summer of 1952, 10-year-old Charles Merkel shared a bus ride with the New York Yankees (10 of whom are shown in an original photograph at top) from Sportsman's Park in St. Louis back to the hotel in which the team and Charles's parents were staying.

The original photograph of Charles Merkel with Mickey Mantle (above) was taken before the start of the game between the St. Louis Browns and New York Yankees at Sportsman's Park in the summer of 1952. The photo was autographed by Mantle when Charles Merkel met him again nearly 40 years later at the Mantle/Ford Fantasy Camp.

An assortment of early 1950s baseball cards and unopened wax packs issued by Bowman Gum, Inc. and Topps Chewing Gum Company are shown in the montage opposite.

"Topps Bubble Gum with Giant Baseball Picture Cards bring you, for the very first time, full-color photographs of famous Big Leaguers in the New Big Size. Each card includes the player's autograph, biography and official, lifetime statistical record. Never offered before, this giant-size, prize collection will be cherished through the years by every lover of the great American pastime. Every kid will want the complete set!"

—Advertisement that was printed on the lid of every retail box of 1952 Topps baseball 5-cent wax packs

After conducting Charles Merkel's interview, I was convinced that the best way to capture the essence of his connection with baseball and his lifetime devotion as a baseball card collector was to allow readers to hear it straight from Charles. This decision was also inspired by my respect and admiration for the work of two renowned authors on baseball,

Lawrence Ritter and Donald Honig. Between 1961 and 1966, Lawrence Ritter, an economist at New York University, traveled throughout the United States and Canada to interview old ballplayers who could tell him what it was like to play in the big leagues from the turn of the century to the 1920s. Ritter published these remarkable interviews in *The Glory of Their Times: The Story of Baseball Told by the Men Who Played It* (1966), which is considered one of the timeless classics in baseball literature. Inspired by Ritter's work, Donald Honig conducted his own set of interviews with ballplayers who played in the majors from the 1920s to the 1940s and chronicled them in *Baseball: When the Grass Was Real* (1975).

Charles Michael Merkel was born on November 2, 1941, in Nashville, Tennessee, but has lived in Mississippi all his life. He attended Ole Miss, where he earned a B.A. in mathematics as well as a law degree, and has been running his own practice as a plaintiff's trial lawyer in

177

MONTY IRVIN
Monford Monte Irvin

DUKE SNIDER
Edwin D Snider

ROBIN ROBERTS
Robin Roberts

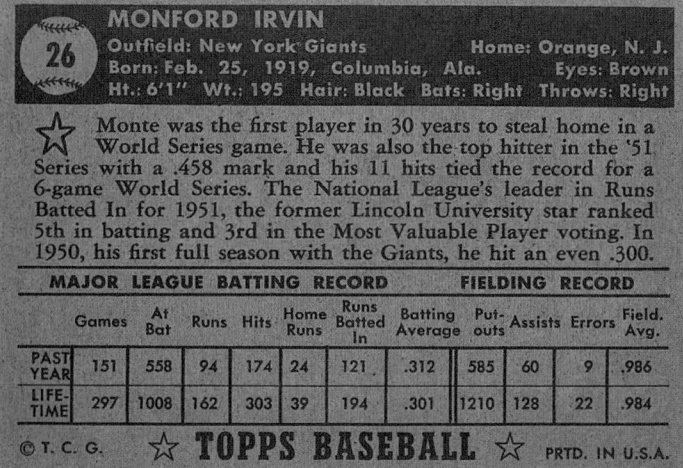

26	MONFORD IRVIN										

Outfield: New York Giants   Home: Orange, N. J.
Born: Feb. 25, 1919, Columbia, Ala.   Eyes: Brown
Ht.: 6'1"   Wt.: 195   Hair: Black   Bats: Right   Throws: Right

☆ Monte was the first player in 30 years to steal home in a World Series game. He was also the top hitter in the '51 Series with a .458 mark and his 11 hits tied the record for a 6-game World Series. The National League's leader in Runs Batted In for 1951, the former Lincoln University star ranked 5th in batting and 3rd in the Most Valuable Player voting. In 1950, his first full season with the Giants, he hit an even .300.

MAJOR LEAGUE BATTING RECORD								FIELDING RECORD			
	Games	At Bat	Runs	Hits	Home Runs	Runs Batted In	Batting Average	Put-outs	Assists	Errors	Field. Avg.
PAST YEAR	151	558	94	174	24	121	.312	585	60	9	.986
LIFE-TIME	297	1008	162	303	39	194	.301	1210	128	22	.984

© T. C. G.   ☆ **TOPPS BASEBALL** ☆   PRTD. IN U.S.A.

As shown on the back of the 1952 Topps card of New York Giant Hall of Famer Monte Irvin (above), each card contained a brief player bio and statistics from previous seasons, a format that Topps continues to maintain today.

In the late 1940s and '50s Brooklyn Dodger fans dubbed their graceful, handsome young centerfielder—Edwin Donald Snider (above, middle)—the Duke of Flatbush. A quick lefthanded pull hitter who still remains the Dodgers franchise record-holder for home runs (389), RBIs (1,271), and extra-base hits (814), the Duke went up against a number of the era's top hurlers including Robin Roberts (above, right), whose Hall of Fame plaque is inscribed with the legend, "Tireless worker who never missed a start in the decade of the fifties." Roberts led the NL in innings pitched (1951–55) and in complete games (1952–56).

An original unopened box of 1952 Topps 5-cent wax packs, the kind that Charles Merkel bought at McClellans five and dime store in Leland, Mississippi, is shown at left. The cards featured on this and the following five pages, which are part of Merkel's collection, are just some of the treasures that were found inside such packs. Each card has been authenticated and graded "Mint 9" condition by Professional Sports Authenticator (PSA). (1952 Topps cards: 2⅝" x 3¾")

Clarksdale, Mississippi, since 1967. He became a lifetime New York Yankee fan and devoted collector of baseball cards in the summer of 1952 after watching the Bronx Bombers play a Sunday doubleheader against the Browns at Sportsman's Park in St. Louis. It was a day to remember for the rest of his life, and the genesis behind one of the world's finest collections of rare, vintage high-grade baseball cards.

"I grew up in Leland, Mississippi, which was a Delta town with signs on the city limits that said '5,000 Nice People and a Few Old Sore Heads.' There were no local baseball leagues and certainly no major-league teams within a thousand miles of there at the time. But my father was a baseball fan, and he loved the Yankees. I guess my earliest memories of baseball were when my dad started throwing ball with me in our backyard when I was about four years old. He pitched to me every time he had a chance and, although he was no great athlete himself, he sure loved it and instilled in me a love for the game at a very early age. From the time I was four until I was about eight, I spent every afternoon of warm enough weather playing sandlot ball in a dirt field on a vacant lot next to the house with eight to twelve neighborhood kids. We also played at school during recess, and every noon hour of the day. I also remember watching my dad get real excited about listening to Joe DiMaggio talking about his various exploits on 'The Game of the Day' that was broadcast on the

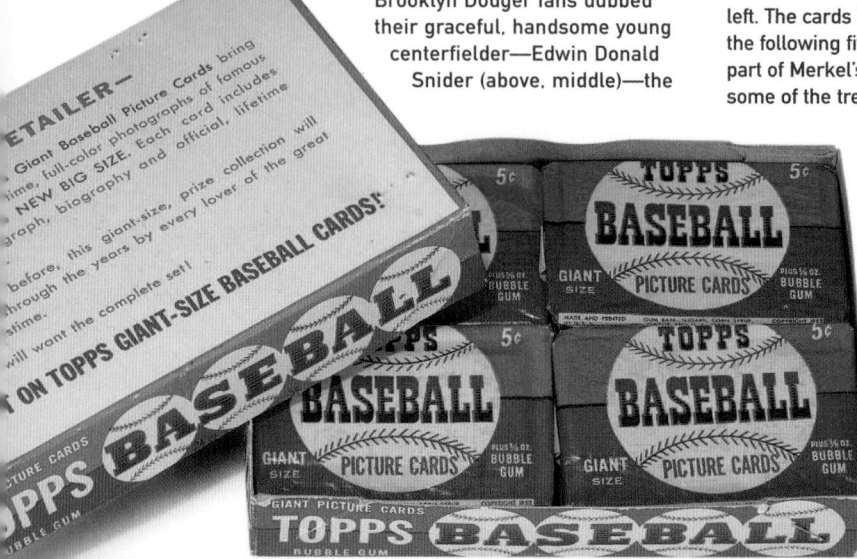

PHIL RIZZUTO

ALLIE REYNOLDS

GIL McDOUGALD

JOHNNY MIZE

radio, long before TV ever made it to Leland.

"By the time I was ten, I'd never been to a major-league ballpark, never even been in a city that had a team. So my folks for a vacation that summer took me to Sportsman's Park in St. Louis to watch a Sunday doubleheader between the Browns and the Yankees. This would have been the summer of '52 because it was the first season after DiMaggio retired. During a previous series that year, I'm not sure at this point whether it was in New York or St. Louis, Billy Martin and Clint Courtney had gotten into a fight underneath the stands, so when the Yankees came into Sportsman's Park, they were booed and the crowd was hostile with lots of animosity.

"At any rate, I showed up at the ballpark with my parents. I brought a baseball, a ballpoint pen, and my Yankee cap, and spent literally hours getting autographs on the ball. We would get to the park before the team came out of the dressing room. In those days, the team passed right through the crowd underneath the stands, as they went from the dressing room door to the field. So you would stand in that area, and the players would stop and sign autographs. You got 'em going to batting practice, you got 'em coming off the field to change, you got 'em going to the game, as well as coming off after the game. My parents took plenty of photographs, and I've got pictures of me standing there with Mantle, Martin, Ford, Berra, Riz-

zuto, Lopat, Raschi, Reynolds, Stengel, and Johnny Mize—the whole gamut of the Yankee greats of that era, with their arms around me, or talking to me and posing.

"By the final day of the series, I was checking the program and roster against the autographs on my ball. The autographs were clear as the dickens unlike most of the scrawls you see today— every one of them was signed with such great care. That's how most of the ballplayers were back then. They knew how much these kind of things meant to the fans, especially to youngsters like me.

"There was a rookie on the team named Andy Carey. I had no clue as to what he looked like since he had never been on a baseball card. I stood, looked, waited, and watched the players coming off the field trying to pick him out or trying to spot his number. The last guy off the field was Gil McDougald, who was at that time a second baseman and shortstop for the Yanks. I remember it like yesterday. Everybody is gone, he's the last player coming in, and he stopped to sign my autograph. But instead of getting an autograph from him, I said, 'Mr. McDougald, do you know where Mr.

After the game between the Browns and the Yankees in the summer of '52, Gil McDougald (top, right) brought Charley into the Yankee locker room at Sportsman's Park so he could obtain Andy Carey's autograph. Along the way, Charley bumped into other Bronx Bombers like shortstop Phil Rizzuto (1950 NL MVP), pitcher Allie Reynolds (1952 AL leader in ERA), and slugger Johnny Mize, whose 6-foot-2, 215-pound frame and short, compact swing helped him belt 359 career home runs and compile a lifetime batting average of .312. "His bat doesn't travel as far as anybody else's," Casey Stengel once said about Mize's swing. "He just cocks it and slaps, and when you're as big as he is, you can slap a ball into the seats. That short swing is wonderful."

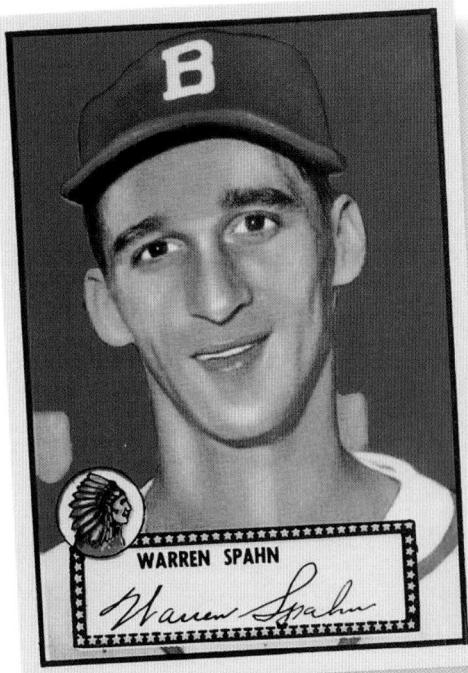

Carey is?' And obviously amused, he said, 'No I don't, but if you come with me young man, we'll go find Mr. Carey.'

"When we got into the dressing room, we went right through all the Yankee ballplayers back to a corner and up to a guy that was taking his shirt off. McDougald said, 'Mr. Carey, for some reason this young man wants your autograph.' So, I asked him and Carey signed my ball. They asked me where I was from, and they all laughed at Mississippi and my accent. Then McDougald walked me back out to the door where my parents were waiting. He said, 'If ya'll aren't in a hurry, why don't you let the kid stay and ride the bus with us back to the hotel.' We were staying at the same hotel as the Yanks, so my folks said fine. I probably spent forty-five minutes or more during the dressing interval chatting it up with all those legends. And the bus ride back to the hotel with them was probably one of the greatest thrills of my entire life. From then on, I was hooked on the Yanks like nothing you can imagine. And baseball cards, having made it to the five and dime store in Leland by that time, became an obsession for me. I just couldn't wait to get my hands on those cards that pictured all my heroes who sat with me on the bus.

"The store was called McClellans five and dime. It was the only place in Leland that you could get cards. So, for my Saturday ritual, I'd take my quarter allowance, go to the movies, and have thirteen cents left over. That bought two packs of '52 Topps cards

The '52 Topps set featured players who were heroes off the diamond as well. Warren Spahn (top, left) served three years as a combat engineer, saw action during the Battle of the Bulge, was wounded in the foot, and survived the collapse of the Remagen Bridge in Germany, which earned him three battle stars, a Purple Heart, and a battlefield commission as second lieutenant, the only major-league player to earn such an honor. Bob Feller became the first big leaguer to volunteer for active duty, enlisting in the United States Navy just two days after the Japanese attack on Pearl Harbor. He served four years of his prime as an anti-aircraft gunner on the battleship *USS Alabama* and fought in battles at Tarawa, Iwo Jima, and the Marshall Islands.

Albert "Red" Schoendienst may have been baseball's rebuttal to "nice guys finish last." His flaming red hair, freckles and often-sunny disposition won Schoendienst many friends in the big leagues. But his Hall of Fame induction was built on merit, not smiles: He led the NL in fielding percentage six times, hit .300 or better seven times, and won the 1950 All-Star Game for the NL with a 14th-inning home run.

and a couple of pieces of some other kind of candy. After that, I was broke for a week. During the course of that summer, I collected all the '52 Topps cards except for those from the last series. Topps issued cards in several series, but the final series, so called the high numbers which are card numbers 311 to 407, never made it to Mississippi. So over the course of that year, and probably the next, I put together the entire '52 Topps set from cards #1 through #310. I continued to buy cards in that set the following year, as the dime store still had some left over, and you could also go to other towns where they would have old inventory as well.

"In those days, cards were not protected like they are nowadays in plastic sleeves and holders. Nobody had card sleeves, and nobody thought about saving them for later on down the road. I mean, they were put in your pocket, or you'd store the cards in boxes with rubber bands around a bunch of them. The first and last card always had rubber band marks. We also played games with our cards on a miniature baseball field we made in a grass area near school. We cut little base paths in the grass, and made a small fence out of old plywood that was about six inches tall to serve as the outfield wall. Home plate to the leftfield and rightfield walls was about ten feet. It was about thirteen feet from home to dead center. We put the cards of the players on the field, according to the ballplayer's actual position in real life: Spahn's card would go on the mound, Joe Garagiola's card behind the plate, Rizzuto's card at shortstop, Monte Irvin's card in the outfield, and so on. The pitcher would

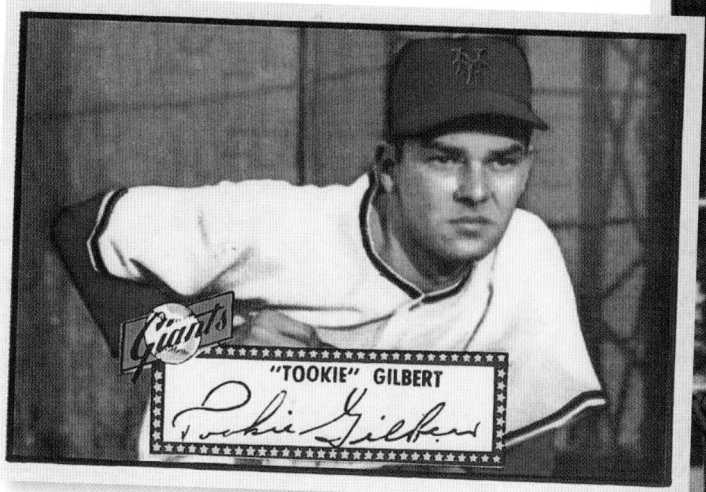

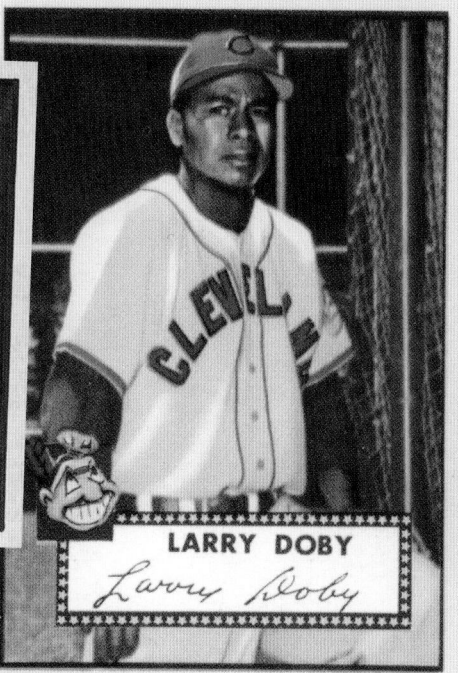

"TOOKIE" GILBERT

LARRY DOBY

GUS ZERNIAL

toss a marble to the batter who used a bat that was a little bigger than a pencil. Play was determined by where the marble landed: if it landed within one hand-span of the outfielder, he caught it; if the marble landed at a slightly lesser distance from an infielder, you assumed he made the play. If it went over the fence, it was a home run. The cards had grit and sand all over them from being out there, particularly the ones that featured the star ballplayers.

"We also traded cards. I would ride around town on a bicycle with a wad of '52 Topps duplicates in my hip pocket, looking for a neighbor who might have a card of somebody for someone I didn't have. You know, like a Robin Roberts for an Allie Reynolds, or Ted Kluszewski for a Bob Feller. The biggest trade I ever made happened in '54. Tookie Gilbert, who was a New York Giant first baseman, was the last card I needed to complete my '52 Topps set of cards #1 to #310. For two years, I had never even seen the card. I finally found a kid who had one, and I offered him a dozen other cards for it. He wasn't interested. I learned he was a St. Louis Cardinals fanatic, but he had no Stan Musial card. None of us knew at the time whether Musial existed in the '52 Topps set because there was no checklist to go by. Well, I managed to find a Musial card from the '54 Red Heart Dog Food set. It took about half a second for the kid to give me Tookie for Musial.

"Fifty-seven was about the last of the years that I ever collected as a boy. By then, I was a sophomore in high school playing sports, and while I still wanted to collect, I wasn't sure it was cool enough to do at that

Tookie Gilbert was the only card Merkel needed to complete his '52 Topps set of cards #1 to #310.

Three months after Jackie Robinson broke major league baseball's color barrier, Larry Doby broke the color barrier in the American League on July 5, 1947. The seven-time All-Star was the AL home run champion in 1952 and '54 and helped lead the Cleveland Indians to a World Series victory (1948) and AL pennant (1954).

One of the more interesting images in the '52 Topps set is that of Gus Zernial, who trailed only Mickey Mantle, Yogi Berra, and Larry Doby in AL home runs in the 1950s.

point. Wasn't sure what the girls would think. So for a period there, I stopped collecting cards. When I went off to college, I didn't want to throw them away, so I stored them in shoeboxes and put them up in the attic.

"I did a lot of litigation in other cities and states when I became a trial lawyer. I guess somewhere around the mid-'70s, I was in Florida for a deposition in an outlying area of Miami. There was a strip mall nearby with a card shop in it. While I was killing time during the noon hour waiting for court to re-adjourn, I went browsing around, and there was a price guide in the store. I think at that time they showed that the '52 Topps set was worth $8,000 in near mint condition. I had no clue what 'near mint' meant, but I was amazed that people were paying that kind of money for cards. The next time I went home where my parents were living, up to the attic I went and dug through the shoeboxes. Sure enough there were my cards, just like they had been when I put them away eighteen years earlier.

"In 1980, when my son was about eight, I started putting together some sets of current card issues with him. It didn't kick in with him like it had with me, but he was interested long enough that I began collecting again. When we would go to the card shop to buy the new cards that he was putting into sets, I would spend my time looking at the older vintage cards: like the 1915 Cracker Jacks with their gorgeous cherry-red colored background, the '33 and '34 Goudeys with their incredible

detailed artwork, the '33 Delongs and the '34 Diamond Stars with their 'art-deco feel,' the '41 Playballs with their rainbow of pastel colors, the '48 Leafs with their toned, unrefined characteristics, and all the Bowman and Topps cards of the early '50s, with their mind-blowing designs and breadth of colors.

"All through the '80s, I started to add to my card collection that had been stored in the attic for all those years. I took my time at first; I wasn't paying much attention to finding the really rare, big-ticket, high-conditioned cards, or the crown jewels, if you will. I was just trying to find a few princes here and there amongst the frogs. But by the early '90s, I kicked it into high gear, and my collection really started to take off—I started focusing more on rarity by building sets with the best conditioned cards I could find.

"This process was facilitated by the folks over at a third-party card-grading service called Professional Sports Authenticator, better known as 'PSA.' They developed a card-grading system whereby cards would be reviewed by experts, and then designated a grade from '1' to '10.' The cards would then be placed into a plastic holder with a label showing the card's grade, a '1' grade representing the worst grade possible, while the '10' grade being the best grade possible. What separates a '1' from a '10' is night and day—a card graded '1,' for example, would have very rounded corners, creases running through it, fading, and sometimes even sur-

At 6-foot-2 and 240 pounds, "Big Klu" (Ted Kluszewski), whose huge biceps and big forearms made him one of the most feared big-league sluggers during his prime, was an intimidating sight in the batter's box: In 10 of his 15 seasons he walked more often than he struck out.

"I'm not sure what the hell charisma is, but I get the feeling it's Willie Mays," Kluszewski once said. This popular card of the "Say Hey Kid" was issued after his inaugural year in the majors, in which he was named NL Rookie of the Year.

The breadth of colors used in the '52 Topps set, like the salmon-orange on the card of Dodger great Gil Hodges, is one of the reasons why this set is widely considered the most popular of the postwar era.

face abrasions. It basically would look like a truck ran over it. A '10,' on the other hand, would look like the card came right out of a pack, with needle-point-sharp corners, shiny gloss, perfect picture registration, and white-colored borders as bright as snow.

"This grading system has really helped to spot those cards that have been trimmed or re-colored by counterfeiters. You know, taking a medium grade card that would look like a '5' or '6,' and fixin' them up to look like an '8,' '9,' or '10.' Well, I didn't want to take any chances so I began focusing on buying only graded cards that earned an '8,' '9,' or '10.' In addition to helping me make sure I didn't buy any doctored cards, I figured the grading system would help establish a sense of scarcity value for the higher conditioned cards. Heck, anybody can find a '52 Topps Eddie Matthews card in a '5' or '6.' But try finding one in a '9.'

"The advent of card grading was certainly not the reason why I became more serious about card collecting. It happened after I experienced something almost as special as that wonderful day at Sportsman's Park back in 1952. It was entirely arranged by my lovely wife Donna. Well, Donna, of course, has known that I have been a baseball nut ever since she's known me. I played varsity ball at Ole Miss, and that's where we met. We were married, and then moved to Washington, D.C. for a few years. The Yanks would play a series there against the Orioles, and one of my old teammates from Ole Miss, Jake Gibbs, who was playing for the Yanks at the time, would come in to town. So, she sort of grew into it with me. I don't think she has ever understood the card business other than I'm a kid at heart who refused to grow up. But besides that, whatever I liked, she always made an effort to like it as well.

"So, on my 50th birthday in 1991 she handed me a packet that contained information for a week in Fort Lauderdale at the Yank's training facility there for the Mantle/Ford Fantasy Camp. Of course, the program suggested getting in some kind of shape, but at that point in time I probably hadn't really thrown a baseball with any purpose for over twenty years. But you could be sure as hell I was going to try.

"I went to Fort Lauderdale and met and played with Mickey, Whitey (Ford), Hank Bauer, Bill Skowran, Enos Slaughter, Johnny Blanchard, and Jake Gibbs, who were all counselors. We played ten games in five days, two games per day. And the Saturday after that, the campers played the Yanks. Just couldn't believe how much I enjoyed playing again after all that time. The counselors and the Yankee batting practice pitchers sort of determined what caliber of player you might be, and they pitched accordingly. I mean, if you were some guy that had never played real ball, they would lob it up there nice and slow. But if they could tell you had the good stuff, Whitey would throw the breaking ball, and he could still drop it off the table.

"Every night you'd sit around and have a few drinks and listen to them talk about the old days. Several things stood out. Number one, they were all tight family then. Mantle talked about his kids being babysat by kids of other players, and vice versa. They would go to the ballpark at 8:30 or 9:00 in the morning for an afternoon game, and then after the game they would sit around and play cards with the families, and then go out to dinner together. The affectionate feelings they shared with each other were just obvious. Very strong, very sincere.

"There were a ton of wild stories of all those antics that made the papers at the time. The papers didn't know anything compared to what these guys would tell you at the camp. There was one great story on the Mick. Whitey had pitched a Saturday game, and they had gone to the Copacabana after the game that night. They came out about midnight because they had a 1:00 P.M. game on Sunday. Since it was raining and Mick was on the disabled list, Whitey said, 'We've got no

BOBBY THOMSON

ED MATHEWS

"COOKIE" LAVAGETTO

Bobby Thomson certainly had a lot to smile about; just one season earlier he hit arguably the most celebrated home run in major-league history—the Shot Heard Round the World that sent the Giants to the 1951 Fall Classic. And perhaps Lavagetto broke a smile for Brooklyn Dodger fans to remind them of his game-winning double off the rightfield wall of Ebbets Field, which broke Bill Bevens's no-hitter in Game Four of the 1947 World Series.

The rookie card of the Braves' legendary slugger Eddie Mathews is considered one of the most difficult postwar cards to obtain in high-grade condition because, as the last card of the set, it typically underwent the same kind of abuse as that inflicted on the first card of a set.

reason to go home, so we can stay out longer. There's not going to be any game tomorrow because it'll be rained out.' So, they stayed till the wee hours of the morning, went home, got to bed, and a couple of hours later the phone rang. Somebody was telling them to get to the ballpark because it had cleared off and they were going to play.

"Whitey said they were sitting on the far end of the bench from Stengel, and in the ninth inning they were down by two. Mantle was sound asleep, snoring and leaning against Whitey. Stengel had two men on base, and yelled down the bench for Mantle to get at bat. Whitey said he had to hit Mantle in the side with his elbow to wake him up and shake him alert. Stengel said, 'Get a bat and get in there and hit for so and so.' Mantle said, 'Skip, I'm on the DL.' Stengel replied, 'No, you came off at midnight last night. Get a bat and get in there.'

"Mick took one pitch and hit the second one into the upper deck down the rightfield line, went around the bases, came into the dugout, and sat back down beside Whitey. Whitey said, 'How on earth did you do that?' Mick replied, 'Hell, slick, I just swung at the ball in the middle.'

"On the plane ride home after that week down in Ft. Lauderdale, I felt like I was on that bus again riding from Sportsman's Park back to the hotel. It was like a dream. And I just couldn't wait to get back to Clarksdale and pull out my cards."

1951 BOWMAN
MICKEY MANTLE
PSA
#253
MINT 9
01125125

VINTAGE BASEBALL CARDS
1915–70

BY KEVIN STRUSS AND STEPHEN WONG • FEATURING CARDS FROM THE CHARLES M. MERKEL COLLECTION

In many ways, baseball card collecting is the backbone of the sports memorabilia hobby. It represents the concept of "collecting" in its purest, most straightforward form. Baseball cards were made specifically to be assembled in a logical, progressive fashion. Generally, they carry numbers, and they come with checklists to enable the orderly recording of one's progress. Although some young consumers may buy the packs of cards to get the gum inside, in the end, every kid's goal is to complete that year's set of cardboard treasures.

Most of us can recall having had to trade a duplicate Mickey Mantle or Hank Aaron card to finally acquire an elusive Vic Wertz or Sam Mele. Thousands of kids all over America made similar, rea-soned sacrifices year after year. The cards came in waves, so that just as a collector finished completing one series, another would soon be out. Those enthusiasts who couldn't wait for the next season could bide their time pursuing football, hockey and occasional basketball sets. By the time smaller productions began to be issued with cereal, hot dogs, desserts, and even dog food, it seemed that a young collector's work was never done!

By the end of 1915, baseball inserts had all but disappeared from tobacco and food products. The second major era of baseball cards was over. Many of the sets from the 1920's were issued with candy. Most of these releases were black and white, and they often shared images with cards from other issues. Abundant

1951 Bowman Mickey Mantle (PSA 9): Let's just call it splendid serendipity that some of the game's all-time greatest stars were in their rookie season when Bowman reached its artistic peak in 1951. In addition to Willie Mays, Bowman signed up this young man from Commerce, Oklahoma. (2 1/16" x 3 1/8")

from this era are cards that were issued in exhibit machines and cards that were sold in dime stores in uncut "strips." These items tended to be very crude in design; they surely held less appeal for youngsters than the colorful cards from the decade before.

The 1930s, and specifically the year 1933, brought the onset of the third great era of baseball cards. Although quite a few manufacturers issued baseball cards along with their gum or candy, the Goudey Gum Company of Boston stole

COBB, Detroit - Americans

1915 Cracker Jack Ty Cobb (PSA 9): The Georgia Peach demonstrates his legendary split-handed grip on the bat, whereby he held his hands apart for better bat control. Faced with a difficult breaking ball, Cobb would drop down a bunt or poke the ball over the infield; given an easier pitch, he would slide his top hand down and swing away.

The back of each Cracker Jack card (right) contained a bio of the player. (1915 Cracker Jack cards: 2¼" x 3")

1915 Cracker Jack Joe Jackson (PSA 8, far right): Shoeless Joe Jackson is captured in his final season with the Cleveland Naps, with whom, between 1910 and 1914, his batting average ranged from .331 to a league-leading .408. In 1915, financially strapped Naps owner Charlie Somers traded Jackson to the White Sox. By decade's end, it would all end in tears for baseball's arguably greatest natural hitter.

30

Tyrus Raymond Cobb, center fielder of the Detroit American League team, was born December 18, 1886, at Royston, Ga. Cobb's professional career began in 1904, when he played for a short time with the Augusta Club of the South Atlantic League. He was purchased by Detroit in 1905. Since then he has been a regular member of the team, and is noted as a marvel for speed and batting.

This is one of a series of pictures of famous Ball Players and Managers in the American, National and Federal Leagues, given Free with Cracker Jack, "The Famous Popcorn Confection," one card in each package. Send 100 Cracker Jack Coupons, or 1 Coupon and 25c. to CHICAGO OFFICE for complete set of 176 Pictures. Handsome Album to hold full set of pictures sent postpaid for 50 Coupons, or 1 Coupon and 10c. in coin or stamps.
RUECKHEIM BROS. & ECKSTEIN
Brooklyn, N. Y.   Chicago, Ill.

The 1915 Cracker Jack set, one of the most beautiful and popular sets of the prewar era, was part of an effort by early 20th-century merchants to distribute baseball cards with products other than tobacco. These thin paper-stock cards were highly vulnerable to molasses stains and other damage from moving around inside the box. (An original Cracker Jack box that once included a card is shown here.) The cards in the montage are part of the highest-conditioned, complete set known to exist.

the show with a magnificent, 240-card set. Measuring 2 3/8" x 2 7/8", the cards were larger than any that most young collectors had ever seen. They were also exceptionally attractive. They were made by means of a silkscreen printing process that enabled the cards to have a wide range of colors (see pages 186–87), and they incorporated selected photographs of ballplayers, including many (such as Benny Bengough, Kiki Cuyler, Paul Waner, Babe Ruth, and Lou Gehrig) by the very talented Charles M. Conlon. The backs of the cards contained player biographies. Nearly every star of the day was represented, and the set's line-up included multi-

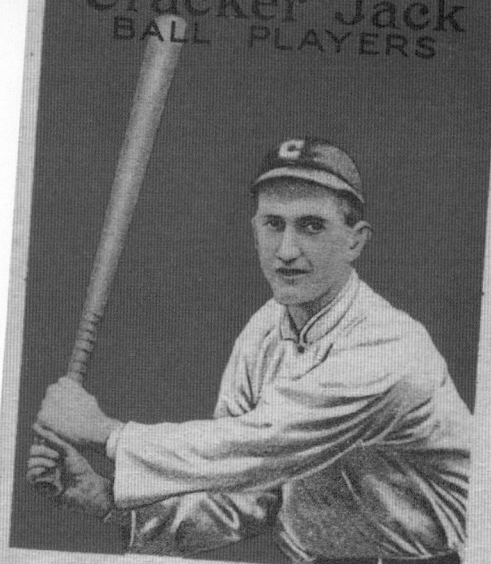

JOE JACKSON, Cleveland - Americans

"My generation knew nothing at all about baseball cards until 1933, when the Goudey Gum Company began issuing them with their gum," recalled author Robert W. Creamer. (1933 Goudey cards: 2⅜" x 2⅞") "You paid one cent for a flat packet wrapped in wax paper; inside were three sticks of bubblegum and a baseball card. The gum was important—I doubt we'd have paid a penny for the card alone—but the cards were desirable, no question about

that. They became our passion. We carried them in our pockets, used them to play games with, tossed them for distance, tossed them for accuracy, flipped them in turn, and captured our opponent's cards if ours landed on his." As shown by the cards of Ted Lyons, Joe Cronin, Rogers Hornsby, and the ones featured in the montage below, Goudey incorporated a rich spectrum of colors matched only by the T206 set of the early 20th century and the 1952 Topps. (PSA 8 and 9)

ple cards of such "big name" players as Dizzy Dean, Jimmie Foxx, and Lefty Grove. Each card carried a number on its reverse side, and each pack contained a note informing one and all that there were 240 cards in the series. In fact, there were only 239. Card #106 was missing from every collection. Goudey had intentionally omitted it in order to send every child in America on a wild-goose chase. Judging from the success of the set— they were so popular that Goudey had to truck the gum to a warehouse so that 300 women could hand wrap the packages—the move was pure marketing genius! In response to complaints from collectors, Goudey finally issued #106 with its 1934 cards and sent an example by mail to those who

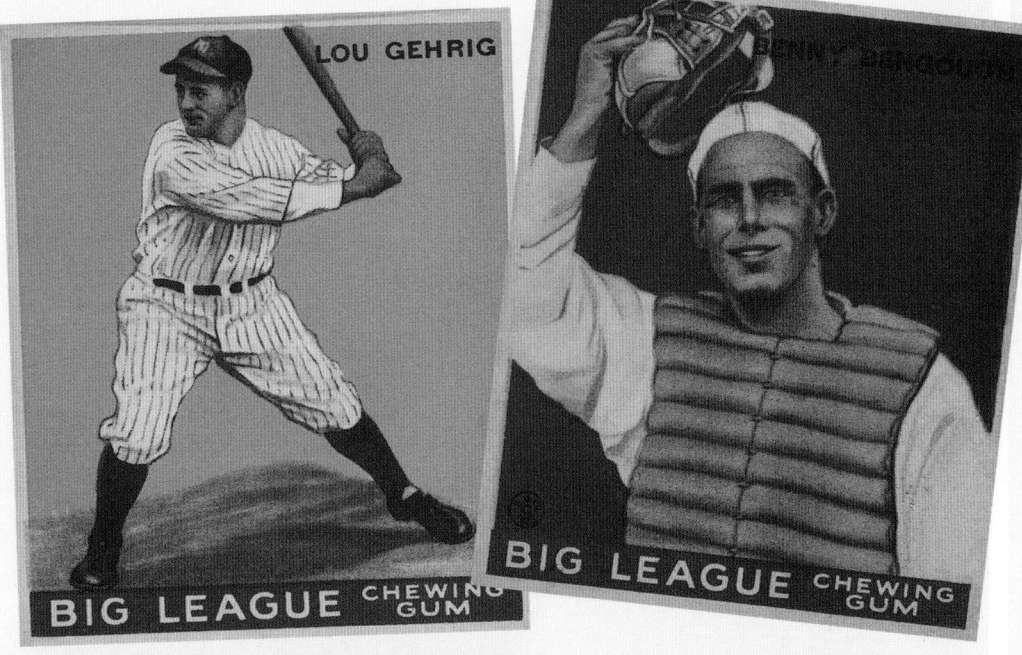

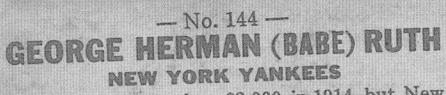

— No. 144 —

GEORGE HERMAN (BABE) RUTH

NEW YORK YANKEES

Cost Red Sox less than $3,000 in 1914, but New York Yankees paid about $125,000 for him six years later. Stepped from industrial school in Baltimore to minor league ball and went to big league in less than a year.

Was star pitcher for several years, but now plays in outfield. Holds big league home run record, 60, made in 1927. Led American League in batting in 1924. Last year batted .341 and hit 41 homers.

Is 39 years old, six feet, two inches tall and weighs 210. Bats and throws left handed.

This is one of a series of 240 Baseball Stars

BIG LEAGUE

CHEWING GUM

GOUDEY GUM CO.   BOSTON

Made by the originators of

INDIAN GUM

When it came to the game's biggest sluggers, Goudey stuck with the work of photographic master Charles M. Conlon, who took both of these full-body images of the Bambino (top, left) and the Iron Horse (top, middle) in 1927 and 1930, respectively. These two cards are among the most popular of all prewar card issues and the Gehrig card (#92), in particular, which has been graded "Gem Mint 10" by PSA, is the highest-conditioned example of this card known to exist. (Ruth card #144, PSA 8)

1933 Goudey Benny Bengough (PSA 9): Although Benny Bengough was only a second-string catcher throughout his career, his name will continue to resonate in the annals of card collecting. As card #1 in the 1933 Goudey set, his permanent place of residence was on top of the stack, carefully protecting the cards of Ruth, Gehrig, Foxx, and Hubbell. His job took its toll over the years, absorbing all the abuse. Shuffled from box to box, bound with corrosive rubber bands, touched first by sticky thumbs and fingers, Bengough was the lid to the treasure chest of 1933 Goudeys. Somehow, this example miraculously escaped the ravages of time: it has been graded in mint condition.

1933 Goudey Napoleon Lajoie (PSA 9): Responding to widespread complaints that the 1933 Goudey set was missing card #106, Goudey printed this legendary card (which contains a 1933-style back) in its 1934 series, and then mailed it to all those who filed a complaint. The card's background contains a silhouette of a baseball diamond and players in action, which was a distinct design in the 1934 Goudey set. It remains a mystery as to why Napoleon Lajoie was chosen for card #106. This is one of only three examples of this card graded in flawless mint condition by PSA.

had requested it. The long-awaited #106 pictured retired Dead Ball–era great Napoleon Lajoie and is now one of the scarcest and most expensive cards in the hobby. Goudey went on to produce several more card sets over the next eight seasons, of which the most notable were the 1934 "Lou Gehrig Says" and "Chuck Klein Says" series and the 1938 "Heads Up" cartoon cards, but none of the later offerings was as popular as the first Goudey issue.

Another significant group of sets, known as the "Play Ball" series, was issued by Gum, Inc. between 1939 and 1941. The 1939 and 1940 sets featured black-and-white photographs and were distinguished by a stellar selection of players that included Ted Williams (on his "rookie" card) and a very young Joe DiMaggio. The company's 1941 offering, with just 72 cards, is one of the most sought-after of all baseball card series. All of the cards are in full color, and they are among the most beautiful cards ever produced. Unfortunately, the shortage of paper during World War II brought about an early end to trading-card manufacturing. Not only were almost no new cards introduced, but many existing collections fell victim to the urgency of the time's patriotically inspired paper drives. World War II has become an informal line of

PEPPER MARTIN, ST. LOUIS CARDINALS

ROBERT (LEFTY) GROVE, PHILADELPHIA ATHLETICS

No. 23, THROWING THE FAST BALL

Few pitchers in major league history have had Lefty Grove's speed. Lefty is an overhand pitcher who makes the most of his six feet height. Legs, body, arms, wrists and fingers go into throwing the fast ball, and not the least of these is the wrist and fingers which impart the final snap. A good fast ball will have a slight rise or upward curve as it approaches the plate, perhaps less than an inch, that is called the "hop." It causes batsmen to pop the ball into the air. However, boys should avoid overworking their arms.

—By Austen Lake,
Baseball Editor, Boston Transcript.

This is one of a continuing series of famous major league players. Each card with a different tip on inside baseball. More sport series to follow.

PLAY BALL GUM is as pure and as fine quality as any made — contains real chicle.

Copyright 1933
DeLong Gum Co.

DeLONG GUM COMPANY,
Boston, Mass.

1933 DeLong Pepper Martin and Lefty Grove (both PSA 8): Harold C. DeLong, who had served as treasurer for the Goudey Gum Company, formed the DeLong Gum Company in Boston and issued a set of 24 baseball cards in 1933. Given the set's relatively small size and limited distribution, it remains as one of the rarest pre-war issues. The set includes 15 Hall of Famers. Each card features a black-and-white player photograph against a color depiction of a ballpark. (1933 DeLong cards: 2" x 3")

Instead of player bios, the backs of DeLong cards provided tips on how to play the game written by Austen Lake, who was an editor at the *Boston Transcript*.

In 1934, Goudey followed its milestone 1933 issue with this beautiful set of 96 cards (below, 2⅜" x 2⅞"), whose stunning artwork was on a par with that of the 1933 issue. Cards #1–72 include a small picture of Gehrig in the bottom border area, along with the scripted words, "Lou Gehrig says. . ." The back of each card contains a brief player summary written by Gehrig. Chuck Klein, the 1933 National League Triple Crown winner, prepared the player summaries on the backs of cards #73–96. His image appears in the bottom border area on the front of these cards. Two albums (shown here) were also available: one to store cards of National League players and the other for cards of American League players.

JOE DI MAGGIO, Yankees

"HANK" GREENBURG

"DOM" DI MAGGIO

"TED" WILLIAMS

Subsequent sets issued by Goudey never matched the aesthetic pinnacle of their 1933 and 1934 issues. Nevertheless, the 1938 "Heads-Up" variety (2⅜" x 2⅞") earned some acclaim for innovation because of the background cartoons which were featured on some of the cards. In addition, Goudey packed the set with a galaxy of notable stars including Joe DiMaggio (far left), Bob Feller, Charlie Gehringer, and Jimmy Foxx. (PSA 8).

Between 1934 and 1936, the National Chicle Products Company issued a baseball card set called "Diamond Stars," which featured distinctive art-deco artwork. During its three-year period of issue, National Chicle used the same images on the front of the cards but different statistics were applied to the reverse. Included among the several Hall of Fame legends whose cards came in this set was a misspelled Hank Greenberg card (left, 2⅜" x 2⅞"). (PSA 8)

14. THEODORE SAMUEL WILLIAMS

Outfielder   Boston Red Sox

Born: San Diego, Cal.   October 30, 1918
Bats: Left   Throws: Right
Height: 6' 3"   Weight: 175 lbs.

Ted Williams proved last year that he was no flash-in-the-pan as one of the outstanding rookies of 1939. He batted a powerful .344, brought in 113 runs and led the league in runs scored for the Boston Red Sox with 134. His drives included 23 home runs, 14 triples and 43 two-base hits, with a total of 193 safe blows. He also improved his fielding percentage by 15 points. An enthusiastic ball player who would rather wield a bat than eat, Williams looms as one of the great hitters of modern times.

PLAY BALL
Sports Hall of Fame
Also ask for BLONY Super Bubble Gum, "the sweet that lasts longer."
© 1941   GUM, INC., Phila., Pa.   PRINTED IN U. S. A.

demarcation in the hobby; today baseball cards are typically categorized as "prewar" or "postwar."

The first postwar set arrived in 1948. Produced by Bowman Gum, Inc., the direct descendent of Gum, Inc., these black-and-white cards were sold in one-cent packs and were not very visually appealing. Subsequently, Bowman remedied this problem. Its 1951 issue is extremely attractive and includes the rookie cards of Willie Mays and Mickey Mantle. Although Leaf Gum, Inc. briefly challenged Bowman in 1948 by

issuing a 100-card set in color, the company faced little competition until Topps Chewing Gum Company of Brooklyn entered the market in 1951. At first, Bowman must have felt quite secure in its market position, since Topps' 1951 cards were physically unimpressive and evidently not too popular with the kids of the day—they didn't even come with bubble gum! But Topps fought back in 1952 with oversized, "giant" cards that surely caught Bowman by surprise. The cards from Topps' 1952 set are generally considered to be

among the most majestic in design, and the most important, of all postwar sets. (See interview with Charles M. Merkel in this chapter.) They were offered in both one-cent and five-cent packages, establishing pack prices that would be maintained for some time. The 1952 series includes the first Topps card of Mickey Mantle, which is now the most sought-after card in the postwar segment of the hobby (see Chapter VIII, "The Marshall Fogel Collection"). Making the Topps cards even more striking was the fact that they

1941 Play Ball Dom DiMaggio (PSA 9) and Ted Williams (PSA 8): Two avatars of the 1940s Red Sox are beautifully depicted on these two Play Ball cards issued by Gum, Inc. in 1941. One card and two sticks of "Blony Super Bubble Gum" came in each wax pack. This would be the last great baseball card set of the pre-war era. Not until nearly a decade later would the artwork and production quality of baseball cards match that of the 1941 Play Ball issue and major sets from the 1930s. (2½" x 3⅛")

1949 Bowman Satchel Paige (PSA 9): After its 1948 black-and-white card issue failed to excite America's youngsters, Bowman added color in 1949. The breadth of colors used in the printing process was still inferior to the Goudeys, Diamond Stars, and Play Balls of the past, and the printing process also resulted in poor image registration on a number of cards. But Bowman's selection of ballplayers was right on the money. This card of the great Satchel Paige, which features him in only his second year in the majors, is one of the most important cards in the set. (2¹⁄₁₆″ x 2½″)

In addition to player bios, the backs of some card sets like 1949 Bowman included advertisements for premium prizes such as metal baseball rings.

1950 Bowman Jackie Robinson (PSA 8): Bowman finally got the aesthetic appeal right with its 1950 card issue. Here is perhaps one of the most beautiful cards in the set—Jackie Robinson at the end of his swing. (2¹⁄₁₆″ x 2½″)

1948 Leaf Babe Ruth (PSA 9): During the summer of 1948, America witnessed the sad deterioration of the Bambino's health from throat cancer. His passing in August of that year left a void in the game's spirit that Leaf Gum Company of Chicago addressed with dignity. Ruth took his place, right where he still belonged, with Joe DiMaggio and Ted Williams, Stan Musial, and Jackie Robinson, and thus continued, for that one, additional season, to be the focal point for the country's vast population of card collectors. (2⅜″ x 2⅞″)

quarters. Additionally, the company created such auxiliary offerings as baseball stamps, pins, tattoos, rub-offs, discs, game cards, and over-sized cards. A determined Topps, almost alone, controlled the market until 1981, when a 1980 antitrust court decision allowed Fleer and Donruss to enter the market. Today, there are literally hundreds of card manufacturers, but Topps is still one of the industry's leaders.

Many adults were re-introduced to card collecting when their offspring began to acquire newly issued, unopened packs. Their children's excitement reminded them of their own childhood collections. Some people are lucky enough to have retained the cards from their youth, but most lost their collections along the way. In countless cases, Mom had tossed the treasures into the garbage can. This was not short-sighted as it may seem in retrospect, since baseball cards typically weren't collected on the basis of intrinsic value; the cards had none. Collecting was simply a hobby, something that all the other kids on the block were doing.

Initially, most collectors try to replicate their childhood collections, and then they start to work their way backward in time, moving on to acquire

measured 2⅜″ x 3¾″ in size, more than 50% larger than Bowman's cards. Even the most loyal Bowman customers must have been awestruck by the sheer size and beauty of the new Topps cards. The large format would remain as Topps' standard through 1956. In its continued attempts to compete, Bowman was compelled to upsize its own cards in 1953 (see card of Yogi Berra, opposite). The two companies' fierce rivalry between 1953 and 1955 gave the hobby several spectacular card sets, but it came to an end when Topps purchased its longtime adversary in early 1956. Thus, Topps began to enjoy the fruits

of a virtual baseball card monopoly that it would retain for a number of years.

In 1957, Topps changed the dimensions of its baseball cards once more to 2½″ x 3½″. The new size found wide acceptance and remains the "universal standard" today (see pages 192–93). Topps sets also became bigger and came to include special items such as Highlights, League Leaders, and All-Star cards. In 1968, Topps also experimented with a set of unique 3-D cards. But due to their high cost of production, the cards were distributed only to a handful of Brooklyn-based candy stores near the Topps company head-

gum cards of legendary star players, such as Babe Ruth and Lou Gehrig, whom they never saw in action but always idolized through books and magazine articles. A bit more research leads collectors to the wonderful tobacco cards, featuring the likes of Ty Cobb and Christy Mathewson. Others begin to reach even further back to the amazing cards of the 19th century. No matter which period one chooses, there are many sets to collect.

Unlike during the fondly-remembered times of childhood, however, it takes considerably more than a penny or nickel to add cards to one's

ED "WHITEY" FORD

JOHN PODRES
pitcher BROOKLYN DODGERS

collection. As with all collectibles, a card's market value is determined by a variety of factors, most notably condition, rarity and popularity. A perfect specimen of Mickey Mantle's 1952 Topps card can sell for a six-figure price, while a beat-up Vic Wertz card would be lucky to bring a dollar or two. Even two identical cards can vary greatly in value, if their condition varies greatly.

The advent of third-party sports-card professional authentication and grading services within the last ten years has taken much of the guesswork out of evaluating a card's condition. Prior to the advent of third-party services, there was an inherent conflict of interest, since the seller of a card was tempted to overstate its condition, and the buyer had the same incentive to downgrade it. Most of the sports-card grading services rate cards on a 1-through-10 scale. While grading is still subjective, and the beauty of a card continues to be judged by the eye of the beholder, professional grading companies have helped to even the playing field so that novices need not be grading experts in order to enjoy the hobby. There are now dozens of grading services. A few, such as Professional Sports Authenticator (PSA), Sportscard Guaranty Corporation (SGC) and Global Authentication Inc. (GAI) are

the field's clear leaders. Their services enable hobbyists to purchase cards with more confidence than before, since an unbiased party has assigned the grade to the card.

Another benefit of third-party grading services is their ability to allow collectors to ascertain the relative quality of their collections. The grading services compile Population Reports that state how many of each card in a particular grade have been authenticated. They also maintain Set Registries, which allow hobbyists to display their collecting achievements by listing the cards that they own, along with the cards' grades. For each collection, an average grade can be calculated to facilitate a comparison between one's sets and those of other collectors. Because of the Set Registries, collecting has become very competitive, and the quest to have the "#1" set of any particular issue can be a difficult but satisfying task.

There is no "right" or "wrong" way to collect. Some people prefer to concentrate on quantity rather than quality, but most of the significant collections have emphasized the latter. Complete set collecting is the most popular way to organize cards, but many hobbyists focus on teams or specific players. Others are happy to locate a single card from as many sets as possible. There are countless variations on these themes so one can con-

1951 Bowman Whitey Ford (PSA 8): Casey Stengel once said of Whitey Ford, "If you had one game to win and your life depended on it, you'd want him to pitch it." Ford earned the highest winning percentage of the 20th century (.690) with 236 wins and only 106 losses. His numbers in the postseason were just as spectacular: Ford's 32 consecutive scoreless innings in World Series play broke Babe Ruth's record of 29⅔ innings, and he holds the most Fall Classic victories (10) and strikeouts (94). Although Ford won nine games for the Yankees in the 1950 season, this 1951 card is the first one ever issued of him. (1951–52 Bowman cards: 2 1/16″ x 3 1/8″)

In 1952, Bowman added facsimile signatures of the players to the cards and maintained its high-quality production standards, as shown by the card of Stan "The Man" Musial. (PSA 9)

Topps's 1953 set featured breathtaking hand-drawn artwork that create the appearance of miniature-sized watercolor paintings (see Johnny Podres card, 2⅝″ x 3¾″)

In response to competition from Topps, in 1953, Bowman issued the first baseball card set ever to feature actual color photographs (see card of Yogi Berra). In addition to also increasing its card size to 2½″ x 3¾″, Bowman included player statistics on the cards' reverse for the first time. (PSA 9)

As shown on the 1952 Topps card of Joe Garagiola, Topps included team logos as part of the cards' design.

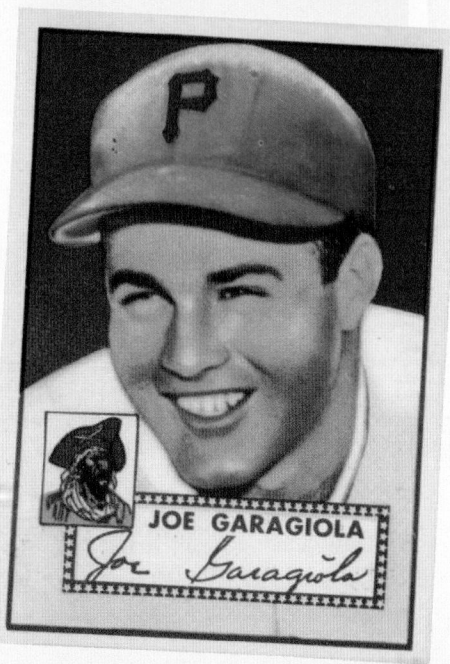

JOE GARAGIOLA

BROOKS Robinson
BALTIMORE ORIOLES   3rd B.

1

WORLD SERIES BATTING FOES
MICKEY MANTLE • HANK AARON

2

bob gibson

Robert Gibson

ST. LOUIS CARDINALS
PITCHER

3

BILL MAZEROSKI   Pittsburgh
Second Base   Pirates

6

1962
ROOKIE

LOU
BROCK
CHICAGO CUBS   OF

7

SANDY
KOUFAX
L. A. DODGERS   PITCHER

8

struct a collection on almost any budget.

Baseball cards can be obtained through a wide variety of sources. Hobby publications have existed for over sixty years and allow dealers to advertise their inventories and collectors to communicate with each other through classified ads. Baseball card conventions are also very popular; nearly every major city hosts several shows a year. The Internet has allowed collectors to trade among themselves easily and dealers to advertise relatively inexpensively. Numerous price guides have been published to assist collectors in determining values of cards (but as their name indicates, they are only guides). The majority of the hobby's significant cards are sold through auctions. Auctions range from those conducted on eBay to auctions held in high-end venues that specialize in sports cards and memorabilia. Auctions are a very efficient way to advance a collection or sell one's holdings, since they allow bidders to decide exactly what an item is worth at a given point in time. And, as always, a piece's true worth is represented by the price that an actual buyer is willing to pay.

Baseball card collecting is one of the nation's most widespread hobbies for a number of reasons. Financially, quality baseball cards have generally proven to be very good investments over the years. But ultimately, collecting needs to be fun, and this is where our hobby excels. Card collecting is a pur-

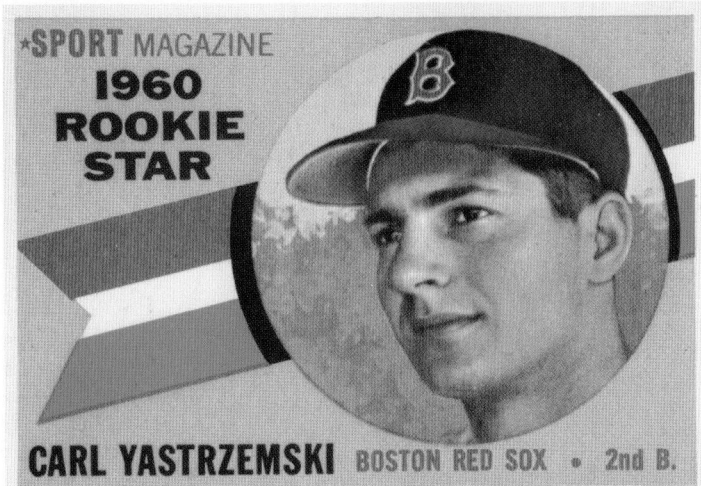

4

5

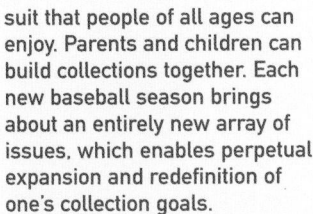

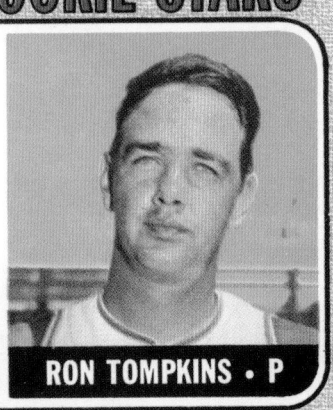

9

10

12

11

suit that people of all ages can enjoy. Parents and children can build collections together. Each new baseball season brings about an entirely new array of issues, which enables perpetual expansion and redefinition of one's collection goals.

Even though other niches of the sports memorabilia hobby may be more glamorous or exotic, the fact is that baseball cards are the impetus for most major collections. Perennially collectable by their design and by their nature, cards can be appreciated by virtually everyone.

In 1957, Topps switched to a slightly smaller card size of 2½″ x 3½″, which has remained the standard size of baseball cards ever since. Here is an assortment of Topps cards which should stir fond memories for those who collected cards from the late 1950s through 1970.

1. 1957 Topps Brooks Robinson

2. 1958 Topps World Series Batting Foes

3. 1959 Topps Bob Gibson

4. 1960 Topps Carl Yastrzemski

5. 1960 Topps Willie McCovey

6. 1961 Topps Bill Mazeroski

7. 1962 Topps Lou Brock

8. 1963 Topps Sandy Koufax

9. 1965 Topps Pete Rose

10. 1968 Topps Rookie Stars (Johnny Bench and Ron Tompkins)

11. 1968 Topps "3-D" Roberto Clemente, a test issue whose only known public distribution took place in a few Brooklyn candy stores close to the Topps Company headquarters.

12. 1970 Topps Nolan Ryan

14

TOKENS OF YOUTH

After eight distinguished seasons playing in the Negro Leagues, Roy Campanella became the first black catcher in major-league history when he joined the Brooklyn Dodgers in 1948. Between 1951 and 1955, he won three National League MVP Awards. The one shown here along with his game-used catcher's mitt was his last. Campy's playing career was tragically cut short by a car accident in 1958, which permanently paralyzed his arms and legs. On May 7, 1959, the Dodgers and New York Yankees hosted "Roy Campanella Night," which included a special tribute exhibition game at Los Angeles Memorial Coliseum, where the largest crowd in major-league history (93,103) turned out to honor the Dodger hero. (Dimension of trophy is 16" in diameter.)

" There's always the temptation to try that one more year, to see if you can wind up the clock again. But you find out soon enough that it's a game where youth dominates. You remember when you came up yourself, full of springtime, and pushed somebody else aside. So you have to be philosophical about it. You'd better be."
—TED KLUSZEWSKI,
Cincinnati Reds (1947–1957), on retirement from major-league baseball

The impressive Ron Leff Family Collection of trophies begins with artifacts from the early 20th century, when manufacturers and merchants sought to capitalize on baseball's popularity by incorporating its images and information into their advertising (see Chapter IV, "The Gary Cypres Collection"). In exchange for additional publicity, many companies offered money or products to players who achieved certain milestones. The American Tobacco Company, for example, awarded $50 to each batter who hit the company's Bull Durham signs, which were displayed on the outfield fences of a number of ballparks across the country. The Allmann Shop in Brooklyn offered a free pair of Stetson shoes to any player who hit its sign painted on the outfield wall of Washington Park, home of the Brooklyn Superbas (later renamed the Dodgers) between 1898 and 1912. In 1910, Hugh Chalmers, president of Chalmers Motor Company of

BATTING CHAMPION 1954
NATIONAL LEAGUE
B.A. 345

GENUINE
WILLIE H MAYS
LOUISVILLE SLUGGER

"There have been only two geniuses in the world," actress Tallulah Bankhead once said. "Willie Mays and Willie Shakespeare. But, darling, I think you'd better put Shakespeare first." With 3,283 lifetime hits (11th of all time), and 560 home runs (fourth of all time), Mays was certainly a genius at the plate. Surprisingly, the 34-inch-long award above is the only Silver Bat that Mays ever won during his magnificent career.

Detroit laid the foundation for major-league baseball's official Most-Valuable Player Award when he announced that he would donate one of the company's automobiles to the player with the highest batting average in the major leagues. But the award's first year generated as much controversy as promotional publicity.

Toward the end of the 1910 season, Napoleon Lajoie was battling Ty Cobb for the Chalmers Award. Lajoie began Cleveland's season-ending doubleheader, against the St. Louis Browns, batting .376, while Cobb, whose average stood at .383, chose to sit out his team's last two games rather than risk his average. This decision was both unsporting and unwise, since Cobb was already detested by almost everyone in the league. Apparently out of spite for Cobb, Browns manager Jack O'Connor ordered his third baseman, Red Corriden, to play deep, near the outfield grass, so that Lajoie could drop down bunts all day to surpass Cobb's batting average. Lajoie, for his part, accepted the questionable gift, going 8 for 8 in the twin bill, with six bunt singles and one hit after a dubious scoring decision on a

wild throw by the St. Louis shortstop. O'Connor was fired following the charade, and Cobb won the title anyway, by one percentage point, after AL president Ban Johnson announced that the official records had contained a "discrepancy" and that Cobb's average was actually higher than Lajoie's. Not wanting to stir further controversy, Chalmers awarded cars to both Cobb and Lajoie. The following year, Chalmers announced that he would give the award to the player in each league whom a panel of sportswriters identified as "the most important and useful player to his club." (The Cobb-Lajoie controversy has a postscript: In 1981, researchers uncovered evidence indicating that the batting title should have gone to Lajoie. Bowie Kuhn's commissioner's committee voted to leave the mistake uncorrected.)

The Chalmers Award lasted only until 1914, but its spirit was revived in 1922 with the American League Award, which was given to one player in each

league who was "of greatest all-around service to his club." League officials chose one sportswriter from each city in the league to vote on the award. The National League followed suit, though with a different method of selection, in 1924. But a combination of fan disinterest, wrongheaded eligibility rules and credibility problems led to the demise of both awards by 1930.

In December of that year, the Baseball Writers Association of America (BBWAA)

One season after Mickey Mantle (opposite, middle, with Ralph Terry, left, and Tom Tresh, right) and Roger Maris electrified the nation with their celebrated 1961 home-run derby, Mantle continued his offensive blitz with the league's highest on-base and slugging percentages, the second highest batting average (.321), and 30 home runs, all of which convinced sportswriters to crown him with his third MVP Award. (16" diameter)

reinstituted the award that Chalmers had started, and ushered in what became the current MVP Award. It appointed a committee of sportswriters for each league to select a "most valuable player." Up until 1937, each committee consisted of one sportswriter from each city represented in that league. The number of sportswriters from each city increased to three from 1938 to 1960; in 1961, it was reduced to two. Each sportswriter nominated and ranked up to 10 players. A first-place vote earned a player 14 points, a second-place vote was worth nine points, and a 10th-place vote counted for one point. The player with the most points after the voting won the BBWAA Most Valuable Player Award.

Presented to one player in each league on an annual basis, the BBWAA Most Valuable Player Award represents the pinnacle of player achievement for a single season and is widely regarded as the most coveted award bestowed on a major-league player. Since 1945, the winner of the BBWAA Most Valuable Player Award in each league has received the Kenesaw Mountain Landis Memorial Baseball Award trophy, named in honor of major-league baseball's first commissioner. The Ron Leff Family Collection, started by Ron and his two sons, Andy and Mitchell, includes two examples of this trophy, which are pictured at left and on page 195. One was awarded to Brooklyn Dodgers catcher Roy Campanella in 1955, when Brooklyn won its first and only World Series. The other trophy went to Mickey Mantle for the 1962 season, in which he helped the Yankees win their seventh World Series since his rookie season in 1951. Campanella and Mantle each won this prestigious award three times. (Only six other players can claim that distinction: Jimmie Foxx, Joe DiMaggio, Yogi Berra, Stan Musial, Mike Schmidt, and Barry Bonds.) The trophies in

the Leff collection are black circular plates made of wood, with an inlaid plaque of sterling silver and 10-karat gold components. The trophies came directly from the players' family estates.

Despite the tepid interest fans had shown in the League Award, leading equipment manufacturers became convinced in the late 1940s and 1950s that sponsoring annual awards given to individual players for outstanding achievements would be an effective advertising platform. Starting in 1949, Hillerich & Bradsby Co. (H&B), maker of the famous Louisville Slugger brand baseball bat, bestowed the Silver Bat award on the player in each league who earned the highest season batting average. The Silver Bats weighed approximately 56 ounces and measured 34 inches in length. They were sterling plated, with the H&B company logo, the player's name, and his batting average engraved on the barrel. H&B officials presented the bats to the winning players at their home ballparks. The Ron Leff Family Collection includes the Silver Bat awarded to Willie Mays in 1954, arguably the best season of Mays's illustrious career. That year, in addition to achieving the National League's highest batting average (.345) and winning the league's Most Valuable Player Award, Mays led the New York Giants to a World Series sweep over the Cleveland Indians. These feats are especially remarkable when you consider that Mays had not played the previous two seasons because he was serving in the Army.

In 1957, Rawlings Sporting Goods of St. Louis established the Rawlings Gold Glove Award to recognize excellence in fielding. The company convened a panel of sportswriters to select the major leagues' most outstanding defensive players in each position. In 1958, players, not sportswriters, began voting for a player from each position in both leagues. In 1965, the selection process changed again, with managers and coaches from each team in both leagues taking over the voting for Gold Glove Award recipients. This process continues today. As the examples

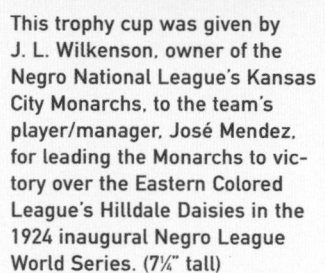

This trophy cup was given by J. L. Wilkenson, owner of the Negro National League's Kansas City Monarchs, to the team's player/manager, José Mendez, for leading the Monarchs to victory over the Eastern Colored League's Hilldale Daisies in the 1924 inaugural Negro League World Series. (7¼" tall)

at right illustrate, the Gold Glove Award features a gold-finished leather glove mounted on a three-tiered walnut stand with the player's face imprinted on a plate above a second plate engraved with the player's name and the year of the award.

Some of major league baseball's most visually distinctive trophies commemorate World Series victories and player milestones. One example is the 12-inch replica of a much larger trophy commemorating the Oakland Athletics' 1972 World Series title. The replica trophy—produced by world-renowned jeweler Balfour—was presented to an Athletics front office executive. These replica World Series trophies have been produced for individual players, including Roberto Alomar and Mickey Rivers (their trophies are pictured on page 200). The gold-plated pennants on the Series trophies are each inscribed with the name of a major-league franchise—every one is represented—and they encircle a silver baseball affixed with a gold band. A golden crown sits above the ball, and a pair of World Series press pins representing the two teams playing in the Series rests in front of the ball.

The 43-inch wooden trophy on page 201 was presented by National League president Charles "Chub" Feeney to Ernie Banks after Banks hit his 500th career home run on May 12, 1970, at Wrigley Field. The 13-time All Star and two-time National League Most Valuable Player became only the ninth player in major-league history to reach the 500-homer plateau. Two plaques at the base of the trophy detail each of Banks's 500 home runs. This is one of only a few 500-home-run trophies known to exist in private collections.

Some trophies in the Leff Family Collection are aesthetically unassuming, but breathtaking in terms of historical significance. From afar, the engraved areas on the seven-inch trophy on this page are hard to decipher through 80 years of tarnish on the silver. A closer inspection reveals that Kansas City Monarchs' owner J. L. Wilkenson pre-

Mike Schmidt led the National League in home runs a record eight times (only Babe Ruth led his league more often) and knocked out 30 or more homers in a season 13 times, a feat surpassed only by Hank Aaron. But Schmidt's glove was as mighty as his bat: he won 10 Gold Gloves (the one shown at left being his first), more than any other third baseman except for Brooks Robinson. (16½" x 17" x 6½")

At left is the last of five Gold Gloves won by the legendary San Diego Padre centerfielder Tony Gwynn. (16½" x 17" x 6½")

Fresh from the triumph of his second World Series championship, Steve Carlton of the Philadelphia Phillies captured his first and only Gold Glove in 1981 (right), to complement the three Cy Young Awards he had already won. (16½" x 17" x 6½")

Ted Williams called Bobby Shantz's curveball the best in the American League. But Shantz (below, right) was an outstanding fielder as well: He won eight straight Gold Gloves from 1957 to 1964, including this one in 1959. "I had to be a good fielder," he once explained. "I nearly got killed a few times." (16½" x 17" x 6½")

sented this trophy to José Mendez of Cuba— one of the greatest pitchers in Negro League history—to commemorate Mendez's efforts in leading the Monarchs to victory over the Hilldale Daisies in the 1924 inaugural Negro League World Series. A lean, wiry righthander with a devastating fastball—one story says his fastball killed a teammate during batting practice—Mendez started his career with the Havana Club in 1908 and produced the most wins in the Cuban League between 1908 and 1911. During exhibition games against some of the best teams in the major leagues, Mendez defeated legendary hurlers such as Eddie Plank and Christy

The 1972 World Series between the Oakland Athletics and Cincinnati Reds generated an unprecedented six one-run games. Even without their star slugger Reggie Jackson (bottom), who had been injured, the Athletics came out on top in seven games. The victory was secured by superb pitching from Rollie Fingers, an extraordinary leaping snag against the leftfield wall by Joe Rudi that robbed Denis Menke of a ninth-inning double in Game 2, and the potent slugging of backup catcher Gene Tenace, who hit four homers in the Series, tying a record shared by Babe Ruth and Lou Gehrig. The trophy below commemorates the Athletics franchise's first World Series title since 1930. (25" tall, 13" in diameter)

The 1978 New York Yankees proved that their 1977 World Series triumph was no fluke by winning again in six games against the Los Angeles Dodgers. In this Series, the Yankees came back from two games down, winning four straight to become the first major-league team ever to do so. This 1978 World Series trophy (right, below) was awarded to New York Yankees center-fielder Mickey Rivers. (12" tall, 7½" in diameter)

Red Sox fans may want to avoid looking at this World Series trophy (left) that was awarded to the 1986 World Series Most Valuable Player, Ray Knight of the New York Mets. In Game 6, Knight scored the winning run when Mookie Wilson's grounder rolled under Bill Buckner's glove. In Game 7, Knight hit a seventh-inning solo homer to give the Mets the lead for good in their 8-5 victory. (12" tall, 7½" in diameter)

The 1992 World Series trophy (below) was given to Toronto Blue Jays second baseman Roberto Alomar, who also was named that year's American League Championship Series Most Valuable Player. (12" tall, 7½" in diameter)

Mathewson. After one game against the New York Giants, John McGraw proclaimed Mendez to be "sort of Walter Johnson and Grover Alexander rolled into one." Hall of Famer John Henry Lloyd said he'd never seen a better pitcher than Mendez. In the 1924 Negro League World Series, despite being at the tail end of his career, Mendez pitched in four games, producing a 1.42 ERA and clinching a shutout victory for the Monarchs in the Series' final game. On the trophy, a wreath of oak leaves surrounds an ornate "M" (for Monarchs), below which is engraved "To Joe Mendez." One side of the base is inscribed "From J. L. Wilkenson—Oct. 20, 1924"; the other side reads, "Worlds Colored Champions" and "Kansas City Monarchs, K. C. Mo."

Baseball history is punctuated with unexpected flashes of greatness. Don Larsen's World Series pitching performance on October 8, 1956, for the New York Yankees is a prime example. In 1953, after serving two years in the Army, Larsen joined the St. Louis Browns pitching staff. He finished the season with a 7–12 record. The following year, Larsen moved with the Browns to Baltimore, where he went a disastrous 3–21, with a 4.37 ERA. He made an impressive turnaround while pitching for the Yankees in 1955 and 1956, going 9–2 and 11–5, respectively, but Bronx Bombers fans could hardly have expected Larsen's performance in Game 5 of the '56 Series. Especially after his dismal outing in Game 2 of that Series, in which he walked four Dodgers and left after $1^2/_3$ innings of work. Larsen's rambunctious lifestyle off the mound did little to boost his image: He smashed his car into a lamp post in Florida after a late-night drinking binge during spring training, and he missed several team trains headed to away games during the 1956 season. Sportswriters had claimed that Larsen showed "more concern for good times than for good games" and that "[he] doesn't give a damn."

Despite his wayward demeanor and poor performance in Game 2, Larsen was untouchable in Game 5. He pitched a perfect game, the first (and still only) World Series no-hitter and the first perfect game in the big leagues in 34 years. Twenty-seven Brooklyn Dodger batters went up to the

Major League Baseball gave this trophy to Ernie Banks to commemorate his 500th career home run. A flyer distributed during Banks's Hall of Fame induction ceremony shows National League President Charles "Chub" Feeney (above) presenting this trophy to Banks. (Trophy: 43" tall, 23½" x 7½" base) (Flyer: 11" x 14")

World Series and Pennant Rings

In addition to trophies, each front-office executive, manager, coach, and player on a World Series championship team or a pennant-winning team typically receives a gold ring. This is part of a tradition that dates back to the early 20th century, when team members were given medallion watch fobs (see the 1906–08 Chicago Cubs gold medallion watch fob in Chapter VIII, "The Marshall Fogel Collection") or gold pendants, in honor of winning the World Series. World Series rings are known to have been awarded as early as 1927. Quite possibly, such rings were awarded even earlier. At a minimum, we know that as early as 1916, a team received gold rings to commemorate a winning streak.

Each of the rings pictured here from The Ron Leff Family Collection, which commemorates a World Series title or a pennant, is made of either 10- or 14-karat gold. They provide a bird's-eye view of some of the beautiful designs and craftsmanship that have been employed by a few of the world's leading jewelers:

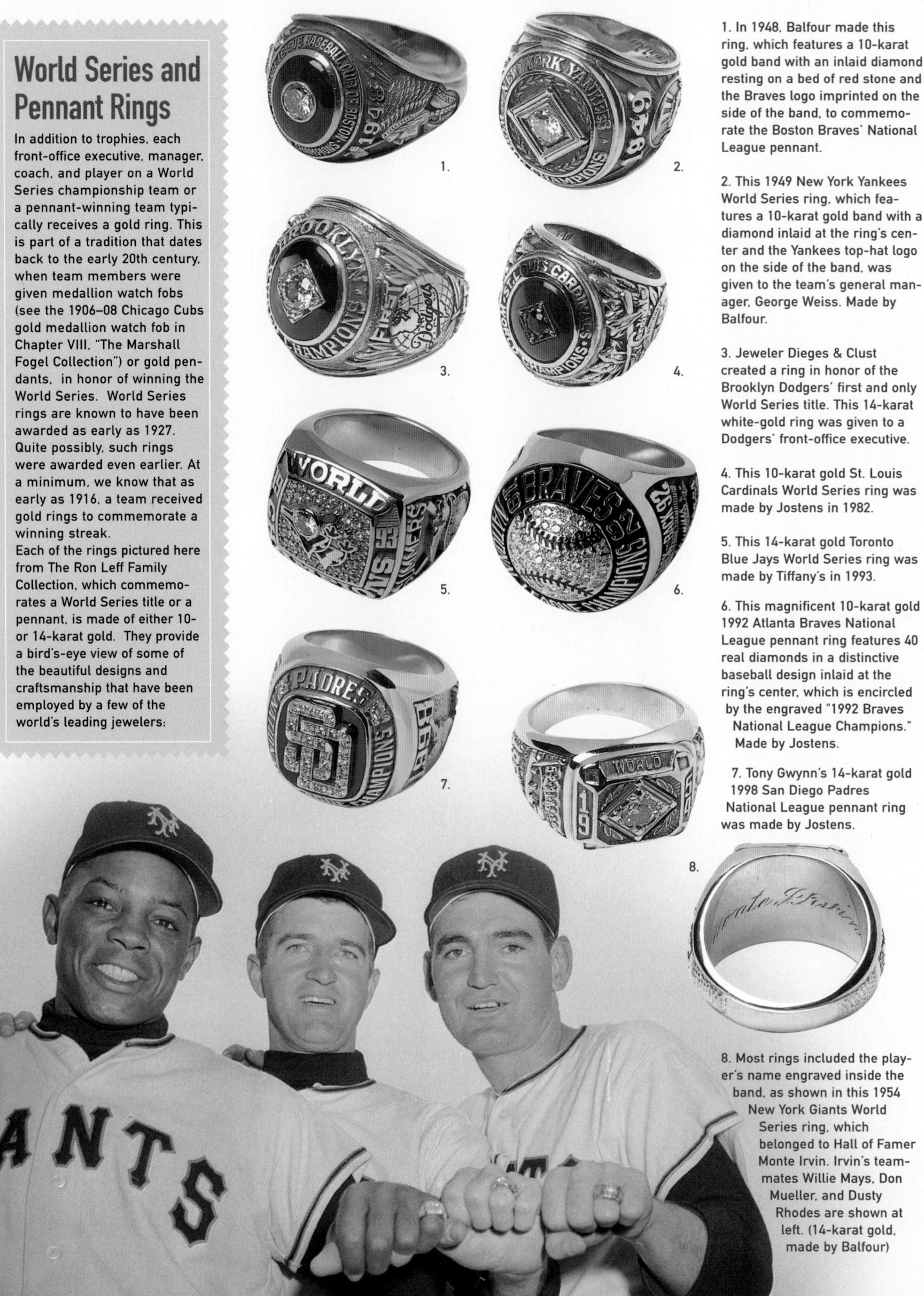

1. In 1948, Balfour made this ring, which features a 10-karat gold band with an inlaid diamond resting on a bed of red stone and the Braves logo imprinted on the side of the band, to commemorate the Boston Braves' National League pennant.

2. This 1949 New York Yankees World Series ring, which features a 10-karat gold band with a diamond inlaid at the ring's center and the Yankees top-hat logo on the side of the band, was given to the team's general manager, George Weiss. Made by Balfour.

3. Jeweler Dieges & Clust created a ring in honor of the Brooklyn Dodgers' first and only World Series title. This 14-karat white-gold ring was given to a Dodgers' front-office executive.

4. This 10-karat gold St. Louis Cardinals World Series ring was made by Jostens in 1982.

5. This 14-karat gold Toronto Blue Jays World Series ring was made by Tiffany's in 1993.

6. This magnificent 10-karat gold 1992 Atlanta Braves National League pennant ring features 40 real diamonds in a distinctive baseball design inlaid at the ring's center, which is encircled by the engraved "1992 Braves National League Champions." Made by Jostens.

7. Tony Gwynn's 14-karat gold 1998 San Diego Padres National League pennant ring was made by Jostens.

8. Most rings included the player's name engraved inside the band, as shown in this 1954 New York Giants World Series ring, which belonged to Hall of Famer Monte Irvin. Irvin's teammates Willie Mays, Don Mueller, and Dusty Rhodes are shown at left. (14-karat gold, made by Balfour)

plate and not one of them made it to first base. "The million-to-one shot came in," wrote *Washington Post* sports columnist Shirley Povich. "Hell froze over. A month of Sundays hit the calendar. Don Larsen today pitched a no-hit, no-run, no-man-reach-first game in a World Series. . . . He did it with a tremendous assortment of pitches that seemed to have five forward speeds, including a slow one that ought to have been equipped with backup lights." Larsen's flash of greatness was forever enshrined by his wife in the homemade, bronzed trophy display (above). The ball that was caught by catcher Yogi Berra for the third and final out in Larsen's perfect game rests on a wooden plaque, along with the glove and spikes Larsen used in the game. Larsen wore a number of caps during the game, one of which rests at the center of the trophy display.

Until Ron Leff acquired it in 2002, this display remained in Larsen's possession for more than three decades after his retirement from the majors in 1967. Campanella and Mantle held on to their MVP trophies until the end of their lives, and their family estates only recently let them go. The same is true for Willie Mays's Silver Bat and Ernie Banks's 500-home-run trophy.

Obviously, baseball trophies represent some remarkable achievements. Don Larsen once said, "Sometimes a week might go by when I don't think about that game, but I don't remember when it happened last." But over time, trophies come to represent more than the achievements they commemorate. They enable honorees to recover a lost bit of time from their youth, a time when, as Ted Kluszewski put it, they were "full of springtime."

The trophy display above commemorates Don Larsen's perfect Game 5 in the 1956 World Series, (12½" tall, 19" square base) which culminated in Yogi Berra's famous leap into Larsen's arms (top, left).

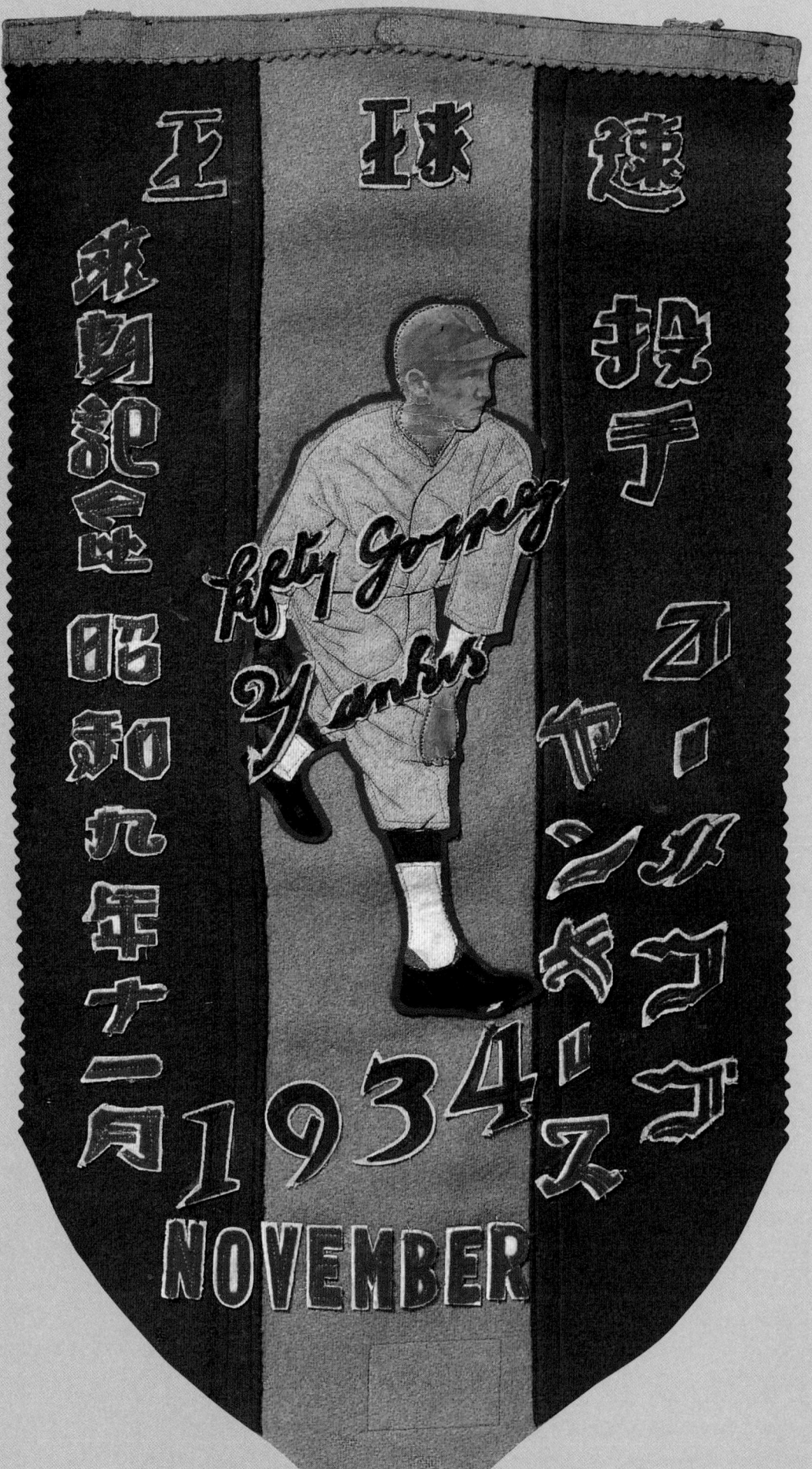

15

BASEBALL ABROAD

Photograph of bearer

This passport, properly visaed, is valid for travel in all countries unless otherwise restricted.

This passport, unless limited to a shorter period, is valid for two years from its date of issue and may be renewed upon payment of a fee of $5 but the final date of expiration shall not be more than four years from the original date of issue.

American citizens traveling in disturbed areas of the world are requested to keep in touch with the nearest American diplomatic or consular officers. American citizens making their homes or residing for a prolonged period abroad should register at the nearest American consulate.

SEE PAGES 6, 7, AND 8 FOR RENEWAL, EXTENSIONS, AMENDMENTS, LIMITATIONS, AND RESTRICTIONS.

5

No. 158188

SPECIAL PASSPORT

United States of America

> "In 1942, members of the Manhattan Project began floating the idea of abducting Werner Heisenberg from Germany. By the time the OSS became involved, these impolite suggestions became two kidnapping missions, where the unspoken option was murder. The first involved a burly former Mexican border patrolman named Carl Eifler. The second designated kidnapper was a man who had once caught for a living—Moe Berg."
>
> —NICHOLAS DAWIDOFF
> *The Catcher Was a Spy*

After learning about the mysterious and colorful life of major-league catcher Moe Berg, Dr. Bill Sear became interested in overseas exhibition baseball tours from 1874 to 1934. A ballplayer who became a spy, Berg was a double anomaly for his time—an Ivy League–educated Jew who played in the majors at a time of widespread anti-Semitism. Berg also had a law degree, which mirrored the Sear family's lineage of district judges, federal prosecutors, and corporate attorneys.

The son of a pharmaceutical merchant who emigrated from the Ukraine to America in 1894, Berg was raised in Newark, New Jersey. He studied seven languages (including Sanskrit) at Princeton University and graduated with distinction in the class of 1923. Berg was also the starting shortstop on the baseball team, and during his senior year, he exploited his penchant for language by communicating in Latin with second baseman Crossan Cooper to confuse opposing runners attempting to steal third base. After graduation, Berg played for the Brooklyn Robins (later renamed the Dodgers) to earn tuition for graduate studies at the Sorbonne in Paris.

In 1930, Berg earned an LL.B. from Columbia Law School and tried his hand at corporate law on Wall Street. But Berg preferred life on the diamond. He spent the rest of the decade as a third-string catcher for the Cleveland Indians, Washington Senators, and Boston Red Sox. As a bullpen catcher during this period, Berg rarely got the chance to play. But this perfectly suited a man whom author Nicholas Dawidoff describes as a "sensualist," who "was making use of baseball to plot a life of wandering curiosity."

The vertical hand-made felt pennant (opposite) made by "Tokyo Japan S. Matsuzama Co." features New York Yankee Hall of Fame pitcher Vernon Louis "Lefty" Gomez, who led the American League in 1934 in seven major categories including wins, ERA and strikeouts, which made him a logical choice as the starting hurler for the All-American squad. These charming keepsakes were presented to each of the 1934 Tour players when they arrived in Yokohama. (21" x 10")

In 1951, Moe Berg officially re-entered government, accepting a role in the NATO defense structure. Above is his passport from that period.

JAPAN VS. AMERICA
Grand Base Ball Match
1931

讀賣新聞社運動部編

日米大野球戰グラフ

定價貳拾錢

世界最強チーム来朝の真相
及來宿の革
市岡忠男……來朝選手歷
鈴木惣太郎
市岡忠男……全日本代表選手小傳

東印刷アロウス（商）共刻

During major-league baseball's exhibition tour to Japan in 1934, Berg did some curious wandering indeed in the city of Tokyo. Because of a last-minute cancellation by Red Sox catcher Rick Ferrell, Berg was invited to make the trip, along with Babe Ruth, Lou Gehrig, Jimmie Foxx, Charley Gehringer, and the rest of the American all-star team. He was to serve as the second-string catcher in a series of 17 exhibition games against Japan's first professional team, the Tokyo Giants, which was made up of the country's best former high school and college players. In Tokyo, half a million fans turned out to witness the mighty Bambino on his first trip to the Land of the Rising Sun. (Two years later, Japan formed its own professional league.) But the thunderous cheers for Ruth belied Japan's growing discontent with the United States, which was largely a result of American politicians' uproar over Japan's increasing military presence within the Asia-Pacific region. Many Japanese felt "hostility and paranoia" towards Americans.

This original sepia-toned photograph of the 1934 All-American team (above) was taken outside the Hotel Ryokwan in Sendaishi, Japan. (See luggage tag from the hotel displayed in the montage, opposite.) Moe Berg is sitting in the front row, second from the left. (8" x 10")

Between 1922 and 1932, a marginal former major leaguer named Herb Hunter played a pivotal role in the spread of baseball to the Far East. In 1922, he helped arrange an exhibition tour to Japan, Shanghai, hina, Korea, and Manila, Philippines, which included Hall of Famers Casey Stengel, Herb Pennock, and Waite Hoyt. Nine years later, he was back in Japan with another tour—this one anchored by Hall of Famers Lou Gehrig, Mickey Cochrane, and Frankie Frisch—which paved the way for future postseason barnstorming tours. At left is the official program for one of the games during the 1931 Tour and it features Lou Gehrig on the cover. (12" x 6 ½")

The circumstances could hardly have been more inviting for an intrepid adventurer like Berg. He skipped out on the game scheduled in the town of Omiya on November 29 and instead played his version of the tourist. Dressed in a kimono and a pair of geta (raised wooden clogs), Berg grabbed his Bell and Howell movie camera and picked up a bouquet of flowers before heading off to Saint Luke's Hospital under the pretext of visiting a U.S. Ambassador's daughter who was giving birth at the time. Upon arriving at the hospital, which was one of the tallest buildings in the city, Berg walked past the reception area unchallenged and rode the elevator to the fifth floor, where he dumped the flowers in a garbage can. Berg then rode to the seventh floor, exited the elevator, and climbed up a narrow staircase to a bell tower that provided a panoramic view of Tokyo. He pulled the movie camera from under his kimono and began filming the city.

Some scholars and historians maintain that Berg was acting on orders from the U.S.

On October 20, 1934, the All-American team set sail aboard the Canadian Pacific Line's *Empress of Japan* from Vancouver bound for Yokohama by way of Honolulu.

An original program from this steamship voyage (above) accompanies four luggage tags issued by the hotels at which the players stayed while in Japan. To the right of the tags is a ticket to one of the 17 games where tens of thousands of ecstatic Japanese fans saw their local heroes take on the Americans, who were led by Babe Ruth, Lou Gehrig, Jimmie Foxx, Lefty Gomez, and Moe Berg, all of whom have signed the Tamazawa Official American League baseball shown in the montage. Special jerseys were made for this tour. The one shown here was worn by Edmund John "Bing" Miller—who earned a lifetime batting average of .312 over 16 major-league seasons—during each of the 17 exhibition games.

This is the actual 16-mm Bell and Howell movie camera (and its original leather case) used by Moe Berg in the bell tower of St. Luke's Hospital to take film footage of Tokyo city. Some baseball historians have suggested that the footage was used in planning the surprise bombing raids on Tokyo, Yokohama, Osaka, and Nagoya, by Lieutenant Colonel Jimmy Doolittle on April 18, 1942. (5½" tall)

State Department to produce the footage and that the footage was used by Lieutenant Colonel Jimmy Dootlittle to plan the April 18, 1942, bombing raids on Tokyo, Yokohama, Osaka, and Nagoya. In 1942, during his tenure with the Office of Inter-American Affairs (OIAA), Berg showed the footage to a number of U.S. intelligence officers within the Office of Strategic Services (OSS)—the forerunner of the CIA—as well as the armed forces. But whether Berg was acting on behalf of the State Department to produce reconnaissance footage and whether Jimmy Doolittle in fact used the footage remains a matter of controversy. Either way, Berg's "hospital visit" provides a noteworthy glimpse into his adventures in espionage. Berg eventually resigned from the OIAA and traveled to Europe as an OSS spy to learn more about Hitler's atomic bomb program. According to Dawidoff, Berg was to determine if there was "indisputable evidence" that a German bomb was imminent; if there was, Berg was to assassinate Werner Heisenberg, the world-renowned German physicist whom the U.S. believed was the most likely candidate to produce an atomic bomb.

Inspired by Berg's mystique, Bill Sear began collecting items associated with the catcher and his life of espionage. In addition to a wealth of baseball artifacts from the 1934 Japan Tour, the Dr. Bill Sear Family Collection includes Berg's personal diaries, his U.S. passport, his OSS identification card, and the Bell and Howell movie camera he used to record his footage from the top of St. Luke's Hospital. The Sear Family Collection also includes hundreds of letters that document Berg's correspondence with various U.S. intelligence agencies. As tangential as Berg's espionage escapades may be to the business of major-league baseball, for Sear they opened the door to collecting memorabilia from international major-league exhibition tours. After all, a baseball game played in front of thousands of spectators in Cairo or Rome in 1888 or '89, or in Hong Kong or Manila in 1913 or '14, was no ordinary event. In more than 10 years of collecting, Sear has accumulated some remarkable relics relating to baseball's unique role in extending American culture abroad.

U.S. baseball teams began launching

The leatherbound album above (inset) was made by members of the Japanese press and presented to each player and dignitary on both the American and Japanese squads. The album includes twenty-four 10" x 12" sepia-toned photographs taken at various stages of the tour in Japan. The photograph shown above depicts the Americans wearing kimonos and being surrounded by geisha girls on board the *Empress of Japan*. The album also includes team-signed sheets from both teams. (14¾" x 10½")

This lithographic print (opposite, above) depicts the chief sponsor of the 1888–89 World Tour, sporting goods magnate Albert Goodwill Spalding, greeting the Prince of Wales on March 12, 1889, at the Surrey Cricket Grounds' Kennington Oval in England, one of the stops on this celebrated tour. Spalding was determined to use the tour to promote his sporting goods business and to advance the notion that baseball was American in origin, not a descendant of English games. (19½" x 13¾")

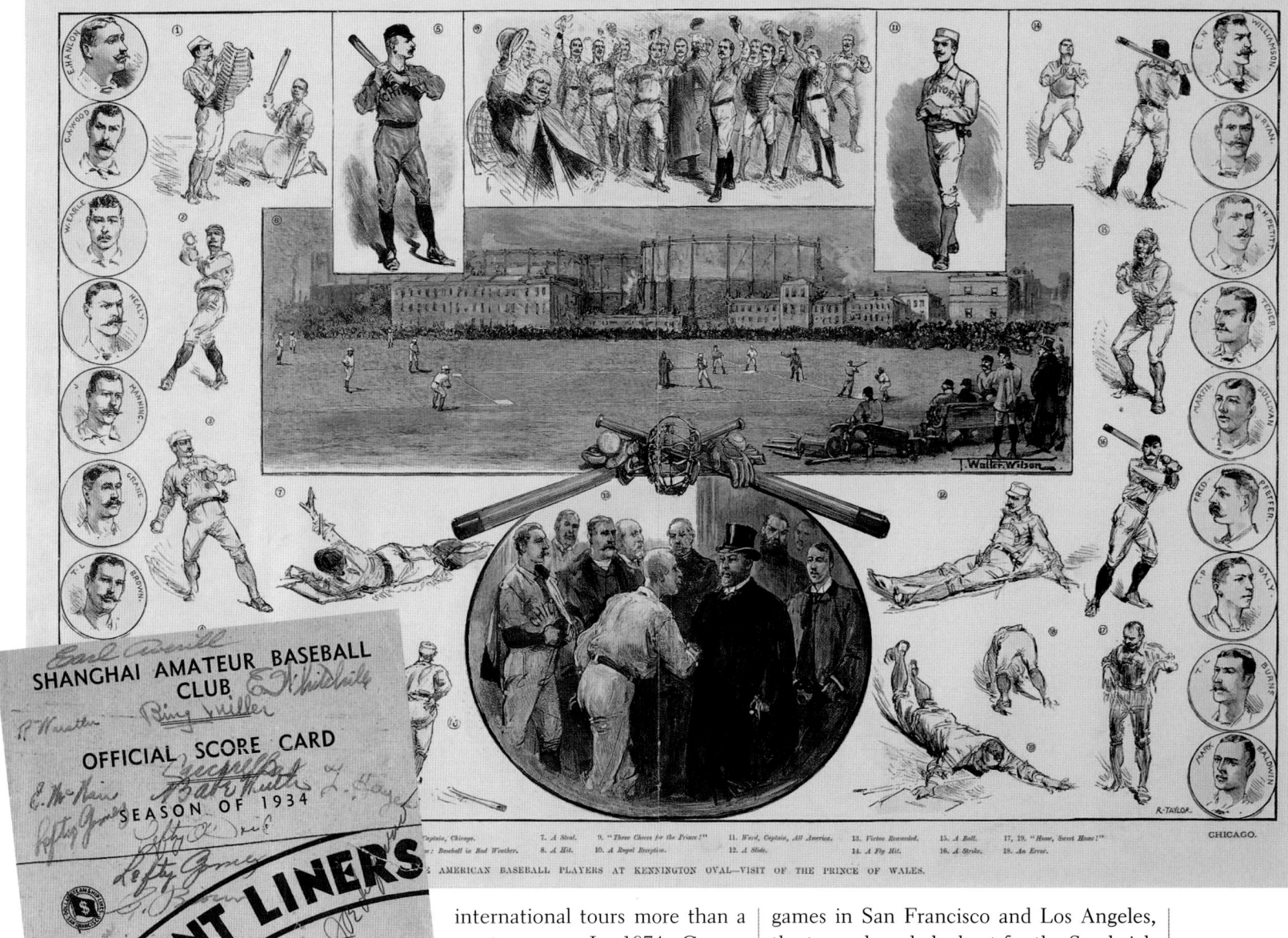

AMERICAN BASEBALL PLAYERS AT KENNINGTON OVAL—VISIT OF THE PRINCE OF WALES.

After the last game in Japan, which was played at Utsunomiya on December 1, 1934, the All-Americans traveled to Shanghai on board the *Empress of Canada* to play one game against the "Pandas," Shanghai's best amateur baseball club. This club had been formed by Liang Fuchu, who is known as the grandfather of Chinese baseball. This is an original scorecard from that game, played on December 5, 1934. Its cover is autographed by several members of the All-American team. (9" x 6½")

international tours more than a century ago. In 1874, George Wright (the legendary shortstop for the 1869 Cincinnati Red Stockings, baseball's first all-professional team) and his older brother Harry (baseball's first professional manager) arranged the first one. They brought teams from Boston and Philadelphia to England in an attempt to convince the British to abandon cricket in favor of baseball. The attempt failed, as the *London Observer* dismissed the American sport as a "rushing, helter-skelter game," but the 1874 England Tour would not be the last of its kind.

Fourteen years later, Albert Goodwill Spalding (who had been a part of the 1874 England Tour) led a tour with the Chicago White Stockings and a rival team of all-stars. The group left Chicago by rail on October 20, 1888, and played games in Iowa, Nebraska, Colorado, and Utah. After staging games in San Francisco and Los Angeles, the teams boarded a boat for the Sandwich Islands (known today as Hawaii), New Zealand, Australia, Ceylon, and Egypt. In Egypt, the players were photographed at the feet of the Sphinx (see page 210). The 1888–89 World Tour continued on to Rome, Paris, and the British Isles. As chief proprietor of baseball's biggest sporting goods business, Spalding sought to use the tour to build recognition for his brand name overseas. But he was also determined to convince observers that baseball was American in origin, and not a descendant of the English game of rounders. According to baseball historian Harold Seymour, "After the Civil War, organized teams became important, and baseball developed into popular show business, enjoying a prestige enhanced by American pride in having a 'national game.' Pride and patriotism required that the game be native, unsullied by English ancestry." Spalding believed the tour could foster this patriotic fervor.

This original sepia-toned photograph by "Fratelli D'Alessandri—Roma" (left) depicts the 1888–89 Tour players posing at the Villa Borghese in Rome before the game played on February 23, 1889. "This afternoon we played a game of ball at the Villa Borghese the beautiful grounds of the Prince," wrote tour member James Ryan in his journal (opposite, top). "During the progress of the game the King and Queen drove through the grounds. A great many Americans and all the students of the American College saw the game." (17" x 22")

Reproduced numerous times in books and periodicals over the years, this original sepia-toned photograph by P. Sebah captures the 1888–89 Tour players in uniform posing on the Sphinx in the Egyptian desert at Giza on February 9, 1889 (far left). "Today is a gala day for us," Ryan wrote, "for a visit has been arranged to the Sphinx and Pyramids . . . We then had our photographs taken sitting upon the face and shoulders of the Sphinx and descending to the plain introduced the game of base ball to the Sheiks and children of Israel upon the desert sands of Egypt. Five innings satisfied us for the fine sand blowing into our eyes made them sore so we mounted our camels and donkeys and rode home to Cairo." (9 _" x 13 _")

Tris Speaker, "Wahoo" Sam Crawford, and Buck Weaver to play in Japan for the first time. The sportswriter Ring Lardner was among the notables who documented the remarkable voyage. After Manila, the group sailed to Australia, Ceylon, and Egypt, where the ballplayers, like the ones before them, were photographed at the feet of the Sphinx. They then crossed the Mediterranean to Naples and continued on to Rome and Paris, with a brief stop along the Riviera. Before leaving Europe, they played one last exhibition game for England's King George V and an enormous crowd at Stamford Bridge, home of the Chelsea Football Club. After returning to the United States aboard *RMS Lusitania*, McGraw and Comiskey commemorated the tour with a gala banquet on March 7, 1914, at the Biltmore Hotel in New York City and another on March 10 at Chicago's Congress Hotel.

The Sear Family Collection includes artifacts and photographic images from these three tours, as well as relics from tours that took place in 1922, 1924, and 1931. Because many of the objects had at one point belonged to individual tour members, they impart a personal story. They also embody extraordinary memories of ballplayers traveling by steamship across the Atlantic, the North Pacific, the Yellow Sea, the Indian Ocean, and throughout the East

In 1913 and '14, New York Giants manager John McGraw and Chicago White Sox owner Charles Comiskey outdid Spalding with an ambitious world tour that included Europe and Asia. This tour marked major-league baseball's first visit to Shanghai and Manila and included the first baseball game ever played in Hong Kong. In addition, the 1913–14 tour brought top-caliber big-league stars such as

In a private room at Smiley Mike Corbett's bar on Chicago's East side in December 1912, John McGraw and Charles Comiskey met to discuss the idea of taking the Giants and White Sox on a world tour. The man who brokered the meeting was Timothy Paul "Ted" Sullivan, a college roommate of Comiskey's and trusted acquaintance of McGraw's. Sullivan was appointed managing director of the tour and wrote his impressions of the event in *History World's Tour Chicago White Sox-New York Giants 1913–14*, an original copy of which is shown opposite. One of the Tour's highlights was a luncheon with Sir Thomas Lipton at the Galle Face Hotel in Colombo (invitation shown center), the capital city of

Handwritten journal text (partially visible):

...currance... turns upon its own... to death. Returning to... dine on board the United States... Essex which arrived in port last eve... ing homeward bound from a three years cruise in the China seas. Many of... our boys found old familiar faces amongst the officers and crew. This afternoon we gave an exhibit... to an audience composed of Amer... English, Hindoos, Cingalese, Turks... Arabians all collected together. After... the Great American game. After... five innings we returned to the... and immediately got under... In passing the Essex the... were all in the rigging bidd... and after many cheers we put to...

James Ryan 1888–89 A. G. Spalding World Tour Handwritten Journal: Spalding's global voyage, which included visits to 13 different countries, started in Chicago on October 20, 1888 and ended there on April 20, 1889. This extraordinary journal, kept by Chicago White Stockings outfielder James Ryan, provides a handwritten account of every single day of this historic tour. Many of his entries provide fascinating details which make one feel as though one is traveling alongside Ryan, Cap Anson, John Montgomery Ward, George Wright, and Ned Williamson, and the other "boys" as they embark on an adventure of a lifetime. (7¼" x 12½")

Ceylon, which was Great Britain's tea plantation. The genius who revolutionized the tea industry, Lipton was an avid baseball fan and saw many games during his time spent in the United States in the 1870s.

When Spalding's Chicago Nationals returned from the 1888–89 World Tour, the magnitude of their accomplishments continued to be celebrated with a beautiful series of 16-page programs that were produced for regular season games during the 1889 season (far right). These programs featured portraits of Chicago players surrounded by four scenes from the World Tour. This example features a bust shot of Chicago catcher Frank "Silver" Flint surrounded by color lithographic illustrations which are titled, "Uncle Sam's Farewell in California" (top left), "Arrival in Australia" (top right), "Reception in England" (bottom left), and "At the Pyramids" (bottom right). (12" x 8½"

Indies to play baseball in distant lands in front of hundreds, sometimes thousands, of bewildered spectators, many of whom had never even heard of the game. Key items in the collection include an original lithograph print of the Prince of Wales greeting Spalding at Kennington Oval during the 1888–89 World Tour, a fine array of vintage photographs from the same tour shot in England, and the aforementioned photos of the players in front of the Sphinx. The Sear collection also includes photos of players at the Villa Borghese in Rome, James Ryan's personal diary of events on Spalding's tour, and the uniforms worn by some of the tour participants, including the one worn by John McGraw on the 1913–14 Tour.

Sear says that the passion and drive behind his collection come from having spent his childhood in New Orleans—a city without a major-league ball club. He bought baseball cards at the local Lorenza's Rexall

Before setting sail across the Pacific to Japan, John McGraw's Giants played Jimmy "Nixey" Callahan's White Sox in 31 exhibition games in 34 days in 27 different cities within the United States. One of these games was played at Oxnard Field, California, on November 11, 1913, where the players were treated to the town's breakfast specialty—roasted ox, lima beans, and beer. Despite the rather heavy start to the day, the White Sox batsmen swung their lumber mightily, forcing Christy Mathewson to rely on his seldom-thrown spitball to squeak out a 3–2 win for the Giants. The entire team is shown at top, including Mathewson and manager McGraw, whose uniform, specially designed for the Tour, is shown at right. (Photograph is 42" x 6¾")

As this vintage pennant (right, above) illustrates, Christy Mathewson was at the peak of his pitching career by midway through the 1913 season: He pitched 68 consecutive innings without giving up a single base on balls from June 13 through July 18. Matty was one of the key drawing cards for the Tour, but he opted not to participate in its overseas leg, preferring to spend the winter with his family in Pasadena, California. (29½" long, 11" wide)

drug store, watched afternoon games of the AAA League New Orleans Pelicans, listened to the "Game of the Week" with Dizzy Dean and Pee Wee Reese on radio, and watched occasional New York Yankees games on television. But it was not the same as rooting for a hometown major-league club at your own ballpark.

For many of his childhood years, Sear wondered what it would be like to sit in a ballpark and see the likes of Hank Aaron, Ted Williams, Mickey Mantle, or Frank Robinson roam the outfield or belt one into the stands. In the spring of 1960, Sear finally got his chance to see big-league players in person. His father brought him to Tad Gormly Stadium in City Park, New Orleans, to see Ted Williams and the rest of the Red Sox play in a spring training game. An hour or so before game time, Sear and his father sat in the lower grandstand between third base and home plate. Six Red Sox players gathered around the batting cage conversing; one or two occasionally turned to spit tobacco juice. Sear caught a glimpse of Williams in the cage, his head and shoulders clearly visible above the other players. Seeing the remarkable fluidity of Williams's swing and the intensity of his concentration at bat for the first time gave Sear tremendous joy.

"Just imagine," he says now, as he holds a baseball autographed by

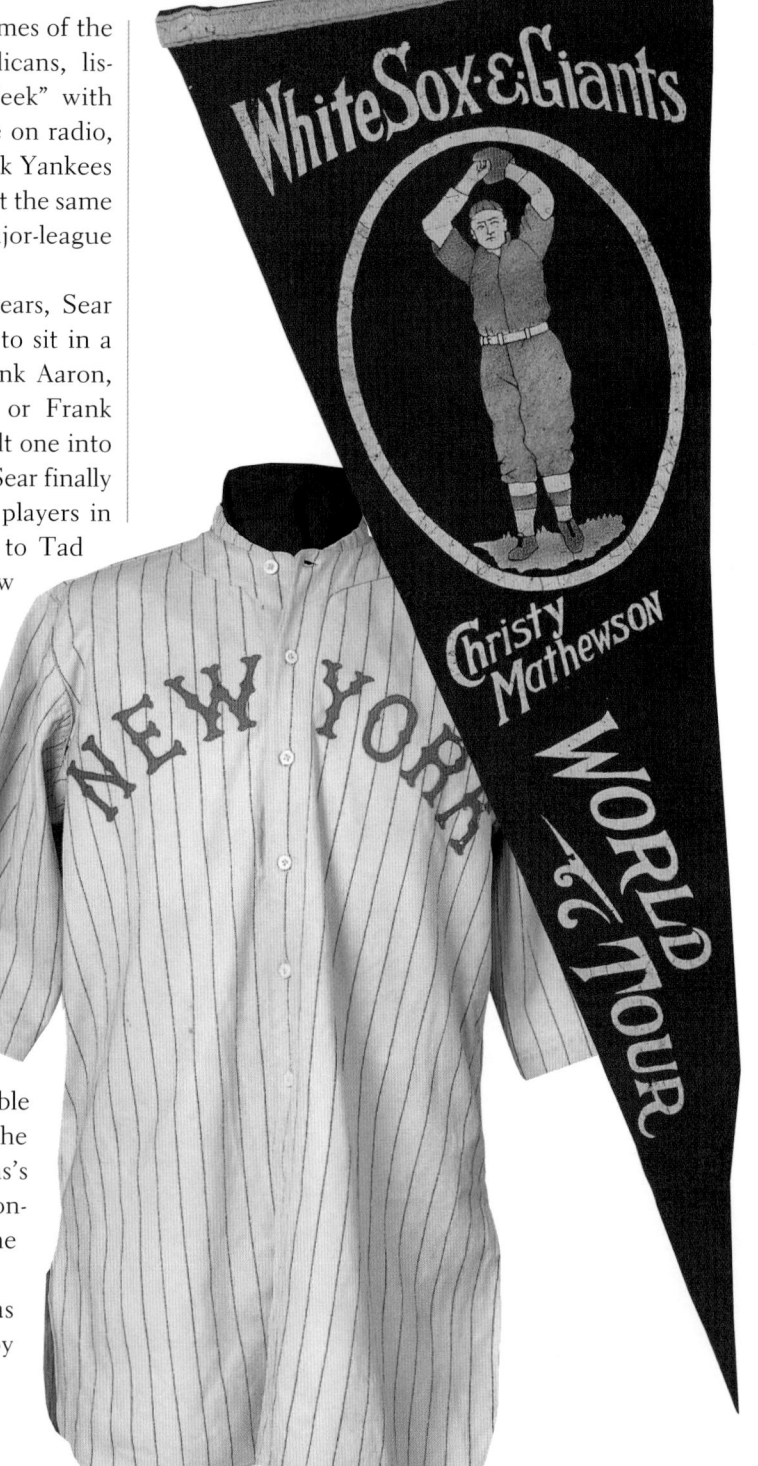

The invitation and program to a gala banquest honoring the World Tourists, held at the Biltmore Hotel in New York City on March 7, 1914, are shown at right. The interior pages of the program list the schedule and complete results from the Tour. The medallion welcoming ribbon was a souvenir keepsake for banquet participants. (Invitation and program, 10¾" x 7¾"; ribbon, 4" x 1¾")

Three days later, on March 10, 1914, Chicago's top brass filled the great ballroom at the Congress Hotel for another festive evening in honor of the returning World Tourists, which is beautifully depicted in this original photograph. (17" x 11½")

members of the 1934 Japan Tour, "what it was like for those Americans stationed overseas for so many years with hardly any source of contact with the game. For them, seeing Speaker, Crawford, Ruth, Gehrig, or Foxx coming off that steamship must have been a pretty darn spectacular feeling, as well. I guess in some way, I can identify with how they felt, and the collection is my way of reaching out to them and preserving those treasured moments." Those treasured moments, and the mysterious ones involving catcher Moe Berg, embody the exoticism and the sense of adventure attending baseball's early foreign tours.

DINNER
IN CELEBRATION OF
THE HOME COMING OF THE
WORLD'S TOUR PLAYERS
MARCH THE SEVENTH
1914
THE BILTMORE

The Trip
Across the Continent

Oct. 18, CINCINNATI, OHIO ....Giants, 11; White Sox, 2
19, CHICAGO, ILL. ....Giants, 2; White Sox, 1
20, SPRINGFIELD, ILL. ....Giants, 3; White Sox, 1
21, PEORIA, ILL. ....Giants, 6; White Sox, 4
22, OTTUMWA, IOWA ....White Sox, 6; Giants, 4
23, SIOUX CITY, IOWA ....White Sox, 7; Giants, 3
24, BLUE RAPIDS, KAN. ....Giants, 6; White Sox, 5
25, ST. JOSEPH, MO. ....White Sox, 8; Giants, 3
26, KANSAS CITY, MO. ....White Sox, 4; Giants, 3
27, JOPLIN, MO. ....Giants, 6; White Sox, 2
28, TULSA, OKLA. ....Giants, 13; White Sox, 12
29, MUSKOGEE, OKLA. ....White Sox, 6; Giants, 0
30, BONHAM, TEXAS ....White Sox, 7; Giants, 1
31, DALLAS, TEXAS ....Giants, 4; White Sox, 3
Nov. 1, BEAUMONT, TEXAS ....White Sox, 10; Giants, 3
2, HOUSTON, TEXAS ....Giants, 3; White Sox, 2
3, MARLIN, TEXAS ....White Sox, 9; Giants, 4
4, ABILENE, TEXAS ....Giants, 11; White Sox, 1
5, EL PASO, TEXAS ....Rain
6, DOUGLAS, ARIZ. ....White Sox, 10; Giants, 3
7, BISBEE, ARIZ. ....Giants, 14; White Sox, 5
8, LOS ANGELES, CAL. ....Giants, 9; White Sox, 1
9, LOS ANGELES, CAL. ....White Sox, 5; Giants, 3 (Tie)
10, SAN DIEGO, CAL. ....Giants, 7; Giants, 3
11, OXNARD, CAL. ....Giants, 4; White Sox, 2
12, SACRAMENTO, CAL. ....Giants, 3; White Sox, 2
13, OAKLAND, CAL. ....Rain
14, SAN FRANCISCO, CAL. ......White Sox, 5; Giants, 2
15, SAN FRANCISCO, CAL. ......White Sox, 3; Giants, 2
16, OAKLAND, CAL. ....Giants, 6; White Sox, 3
16, SAN FRANCISCO, CAL. .....White Sox, 12; Giants, 8
18, PORTLAND, ORE. ....White Sox, 4; Giants, 2
18, MEDFORD, ORE. ....Giants, 3; White Sox, 0 (6 innings)
19, SEATTLE, WASH. ....White Sox, 2; Giants, 0
.....................................Rain

Sailed night of Nov. 19 from Vancouver for Japan.

Dec. 6, TOKIO, JAPAN ....White Sox, 9; Giants, 4
7, TOKIO, JAPAN ....White Sox, 12; Giants, 9

Sailed thence to China.

Dec. 14, HONG KONG, CHINA ....Giants, 7; White Sox, 4

Sailed thence to the Phillipine Islands.

Dec. 17, MANILA. ....White Sox, 2; Giants, 1
18, MANILA ....White Sox, 7; Giants, 4 (7 innings)

Sailed thence to Australia.
1914.

Jan. 1, BRISBANE, AUS. ....Giants, 2; White Sox, 1
3, SYDNEY, AUS. ....White Sox, 15; Giants, 6
5, SYDNEY, AUS. ....White Sox, 10; Giants, 5
7, MELBOURNE, AUS. ....Giants, 12; White Sox, 8
8, MELBOURNE, AUS., Giants, 4; White Sox, 3 (11 inn'gs)

Sailed thence to Ceylon.

Jan. 22, COLOMBO, CEYLON ....White Sox, 4; Giants, 1

Sailed thence to Egypt.

Feb. 1, HELIOPOLIS (CAIRO) .Giants, 3; White Sox, 3 (Tie)
2, HELIOPOLIS (CAIRO) ....Giants, 6; White Sox, 3

Sailed thence to Italy.
No game possible in Rome on account of rain.

Traveled thence to France.

Feb. 16, NICE, FRANCE ....White Sox, 10; Giants, 9

Traveled thence to Paris.
No game possible on account of rain.

Traveled thence to London.

Feb. 26, LONDON, ENG. ..White Sox, 5; Giants, 4 (11 inn'gs)

Feb. 28, Sailed for home.

Other Games

Dec. 7, TOKIO, JAPAN ....Giants-Sox, 16; Keio, 3
Jan. 3, SYDNEY, AUS. ....White Sox, 10; Australians, 4
5, SYDNEY, AUS. ....Giants, 15; Australians, 2
7, MELBOURNE, AUS., Giants, 18; Victoria, 0 (7 innings)

IT ALL STARTED AT GEROLOMAN'S

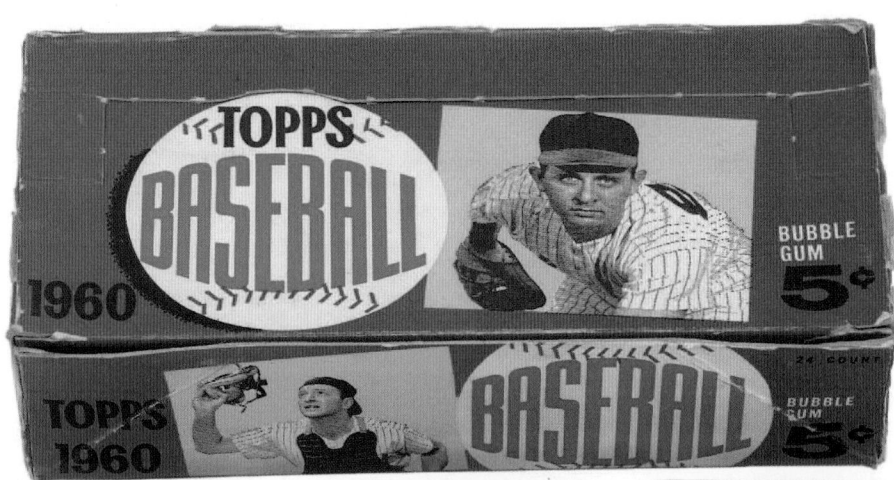

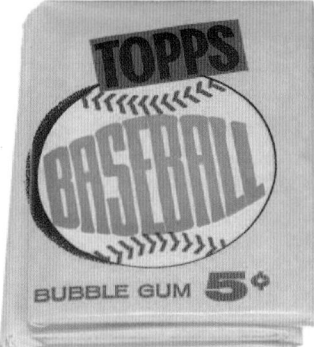
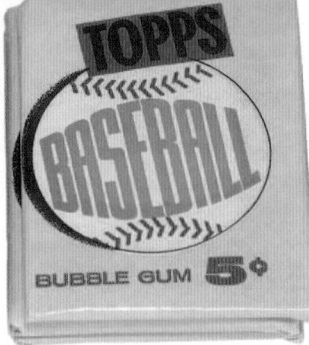
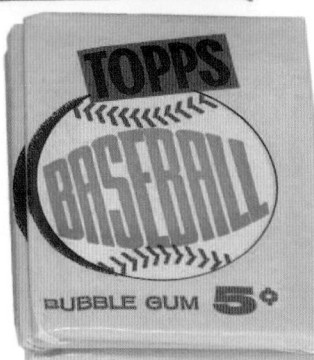

It was a shiny red box of 1960 Topps 5-cent wax packs (left) that captivated a seven-year-old Bill Mastro from inside the candy case at Geroloman's, and set him on his life's course.

Collectible artifacts related to Babe Ruth (opposite) are practically an industry unto themselves, ranging from postcards, books, and tobacco tins to autographed baseballs, pin-back buttons, watch fobs, and much more. In 1928, Babe Ruth invited a thousand orphans to a party in Boston given in his honor, and the Fro-Joy Ice Cream company provided cones for all of the kids. In the curious ad copy produced for the occasion, Ruth "wrote," "I understand your Fro-Joy Ice Cream is Chock-full of Youth Units and that Fro-Joy Cones are pure and wholesome. I want to give each one of these thousand orphan boys a Fro-Joy Cone filled to the brim with Fro-Joy Ice Cream." Leaving aside the question of what, exactly, a "Youth Unit" is, this excerpt (opposite, top left) points to why Babe Ruth appeals to so many collectors. He transcended the game, becoming a cultural icon and a hero to children. Paul Gallico once wrote that Ruth was "God himself" to children: "God with a flat nose and little piggy eyes and a big grin, and a fat, black cigar sticking out of the side of it."

> "Midsummer baseball feels as if it would last forever; late-season baseball becomes quicker and terser, as if sensing its coming end, and sometimes, if we are lucky, it explodes into brilliant terminal colors, leaving bright pictures in memory to carry us through the miserable months to come."
>
> —ROGER ANGELL

Do you remember opening your very first pack of baseball cards? Bill Mastro opened his in April 1960. Since then, he has spent 45 years turning his childhood passion for baseball cards and memorabilia into a lifetime vocation. Mastro was an integral part of the grassroots era of card collecting in the 1960s and 1970s, and he was a pioneer in the Americana and sports memorabilia auction industry. Along the way, he also managed to assemble a remarkable collection of artifacts that were once widely underappreciated but now form the cornerstones of memorabilia collecting—advertising-related ephemera, vintage photography, and other forms of memorabilia related to baseball players or events. Here is how it all began . . . .

In the spring of 1958, Julius and Judy Mastro decided they needed a bigger home in which to raise their two young boys, Bill and Randy. The couple built a beautiful new house on a one-acre plot of land in the small

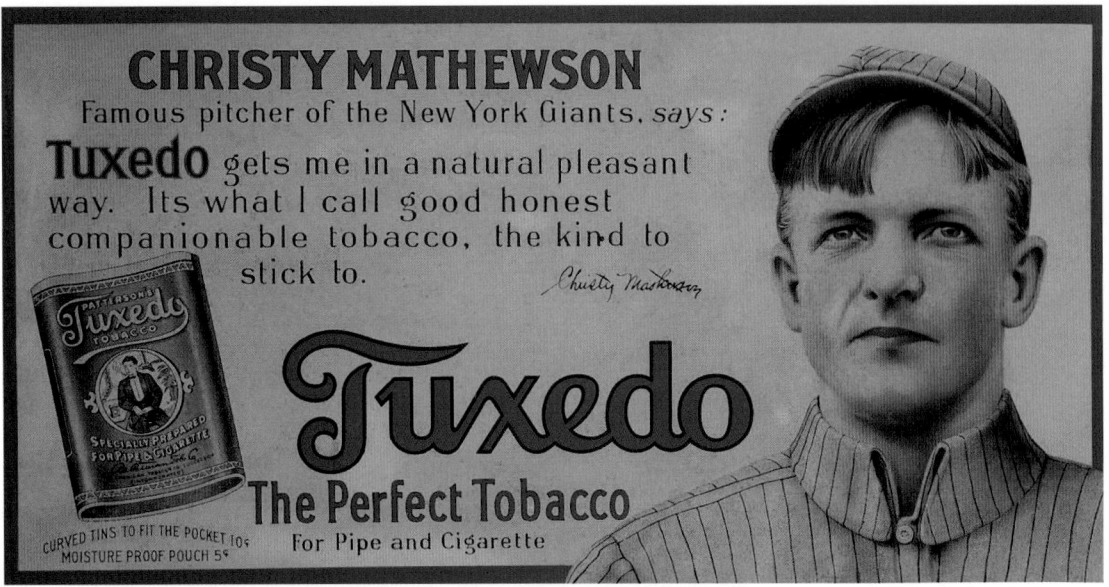

CHRISTY MATHEWSON
Famous pitcher of the New York Giants, *says:*

Tuxedo gets me in a natural pleasant way. Its what I call good honest companionable tobacco, the kind to stick to.

Christy Mathewson

Tuxedo
The Perfect Tobacco
For Pipe and Cigarette

CURVED TINS TO FIT THE POCKET 10¢
MOISTURE PROOF POUCH 5¢

Hall of Fame pitcher Christy Mathewson lent his likeness to a Tuxedo Tobacco advertisement (left) that appeared in trolley cars circa 1910. The move gently contradicted the press's persistent portrayal of Mathewson as a paragon of virtue, an image his wife, Jane, was known to deflate herself, pointing out from time to time that Mathewson was "no goody-goody." In addition to not being above accepting an endorsement check from a tobacco firm, Mathewson enjoyed gambling with his own checkerboard, sometimes cussed, and in 1905, punched a lemonade boy in the mouth for making a snide remark about a teammate. (11" x 20")

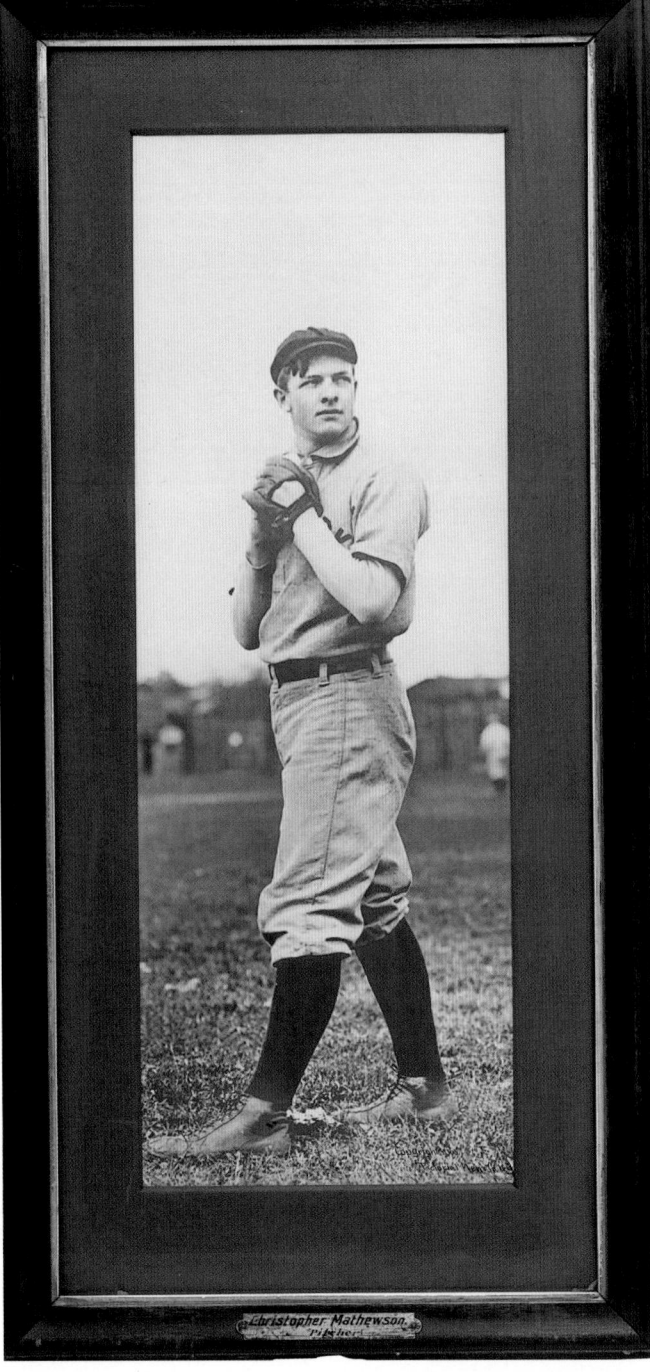

An original silver gelatin photograph of legendary righthander Christy Mathewson (left), taken in 1906 by New York-based photographer N. W. Penfield, hung in the office of Harry Moseley Stevens before Mastro acquired it. Baseball's pioneer concessionaire, Stevens is credited with inventing two staples of the national pastime: the scorecard and the hot dog (see Chapter IX, "The James and Lauren Clister Collection"). The image of Mathewson also appears on his T206 baseball card (see Chapter V, "The Brian Seigel Collection"). The photograph sits in its original frame, which includes a brass plate at the bottom engraved with Mathewson's name and position. (17" x 35")

On March 5, 1903, 23-year-old Christy Mathewson wed Jane Stoughton, a native of Lewisburg, Pennsylvania, and a 1902 graduate of the Lewisburg Female Institute. Among the 150 guests at the reception were 23 members of the Delta Chapter of the Phi Gamma Delta fraternity, of

"Christy" Matthewson
New York's great baseball pitcher . . . . .

And Newly Wedded Wife
ARE ON
....THIS TRAIN....

Make them feel at home as there may be . . . .
"SOMETHING DOING."

Note :

He will be easily recognized by his boyish countenance and Apollo like form. . . . .

which Mathewson was a member. When the newlyweds boarded a train en route to their honeymoon, Mathewson's fraternity brothers distributed hundreds of humorous handbills (above) to the couple's fellow passengers. Notifying everyone on board that there may be "something doing" between the newlyweds, and to recognize the star pitcher by his "boyish countenance" and "Apollo like form," the brothers strike a playfully teasing note in the "announcement."

In 1905, Honus Wagner (left) became the first ballplayer to have his signature branded on a Louisville Slugger. By 1912, when Mastro's extraordinary studio portrait was taken, Wagner was in a class by himself. Manager John McGraw told a Pittsburgh sportswriter that year, "You can have your Cobbs, your Lajoies, your Chases, your Bakers, and all the rest, but I'll take Wagner. He does everything better than the ordinary star can do any one thing. He is the most wonderful ball player who ever lived." Wagner's autograph appears below the image. (16" x 13" framed)

An intimate portrait of Honus Wagner (above) circa 1913 is another jewel in Mastro's fine assortment of artifacts. Taken by Charles M. Conlon, the image provides a close-up of one of baseball's all-time greats. In 21 seasons (1897–1917), Wagner led the National League in batting a record eight times and hit .300 or better in a record 17 consecutive seasons. (5" x 7")

Mastro's Ty Cobb Golden Sporting Shoes advertising display (right) is the only one of its kind known to exist. (16" x 9¾")

hamlet of Bernardsville, New Jersey. Perched atop a bucolic hillside along a winding road, the property was flush with giant oak trees, and gorgeous rows of daffodils, tulips, and azalea bushes. A wooden fence ran along the landscape's perimeter in the spacious backyard.

"Our homestead was the most phenomenal baseball field in Bernardsville," says the Mastros' eldest son, Bill, who is the chairman and CEO of MastroNet, Inc., a premier auction firm for rare and significant Americana and sports memorabilia. Bill and his younger brother, Randy, dug long ditches along the rows of daffodils and used them as base paths. The tulip and azalea bushes became bases, and the boys fashioned a scoreboard and a strike zone in black chalk on the walls of the white house and the garage door. The young Mastro boys played every day. While Bill now regrets the damage he and his brother inflicted on their parents' lawn, he is comforted to know that Mom and Dad took great pride in the long-term benefits of the boys' passion for baseball, landscaping carnage aside.

In 1960, as a boisterous, adventuresome seven-year-old, Bill spent his spring and summer afternoons following baseball games on television and radio, playing stickball with Randy and the neighborhood kids, and riding his bicycle through the woods of Bernardsville, hunting for frogs and fishing for trout. He loved to ramble through all sorts of activities as a kid, but baseball was Mastro's passion. He could not get enough of it. When the long, cold winter months set in, he yearned for the bliss of the baseball and stickball season. That's where Geroloman's "Good ol' Geroloman's came to the rescue," Mastro fondly recalls.

Carl Geroloman—a lanky middle-aged gentleman, forever dressed in a plaid woolen V-neck sweater—owned Geroloman's, a grocery store just down the road from the Mastro home. When Bernardsville youngsters entered Mr. Geroloman's store, their attention sailed right past the nectarines, the cornstarch, the canned olives and all the other provisions in the small shop, and settled, in rapt fashion, upon the contents of the large glass case in front of the cash register. Behind the glass lay a profusion of penny candy in dazzling colors. It was a child's idea of heaven: PEZ dispensers, Necco candy wafers, licorice whips, green wax lips, peppermint balls, spearmint leaves, chocolate-

covered raisins, Bazooka bubble gum, Smarties, and taffy—all arrayed in tantalizing horizontal rows.

One mid-April afternoon in 1960, Bill took up his usual position in front of the case, his forehead and two hands pressed against the glass. "All right, kid," Mr. Geroloman said. "What do you want? And make it quick, I don't have all day." Bill examined every row of the case's delightful interior, inch by inch. And then he stopped. His eyes locked on a fresh red cardboard box of 1960 Topps baseball card packs. They were tucked between a carton of cherry lollipops and malted milk balls. Bill withdrew his entire week's allowance—a quarter—and placed it on the counter.

He came running out of Geroloman's with five packs in his pocket and, poring over

penders company (below) is unique for two reasons. First, it demonstrates the wide range of products that associated themselves with the national pastime in the early 20th century, and second, it features a woman as its central figure and pitch-person, which was quite rare for baseball-related products of the time. (30" x 12½")

Touting a BALL PLAYER'S PICTURE IN EVERY PACKAGE, a circa-1910 advertisement for Colgan's Chips chewing gum (below) features the likeness of legendary Pittsburgh shortstop Honus Wagner. Between 1909 and 1911, John Colgan, a former druggist from Louisville who is credited with improving the flavor of chewing gum, issued a baseball card set to augment sales of his "Colgan's Chips—The Gum That's Round." Mastro's original paper-stock advertising display was designed to fit in the corner of the window of candy stores, and the series featured a handful of other ball players as well. (20" x 26")

Featuring an illustration of an apple-cheeked lass enjoying a Coca-Cola at a baseball game, Mastro's 1922 calendar issued by the soft-drink giant is a fine example of the color lithographic graphics of the period. Coca-Cola calendars depicting baseball are quite rare. (30½" x 12")

Mastro's circa-1910 baseball-themed advertising display from the Utica sus-

the crisp new cards in the bright April sunlight, Mastro marveled at the portraits of many of the big leaguers he and his brothers emulated in stickball—Frank Howard, Nellie Fox, Bob Gibson, Bill Mazeroski, and Willie Mays, they were all there. Each pack came with a pink strip of bubble gum, which young Bill eagerly devoured. At home in his bedroom, he displayed the cards on top of his dresser and toy trunk.

He would go on to keep checklists of all the cards he owned and the ones he needed to complete the set, and he organized his cards numerically in drawers and P-F Flyer shoeboxes. He even placed them under his pillow at night. A new form of baseball passion had arrived in town, and it provided Bill with a way to make the it through the long Bernardsville winters.

"There was no way on earth that I was going to survive on a 25-cent weekly allowance after that day," Mastro recalls. He started collecting empty soda bottles and trading them in for their five-cent deposits to

An Old Gold Cigarettes advertisement from the 1930s featuring Babe Ruth (top right) would typically appear in a drugstore window display (top left). When the American Tobacco Company dissolved in 1911, Old Gold cigarettes became the property of the P. Lorillard Company, the oldest tobacco company in the United States. Lorillard reblended and relaunched Old Gold cigarettes in 1926, creating one of the most popular brands of the 1930s and 1940s. Lorillard spared no expense in advertising, as demonstrated by the heavy cardboard, three-panel display of the ultimate pitchman, the Bambino. (38" x 52")

To promote its P-F Canvas Shoes, the B.F. Goodrich footwear company sponsored a television interview series featuring the baseball stars of the day, including, as the heavy cardboard display (above right) indicates, Willie Mays, Pee Wee Reese, Stan Musial, and other future Hall of Famers. The "P-F" in the shoes' name stands

for Posture Foundation insole, which the company patented in 1933 and billed as "an innovation in comfort and performance." By the mid-1950s, P-F canvas shoes had become one of the most popular brands in America—remember P-F Flyers?—largely due to the TV-interview campaign. Television was still a relatively new medium, and it enabled millions of Americans (many for the first time) to see their favorite entertainers and athletes on a weekly basis. (30½" x 23")

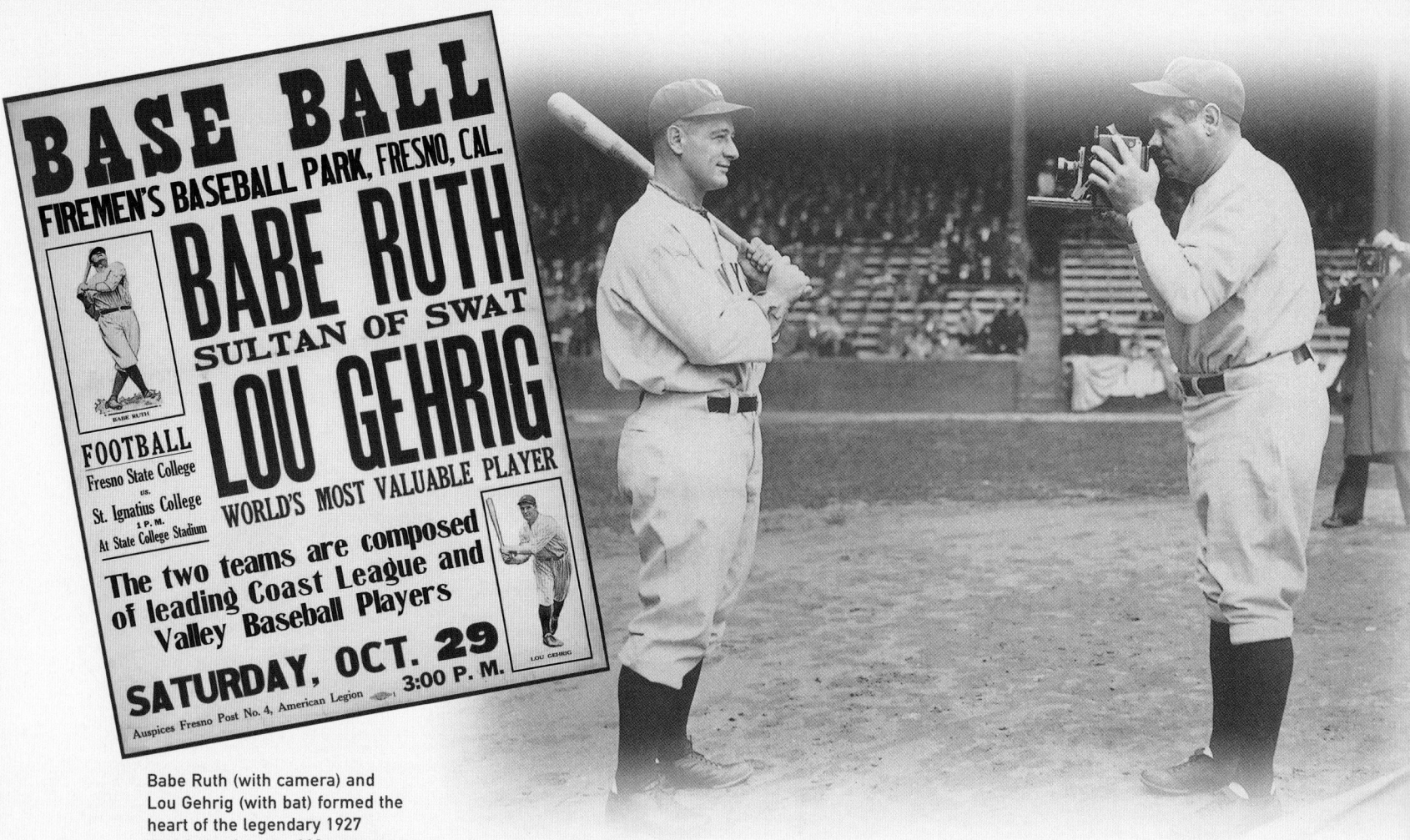

BASE BALL
FIREMEN'S BASEBALL PARK, FRESNO, CAL.
BABE RUTH
SULTAN OF SWAT
LOU GEHRIG
WORLD'S MOST VALUABLE PLAYER

FOOTBALL
Fresno State College
vs.
St. Ignatius College
1 P.M.
At State College Stadium

The two teams are composed of leading Coast League and Valley Baseball Players

SATURDAY, OCT. 29   3:00 P. M.

Auspices Fresno Post No. 4, American Legion

Babe Ruth (with camera) and Lou Gehrig (with bat) formed the heart of the legendary 1927 Yankees, who won 110 games and swept the Pittsburgh Pirates in the World Series. After that landmark season, Ruth and Gehrig embarked on a national tour, appearing in games with regional teams from coast to coast. Mastro owns a broadside (above) advertising one of the tour's last stops, in Fresno, California. The piece is one of only two known to exist, and it was originally a part of the Lou Gehrig family scrapbook. (20¾" x 28")

fund more packs of baseball cards at Geroloman's. He earned more money from his father, who promised him a nickel for every dandelion he plucked from the garden. "Day and night, I was out there plucking away," Mastro says. "And every time I found one, all I could think of was those marvelous packs waiting for me at Geroloman's." In 1965, Bill applied his entire savings to buying more than 2,000 1965 Topps packs, which pushed his collection past the 10,000-card mark.

Still, Bill was missing one card to complete the 1965 set of 572 cards: that of New York Yankees third-string catcher Bob Schmidt. But the case at Geroloman's was already stocked with football cards! To a 12-year-old who had come within one single card of completing an entire 1965 set, this was nothing short of a tragic set of circumstances. Amid the waist-high stacks of cards scattered across his bedroom floor, young Bill raged in frustration.

"I was absolutely miserable," Mastro recalls. "It was as if God was finally torturing me for tearing up my parents' yard. Not even one Bob Schmidt in over 2,000 packs! But,

come to think of it, missing that particular card was probably a blessing in disguise. Since there were no more packs left at Geroloman's, I had to look for other ways to get the Bob Schmidt card. During this search, I happened to discover a whole new area of the hobby that I never knew existed. I actually started to dream about making a living out of this stuff some day." Needless to say, that dream became a reality.

Back in his room, cursing the fates, and a third-string Yankees catcher, Mastro picked up an issue of *The Sporting News* that was lying under one of the card stacks. Inside, he found a tiny rectangular advertisement for Woody Gelman's The Card Collectors Company of Franklin Square, New York, that suggested, SEND 15 CENT STAMP AND QUARTER TO GET CATALOGUE. The catalog listed thousands of T206 tobacco cards—a major set issued by the American Tobacco Company between 1909 and 1911—as well as cards issued by prominent bubble-gum-card companies like Goudey, Topps, and Bowman.

Mastro ordered the Bob Schmidt card

from Gelman and then began wheeling and dealing with other card merchants listed in *The Sporting News*. It was the grassroots era of collecting; baseball cards were still a long way from becoming commercial, mainstream collectibles. Transactions were conducted by mail and often took several weeks, sometimes months, to complete.

Children weren't the only ones who enjoyed baseball cards in these early days—a group of devout hobby veterans, many of whom had been collecting cards since the 1930s and 1940s, also cherished them. New card issues and "new finds" of collections were frequently surfacing in basements, attics, flea markets, yard sales, and antique bazaars across the country.

Mastro's card collection grew exponentially, as did his circle of friends in the hobby. In 1966, he met Frank Nagy, whom many collectors regard as the father of modern card collecting. Owner of one of the largest collections in the Midwest, Nagy was an associate editor and writer for one of the hobby's leading publications at the time, *The Sport Hobbyist*. He took Mastro under

Mastro owns an original news service photo of Hack Wilson (below) as well as a series of photographs (above) showcasing the softer sides of some of baseball's greatest stars. The top row (l to r) features Walter Johnson holding his daughter on a giant novelty baseball mitt, Jackie Robinson sharing a few batting tips with his son, and Yankees great Waite Hoyt with his son Harry on opening day, 1924. In the middle row (l to r), the famously prickly Ty Cobb is captured in a rare moment of affection, with his son Ty Jr., Gil Hodges steals a taste of his son's ice cream cone, and Roy Campanella tries to figure out if his son will follow in his foot-steps. The bottom row (l to r) shows Phil Rizzuto posing with his family, Walter Johnson teaching his three sons and daughter how to pitch, and Eddie Collins horsing around on the lawn with his two sons.

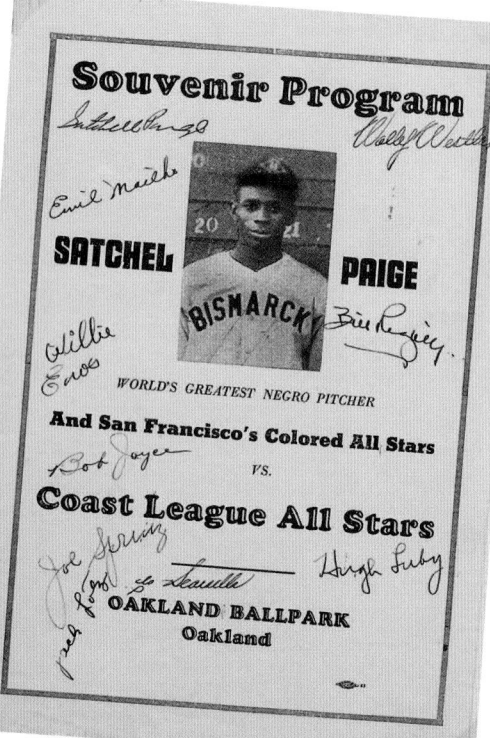

his wing, offering advice on how to collect, what to buy, and what to look out for. Mastro also learned from other hobby veterans like Fred McKie, Bill Haber, and Charles Bray. He attended baseball collecting's first organized assembly, which took place in the spring of 1969 in the upstate New York basement of veteran collector and dealer Mike Aronstein. It was the first time collectors from all over the country gathered in one place to trade, buy, and sell sports cards. Now, they descend upon the National Sports Collectors Convention, the industry's premier event, which is held in a different major city every year and draws tens of thousands of collectors, exhibitors, corporate sponsors, sports fans, and old friends.

By 1981, however, the sense of adventure and the mystique that characterized card collecting in the 1960s and 1970s had started to fade for Mastro. He already owned almost every significant card there was. Other forms of memorabilia seemed just as appealing as cards, Mastro thought, but were not appreciated nearly as much. He felt that very few people paid attention to collectible items such as vintage, first-generation photographs of Babe Ruth and Lou Gehrig, or large colorful advertising display pieces featuring portraits of ballplayers

like Ty Cobb, Christy Mathewson, or Ted Williams.

"Here were these incredibly visual artifacts with breathtaking artwork, craftsmanship, and eye appeal that pertained to all the legendary ballplayers from just about every era in baseball history," Mastro recalls. There were other relics, too: baseballs autographed by Jimmie Foxx or the 1955 Brooklyn Dodgers; postcards with images of Satchel Paige, Josh Gibson, or Cool Papa Bell, the list went on and on. "The items were much rarer, and larger in size, than any baseball card that I have ever owned," says Mastro. "And they could be easily displayed in an open forum and shared with everyone. This was in stark contrast to my baseball card collection, which was stored entirely in albums that were tucked into shelves or stacked in the closet."

The realization opened up a new world to Mastro. "Here was this whole new reservoir of amazing artifacts that had yet to be discovered and appreciated by anyone, let alone me," he recalls. "I felt as though I was looking inside the Geroloman's candy case once again, like that wonderful day back in April 1960."

Indeed, today Mastro's cavernous memorabilia display room resembles nothing so much as baseball's version of Geroloman's candy case. The walls are hung with ornately-framed rare baseball photographs, baseball-themed advertising displays, and cases full of memorabilia ranging from

Mastro owns an assortment of Negro League ephemera, including postcard portraits of the 1931 Homestead Grays (above left, sepia-toned card), who are widely regarded as the best Negro League team of all time, and the 1932 Pittsburgh Crawfords (top left), known as the "Black Yankees" for their formidable lineup that included future Hall of Famers Oscar Charleston, Satchel Paige, and Josh Gibson. As a rookie playing for the Grays in '31, Gibson (top row, fourth from the right in Grays photo) hit 75 homers and helped his team to a 163–23 record.

While Negro League stars were banned from playing major-league ball, they did occasionally play in major-league parks, such as Comiskey and Wrigley, as Mastro's tickets (above middle) document.

A souvenir program (above right) from an early 1940s game between "San Francisco's Colored All Stars" and the Coast League All Stars featured legendary Negro League pitcher Satchel Paige on its cover. "Age is a case of mind over matter," Paige once quipped. "If you don't mind, it don't matter." And Paige didn't: His career spanned four decades (five if you count three shutout innings he pitched against Boston in 1965), and his abilities were lavishly praised by such stars as Joe DiMaggio and Bob Feller. (10" x 7")

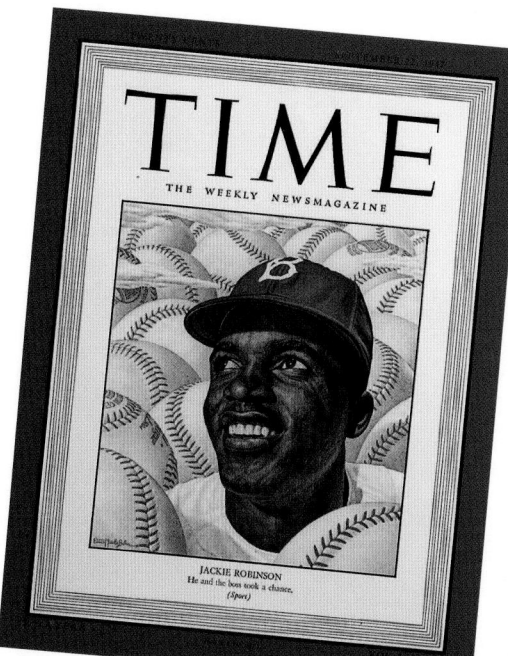

watch fobs, match books, and cigar labels, to ashtrays, flip books, and store-model bats. Most of Mastro's photographs are original first-generation black-and-white or sepia-toned prints shot by prominent baseball photographers from the early 20th century through the 1950s. The images are striking, and they run the gamut of famous ballplayers from almost every era. But the most intriguing aspect of the photograph collection is the uniqueness of a number of the images: renowned photographer Charles Conlon's close-up image of Honus Wagner's face, Babe Ruth snapping a photograph of teammate Lou Gehrig; Hack Wilson standing next to a stack of wagons made in his honor, to name just three.

It was a natural progression for Mastro to move from collecting baseball cards to collecting vintage photographs. "When I look at a specific piece of memorabilia, I want to feel as though I am actually going back in time," Mastro explains. Photographs can evoke this sensation like no other form of memorabilia. Certain images, such as the Conlin close-up of Wagner's face, tend to link the present with the past.

Many vintage advertising posters and cardboard display pieces wield similar emotional power. Each piece's typography, design, use of color, and slogans reflect the era in which it originated. The advertisements for Colgan's chips (1909), Tuxedo tobacco (1910), and Utica athletic suspenders (1910), as well as the Coca-Cola calendar (1922), feature the beautiful color lithographic artwork that was customary in early-20th-century advertising. By contrast, the P-F canvas shoes and Jell-O gelatin dessert displays draw on the mass-produced art typical of the 1950s and 1960s.

Picking up a copy of the premier sports auction catalog produced by Mastronet, the company he founded in 1996 with lifelong friend and hobby veteran Don Steinbach, Mastro flips through its pages and stops at Lot 1249, which features an unopened box of 24 1960 Topps five-cent wax packs, the same kind that Mastro bought from Geroloman's candy case more than 40 years earlier. "It's been an incredible journey," he says. "I am truly grateful to have had the opportunity to be a part of this remarkable industry of ours. There are so many wonderful baseball objects to collect nowadays. . . . It's come a long way since the days of Woody, Nagy, McKie, Haber, Bray, and Aronstein."

He looks at a framed photograph of his mother and father on top of his desk. "I'm also grateful to them, and hope they have forgiven me for tearing up the yard."

20TH-CENTURY BASEBALL MEMORABILIA

BY BILL MASTRO

There are many factors you could consider before launching a collection of 20th-century baseball memorabilia, but first and foremost, collect what you like! Although many hobbyists zero in on Babe Ruth or the Yankees, on pins or postcards, or on similarly defined areas of interest, you do not have to limit yourself to a specific team or player or type of collectible. As you collect, don't worry so much about investment. Sometimes you'll get a deal, and sometimes you'll overpay, but if you always buy what you like, it doesn't really

Falling outside the scope of more traditional collectibles, 20th-century baseball memorabilia (above) come in a wide range of unique objects, including catalogs, unused tickets, postcards, pins, matchboxes, cocktail menus, cigar boxes, statues, ashtrays, drinking glasses, and many more artifacts. World-class collector Bill Mastro suggests that you let your personal taste, more than anything else, guide you when you embark on a collecting hobby. That way, you'll enjoy every item you acquire, regardless of its market value.
The Bill Mastro Collection.

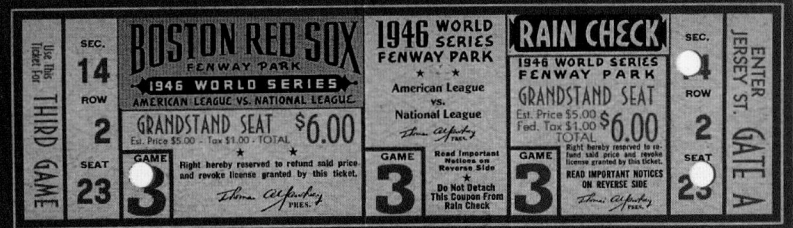

An unused ticket to Game 4 of the 1927 World Series (left, top, 7½" x 2¼") prompts the question of why its original owner opted not to attend the game, passing up a chance to see the mighty '27 Yankees complete a sweep of the Pittsburgh Pirates and cap arguably the greatest season in franchise history. The Series ended when Pittsburgh's Johnny Miljus threw a wild pitch—his second one of the inning—with the bases loaded in the bottom of the ninth and New York outfielder Earle Combs raced home with the Series-clinching run. The Marshall Fogel Collection.

The first World Series game played at Fenway Park since 1918, Game 3 of the 1946 Fall Classic was a 4–0 victory for Boston over St. Louis, but one fan chose to pass on the historic game, as an unused six-dollar ticket (left, bottom, 7½" x 2¼") attests. The Wong Family Archives Collection.

matter what it's worth down the line. At least you'll have items you enjoy.

Personally, I am always intrigued to see baseball gloves still lying undisturbed in original tissue paper, never having been removed from their cardboard boxes for so much as a game of catch. When I was a kid, a new glove got beaten to a pulp in the old Woody Wagon before we even got home. And the box, forget about it! Who ever saved a box of Jell-O or Bazooka bubble gum? Today, the sight of these survivors, featuring a likeness of Roger Maris or Mickey Mantle, still captivate us as they did the youngsters who saw them on the grocery store shelves decades ago.

In addition to collecting relics that evoke stories of great baseball players, or memorabilia items that have defied the passage of time, it is rewarding to collect conversation pieces. People might ask, "How does that still exist?" or "Where did you get that?" And these marvelous pieces of history don't have to cost a fortune. It can be just as rewarding to own a postcard or cocktail menu or a water glass from Joe DiMaggio's Fisherman's Wharf Restaurant in the 1940s as it is to own a baseball signed by Babe Ruth. If you visited San Francisco back in that day, DiMaggio's eatery was a mandatory stop. "I remember those," visitors often say when they see the water glass with Joe's silhouette on the side. It doesn't cost much to put that little glass

into a collection, and it sure brings back memories.

The beauty of being a generalist, or "mainstream" collector is that very few limits are placed on your passion. You can expand your collection whenever you encounter an appealing item, regardless of its category. Bats, balls, pins, cigar boxes, ad pieces, and many other items showcase baseball.

Sure, a Babe Ruth collectible is easier to explain, and will draw more attention, than, say, a Babe Dahlgren piece, but the occasional offbeat item slips nicely into the mix. (A piece involving lefthander Don Mossi, for example, is a welcome addition to any collection—especially one that shows off his big ears!) A championship team panorama is usually more intriguing than a photo of a cellar dweller, unless the cellar dweller has some

interesting feature—a Hall of Fame star, or a unique character playing shortstop.

Rarity is nice, but "one-of-a-kind" is overrated if there are only three people on Earth who can relate to it. Still, you can stray off the path occasionally if you wish. It's your hobby, after all. As your collection grows, it will all come together.

One personal story about the unpredictable nature of

A cocktail menu (above, 5" x 3½") and a postcard (left, 5½" x 3½") advertise Joe DiMaggio's Restaurant in San Francisco during the early 1940s. The postcard features the likenesses of the three DiMaggio brothers (l to r), Vincent, Joe and Dom, all of whom played it the major leagues. The Marshall Fogel Collection.

Considering the highly disposable nature of candy wrappers, it's a minor miracle that one from Ruth's Home Run candy (below)—which was produced in 1928 only by the George H. Ruth Candy Co.—would still exist, much less in such remarkable condition. (7" x 5") The Wong Family Archives Collection.

A circa-1909 Hans Wagner oval cigar box label and band (above) show so little evidence of wear, that they may have never been used for their intended purpose. Perhaps Wagner had second thoughts about allowing his likeness to market a tobacco product, much as he did when he refused to allow the American Tobacco Company to use his likeness in its T206 baseball card set. (label, 4¼" x 3¼"; band, 3" x 5/8") The Wong Family Archives Collection.

memorabilia comes to mind. I got carried away with Babe Ruth's handprint at a particular auction. After a seemingly interminable bidding period (and some astronomical price jumps), I took the print home to add to my collection. Proudly, I put the sheet under glass on a book pedestal that stands in my hobby room. To date, not a single person, including the handyman and the exterminator, has ever entered that room without placing a palm atop the Bambino's paw print. Now that's a conversation piece!

Figuring out how to display your collection is a bit like interior decorating. There is an artistic component to presenting the items in a manner that invites appreciation of their unique aesthetics. To enhance the viewing experience, be creative. Rather than storing two-dimensional pieces in albums, frame and display them for everyone to see. Be sure to keep the edges and corners of the piece visible.

Frame particularly important items between two pieces of glass, so that the back can be seen. You might arrange smaller framed pieces decoratively around the room to enliven a variety of surfaces. Also, try designing your own, custom-made display cases and hangers for caps, balls, and bats.

Many "sports rooms" use every inch of available space. Hobby display areas may be laid out in intricate, jigsaw-puzzle fashion, like a kaleidoscope of sports collectibles. Remember, there's always room for refinement. Upgrade, reconfigure, and rework your collection. It can be a work in progress that never comes to a completion but always captivates the viewer and never grows stale.

Try to collect things in exceptional condition, as close to perfect as possible. A dealer sometimes will attempt to sell a damaged item to a collector by declaring, "It's as good as it gets." Frankly, condition is a big part of an item's appeal. Over the years, most enthusiasts will come to regret having compromised on a condition standard. It may be acceptable to tolerate a tiny flaw or two, but many collectors aren't truly happy unless the piece sparkles and amazes. Of course, there are occasions when rarity or value trumps condition, but, generally, a col-

A 1920s Wilson fielders glove (left), endorsed by Rogers Hornsby, appears in its original box. (5½" tall, 9½" square base) The Greg Gallacher Collection.

In 1958, one year after the Milwaukee Braves won the World Series, a small plastics company based in Hartland, Wisconsin, decided to capitalize on the popularity of the Braves by making lifelike statues of Hank Aaron, Eddie Mathews, and Warren Spahn. (The company also produced statues of Yankees legends Babe Ruth and Mickey Mantle.) They became so popular with kids that Hartland added statues (above with the original boxes in which they were sold) of stars from Chicago teams—Ernie Banks (Cubs), Nellie Fox (White Sox) and Luis Aparicio (White Sox). Produced from detailed drawings of the players and coming in a variety of poses, the Hartland statues were sold in dime stores and major-league ballpark concession stands. (7" tall) The Ron Leff Family Collection.

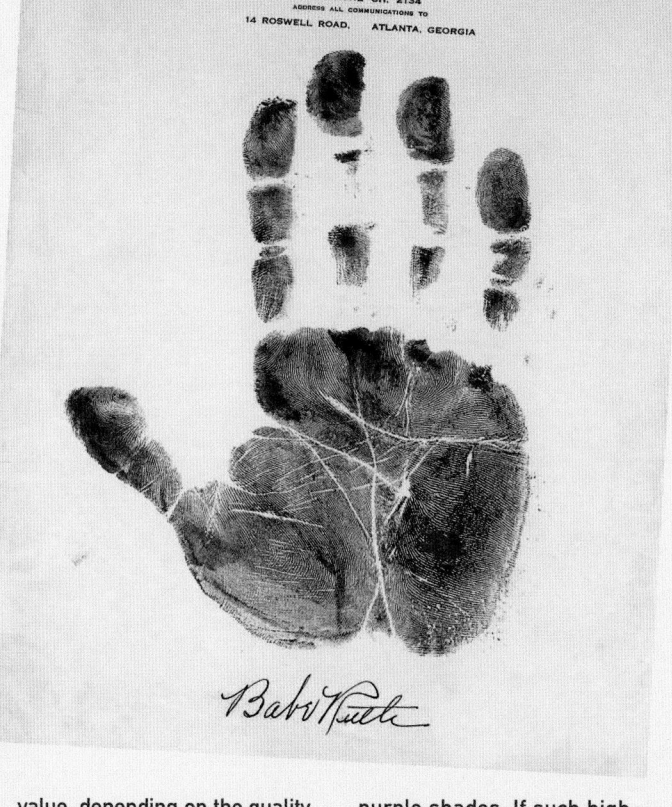

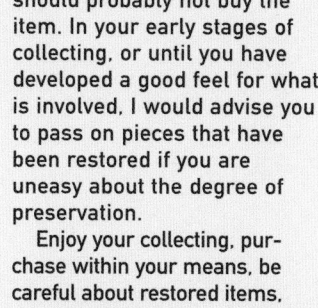

A heartwarming letter (above) from Roger Maris to a boy named Bobby evokes a simpler time, when ballplayers responded to letters from fans requesting autographed pictures or simply asking questions. Maris discusses Babe Ruth's single-season home run record, which he had recently broken, and gives the youngster a bit of fatherly advice. (8" x 6") The Marshall Fogel Collection.

In the late 1920s, *Baseball* magazine published a story exploring the reasons behind Babe Ruth's hitting prowess. Ruth submitted to a variety of tests, including a hand and fingerprint analysis. The Babe's original handprint (above right) was featured in the article, on the letterhead of a "Character Analysis" agent, with the Bambino's signature at the bottom of the page. (8½" x 11") The Bill Mastro Collection.

lector wants an item in the best condition possible.

When appropriate, consider restoration. Our hobby has matured greatly over the past few decades, and standards have changed. Restoration is now generally acceptable. In today's highly sophisticated collecting community and big-ticket display-piece world, some degree of restoration is performed on the vast majority of pieces. Some ground rules exist, however: It is commonly understood that restoring baseball cards is taboo, and you should also be aware that the restoration of autographed baseballs is highly fraudulent and should never be done. Collectors tend to be much more tolerant of restoration in more sizeable items. Display pieces, such as cardboard ads, original photos, boxes and packaging, movie posters, and

larger pieces are generally acceptable items for enhancement, provided the restoration is done subtly and professionally. Each collector must make an individual decision about what constitutes restoration and what borders on the re-creation of a piece. If overdone, the restoration of a collectible markedly reduces its value, but subtle and even moderate professional restoration may significantly enhance a piece's value.

As a collector, you have the right to know if an item has been restored. In certain instances, cleaning, erasing, and general "sprucing up" of pieces is almost undetectable. But any restoration should be disclosed to potential buyers. Trimming, color touching, inpainting, paper filling, and Japanese tissue-paper reinforcement in varying degrees require disclosure. They may or may not affect the item's

value, depending on the quality of workmanship. Most collectors prefer to avoid drastically restored pieces, even if the restoration eludes easy detection.

But how does one determine whether a piece has been restored? A five- or 10-power magnifier under bright lights usually reveals the degree of pattern interruption and the places where restoration begins and ends. A portable black light in a dark room will also give a clear picture of any restoration. The retouched areas will glow in

purple shades. If such highlighting is extensive, you should probably not buy the item. In your early stages of collecting, or until you have developed a good feel for what is involved, I would advise you to pass on pieces that have been restored if you are uneasy about the degree of preservation.

Enjoy your collecting, purchase within your means, be careful about restored items, and place no limits on what you seek to acquire. The mainstream memorabilia hobby can be the most rewarding of all of the fields of baseball collecting, and once you enter it, you'll never run out of delightful items to discover and collect.

A Topps's Bazooka bubble gum box with a jumbo-sized baseball card of Mickey Mantle on the bottom (left) would not have been an uncommon sight at the local candy store to a youngster in 1959, the year Bazooka issued the series. Mantle hit .285 with 31 homers in 141 games that season, a slight step down from his league-leading 42 home runs and .304 average of the previous season. (5¾" x 3½" x 1½") The Bill Mastro Collection.

17

COMING HOME

Bill DeWitt Jr. owns an original photograph (opposite) of one of his most cherished childhood memories—that of meeting the great Babe Ruth at Sportsman's Park in St. Louis when he was six years old. The Bambino autographed the photo in the lower right corner, writing, BEST WISHES TO BILLY, SINCERELY, BABE RUTH, JUNE 19, 1948. (8" x 10")

" Some baseball is the fate of all of us."
—Robert Frost

William Orville DeWitt Sr., the father of Bill DeWitt Jr., devoted 64 years of his life to major-league baseball. In his remarkable career, he created the family legacy that for three generations has been devoted to the national pastime. The DeWitts' experience informs the family's marvelous collection of baseball-related mementos—a rich repository that both reflects the DeWitts' baseball life and celebrates some of the game's unique moments.

On April 12, 1892, the St. Louis Cardinals franchise (known as the Browns until 1899) made its National League debut with a 14–10 loss to the Chicago Colts (later renamed the Cubs) at Sportsman's Park in St. Louis. Located at Grand Avenue and Dodier Street, Sportsman's was being rebuilt following a fire that had destroyed it a year earlier. St. Louis finished its inaugural National League season with a dismal 56 wins and 94 losses, a record that put the team in second-to-last place, 46 games behind the first-place Boston Beaneaters (later renamed the Braves). The Browns' unsuccessful National League baptism, on top of the loss of their park to the fire, seemed to foreshadow the seasons to come. During the next 24 years, the franchise produced only three winning seasons.

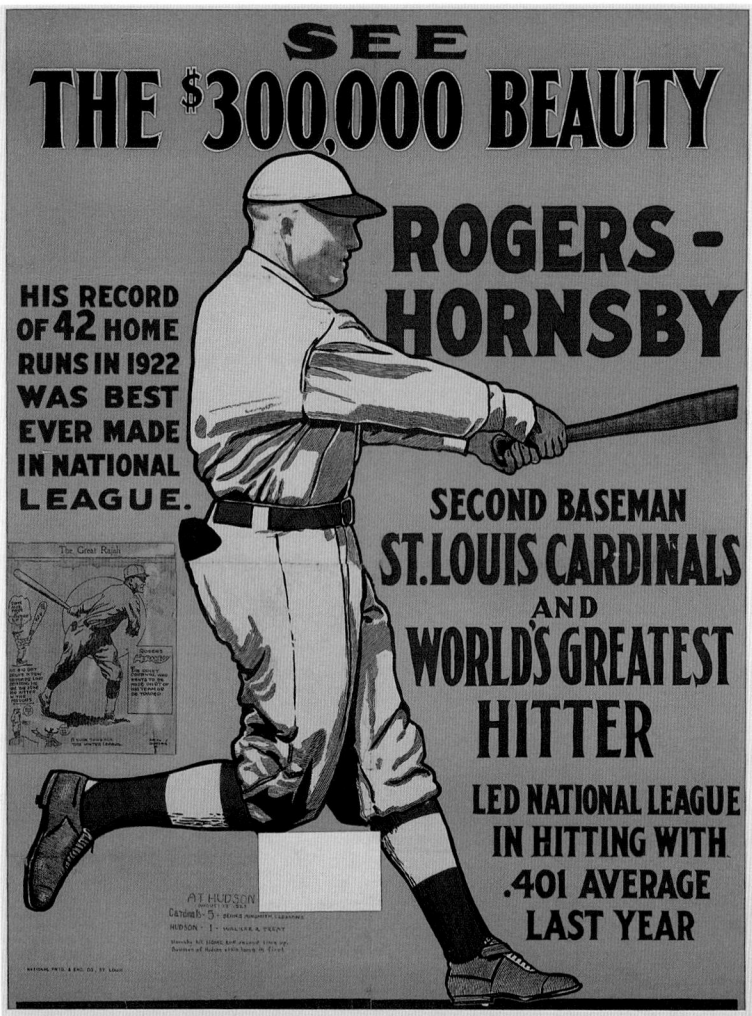

New York—Dizzy and Daffy Dean, pitching aces of the St. Louis Cardinals—world champion baseball team—have entered the movies. They are now making a Warner "short" on a Brooklyn Field. Left to right, Dizzy and Daffy Dean, Sam Sax of Warner Brothers and William DeWitt, treasurer of the Cardinals.

INTERNATIONAL NEWS PHOTO.

A spectacular multi-colored broadside (above) heralds Cardinals legend Rogers Hornsby's appearance in an exhibition game on August 23, 1923. Hornsby's first full season with the Cardinals was in 1916, the same year that Bill DeWitt Sr. started selling soda pop in the grandstands of Robison Field. In addition to the acheivements listed on the broadside, Hornsby led the National League in hitting for three consecutive seasons before 1923, and in 1922 he won the Triple Crown. (26" x 35")

Bill DeWitt Sr. appears in a paper-stock broadside (above, right) alongside Cardinals pitchers and brothers Dizzy and Daffy Dean and Warner Brothers executive Sam Sax. The photograph, which ran in the *Chicago Herald and Examiner*, touted a short film featuring the colorful St. Louis pitchers. Dizzy Dean, who led the National League in strikeouts for four consecutive seasons (1932–35), appealed to Hollywood as much for his fre-

quent interesting turns of phrase as for his prowess on the mound. "It puzzles me how they know what corners are good for filling stations," Dizzy once remarked. "Just how did they know gas and oil was under there?" After getting hit in the head by a ball during the 1934 World Series, Dizzy was asked what the doctors had said. He replied, "The doctors x-rayed my head and found nothing." (11" x 9")

Then came 1916, a season almost as bad as the Redbirds' National League debut. St. Louis finished 60–93, but there was a silver lining: the full-season debut of second baseman Rogers Hornsby, who would go on to become arguably the greatest righthanded batter in baseball history. Hornsby had played 18 games for St. Louis the previous season, hitting an unimpressive .246, but, given the chance to play every day in 1916, he blossomed, batting .313 and launching what would become an eminent

hitting career marked by six consecutive batting titles and two Triple Crowns. His annual batting average would fall below .300 only once in the next 15 years, and he would finish his 23-year career with a .358 average, the second highest career average in baseball history, behind Ty Cobb.

Apart from Hornsby's fine season, though, 1916 was a glum year for St. Louis, and in October the team's owner, Helene Hathaway Robison Britton, sold the club to a group of fan-stockholders headed by her attorney, James C. Jones. One of Jones's first moves as the club owner was to hire a new vice president and general manager, 35-year-old Wesley Branch Rickey. Rickey, of course, would go on to make history with the Dodgers in 1945—when he signed Jackie Robinson to a minor-league contract and, two years later, helped break Major League Baseball's color barrier—but he faced monumental challenges when he

ST. LOUIS BROWNS 1944

Top Row... WEST, P... SHIRLEY, P... MUNCRIEF, P... HAFEY, of... HAYWORTH, C... KRAMER, P... HOLLINGSWORTH, GALEHOUSE, P... KREEVICH, of... JAKUCKI, P...

Center Row... C. DEWITT, Traveling Sec'y... CASTER, P... BAKER, If... POTTER, P... ZARILLA, of... LAABS, of... McQUINN, 1f... CHRISTMAN, 1f... BYRNES, of... STEPHENS, If... BAUMAN, Trainer... HANLEY, Property Man...

Bottom Row... PAUL, P... ZOLDAK, P... CLARY, If... HOFMAN, Coach... SEWELL, Mgr... TAYLOR, Coach... CHARTAK, of... MANCUSO, C... MOORE, of... GUTTERIDGE, 2f... BOB SCANLON, Bat Boy...

PHOTO BY. GEO DORRILL

joined the Cardinals' front office in 1917. Given the organization's scant financial resources, the Cardinals could not afford to compete with other clubs in purchasing the best talent from independent minor-league teams. Rickey, the budding visionary, decided to "grow his own" talent through a team-owned, minor-league farm system. He envisioned a Cardinals network of minor-leagues whose purpose was to produce talent for the big-league team as well as surplus players whom they could sell to other teams at a profit. Rickey's farm-system plan was a monumental undertaking that involved tracking and evaluating players in every organization, hiring a network of scouts, building and operating minor-league tryout camps, and developing a systematic method of training players.

But by the early 1920s the Cardinals' farm-club system was flourishing: Up to 800 players were under contract with 32 teams.

The results were as revolutionary as the man behind the plan: Between 1919 and 1942, under Rickey's stewardship, the Cardinals won six National League pennants and four World Series titles. The rest of the league eventually followed Rickey's lead, and today, farm clubs are standard (though each team operates only five or six minor-league teams).

To successfully implement and operate a system of such magnitude required a lot of trusted lieutenants. One of Rickey's protégés during this pivotal period of Cardinals' history was William Orville DeWitt, who went on to become one of baseball's most prominent front-office men himself. Born in 1902 and raised in North St. Louis, DeWitt was a hardworking boy who loved the game of baseball and revered the Cardinals. After attending grade school and briefly helping his parents at their small family-owned grocery store, DeWitt

An original sepia-toned photograph of the 1944 St. Louis Browns (above)—the team that won the club's first and only American League pennant—resides in DeWitt's remarkable collection. His uncle, Charlie DeWitt, who was the club's traveling secretary at the time, stands on the far left, wearing a tie. (9½" x 7¼")

OLD JUDGE COFFEE
SETTLES THE QUESTION

decided it was time to put his work ethic to use with the team he so admired. In 1916—the year Hornsby blossomed and James Jones approached Rickey—DeWitt took a job selling soda pop in the grandstands of Robison Field, located between Vandeventer and Natural Bridge Avenues, which was the Cardinals' home from 1893 to 1920. (The team left Sportsman's Park after that 1892 season, and returned to a rebuilt version of it in 1920.)

DeWitt's good-natured demeanor and hustle in the grandstands drew attention. Within a few months, the team asked him to join the front office as an office boy. Impressed by the youngster's capabilities, Rickey eventually took DeWitt under his wing and taught him the art of persuasive rhetoric and the nuances of front-office decision-making. He also encouraged his young charge to pursue a college education and a law degree. Following his mentor's advice, DeWitt earned undergraduate and law degrees at night from St. Louis's Washington University and St. Louis University, respectively. During the day, he worked his way up the Cardinals organization's ladder, including a stint as director of the farm system—during which he helped Rickey oversee the construction and operation of minor-league ballparks throughout the St. Louis system—and a period as head of player development. During the 1930s—a Golden Age in Cardinals history, when the team won three pennants and one world championship—DeWitt served as vice president and treasurer of the franchise. The team from that era, known affectionately as "the Gashouse Gang," featured such colorful characters as Dizzy and Paul Dean, Ducky Medwick, Pepper Martin, and Frankie Frisch.

By 1939, DeWitt's front-office acumen had landed him a position as CEO and general manager of the city's other major-league ball club, the Browns of the American League. (The Milwaukee Brewers, charter members of the AL, had moved to St. Louis after the 1901 season and become the Browns.) In that capacity, DeWitt was named Major League Executive of the Year in 1944, the year the Browns won their first and only American League pennant. In

In 1935, the David G. Evans Coffee Company of St. Louis, manufacturers of Old Judge Coffee, produced a set of four stunning wall-display calendars in honor of the four St. Louis Cardinals championship teams between 1931 and 1944. DeWitt owns the one issued in 1935 (opposite) to pay tribute to the Gashouse Gang's 1934 World Series victory over the Detroit Tigers. Included on the calendar is a black-and-white composite photograph of the entire team, including Bill DeWitt Sr., who was the team's Vice President and Treasurer. (15" x 35")

Browns owner Bill Veeck's stunt involving the diminutive Eddie Gaedel came during a gala celebration of the American League's Golden Anniversary at Sportsman's Park, yet despite the occasion, it's unlikely that any photographers would have turned up to document the event: It was mid-August and St. Louis was well out of contention. But Veeck had tipped *St. Louis Post-Dispatch* reporter Bill Broeg about his plan, and Broeg sent *Post-Dispatch* photographer Jack January to the game. January snapped the only photo of Gaedel at the plate (top right).

Gaedel wore a Browns jersey (inset) that belonged to the team's nine-year-old batboy, Bill DeWitt Jr. Although many observers found the stunt entertaining, American League president Will Harridge was not one of them. He banned "midgets" from appearing in any future games. "Fine," Veeck said. "Let's establish what a midget is in fact. Is it three-feet-six inches? Eddie's height? Is it four-feet-six? If it's five-feet-six, that's great. We can get rid of [Phil] Rizzuto."

Gaedel made his entrance by popping out of a giant anniversary cake made of papier-mâché, a moment captured in DeWitt's original news service photograph from the day (above, right). The PA announcer declared: "As a special birthday present to manager Zack Taylor, the management is presenting him with a brand-new Brownie." (8" x 10")

1948, DeWitt and his brother Charlie bought the team, which they owned until financial pressures forced them to sell to Bill Veeck Jr. in 1951. Bill DeWitt remained General Manager under Veeck until the team moved to Baltimore in 1953.

The years DeWitt spent with the Browns franchise produced some unforgettable moments, according to his son, Bill DeWitt Jr., who is the current principal owner, chairman, and CEO of the St. Louis Cardinals. Chief among Bill Jr.'s treasured memories is Babe Ruth Day at Sportsman's Park on June 19, 1948. The day was part of a season-long promotional tour of major league ballparks that featured the Babe

teaching kids how to hold and swing a bat. In each stadium, one child was chosen to stand next to the legendary Bambino as he demonstrated the art of hitting the long ball.

It was six-year-old Bill Jr.'s lucky day. He stood next to the barrel-chested Sultan of Swat and looked up at the Babe's iconic mug against the powder-blue sky. Bill Jr. stood motionless in front of the thousands of fans packed into the park. Suffering from throat cancer at the time, Ruth spoke slowly, in a hoarse, baritone voice, which, amplified over the loudspeakers, sounded like the chant of an old sage. "Now Billy," Ruth instructed Bill Jr., "keep your paws nice and

An original photograph, taken on January 24, 1956, shows Bill DeWitt Sr., Assistant General Manager of the New York Yankees, signing Mickey Mantle to his contract for the 1956 season (above, left). That season would turn out to be one of Mantle's finest: he won the American League MVP and the Triple Crown, belting 52 homers, driving in 130 runs, and batting .353. The photo was autographed by Mantle, who wrote, TO BILL DEWITT, MY BEST WISHES, MICKEY MANTLE. (8" x 10")

With Bill DeWitt Sr. and Yankees general manager George Weiss looking on, Yogi Berra signed his contract for the 1956 season (above, right). "He'd fall in a sewer and come up with a gold watch," Casey Stengel once said about his star backstop. Berra may not have possessed the grace of Joe DiMaggio, but the Yankees always seemed to win with him behind the plate. When a sportswriter asked Stengel about the secret to his success in managing the Bronx Bombers, Stengel said he never started a game without "my man"—his man being Berra, who had already won three American League MVPs by the time this original photograph was shot. (8" x 10")

snug near the knob, pick a good one, and sock it." Ruth certainly was not the force he had been in the days of Murderers' Row, the heart of the dominant New York Yankees teams of the late 1920s. But to Bill Jr., it didn't matter: he knew this was a moment he would never forget. He has a photograph from the day, of himself standing next to the Bambino, autographed by Ruth—it's one of many invaluable personal mementos in the DeWitt Collection.

Meeting the biggest star in the history of the game tops DeWitt's list of fond memories, naturally, but he has another cherished recollection, from baseball's quirkier side. By the early 1950s, attendance at major-league ballparks had begun to slip significantly. This was not a sign that the game was losing popularity, but rather the result of three unrelated factors: the growing prevalence of television, the dominance of the three New York teams (which disheartened fans who didn't root for the Giants, Yankees, or Dodgers); and the steady migration out of cities and into suburbs, away from big-league ballparks. Paid attendance for major-league games had fallen from almost 21 million in 1948 to 17 million in 1952; approximately 25 percent of the paying fans of 1948 were now staying away from the ballpark. The situation was even worse for struggling teams like the Browns, who had finished no better than third place for five consecutive seasons before 1951.

Desperate times called for desperate measures, and club owners scrambled to find new ways to bring fans back to the ballpark. Veeck Jr., who had bought the Browns from Bill and Charlie DeWitt in July 1951, quickly blossomed into a promotional wizard. A month after taking over the team, he came up with an idea that led to another experience Bill DeWitt Jr. will never forget. It involved a ballplayer literally half Babe Ruth's size.

At the start of the 1951 season, Rawlings, the manufacturer of the Browns' uniforms, had made a special child-sized jersey for Bill Jr., who was the team's batboy. On August 19, 1951, during a Sunday doubleheader between the Browns and the Detroit Tigers, Sportsman's Park staged a dual anniversary celebration for the Browns' radio sponsor, Falstaff Brewery, and the American League's 50th year of existence. The celebration featured stuntmen, antique cars, a trampolinist, a band made up of Browns players (including Satchel Paige), and, for the grand finale, a giant anniversary cake.

But the ever-imaginative Veeck had a surprise for everyone: He planned to send 3'7", 65-pound Eddie Gaedel to bat during the first inning of the second game. Gaedel needed a jersey small enough to fit his tiny frame, so Veeck borrowed nine-year-old Bill Jr.'s batboy uniform, removed the number 6 from the back of the jersey, and replaced it with "$^1/_8$". It would be Gaedel's only appearance in a

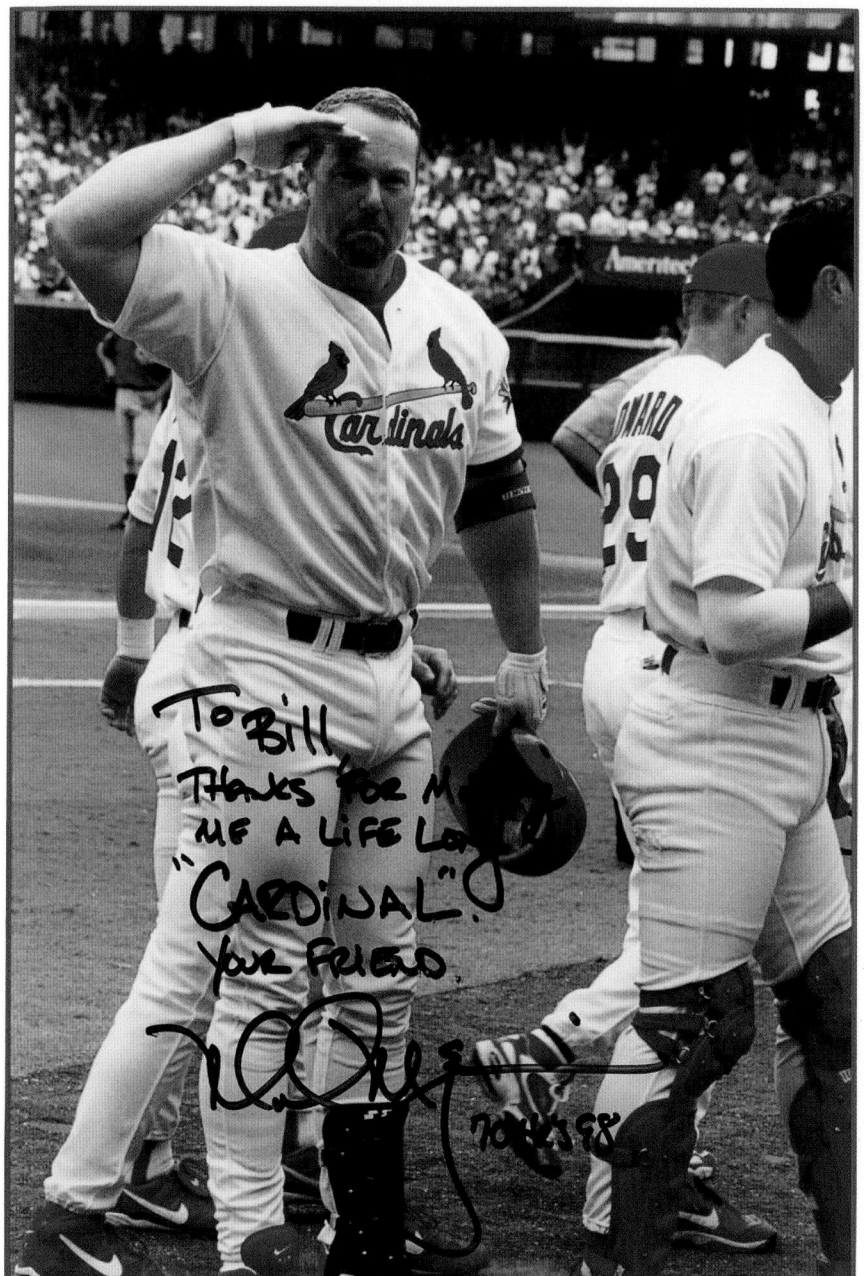

Mark McGwire (left) saluted DeWitt Jr. and the owner's box after he hit his 61st home run of the 1998 season to tie Roger Maris's single season home run record, set in 1961. "It's been quite something ever since Mark arrived," DeWitt said of McGwire, who joined the Redbirds in July 1997. "The fans came out in droves. I don't think it necessarily would have happened in other places. St. Louis has such a wonderful tradition with great players and so many Hall of Famers, 15 pennants, and the second most number of world championships, that they really gravitated to him, knowing this was an epic figure in the history of baseball." DeWitt's photograph of the historic moment is inscribed, To Bill, thanks for making me a lifetime "Cardinal." your friend Mark McGwire—70 Hr's 98. (12" x 8")

Cardinals legend Stan "The Man" Musial posed for the camera with Bill DeWitt Sr. in the mid-1970s. He later inscribed the photograph, To Bill, a dedicated baseball man—best wishes from your friend Stan Musial. (8" x 10")

major-league game, and his sole objective was to reach first base on a walk. He would then be replaced by pinch runner Jim Delsing. Under no circumstances was Gaedel to swing at a pitch. To drive that point home, the jovial Veeck told Gaedel that he would be up on the roof of the stands with a high-powered rifle, and would fire at him if Gaedel dared swing the bat. Gaedel drew the walk on four pitches (all high, of course) and, in Veeck's words, "trotted down to first base to the happy tune of snapping cameras." He also walked his way into baseball immortality as the ballplayer with the highest on-base percentage of all time, and he became an instant celebrity as the star of baseball's most bizarre promotional endeavor, one that remains a touchstone today. In the months that followed, Gaedel appeared on a number of television programs, including the Ed Sullivan and Bing Crosby shows. When he died in 1961, the *New York Times* ran his obituary on the front page. As for his jersey, it was given back to Bill Jr., who still owns it. The jersey is currently on loan to the National Baseball Hall of Fame and Museum.

Between 1955 and 1980, Bill DeWitt Sr. continued his front-office career with a number of top-brass positions with teams other than the Cardinals and Browns. As assistant general manager of the New York Yankees (1955–57), he oversaw the contracts of Mickey Mantle, Yogi Berra, Phil Rizzuto, Billy Martin, and other Bronx Bombers. He then served as presi-

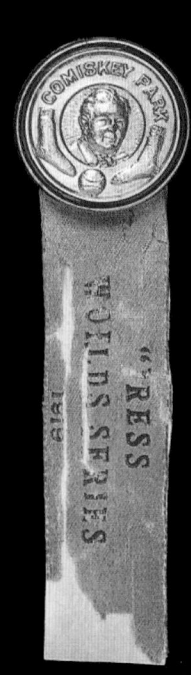

World Series Press Pins

The 1908 National League regular season ended in a tie between the New York Giants and the Chicago Cubs. On October 8, the two teams met in a playoff game at the Polo Grounds to determine the pennant winner, who would go on to play the Detroit Tigers in the World Series. The Polo Grounds had never seen a crowd so large. Cubs ace hurler Mordecai Brown recalled, "The Polo Grounds quit selling tickets about one o' clock . . . and thousands who held tickets couldn't force their way through the street mobs to the entrances. By game time there were thousands on the field in front of the bleachers, the stands were jammed. . . . The elevated lines couldn't run because of people who had climbed up and were sitting on the tracks." Members of the press went down to the field to conduct their usual interviews with the players before the start of the game. While they were there, Giants manager John McGraw invited a number of his friends to sit in the press box. When the sportswriters returned, they discovered they had no seats. Six days later on October 14, 1908, during the final game of the World Series at Detroit's Bennett Park, sports reporters were again upset at seating arrangements. These two events led a group of sportswriters to form the Baseball Writers Association, which established the requirement of press pins and credentials for admission into the press box. The press pin soon evolved into a token of good will between the hosting team and the media, while simultaneously allowing the bearer special privileges and access before, during, and after games. Each team playing in a World Series issued its own press pin.

The Philadelphia Athletics issued the very first World Series press pin, in 1911 (opposite, top row, far left), which features an ornate pin bar made of blue enamel, a blue ribbon, and a gold medallion with an elephant (part of the Athletics' team logo) standing on top of a ball and crossed bats. But these stunning ribbon-style designs would only last for a few more years. In 1918, raw-materials rationing in support of World War I would put an end to the lavish designs introduced by the Athletics and perpetuated by other teams in the following years. Although the war ended in 1919, Charles Comiskey, the owner of the Chicago White Sox and a man with a reputation of stinginess, refused to reinstate the former glory of press pin craftsmanship. From 1920 onward, press pins would be designed in the small nickel-sized format that is standard even today.

The pins featured on the opposite page are exceptionally rare, with only a few examples of each known to exist.

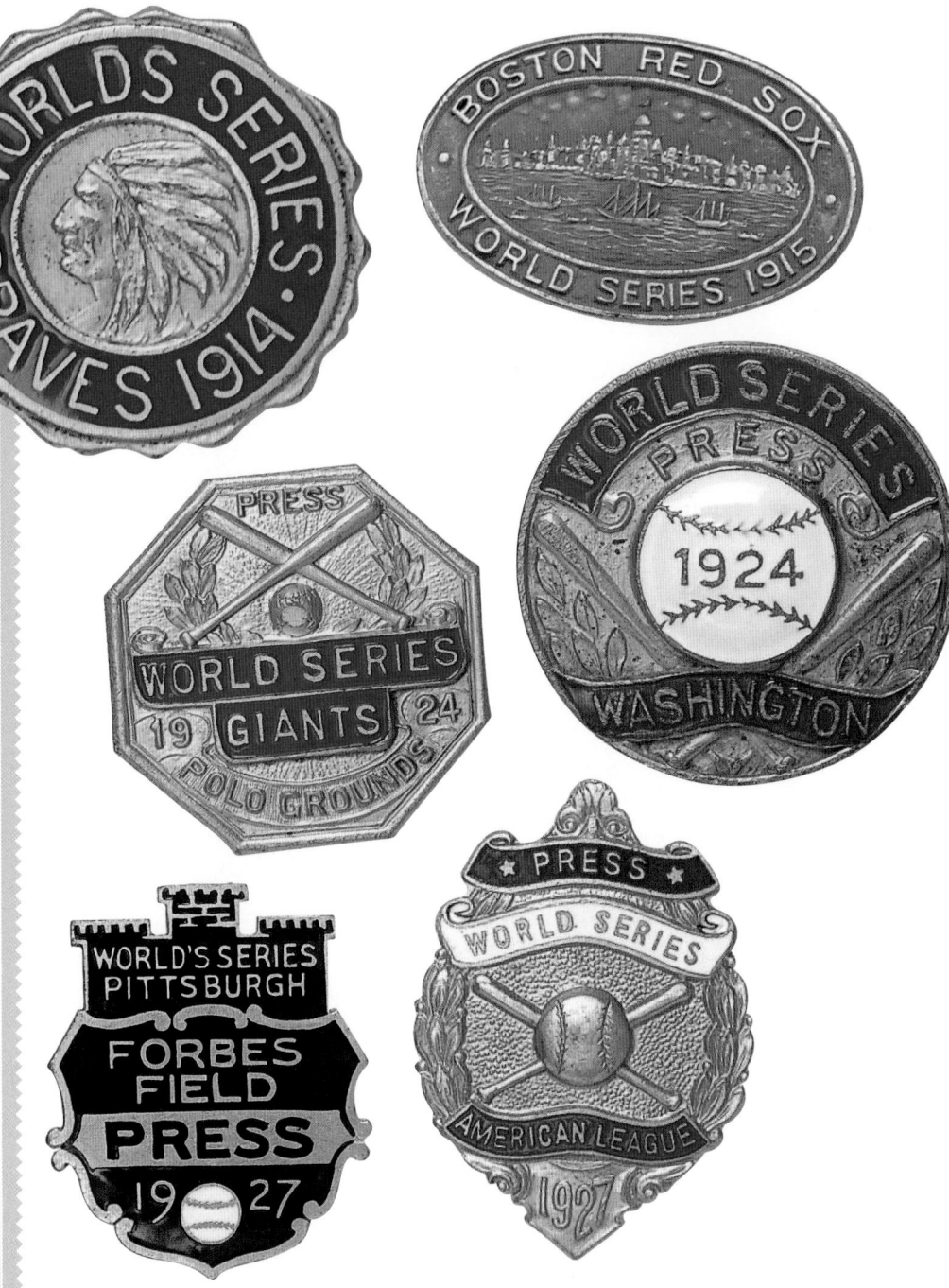

dent, CEO, and part owner of the Detroit Tigers (1959–60), as well as president, CEO, and sole owner of the Cincinnati Reds (1961–67). In 1961, he was again named Major League Executive of the Year, after the Reds won the pennant. DeWitt Sr. concluded his illustrious career in baseball as chairman and part-owner of the Chicago White Sox, in which capacity he was reunited with his old pal, Veeck, who was the principal organizer of the group. DeWitt Sr. stayed active in the game as a member of major-league baseball's Executive Council from 1976 to 1980. He died in 1982, at age 80.

According to baseball historian John Thorn, "The imperative for Americans has always been to forge ahead, in search of the new; base-

As an executive in Major League Baseball, Bill DeWitt Sr. attended a number of World Series and All-Star games. He was given a press pin for each event, and he ended up saving every one of them as mementos. A number of them are shown here, along with several others that Bill Jr. has acquired for his family collection.

In 1938, five years after the first All-Star Game, baseball began issuing press pins for the annual midseason exhibition. (World Series press pins had been standard since 1911.) DeWitt owns one from the first set of All-Star Game pins, a celluloid-based disc (above) made for that year's game at Crosley Field in Cincinnati.

The sportswriter who wore the press pin from the 1941 All-Star Game (inset, middle) saw one of baseball's greatest moments: In the bottom of the ninth, Ted Williams hit a three-run homer to give the AL a 7–5 victory at Briggs Stadium in Detroit. The pin represents the second set of All-Star Game press pins (none were produced in 1939 and 1940).

DeWitt owns the World Series press pins issued by both teams for the 1935, '46, '48, '52, '59, '69, and '83 World Series (top right, and far right):
-1935 Chicago Cubs and Detroit Tigers
-1946 St. Louis Cardinals and Boston Red Sox
-1948 Cleveland Indians and Boston Braves
-1952 New York Yankees and Brooklyn Dodgers
-1959 Los Angeles Dodgers and Chicago White Sox
-1969 New York Mets and Baltimore Orioles
-1983 Toronto Blue Jays and Philadelphia Phillies

ball has always been about the past. In this daunting land of opportunity, a man must venture forth to make his own way. Baseball is about coming home." In 1996, 60 years after Bill DeWitt Sr. left his beloved Cardinals to continue his front-office profession with other teams, Bill DeWitt Jr. led a group of local investors in the purchase of the Cardinals franchise from Anheuser-Busch. In both a real and a symbolic sense, the purchase represented a "coming home" for Bill DeWitt Jr.

One of his most important projects as Chairman and CEO of the Cardinals is the development of a new stadium that will celebrate the team's great tradition and also create an opportunity for adjacent development in downtown St. Louis. The complex, to be named Ballpark Village, calls for office, residential, and retail facilities, as well as a new Cardinals team museum. The new museum will house priceless artifacts from more than a century of Cardinals baseball, including many personal mementos from the Bill DeWitt Family Collection. Fittingly, all four of Bill Jr.'s children—Katie Kern, Bill DeWitt III, Andrew DeWitt, and Margot Good—are Cardinals shareholders. Bill III and Margot work for the team and are involved in the new stadium and museum project. They are carrying on the family legacy in baseball begun almost a century ago by their grandfather.

SMITHSONIAN BASEBALL: INSIDE THE WORLD'S FINEST PRIVATE COLLECTIONS

The White Sox issued a diamond-shaped pin, complete with replica grandstand (top) for the 1950 All-Star Game at Comiskey Park in Chicago.

The 1949 All-Star Game press pin (above, middle) was a handsome, if understated, nickel-sized affair. The game, which took place at Ebbets Field in Brooklyn, was the first All-Star Game to include black ballplayers.

The Indians went all-out for their press pin for the 1954 All-Star Game at Cleveland Stadium (above), issuing a replica stadium design topped by the maniacally smiling Chief Wahoo and a galaxy of stars.

DeWitt owns press pins for all of the St. Louis Cardinals World Series appearances and all of the times the team hosted the All-Star Game (left). The Cardinals have the second-most World Series victories in baseball history. (The Cardinals' 2004 World Series pin is not pictured.)
World Series: 1926, 1928, 1930, 1931, 1934, 1942, 1943, 1944, 1946, 1964, 1967, 1968, 1982, 1985, 1987.
All-Star Games: 1948, 1957, 1966.

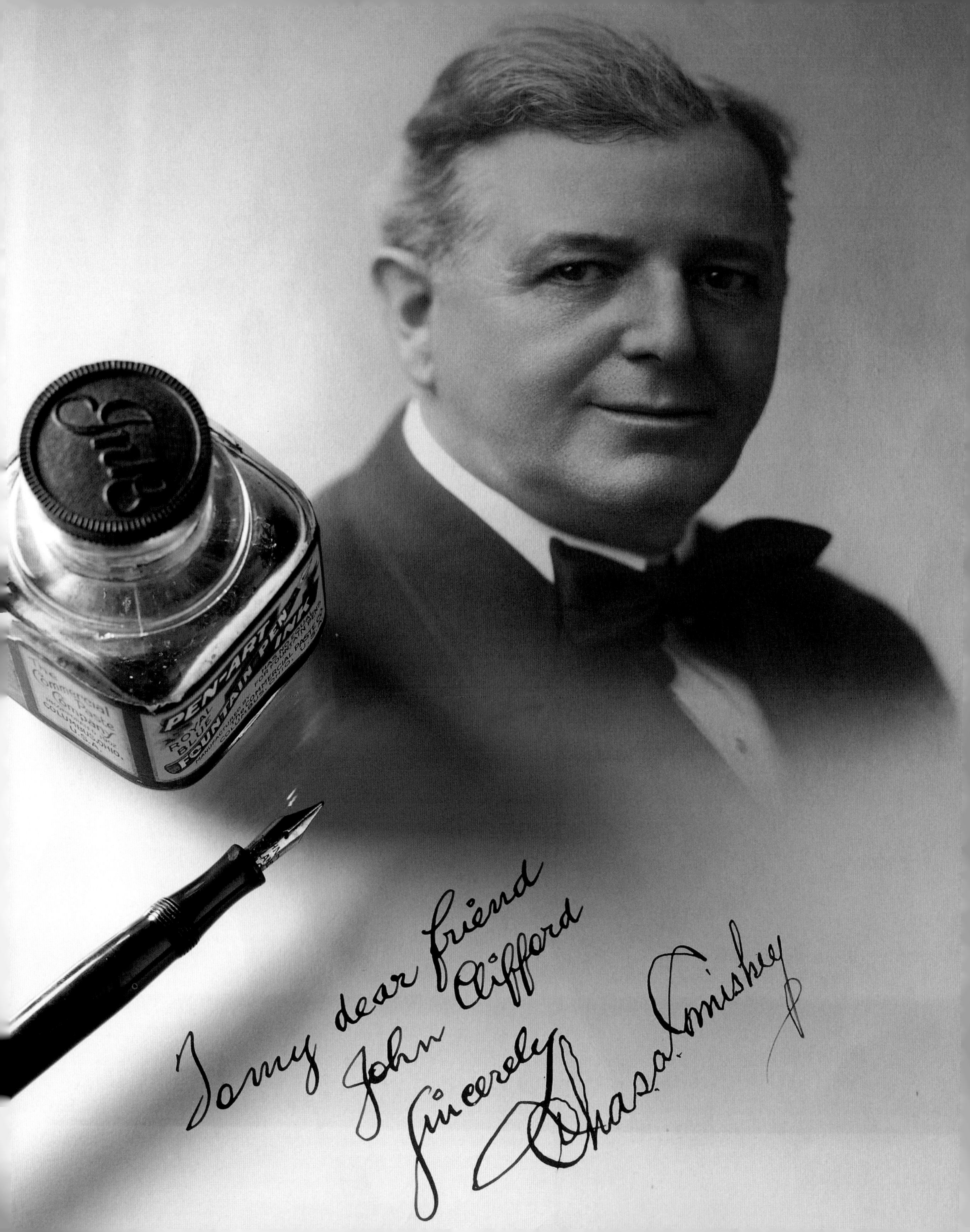
PEN-ART
ROYAL BLUE
FOUNTAIN PEN INK
The Commercial Paste Company
COLUMBUS, OHIO.
U.S.A.
To my dear friend
John Clifford
Sincerely
Chas. A. Comiskey

THE LANGUAGE OF AUTOGRAPHS

"Strange, that the mere identity of paper and ink should be so powerful. The same thoughts might look cold and ineffectual, in a printed book. Human nature craves a certain materialism and clings pertinaciously to what is tangible, as if that were of more importance than the spirit accidentally involved in it. And, in truth, the original manuscript has always something which print itself must inevitably lose. An erasure, even a blot, a casual irregularity of hand, and all such little imperfections of mechanical execution, bring us close to the writer, and perhaps convey some of those subtle intimations for which language has no shape."

—NATHANIEL HAWTHORNE,
A Book of Autographs (1844)

Since the early days of baseball, devout fans have always showered their favorite players with affection and adulation. As far back as 1860, fans turned out by the thousands in upstate New York, Pennsylvania, Maryland, and Delaware to see baseball's first real superstar, pitcher James Creighton (see Chapter I, "The Corey R. Shanus Collection"). When Boston acquired legendary Chicago White Stockings outfielder Mike "King" Kelly in 1886, Beantown fans were so delighted that they purchased a new house for him and a horse-drawn carriage to take him to and from the ballpark. Fans also bestowed gold pocket watches and silver-dollar coins on their hometown favorites (see Chapter VIII, "The Marshall Fogel Col-

lection"). By the early 20th century, fans had organized themselves into rooting clubs like Boston's Royal Rooters, the White Sox Rooters Association, the Cleveland Bards, and the Pittsburgh Stove League.

The list of baseball stars and legends is as long as the rich and colorful history of the game itself. Dozens of players from bygone eras remain as important to us as contemporary stars like Tony Gwynn, Roger Clemens, or Ken Griffey Jr. As author Thomas Boswell explains, "In this country we respect the players of earlier baseball generations perhaps more than we respect other generations in other fields. We've been called a disposable society. But we don't dispose of Babe Ruth or Walter Johnson. We treat them as though

Autograph seekers have always been a part of baseball—a clutch of youngsters waiting reverently for the signature of Lou Gehrig (above) is a baseball tableau as iconic as the Yankee Stadium facade or leftfield at Fenway.

The legendarily penurious Charles Comiskey (opposite) splurged on a studio portrait of himself, circa 1910, which he inscribed and presented to his friend John Clifford. (13" x 16")

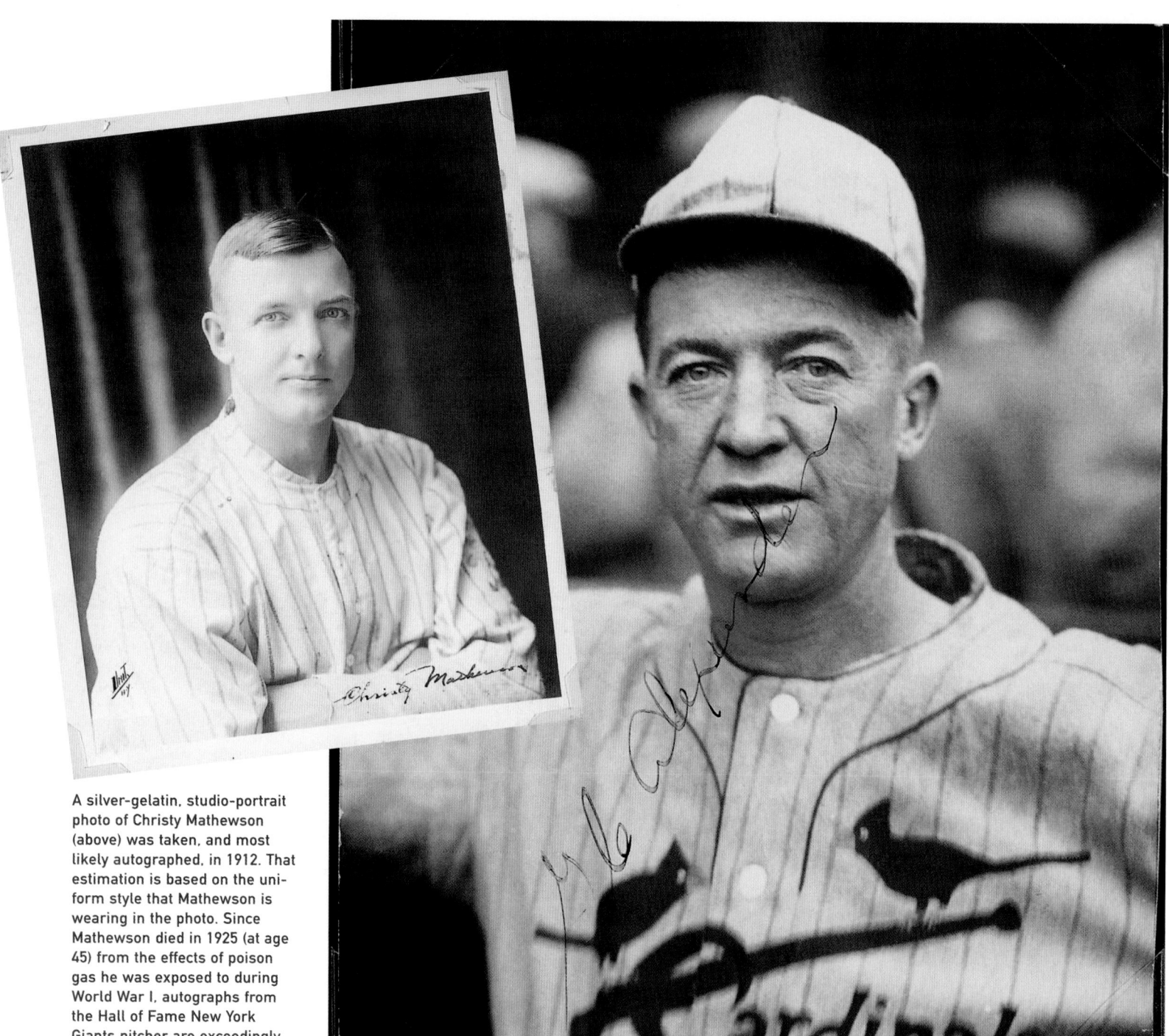

A silver-gelatin, studio-portrait photo of Christy Mathewson (above) was taken, and most likely autographed, in 1912. That estimation is based on the uniform style that Mathewson is wearing in the photo. Since Mathewson died in 1925 (at age 45) from the effects of poison gas he was exposed to during World War I, autographs from the Hall of Fame New York Giants pitcher are exceedingly rare. (14" x 11")

Grover Cleveland Alexander (above right), the co-holder of the National League record for career pitching victories (373), must have smiled when he signed this photograph, which was taken by Charles M. Conlon in 1926, when Alexander was at the tail end of his remarkable career, but near the peak of his status as a legend. In Game 7 of the '26 World Series, the 39-year-old Alexander, who was alcoholic, nearly deaf, and subject to seizures, found his old-time magic one last time to strike out

Yankee slugger Tony Lazzeri in the bottom of the seventh to help win the Series for the St. Louis Cardinals. Rebutting allegations that Alexander had been nursing a hangover when he entered the game, St. Louis manager Rogers Hornsby retorted: "I would be a hell of a manager if I put a drunken pitcher in to save the last game of a World Series, wouldn't I?" (8" x 6")

they were equal and contemporary, though they are dead."

We have all kinds of access to contemporary players. We can read or hear about their exploits in various media hour by hour. We can see and hear them at games and shake their hands at autograph-signing sessions. Access to deceased baseball stars is another story. Memorabilia such as baseball cards, prints, periodicals, books, and other

The managing abilities of Walter Johnson (left) never quite matched his considerable talent as a pitcher. In 1935, when Bowen's autographed photo was taken, Johnson was piloting the Cleveland Indians to a third-place finish. He knew that his days as a big-league manager were numbered, a certainty perhaps reflected in his gloomy eyes. But fans like Mrs. Jameson, to whom the autograph is dedicated, still admired the Big Train, who, one year later, became one of the first five inductees into the Baseball Hall of Fame. (16" x 20")

Casey Stengel called Paul Waner (below) the best rightfielder he ever saw in the National League. "He had to be graceful," Casey recalled, "because he could slide without breaking the bottle on his hip." Waner was known to be a heavy drinker but, as was the case with Grover Cleveland Alexander, alcohol never impaired his abilities on the baeball field. Waner was the seventh player in baseball history to reach 3,000 lifetime hits and finished his 20-year career with a .333 lifetime batting average.

artifacts provide us with images and information, as does old footage of certain games or events. Yet another powerful way to get a sense of the human side of these players is to collect autographed photographs.

As discussed in Chapters VIII ("Collecting Rare and Important Photography") and XVI ("The Bill Mastro Collection"), photographs feed our imaginations. Through photos of our favorite players, we can join them in the dugout or out on the field. The technical attributes of a photograph, such as clarity, contrast, tonal scheme, and angle of the shot, all play a part in these fantasies. As with the Honus Wagner "eyes" photo by Charles M. Conlon that appears in Chapter XVI ("The Bill Mastro Collection"), the subjects in David Bowen's collection are looking straight into the camera's lens. We can imagine ourselves face to face with legendary players like Christy Mathewson, Grover Cleveland Alexander, and Walter Johnson. An autograph brings us even closer. By providing tangible evidence that the player touched and held the photo, the autograph transforms the photograph and the experience of viewing it.

Some inscribed photos reveal relationships between players and famous executives or other players. In the original photo of legendary New York Giants skipper John McGraw on page 244, we see McGraw's handwritten inscription and signature, "Merry Christmas To Harry M. Stevens

A studio-portrait photo of John J. McGraw (above left) is inscribed to scorecard inventor Harry M. Stevens. (17" x 12½")

Inscribed to the baseball pioneer's granddaughter, Bowen's portrait of Henry Chadwick (above) shows the man's gentler side. (6" x 9")

Joe DiMaggio (opposite) autographed a vintage news service photo to New York Yankees coach John Schulte, writing, "To John Schulte with best wishes to one of our classy coaches to the Yanks. Sincerely, Joe DiMaggio." (9½" x 7¾")

According to Mike Royko of the *Chicago Sun-Times*, Hall of Fame pitcher Rube Waddell (above) "loved pitching, fishing and drinking. When he died, they found him in a gin-filled bathtub with three drunken trout." Waddell also liked

hunting for quail, as his inscription on the back of Bowen's original cabinet photo from 1909 suggests: "Compliments of G. E. Rube Waddell . . . Ed Beck quail shooting Dec. 25, 1909 . . . Merry Xmas." (5¾" x 9")

11/25/23 From John J. McGraw." Stevens helped commercialize and popularize the scorecard (see Chapter IX, *The James and Lauren Clister Collection*). In 1894, he became the Polo Grounds' chief purveyor of concessions, selling peanuts, hot dogs, soft drinks, and souvenirs, in addition to scorecards. During the next 20 years, Stevens developed a strong friendship with McGraw, which is commemorated by this autograph.

The autographed photo of Philadelphia Athletics catcher Mickey Cochrane on page 246 gives us an intimate glimpse of one player's respect for a teammate's achievement. In 1929, the Athletics made their first

To John Schultz.
With Best Wishes.
to one of our classey
coaches with the
yanks.
Sincerely
Jo Di Maggio

For a player known as the Beast, Jimmie Foxx (above) broke a smile and made a surprisingly effusive inscripton to a friend on Bowen's autographed photo. (8" x 10")

Gabby Hartnett, who was the Chicago Cubs' legendary catcher for 19 seasons and the 1935 National League MVP, wrote a particularly moving autographed inscription because it reminds us of a bygone era in which ballplayers actually took the time and effort to express their emotions to fans: "To 'Kelly the Owl,' here's hoping he'll enjoy many happy times of the day, formany, many years to come, but when it's all over, I'll be in hell making it hot for him, and many of his friends. Trusting that I'll always remain a heartfelt friend Leo "Gabby" Hartnett Chgo Cubs 1929." (19½" x 11¾")

An original news service photo autographed by Mickey Cochrane (above right) highlights one of the greatest moments in the career of Philadelphia Athletics outfielder Bing Miller. (8" x 10")

World Series appearance in 15 years. With President Herbert Hoover and the First Lady in attendance at Shibe Park for Game 5 of the Series, the A's were keen to make a good showing and finish off the Chicago Cubs. The Cubs held a 2–0 lead going into the bottom of the ninth inning, when Philadelphia's Max Bishop singled and George "Mule" Haas homered to tie the game. With two outs in the inning and the score still tied, Al Simmons doubled. Cubs pitcher Pat Malone then intentionally walked Jimmie Foxx to get to Bing Miller. Miller hit a double off the rightfield scoreboard to win the game and the World Series. Cochrane (for whom Mickey Mantle was named) autographed the photo for his teammate and friend Miller, writing, "To Bing, who knocked in the winning run in the first World's Series 1929. 'Mickey' Cochrane." (The "first" in Cochrane's inscription presumably refers to Miller's first World Series appearance, which this was, and

not the inaugural Fall Classic, which came in 1903, or the Athletics' first Series, which was in 1905.)

Some inscriptions show the personal side of key baseball figures and players. Consider the 1906 original cabinet photograph of Henry Chadwick on page 244. Chadwick has been described variously as "one of the founding fathers of baseball," "pioneer of player statistics," and "inventor of the newspaper box score." The autographed inscription Chadwick made below the image shows him to be a proud and loving grandfather as well: "To my first born grandchild Jennie Eldridge from her loving old grandpa Henry Chadwick . . . Washington's birthday February 22, 1906."

The inscription on the photograph of Jimmie Foxx (above left) shows a different side of the prodigious slugger known as the Beast. A star for the Athletics and the Boston Red Sox, Foxx performed miracles with his bat, and

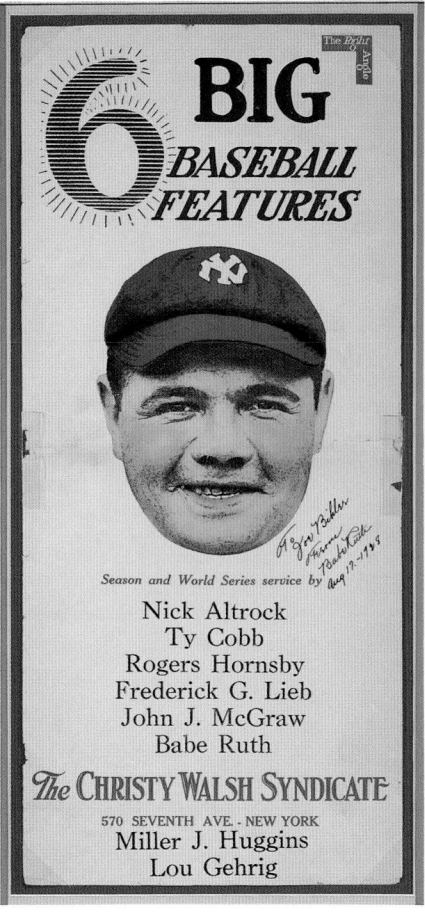

Babe Ruth
training in Hollywood, Calif.
· 1927 ·

Bowen owns five sepia-toned original photos (above) of Babe Ruth "working out" in Hollywood in 1927. The Bambino may have been taking a break from shooting *Babe Comes Home* (1927)—his second feature film after *Headin' Home* (1920)—in which he plays "a ball-playing galoot on his way to marrying a prim and proper miss." (29" x 19")

In 1928, Babe Ruth autographed the cover of a large advertising brochure for *The Christy Walsh Syndicate* (right), making it out to his personal secretary, Joe Bihler. Celebrated *Washington Post* sports columnist Shirley Povich described the *Syndicate*'s operation thus: "My neighbor in the press box, according to the seating plan, was to be, of all

people, Babe Ruth. He had signed on to cover the [1924] World Series for *The Christy Walsh Syndicate*. That sort of thing was commonplace for the game's big stars. They would be provided a press box seat, along with a ghostwriter and telegraph operator, and never set their pen to paper." (9½" x 21½")

thousands and thousands of fans paid to see him at the ballpark. The photo shows a player with massive biceps holding his bat—an image of one of the most feared sluggers in major-league history. "Even his hair has muscles," said Yankees pitcher Lefty Gomez. The inscription ("Jerry—you are a Grand Guy— It's a pleasure to know you . . . Sincerely, Jimmie Foxx"), on the other hand, conveys a warmhearted enthusiasm and sincerity. It allows us to appreciate and identify with the softer side of Jimmie Foxx—a side that major-league pitchers certainly never got to see.

Some autographs and inscriptions tell stories. On September 23, 1947, a number of Jackie Robinson's fans and admirers staged "Jackie Robinson Day" at Ebbets Field to honor the Brooklyn Dodgers' second baseman for breaking major league baseball's color barrier earlier that year. Fans presented Robinson and his wife, Rachel, with a new Cadillac and an inscribed Tiffany gold wristwatch from legendary tap dancer and entertainer Bill "Bojangles" Robinson, among other gifts. Jack Semel, a Dodgers season ticket holder, presented Jackie with a plaque to commemorate the beginning of interracial goodwill in major-league baseball. Yet non-black supporters of Robinson were generally few and

Jackie Robinson (above left) signed an original studio-portrait photo to a supportive friend during the Brooklyn second baseman's difficult rookie year. (9¼" x 7")

Roberto Clemente (above) inscribed a poster to the Pittsburgh Pirates groundskeeper Joe and his wife Emma. (22" x 34")

Bill Klem (left) had a distinctive umpiring style that made him a legend early in his career. During one game in the American Association, an outfielder named

Frank Hemphill charged Klem after a disputed call. Klem drew a line in the dirt and turned away. Hemphill stopped at the line and continued to berate Klem. From then on, Klem continued this act of drawing a line in the dirt, punctuating the action with the words, "Don't cross the Rio Grande!" Any player who did was ejected from the game. Widely respected as an umpire, Klem autographed Bowen's original photo, "To Lee Ballanfant with well wishes 'Good luck and better luck' Yours truly, Bill Klem." (8" x 10")

far between, especially during his rookie season ("Jackie Robinson is the loneliest man I have ever seen in sports," sportswriter Jimmy Cannon wrote in 1947). Robinson showed his appreciation for Semel's support during his difficult first season by inscribing a studio-portrait photo of himself, "To my good friend Jack Semel with appreciation for all you have done... Sincerely Jackie Robinson."

As Nathaniel Hawthorne observed in A

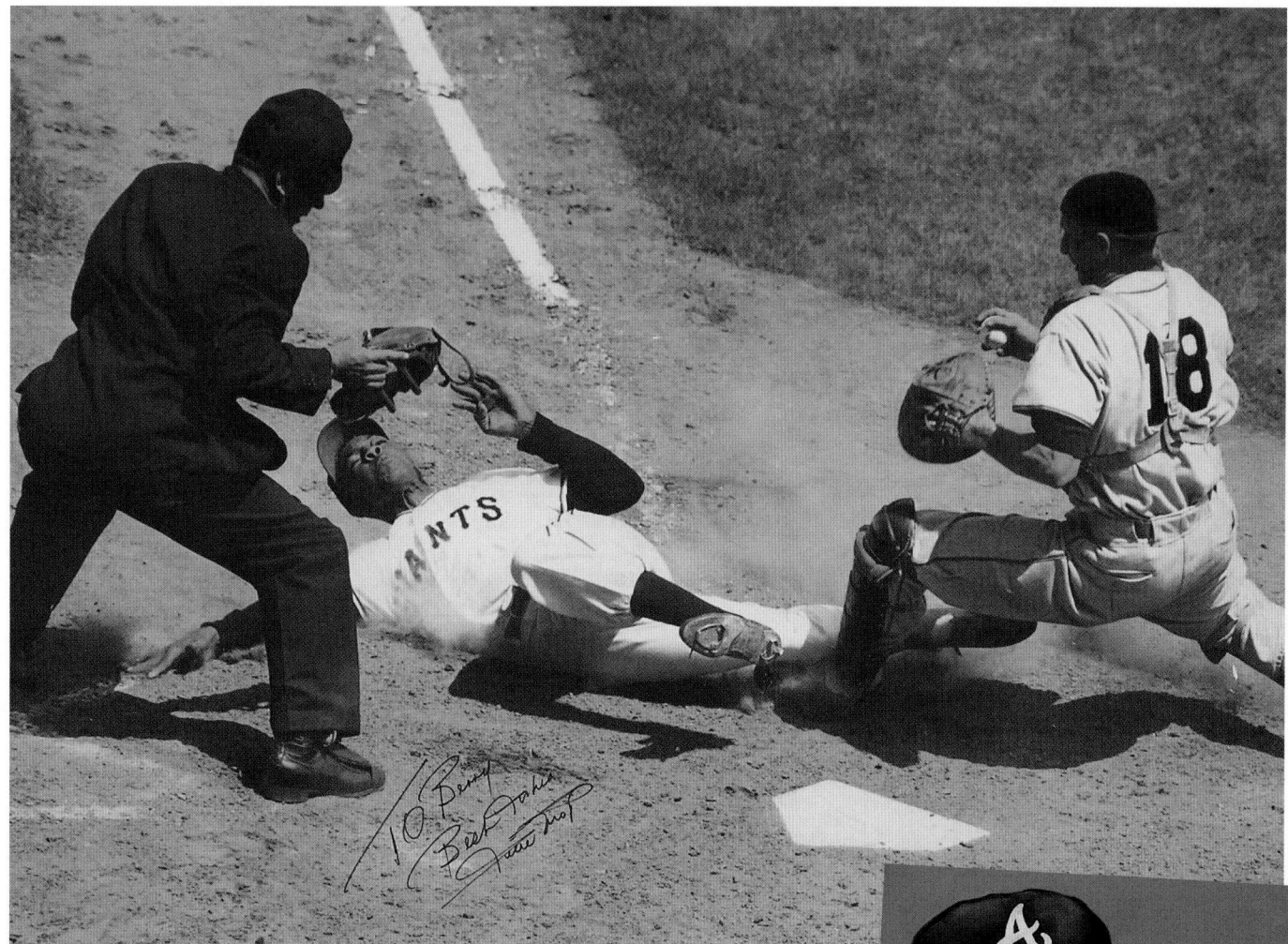

Book of Autographs (1844), penmanship can "bring us close[r] to the writer" and convey "subtle intimations for which language has no shape." The boldness of the black fountain pen ink and lilting style of Charles Comiskey's handwriting on the original photograph on page 240 suggest that he exercised great care in preparing the inscription and signature ("To my dear friend John Clifford Sincerely Chas. A. Comiskey"), probably because John Clifford was a prominent figure in society. Comiskey's care is further evident in the wobbly line of the "h" in "Chas," a characteristic often associated with slower handwriting as opposed to a swift scrawl. The style of the autograph also suggests that it belonged to a proud and accomplished man. Comiskey had helped Ban Johnson co-found the American League in 1900; constructed the "Baseball Palace of the World," Comiskey Park, in 1910; and owned the Chicago White Sox from 1901 until his death in 1931.

On the face of it, fans' adulation for legendary players seems unrequited: the fan idolizes the baseball star because of his skill and greatness, while the star may not even know the fan. But the situation in fact involves an exchange between the player and the fan. After all, without the fans, ballplayers would not be stars in the first place, no matter how proficient they might be at the game. The reciprocity of the relationship is visible in many of the autographs in this collection: Walter Johnson expresses his best wishes to Mrs. Jameson; umpire Bill Klem wishes luck to a fan named Lee Ballanfant; and Roberto Clemente offers best wishes to Emma and Joe. These autographed and inscribed photos are more than simple artifacts once touched by some of the game's greatest legends. They embody the bond between players and fans that has always been an integral part of the grand old game of baseball.

Bowen owns an original painting of Hank Aaron (above) by artist Doug West. The Hall of Fame slugger has signed it. (15¼" x 19")

A hand-colored, black and white photo of Willie Mays sliding into home plate (top) reads, "To Barry Best Wishes. Willie Mays." (39½" x 39½")

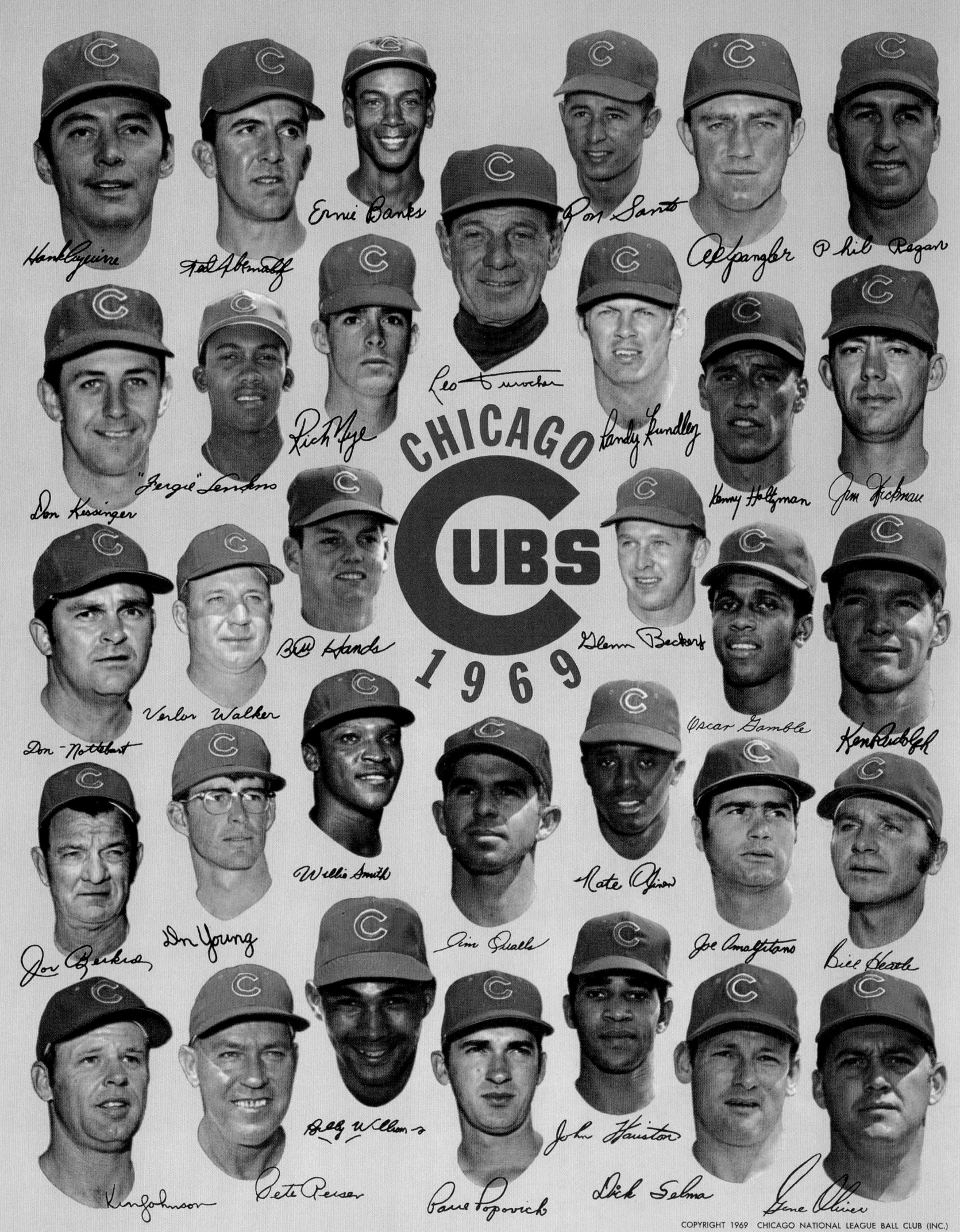

CHICAGO **C**UBS 1969

Hank Aguirre
Ted Abernathy
Ernie Banks
Leo Durocher
Ron Santo
Al Spangler
Phil Regan
Don Kessinger
"Fergie" Jenkins
Rich Nye
Randy Hundley
Kenny Holtzman
Jim Hickman
Don Nottebart
Verlon Walker
Bill Hands
Glenn Beckert
Oscar Gamble
Ken Rudolph
Joe Becker
Dr. Young
Willie Smith
Jim Qualls
Nate Oliver
Joe Amalfitano
Bill Heath
Ken Johnson
Pete Reiser
Billy Williams
Paul Popovich
John Hairston
Dick Selma
Gene Oliver

THE SUMMER OF '69

" It's because on the Cubs it was, 'I for you, we're all in this together, win, lose, and draw.' There was a sense of camaraderie. We were brothers. We cared about each other."

—*CATCHER GENE OLIVER, on why he remains so close to the Cubs despite only playing for them for two seasons of his 10-year major league career.*

Dan Knoll began collecting memorabilia related to the 1969 Chicago Cubs during the summer of that heartbreaking season. While collectors typically focus on artifacts related to popular, championship teams, such as the 1927 New York Yankees, the 1960s Los Angeles Dodgers, or the 1975 Cincinnati Reds, Knoll chose to commemorate a team that failed—and did so spectacularly. With a talented roster featuring future Hall of Famers Ernie Banks and Billy Williams, as well as consistent 20-game winner Fergie Jenkins, the '69 Cubs led the New York Mets by 8 ½ games in the National League East on August 13 of that season, only to drop seven straight games in September and lose the division title by eight games. Knoll's collection underscores the notion that there is much more to baseball collecting than celebrating greatness and victory. Sometimes, it's about remembering the struggles of a particular season, or preserving the memories of the moment you bonded with your team or when you first set foot in a major-league ballpark with your dad or brother. Knoll relives the 1969 Cubs season that made a collector out of him:

HOW DID YOU BECOME A 1969 CUBS FAN?

"I am often asked, 'Why the lifelong love affair with the 1969 Cubs?' They were a team that, in the end, lost. I am immediately

led to quote author Roger Kahn, who so simply, yet so beautifully wrote, 'You may glory in a team triumphant, but you fall in love with a team in defeat.' That may sound sappy to some. But it sums up my experience of that memorable season. It was a season that turned me into a lifelong baseball fan, a season in which I discovered the essence of baseball and in which I first experienced the sense of foreboding that forever seems to shadow the Cubs.

"I grew up on Chicago's South Side, where the White Sox had been fielding good teams pretty much since 1955. The Cubs, on the other hand, had not been a pennant contender once during that same time span. Despite the Cubs' lack of success and our geographic proximity to the White Sox, my father, who also grew up on the South Side, vehemently pledged his allegiance to the

Knoll (above) purchased a Chicago Cubs team-composite print (opposite) during one of the games he attended at Wrigley Field in the spring of 1969. (14" x 11")

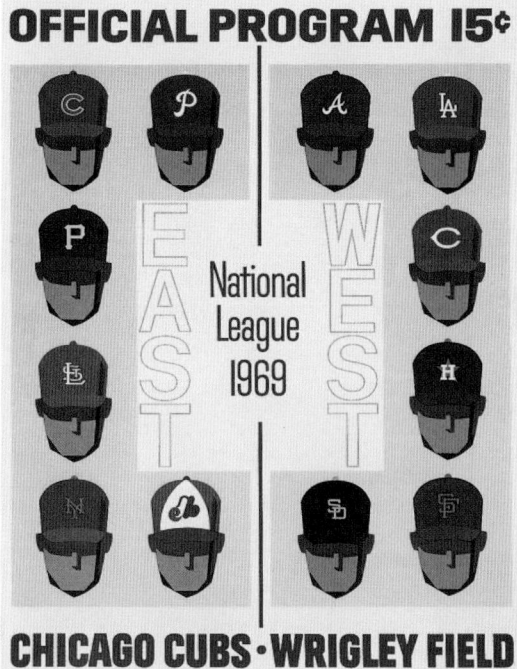

OFFICIAL PROGRAM 15¢

National League 1969

EAST WEST

CHICAGO CUBS · WRIGLEY FIELD

Add to the fun of watching the game.

you'll enjoy the high quality favorites served at Wrigley Field.
- Heileman's Old Style . . . the finest light lager beer
- Oscar Mayer All Meat Wieners . . . mild, tender and juicy
- Coca-Cola . . . Coke has the taste you never get tired of
- Borden's Frosty Malt . . . a ready made Chocolate Malt
- Burny Bros. . . . finest and freshest Baked Goods
- Schlitz . . . "When you're out of Schlitz, you're out of beer."

With its smiling concessionaire on the back cover, the official program from the May 12, 1969, game between the Cubs and the San Diego Padres (left) reflects the high spirits at Wrigley in the early part of that fateful season. (front and back cover) (11¾" x 8½")

Knoll's collection includes a ticket to opening day of the Cubs' 1969 season, as well as a packet of season tickets, a schedule, and a season pass.

unfortunate Cubs. Because Comiskey Park was close to our house, my older brother and I had attended some White Sox games. But we secretly pulled for the north-side Cubbies. As far back as I can remember, our dad told us bedtime stories about the heroic Cubs of the past. He told us about guys named Orval, Tinker, Grover, Gabby, Hack, Kiki, Riggs, Pafko, and Peanuts. We believed in the Cubs, but their losing record, and peer pressure, or a mix of both, relegated the Cubs T-shirts and caps that dad gave us to the recesses of our drawers, far away from the view and ridicule of our neighborhood buddies.

"In the spring of 1969, a number of local and national sportswriters predicted that it just might be the Cubs' year. The team was armed with a handful of future Hall of Famers and managed by the great Leo Durocher. Cubs fans anticipated the coming season as they had not for decades, my father among them. He announced on opening day that this year we'd see our first Cubs game at Wrigley Field. By that first day of the season, I, too, had contracted Cubs fever. I convinced my mom that I had a cough and should not go to school. But by 1:15 in the afternoon of opening day, I had made a miraculous recovery.

"Popcorn in one hand and a Pepsi in the other, I watched the television broadcast of the Cubbies battling the Philadelphia

Phillies. I cheered on Don Kessinger, Randy Hundley, Ernie Banks, and the rest of the squad. To my 11-year-old mind, this game would be a test of the team's true talent and a barometer for the season's success. When Philadelphia tied the game in the ninth inning, I began to feel a little less perky. But Willie Smith's dramatic, game-winning home run in the bottom of the 10th inning brought Cubs fans to their feet. The victory seemed to be a propitious start to their year of destiny. The next day, I proudly wore my Cubs T-shirt and cap. For the first time that I could recall, splashes of Cubby blue decorated our neighborhood. From porches and

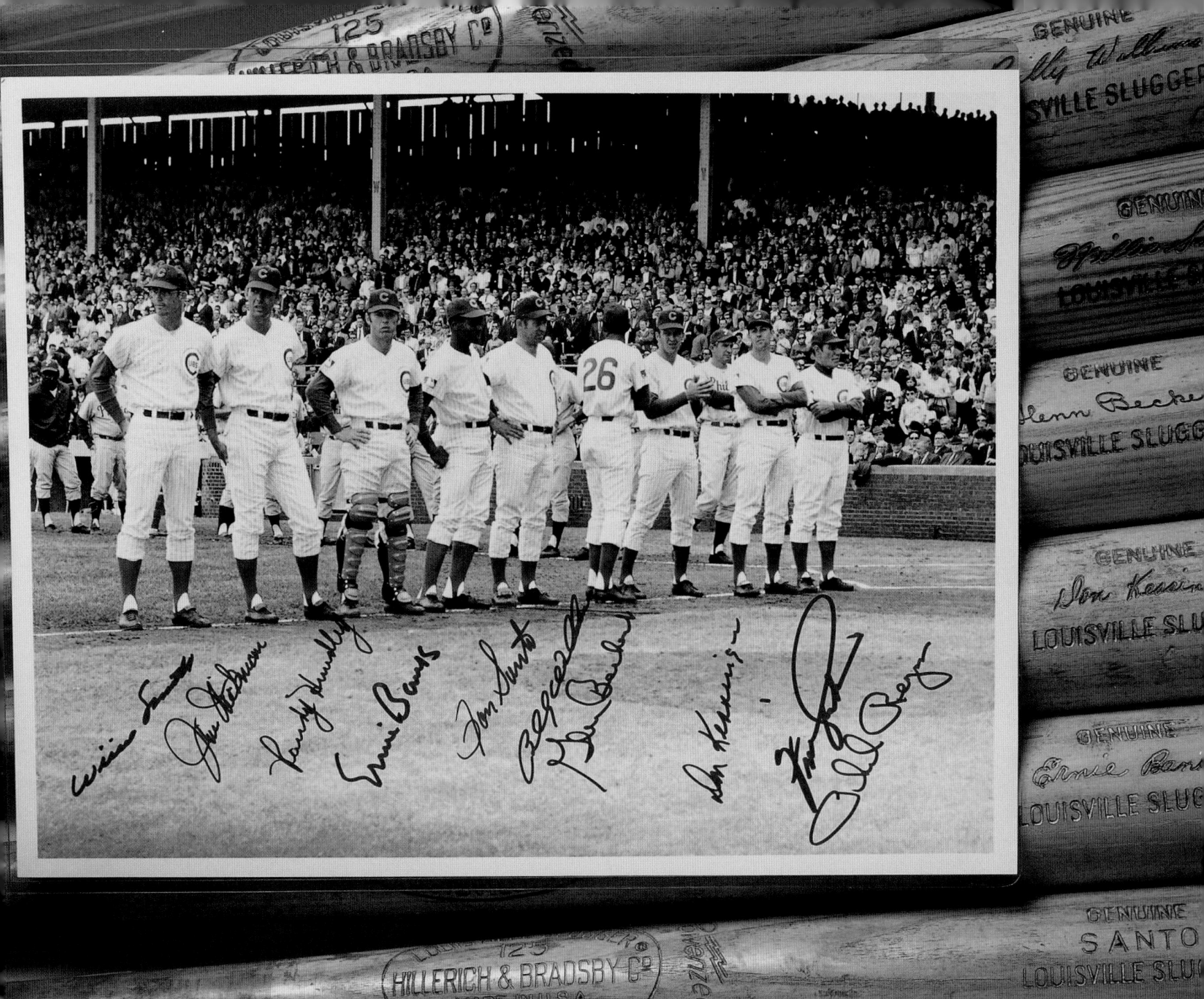

Knoll's autographed 1969 Chicago Cubs opening-day team photograph (above) rests on top of the bats used by each player in the starting nine that day. (photo 9" x 11")

garages, radios were blasting the Cubs pregame theme song: 'Hey, hey, holy mackerel, no doubt about it, the Cubs are on their way.' Cubs fans had come out of hiding.

"Having claimed first place on opening day, the Cubs led their division by seven games at the end of May. On a glorious early June morning, I came downstairs to find my father still home. It could only mean one thing: We were going to Wrigley Field. My brother and I grabbed our gloves in hopes of snagging a foul ball in the stands, perhaps even a game-winning homer. It was a morning to remember—sunny blue skies and a pregame pancake breakfast with dad at the restaurant his father used to take him to

before games. Outside the park, my father handed us each a ticket and led us to the Clark and Addison Street entrance. With one push of the turnstile, I entered the park feeling as if I had been catapulted into a fantasy world. The air smelled of cigar smoke, hot dogs, and stale beer. A short flight of concrete steps led from the lower concourse to the seating area. Emerging from the stairwell, I was immediately struck by the magnificence of the historic ballpark. My father's bedtime stories became reality. The landscape where history had been made so many times looked just like the pictures in the books. Even the buildings of Wrigley's turn-of-the-century backdrop appeared as they had during the

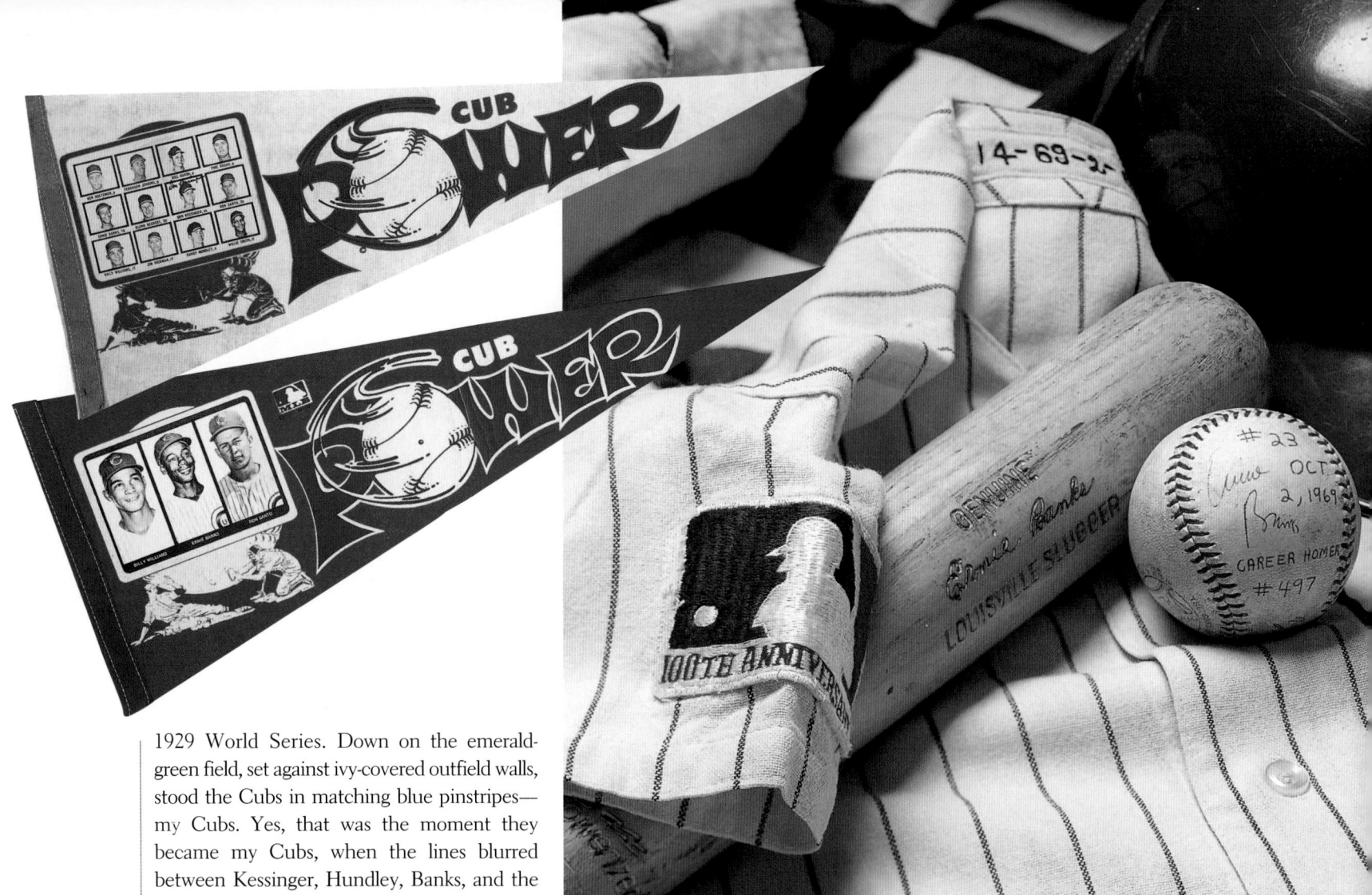

1929 World Series. Down on the emerald-green field, set against ivy-covered outfield walls, stood the Cubs in matching blue pinstripes—my Cubs. Yes, that was the moment they became my Cubs, when the lines blurred between Kessinger, Hundley, Banks, and the remaining 23 men, and I focused on the entire team that took the field in those famous blue-and-white uniforms.

"As we basked in the afternoon sun, a slugfest between the Cubs and the visiting Cincinnati Reds unfolded. Chicago prevailed 14–8. By the final out, my brother and I could recite the entire Cubs lineup, uniform numbers and all. I was hooked, and plans were set to attend the Cubs-Cardinals double header at Wrigley in a few weeks."

WHO WERE THE BLEACHER BUMS?

"What made the 1969 Cubs so special was that the same affection and camaraderie that they showed for one another they shared with their fans. I saw it with my own eyes during my next game, the Cubs-Cardinals doubleheader on June 29. The Cubs' front office was honoring Billy Williams, the quiet, unassuming outfielder, that day. By playing in his 896th consecutive game, Williams, a favorite of my dad's, would break the legendary Stan Musial's National League record of most consecutive games played. ('Sweet Swingin' Billy is still considered by many to be the finest natural hitter ever to wear a Cubs uniform.) More than 41,000 fans packed Wrigley to cheer Williams and watch Chicago battle their archrivals, the Cardinals. The atmosphere was crazy. Cubs pitchers Dick Selma and Hank Aguirre were standing by the outfield wall waving white towels and leading cheers for a rowdy group of diehard fans known as the Bleacher Bums.

Every time I go to town,
The boys all kick my dog around.
Makes no difference if he's a hound,
You better stop kickin' my dog around.

"Affectionately regarded by both the players and Durocher, the Bums helped rally the Cubs when needed. And the Cubs helped rally the Bums. Durocher would say, 'Hey Selma, get those Bums going.' And he would. The Bums, who often donned brightly colored construction helmets, were always there for the team. The Cubs knew that and considered these fans, and others, integral to their season."

The Cubs produced "Cub Power" team pennants (top left) for sale at Wrigley Field during the 1969 season. The pennants include a photo composite of some of the team's star players. (28½" long)

Knoll's red "Cub Power" pennant from the 1969 season (above left) features black-and-white portraits of (l to r) Chicago outfielder Billy Williams, first baseman Ernie Banks, and third baseman Ron Santo. Leo Durocher once said about "Sweet Swingin'" Billy Williams, a .290 lifetime hitter who belted 426 career home runs: "In spring training I said, 'Well this year I'm going to give him a rest.' . . . But every time I made out my lineup card, I had to put him in there. It would have been like scratching Whirlaway and Seabiscuit from a big race." (28½" long)

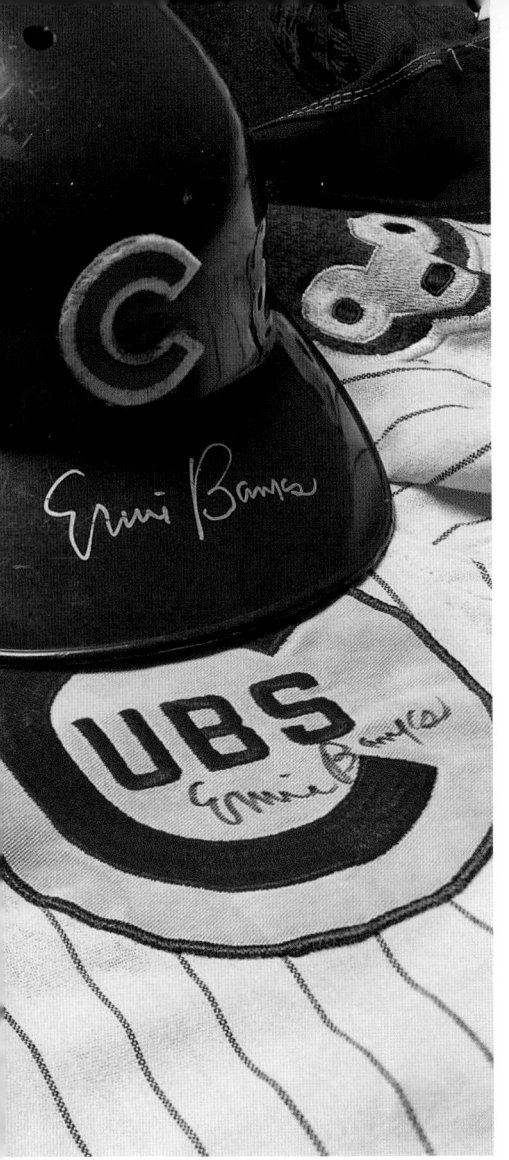

As a devout Cubs fan, it's only fitting that Kroll would own some priceless Ernie Banks memorabilia (left), including the Hall of Fame infielder's game-worn home jersey from the 1969 season, his game-used bat, his game-worn batting helmet, and the baseball he hit for his 497th career home run on October 2, 1969. Voted the "Greatest Cub of All Time" by Chicago fans upon his retirement in 1971, Banks won two National League MVP Awards (1958 and 1959) and belted 512 career home runs. He never played in a World Series (he was a Cub, after all) but he also never lost his boundless exuberance for the game, as exemplified in the words that became his catchphrase: "It's a great day for a ballgame. Let's play two!"

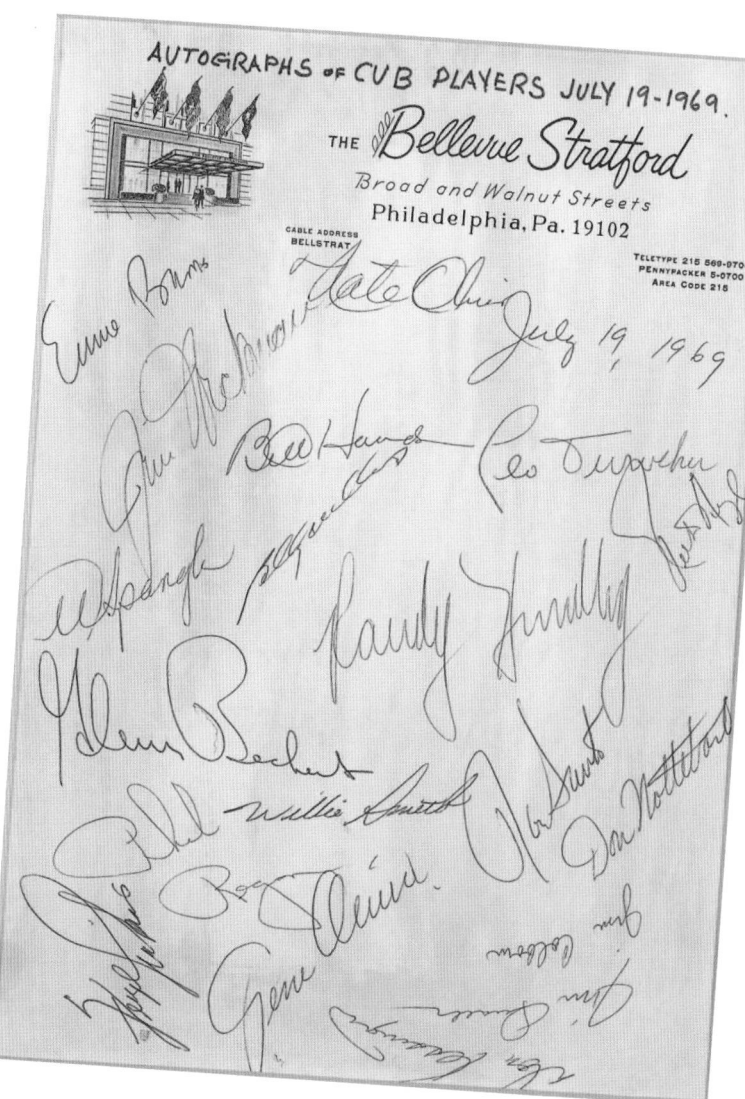

During a four-game set with the Philadelphia Phillies at Shibe Park in July 1969, the Cubs stayed at the Bellevue Stratford Hotel in downtown Philadelphia, taking time out on July 19 to autograph a sheet of hotel stationery (above). (9" x 11")

WHAT HAPPENED TO THE CUBS THAT SEASON?

"Games at Wrigley took on new meaning in the summer of 1969. Cubs mania consumed Chicago fans. Visions of the Cubs' first World Series appearance since 1945 danced in their heads. But baseball is full of superstition, especially when it comes to the Cubs (and, until their historic 2004 season, the Red Sox). The Cubs' encounter with the Mets at Shea Stadium on July 8 was a harbinger of bad ends, of a cruel fate—the stuff of Cubs lore. Fergie Jenkins, the easygoing pitcher seeking his third 20-win season since joining the Cubs, carried a 3–1 lead into the bottom of the ninth. Pinch-hitting for Mets starter Jerry Koosman, Ken Boswell popped what most observers believed to be a catchable fly ball into right center. It dropped for a double. One out later, New York's Donn Clendenon hit a deep drive to left center. The ball appeared to be in rookie Don Young's glove, but it fell to the ground as Young crashed into the outfield wall. The Mets ultimately took the game from Jenkins, 4–3.

"In August, the Cubs were in first place by 9½ games. But the Mets were making noise. They swept the San Diego Padres in consecutive doubleheaders, jumpstarting a remarkable surge of 12 wins in thirteen games. On August 19, Cubs pitcher Ken Holtzman seemed to turn things back in the Cubs' direction when he threw a no-hitter against the Braves and the Cubs won 3–0. But Chicago dropped seven of its next nine games, all in the blistering heat of Wrigley Field. The Mets had climbed to within four games of the Cubs.

"The way I saw it, the Pirates' Willie Stargell drove a nail in the coffin on September 7 in Pittsburgh. With the Cubs standing one strike away from a much needed victory, Stargell knocked a curve ball from Phil Regan out of the park to tie the game in the top of the ninth, and the Pirates went on to win. The Cubs never recovered.

"The following day, the Cubs traveled to New York to face the Mets, holding a tenuous 2½-game lead. Both sides threw bean balls,

including one aimed at Mets slugger Tommie Agee. In Agee's next at bat, he clouted a two-run homer over the centerfield wall. With the score tied 2–2 in the Mets' half of the sixth inning, Agee came up again and belted a double. Wayne Garrett followed with a single to right. Jim Hickman fired the ball home. Every Cubs fan watching the game swore that Hundley tagged the onrushing Agee at the plate, but umpire Satch Davidson called Agee safe, and the Mets had a controversial victory. The Cubs were devastated.

"With their lead down to $1^{1}/_{2}$ games, the Cubs faced Tom Seaver and a confident Mets team the following evening. It was a game Cubs fans would never forget. I know I haven't. In the early innings, with Ron Santo on deck, a black cat appeared on the field in front of the Cubs' dugout, and strolled past the Chicago bench. Sure enough, Seaver and the Mets dominated, winning 7–1. The Cubs clung to a half-game lead.

"After owning first place for 155 consecutive days, since opening day, the Cubs completely fell apart. They lost eight in a row in September and finished eight games behind the Mets in the division. I will never forget the sight of that black cat!"

THE CUBS HAVE NOT WON A CHAMPIONSHIP SINCE 1908, AND ARE SAID TO BE A CURSED TEAM. WHAT IS THE HISTORY BEHIND THE CURSE?

"Perhaps if I'd known about the "Billy Goat Curse" back in 1969, it might have consoled me. My father had never spoken of the curse, maybe because he was never one for excuses. But the Billy Goat Curse has been a mainstay of Cubs lore since 1945. I would have to wait until 10 years after the black-cat season of 1969 to learn the story of the curse.

"It was the summer of 1979. I was home from college and about to start a summer job as a laborer for a concrete company. A day's worth of Cubs baseball in the sun-drenched bleachers of Wrigley Field, I thought, would revitalize both body and mind for the weeks of 10-hour workdays that lay ahead. And since the Cubs were playing .500 ball, a victory over the first-place Phillies was not out of the question.

"It was an unusually gusty day, even for the Windy City. The game began with an explosive first inning by the Phillies. When the third out finally came, the score was 7–0. Undaunted, the Cubs roared back with six runs of their own, leaving the bleachers section where I sat in a delightful state of bedlam. Our celebration was short-lived, however. The Phillies increased their lead by 11 runs during the third inning. Yet by the end

Knoll's 1969 Cubs team poster (above) came as a premium in Topps Chewing Gum packs in 1969. (15" x 12½")

No baseball season would be complete without Topps baseball cards, like the ones Knoll bought during the 1969 season (above left). That year Topps also included premium stamps in the packs (the smaller items beneath the Ernie Banks, Randy Hundley, and Rich Nye cards are stamps). An original unopened 5-cent wax pack containing five cards and a stick of bubble gum sits below a display box that housed wax packs.

of the sixth, the Cubs had miraculously rallied to within two runs, getting a grand-slam homer from Bill Buckner. A lone Philadelphia run in the top of the seventh was followed by a scoreless Cubs' at bat, leaving bleacher fans to wonder if both teams' firepower had run its course.

"But the hits kept coming. Five of them for the Cubs in the eighth tied the game, incredibly, at 22–22. The bleachers went wild, with perfect strangers slapping hands, hugging, and buying each other beers. This had to be the Cubs' year! During the next inning, I had visions of coming home from college in the fall to attend as many playoff and World Series games as possible. But then, like a predawn alarm clock, the crack of Mike Schmidt's bat in the top of the 10th snapped me from my reverie, and put the Phillies back in the lead.

"'Billy Goat,' I heard the man next to me shout, pointing his finger in the direction of our ace reliever, Bruce Sutter, who stood by the mound lamenting the 'fat one' he had just served up to Schmidt. 'Billy Goat,' the man said again, this time revealing a slight accent. He was stately looking, perhaps 50 years old, and dressed in a suit and tie. His erect posture on the bleacher plank called to mind a piano student at a recital. Until now, he had watched the game in silence. 'Why you callin' Sutter Billy Goat, pops?' asked an unshaven fan wearing sunglasses and a bandana. The gentleman explained how William Sianis (nicknamed 'Billy Goat' because of the goatee he wore), owner of the Billy Goat Tavern in Chicago, had attempted to enter Game 4 of the 1945 World Series with his pet billy goat. He had been permitted to bring his goat to past Cubs games, and he had a ticket for both himself and the animal, yet on this occasion he was denied access to Wrigley Field. Sianis appealed his case directly to Cubs owner P. K. Wrigley, who supported the decision to bar the goat from entering the park. When Sianis demanded a reason, Wrigley told him that the goat smelled. Sianis, a longtime Cubs supporter, raised both hands in the air

and proclaimed that the Cubs would not play in another World Series at Wrigley Field. Detroit won the next three games to take the 1945 World Series. When it was over, Sianis reportedly sent Mr. Wrigley a telegram asking, 'Who smells now?'

"I thought it unusual that such an articulate, well-dressed man would believe in the curse's power. But in the bottom of the 10th, the Cubs went down without scoring. The four-hour, 23–22 marathon loss was over, and I was left to contemplate the power of the curse.

"Curse or no curse, World Series or no World Series, the power and the wonder of the 1969 Cubs have never left me. Thirty-five years later, most of the players from that team look back to that season, despite its disappointment, as the fondest of their major-league careers. They, like many of us, have come to understand that baseball is not as much about the outcome as it is about the journey. This belief, shared by both athlete and fan, tells us we are right to remember that very special season."

The game-worn jerseys from the 1969 season of Cubs third baseman Ron Santo (above left), shortstop Don Kessinger (middle), and manager Leo Durocher (right) reside in Knoll's impressive collection dedicated to that melancholy season, which began so well: The entire Chicago infield of Ernie Banks (first base). Glenn Beckert (second base). Randy Hundley (catcher). Kessinger, and Santo made the National League All-Star team in July. Durocher also made the team as one of the two skippers for the NL.

RESURGENCE OF HEROES

" A hero is someone who understands the responsibility that comes with his freedom."
—BOB DYLAN

Home runs have captured the imagination of generations of baseball fans. They wield the power that turns impending defeat into jubilant victory, optimism into utter despair, and ordinary men into legends. The mystique of home runs hit long ago transports us back in time. The majestic arc of the ball's flight off the bat is a cultural touchstone, sure to be part of the American psyche for decades yet to come.

Babe Ruth's home run in the first game played at Yankee Stadium, on April 18, 1923, was a perfectly appropriate "christening" moment. After all, it was the legendary slugger's spectacular seasons of 1920 (54 homers, 137 RBIs), '21 (59, 171), and '22 (35, 99) that revitalized interest in baseball after the "Black Sox" scandal of 1919. Ruth drew paying customers back to ballparks in droves, and made it possible for such a cathedral as Yankee Stadium to be built. Following his famous clout in the new park, sportswriter Fred Lieb dubbed the stadium "The House that Ruth Built."

Ruth's was one of the first in a long line of memorable home runs. Think of Ted Williams's ninth-inning long ball with two out and two on that won the 1941 All-Star Game for the American League. Or Bobby Thompson's electrifying Shot Heard 'Round the World, the "Miracle of Coogan's Bluff," arguably baseball's most famous round-tripper. It was a three-run shot that gave the New York Giants a dramatic come-from-behind win over Brooklyn in the final game of a three-game playoff for the 1951

National League pennant. Fans from the 1970s remember Hank Aaron's majestic 715th career home run on April 8, 1974, which made Aaron major-league baseball's new career home run king, supplanting Ruth. In the 1980s, Kirk Gibson came off the bench limping with a sore left hamstring and a swollen right knee, but left the field triumphantly after belting an improbable game-winning homer for the Los Angeles Dodgers in Game 1 of the 1988 World Series.

Then came 1998, when two National League sluggers defied the boundaries of ballparks around the country. Mark McGwire opened the St. Louis Cardinals' season with a grand slam off the Los Angeles Dodgers' Ramon Martinez. The towering moon-shot into the leftfield stands was not only the first opening-day grand slam in Cardinals franchise history, but also a propitious start to one of the most monumental seasons in the history of the game. The burly redhead, who had bulked up noticeably since his rookie year with Oakland in 1986, launched a 12th-inning rocket into the upper deck of Busch Stadium in the next game. In both the third and fourth games of the season, against the San Diego Padres, McGwire homered again. On April 14, he extended his legacy by becoming the first Cardinal to hit three home runs in a single game at Busch Stadium. He repeated the feat against the Philadelphia Phillies on May 19. By the end of the month, McGwire had 27 home runs, putting him in contention to break Roger Maris's single-season home run record of 61—the most coveted record in major-league baseball—which had stood for 37 years.

But if April and May belonged to McGwire,

The baseball on the far left in the montage on the opposite page is the one Mark McGwire hit for his 70th home run of the 1998 season off Montreal Expos reliever Carl Pavano in the seventh inning on September 27, 1998, the last day of the season. The ball on the right side of the montage is the one Sammy Sosa hit for his 66th home run, also in 1998. A 462-feet moon shot into the third deck of the Astrodome in Houston. Number 66 came off Sosa's friend and fellow Dominican Jose Lima in the game's fourth inning on September 25, 1998. That homer would put Sosa in the home-run derby lead for just a few innings, as McGwire clouted #66 in St. Louis forty-five minutes later. On October 7, 2001, the San Francisco Giants played the Los Angeles Dodgers in the last game of the season. In the bottom of the first inning, Barry Bonds, who was facing knuckleballer Dennis Springer, swatted a 3-2 pitch over the rightfield wall of Pacific Bell Park for home run #73, his last one of the season, and still the single-season home run record. Bonds's batting performance in 2001 is widely regarded as one of the most outstanding in major-league history. The ball that added a final exclamation point to Bonds's unprecedented season appears in the center of the montage. Behind each ball is a Major League Baseball Sports Picks action figure produced by Todd McFarlane's company.

Sosa (above) and McGwire (opposite) electrified the nation and brought thousands of fans back to baseball with their stirring homerun race in 1998.

then June belonged to his challenger, Sammy Sosa of the Chicago Cubs. Having entered the league in 1989 as a 165-pound whippet, Sosa had transformed himself into a 220-pound slugger by 1998. He signaled his own determination to break Maris's record by hitting 20 home runs during the month of June—the most home runs ever produced by a major-league player in a single month. Sosa's momentum continued through the summer. On September 2, he hit his 56th to tie Hack Wilson's 68-year-old record for the most home runs by a Cub in a single season. On September 13, Sosa passed Maris's record. But McGwire had already broken it five days earlier and was on his way to finishing the season with a staggering 70 homers, making him baseball's single-season home run record holder. Sosa ended the season with 66, placing him second on the all-time list. (Three years later, San Francisco slugger Barry Bonds ran away with the home run race, and McGwire's record, smacking 73 for the Giants.)

Todd McFarlane's collection of 10 home run baseballs from the historic 1998 derby includes McGwire's first and 70th as well as Sosa's 66th of the season. In a pleasing turn of fate, McFarlane was born in 1961, the year that Maris broke Babe Ruth's single-season home run record of 60, set in 1927. A producer and director who created the action hero Spawn, McFarlane has won both a Grammy Award and an Emmy Award. He played varsity baseball in college and almost made the cut as an outfielder for the Toronto Blue Jays' farm team in 1983. "Most fans can't imagine how tough it is just to hit a 95-mile-an-hour fastball or a slider that sinks two feet toward your ankles," McFarlane says, while gripping an Easton aluminum bat from his college playing days. "Many consider this the toughest feat in all of sports. Now imagine trying to knock that pitch over the outfield wall of a major-league ballpark; not just once, but over 65 times in one season! Only three men have done it in the history of the game—Sosa, McGwire, and Barry Bonds."

It took 34 years for someone to break Babe Ruth's record of 60 home runs in a season. During this long stretch, only three men—Hack Wilson (56 in 1930), Jimmie

Foxx (58 in 1932), and Hank Greenberg (58 in 1937)—posed any threat to the Bambino's record. Ken Griffey Jr.—with 56 home runs in both 1997 and 1998—is the only player other than McGwire (58 homers in 1997) between 1961 and 1997 to even approach Maris's record. Although Willie Mays, George Foster, Cecil Fielder, Greg Vaughn, Albert Belle, and Brady Anderson each hit between 50 and 52 long balls in single seasons during this period, baseball's cognoscenti will agree that there is a big difference between 50 and 60. Anything above 65 was not even in the realm of contemplation before the end of the 1998 season. But McFarlane's home run ball collection is more than a tribute to the incredible accomplishments of Sosa and McGwire. For McFarlane, it commemorates the importance of the home run and its role in rescuing professional baseball from the negative repercussions of the 1994–95 players' strike.

Nineteen ninety-four should have been a signature year for baseball. Attendance and profits had reached all-time highs. But the labor agreement between players and owners had expired on December 31, 1993, and the 1994 season began without a signed contract in place. Owners insisted on implementing a salary cap on each team's payroll. The players' union refused to consent, resulting in a players' strike that cut short the 1994 season, canceled the World Series, and delayed the start of the 1995 season. Baseball historian Eric Enders calls the strike "one of the great black marks in the game's history . . . and a travesty equaled only by the Black Sox scandal." As Ruth did in the early 1920s following that infamous World Series fixing scandal, McGwire and Sosa belted long balls by the bushel in '98, helping baseball regain its appeal and reach new heights in popularity.

But home run statistics alone do not reveal how Sosa and McGwire managed to inspire the baseball nation. Historian Harold Seymour maintains that "idolization of ballplayers lies in man's urge to create heroes." Some people see in baseball players "living evidence that certain values and assumptions deep in the American psyche still have validity." This may help explain the euphoria surrounding the 1998 home run derby. Sosa's and McGwire's mutual respect, unfailing sportsmanship, and gracious behavior under immense pressure have been well documented. "It doesn't matter if [McGwire] plays for the Cardinals and I play for Chicago," Sosa remarked after a Cubs-Cardinals game, "we still have a relationship as people, as friends." According to author Peter Golenbock, "Kids across America saw something very rare in sports, a display of sportsmanship, along with a strong feeling of deep respect between opponents," In "A Tribute to Mark McGwire," published in *Suburban Journal West County* on October 4, 1998, a fan wrote:

Dear Mark,
You are a real honest, good person who is responsible for the rebirth of baseball. I am eighty-six years old and have been watching the Cards, Browns, and Chicago Cubs for over seventy years as my favorite teams. But when the million-dollar prima donnas went on strike, I quit watching and going to the games. The league owners should put you on a pedestal. You made a fan out of thousands of people again. You have a love for the game and the fans. I wish we had people like you in Washington, D.C. God bless you and your family and bless Sammy also.

This fan's sentiment resonates with McFarlane. "The ballplayer behind the home run is what really interests me," he explains, as he looks at the Sosa and McGwire action figures manufactured by his company. "By their behavior throughout the 1998 season, I think Sosa and McGwire symbolized what we all yearn to see in professional athletes, but often times do not get—a good role model that we can look up to from time to time."

Recent revelations about steroid use in major-league baseball have dimmed some of the luster of that memorable season, and subsequent ones, but the fact remains that McGwire and Sosa handled themselves with grace and class during that pressure-packed summer. In the new millennium, a cavalcade of power hitters has emerged, deepening suspicions about the source of their power. Leading the way is Bonds, who continues to transform baseball's power game at age 40. When he broke McGwire's

single-season home run record in 2001, Bonds produced one of the greatest offensive seasons in baseball history, batting .328, driving in 137 runs, and breaking Ruth's longstanding records for walks (177) and slugging percentage (.863). Bonds' career has had an eyebrow-raising twilight: He finished the 2004 season with 703 career home runs (third on the all-time list, behind only Aaron and Ruth), six MVP Awards, and eight Gold Glove Awards. The single-season home run record may be the most eye-catching, though, and the ball that sailed out for homer No. 73 is in McFarlane's collection, too.

"It completes the trilogy of my collection," McFarlane says of the famous ball. He now owns Sosa's 66th, McGwire's 70th, and Bonds's 73rd—the crown jewels of home run ball collecting.

IMMORTAL BRETHREN

M. BROWN.   J. PFEISTER   A. HOFMAN   C.G. WILLIAMS   O. OVERALL.   E. REULBACH.   J. KLING.

H. GESSLER.   J. TAYLOR.   H. STEINFELDT.   J. McCORMICK.   F. CHANCE.   J. SHECKARD.   P. MORAN.   F. SCHULTE.

C. LUNDGREN.   T. WALSH.   J. EVERS.   J. SLAGLE.   J. TINKER.

CHICAGO NATIONAL LEAGUE BALL CLUB 1906

Franklin P. Adams wrote "Baseball's Sad Lexicon" (see below in text) after the Cubs and their "Tinker-to-Evers-to-Chance" double plays kept defeating his favorite team, the Giants, during the 1908 season. The trio played side by side for most of eleven seasons and led the team to four pennants and two Worlds Series championships, including the last one ever won by the Cubs in 1908. (See original photos of the 1908 team, opposite, top left, and the 1906 team, left, 16¾" x 12¾") Under the T205 cards are season passes for 1909 and 1910. Tinker and Evers wore these pinstriped jerseys during road games throughout the 1909 season. Chance wore the white jersey during home games throughout the same season. Tinker used this bat during this period, as evidenced by side writing and the style of the centerbrand.

" *Fanaticism? No. Writing is exciting and baseball is like writing. You can never tell with either how it will go or what you will do.*"

—MARIANNE MOORE,
Baseball and Writing

One Sunday afternoon in the autumn of 1982, during my sophomore year at The Lawrenceville School in New Jersey, I wandered into the basement of the school library to find some books for a history paper. Walking through one of the aisles, I noticed that several of the bookshelves were stacked with volumes of the school yearbook, which was (and still is) called *Olla Podrida*. I was staring at an archival collection of almost every yearbook since the 1885 inaugural issue, and I was fascinated. I began flipping through a number of them, starting with the 1967 edition, because I wanted to see what pop star Huey Lewis (Lawrenceville class of '67) looked like as a sen-

ior in high school. Gradually, I made my way back to the books from the early part of the 20th century. In one of these yearbooks, stuck between two pages, I came across a brittle newspaper containing the following poem:

These are the saddest of possible words:
"Tinker to Evers to Chance."
Trio of Bear Cubs and
fleeter than birds,
"Tinker to Evers to Chance."
Ruthlessly pricking our gonfalon
bubble,
Making a Giant hit into a double,
Words that are weighty with
nothing but trouble:
"Tinker to Evers to Chance."

I had no idea who Tinker, Evers, and Chance were, nor did I understand what "gonfalon bubble" meant. But being a former Little Leaguer, a San Francisco Giants fan, and an avid buyer of contemporary baseball cards,

ED M^cFARLAND C   JAMES HART C   FRANK ISBELL 2B   C.A. COMISKEY   L. FIENE P   W^M SULLIVAN C   DR WHITE P
F.A. JONES CAP MGR CF   FRANK SMITH P   LEE TANNEHILL 3B   FRANK ROTH C   ED HAHN RF   GUS DUNDON 2B   JOHN DONOHUE 1B   JOHN O'NEILL RF
ED WALSH P   JAY TOWNE C   NICK ALTROCK P   FRANK OWEN P   GEO DAVIS SS   GEO ROHE 3B   ROY PATTERSON P   PAT DOUGHERTY LF

CHICAGO AMERICAN LEAGUE CLUB
WHITE SOX

Before Boston's "Miracle Braves," New York's "Murderers' Row," St. Louis's "Gashouse Gang," and Brooklyn's "Bums," there were the "Hitless Wonders," a sobriquet aptly attached to the World Champion 1906 Chicago White Sox (above). Prominent early-20th-century baseball photographer George R. Lawrence captured the team that was called "Hitless" because they recorded the lowest team batting average (.230) of any pennant-winning ball club in baseball history. Nevertheless, the team still managed to achieve "Wonders." In the 1906 World Series, despite a paltry team Series batting average of .198, the White Sox defeated their heavily favored cross-town rivals, the Chicago Cubs—winners of a record 116 games—who breezed to the National League pennant, 20 games in front of the second-place New York Giants. The victory came on the back and shoulders of the team's pitching staff of "Big" Ed Walsh, Nick Altrock, Frank Owen, and Harry "Doc" White, which posted a dominant 1.50 ERA during the Series. (16⅜" x 12¾")

I knew the poem had to do with baseball; and the names of the three players, along with the lilting rhythm of the poem, greatly appealed to me.

This little poem piqued my curiosity. Who were these three players, and why were they important enough to be the subjects of a poem? What was the "gonfalon bubble"? To find out, I went to a bookstore in nearby Princeton and bought a copy of Lawrence Ritter's *The Glory of Their Times*, which I had heard was a wonderful book based on interviews with ballplayers who played in the early 20th century. From reading an interview with Fred Snodgrass, who played for the New York Giants between 1908 and 1915, I learned that Tinker, Evers, and Chance were the shortstop, second baseman, and first baseman, respectively, for the Chicago Cubs during that era. They were celebrated, across the baseball world as well as in the poem, for their uncanny ability to turn double play after double play. In his interview, Snodgrass recalled, among other memorable plays, Evers's role in the famous "Merkle's Boner" play, in which Giants baserunner Fred Merkle forgot to touch second base, a gaffe that ultimately cost the Giants the pennant in 1908. Not only did Evers notice that Merkle failed to touch second, he also made sure that the umpire was aware of it.

Although it should not have been such a surprise to me that there was more to baseball and baseball players than meets the eye on television broadcasts, somehow this "behind-the-

scenes" perspective was a revelation. Rather than satisfying my curiosity about Tinker, Evers, and Chance, Ritter's book left me wanting to know more. I wanted to learn not only about the 1908 Chicago Cubs, but also about players and teams that I already knew were legendary, such as Shoeless Joe Jackson and the 1919 Chicago "Black Sox," Christy Mathewson and the early-20th-century New York Giants, and Jackie Robinson and the 1950s Brooklyn Dodgers. So I began to read other classics, including W. P. Kinsella's *Shoeless Joe*, Eric Rolfe Greenberg's *The Celebrant*, and Roger Kahn's *The Boys of Summer*. During college and law school, I spent weekend afternoons curled up with A. Bartlett Giamatti (*The Green Fields of the Mind*), Gay Talese (*The Silent Season of a Hero*), and John Updike (*Hub Fans Bid Kid Adieu*), as well as what W. P. Kinsella calls the "sun-drenched baseball prose" of Roger Angell, which appeared in *The New Yorker* from time to time.

For many baseball fans, watching all of their teams' games is all it takes for them to "live and breathe" baseball. For others, the passion grows into a desire to collect the physical objects involved in the game, as well as the objects made to commemorate baseball and its players. I know; this happened to me. In the decade after I found the "Tinker to Evers to Chance" poem and read Ritter's book, I read every baseball book I could get my hands on, and started to purchase old baseball cards so I could see images of the players I had been reading about. I also started to buy old scorecards at baseball memorabilia conventions because I loved the nostalgic advertisements they featured. Collecting baseball memorabilia was not nearly as popular in the 1980s as it is today, so prices were laughably low, and I was able to acquire many items even though I was still a student.

Soon after these acquisitions, I decided to focus my collection on the profound relationships that underlie some of baseball's most legendary pairings: those groups of two or more ballplayers that largely define a team's dominance within a particular era of baseball history. I was interested in the unique bonds between ballplayers, bonds that could be manifested through the repetitive, seamless execution of the double play (Tinker, Evers, and Chance), or through blood (Dizzy and

Daffy Dean), or friendship (Bobby Doerr, Ted Williams, Dominic DiMaggio, and Johnny Pesky). Other such bonds were made by mutual achievement (Joe DiMaggio and Ted Williams), or through social integration (members of the 1950s Brooklyn Dodgers). The Wong Family Archives Collection evokes the emotions these teammates and peers shared during their careers, in the many hours they spent together not only on the diamond, in dugouts and locker rooms, but also on trolley cars, trains, and buses, and at diners, speakeasies, bars, and hotels.

Four writers in particular have inspired parts of my collection: Franklin P. Adams, J. Roy Stockton, David Halberstam, and Roger Kahn. Their work has captured the following groupings of players, and those players' profound individual relationships with each other, better than I would think words capable.

ME AND PAUL
(DIZZY AND DAFFY DEAN)

J. Roy Stockton, a longtime *St. Louis Post-Dispatch* sportswriter and former president of the Baseball Writers' Association of America (1931), served as Dizzy Dean's ghostwriter for a number of articles that appeared under Dean's byline in newspapers before and during the 1934 World Series, in which the St. Louis Cardinals faced the Detroit Tigers. When Stockton asked Dean who was going to win the Series, the player assured his readers in no uncertain terms that the Tigers had no chance. Stockton included some of Dizzy's responses in *The Gashouse Gang and a Couple of Other Guys*, which he wrote in 1945. They highlight the bravado that made Dizzy one of the most charismatic individuals in baseball history.

"I don't want to make the people think I'm a big windbag, but I want to tell the truth, so just say that the Cardinals will take them Tigers like a bulldog takes a pussy cat, and that if they get a good foul off me and Paul, they can consider themselves lucky. I'll pitch the first game, of course, because pinches is duck soup for me and I'll knock 'em off easy.

"That won't sound like braggin', will it? The way I sees it, braggin' is where you do a lot of poppin' off and ain't got nothin' to back it up. But I ain't braggin'. I know me and Paul is gonna win four games in this here series—if Detroit is good enough to win a couple when we ain't pitchin'—and you might just as well be honest and tell the public all about it. They pays our salary and it's nothin' but fair that we tell 'em just what's goin' to happen...."

In addition to printing Dizzy's animated responses, Stockton provided insight into the origins of his bravado.

"Dizzy meant every word he said. He has the natural showman's love and appreciation of exaggeration, but when he tells you how good he is, he considers it no exaggeration.

"The nickname 'Dizzy' is a transferred epithet. He was striking out Chicago White Sox hitters in an exhibition game in Texas and had the batters groggy. He was giving Chicago a headache. He was a pitcher of dizziness. Somebody called him Dizzy and it stuck.

"Characteristics that make the name appropriate are natural when you consider his origin and his meteoric rise to fame. His father was a cotton picker and a farm hand. Dizzy didn't have an entire pair of shoes until he joined the Army for a three-year stretch. He spent his boyhood as a nomad of the cotton fields, doing hard manual labor at fifty cents a day. His schooling was a smattering; the fourth grade was as far as he went.

"Then suddenly the boy found that he had a valuable right arm, that he could throw a baseball with confounding speed and make it do tricks. Small as the salary was in his first contract, it was more money than he had ever expected a Dean to have at one time. Where a few dollars had been considered affluence, one hundred in the pocket at one

This original news service photo shows the heart of the Boys of Summer (Duke Snider, Gil Hodges, Jackie Robinson, Pee Wee Reese, and Roy Campanella) flashing their weapons on the dugout steps at Ebbets Field on June 6, 1951. (8" x 10")

Dizzy and Daffy Dean had every reason to be smiling and waving their caps in the air in this original news service photo taken on September 30, 1934. According to the caption tag on the reverse, Dizzy had just won his 30th game of the regular season, bringing the total number of victories between him and his brother Paul to 49. At the start of the season, Dizzy had predicted that they would win between 45 and 50 games. The Cardinals were also en route to meet the Detroit Tigers in the World Series. (8" x 10")

The 1934 Detroit Tigers, shown in a team photo at right (19½" x 13"), also boasted a formidable pitching staff led by Lynwood "Schoolboy" Rowe. In 1934, Rowe won 16 consecutive games, which tied the American League record set by Walter Johnson, Smokey Joe Wood, and Lefty Grove. Rowe won Game 2 of the 1934 Series in 12 innings, shutting out the Cardinals after the fourth inning and retiring 22 consecutive batters at one point. Rowe wore this home-style jersey (right, below) during his rookie 1933 season. Aside from being friendly rivals in the classic 1934 World Series, Dizzy and Schoolboy will forever be remembered by the following poem, which was featured in the HBO documentary film *When It Was a Game* (1992):

*Who says romance is
   gray with age
That men no longer
   battle odds
When two raw kids
   from brush and sage
Still face the lightning
   of the gods
Can life be stupid, drab
   or slow
With Dizzy Dean and
   Schoolboy Rowe?*

time naturally made him feel like a Croesus."

In the montage on the opposite page, Dizzy's game-worn jersey from the 1934 season, in which he was named National League MVP, and Paul Dean's game-worn jersey from the 1936 season rest on top of a circa-1934 Beech Nut tobacco cardboard advertising display that depicts the two siblings. Also displayed are ticket stubs from each of the seven games of the 1934 World Series, in which the Cardinals beat the Tigers: Dizzy won Games 1 and 7 while Paul won Games 3 and 6.

A PORTRAIT OF A FRIENDSHIP

It was quite a pleasant surprise when David Halberstam's *The Teammates: A Portrait of*

a Friendship appeared on my Amazon.com "Book Recommendations" list in the spring of 2003. Part of my collection had already been dedicated to commemorating the unique relationship among the four ballplayers who formed the cornerstone of the 1940s Boston Red Sox: Ted Williams, Bobby Doerr, Dominic DiMaggio, and Johnny Pesky. But Halberstam, one of America's most renowned journalists and historians, provided so much fresh insight into the foundations of their lifelong friendship that this particular part of my collection has become one of my personal

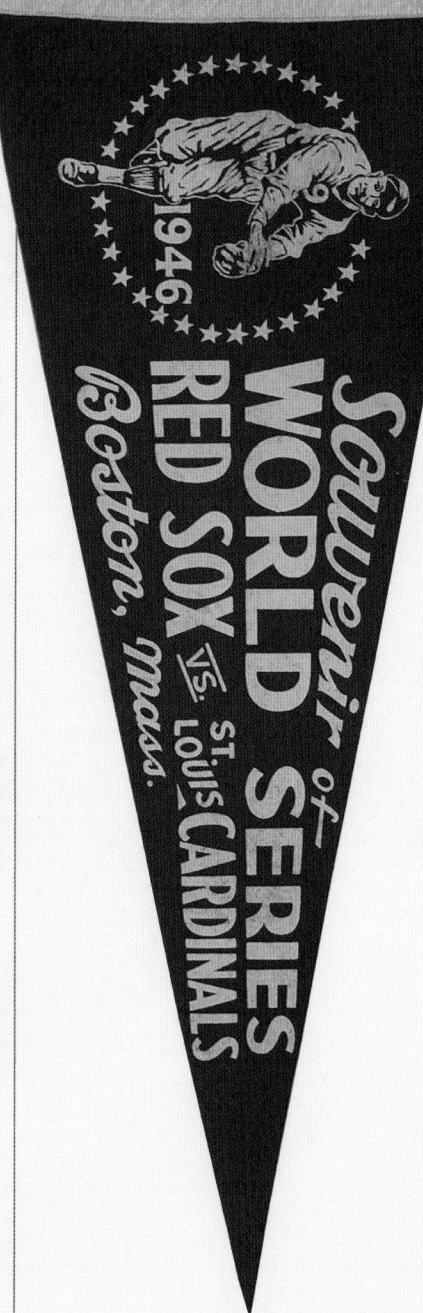

favorites. The following excerpts from *The Teammates* may explain why some fans yearn for the baseball of yesteryear.

"They had, the four of them—Ted Williams, Dom DiMaggio, Bobby Doerr, and Johnny Pesky—played together on the Red Sox teams of the 1940s; Williams and Doerr went back even further: They were teenagers together on the San Diego Padres, a minor-league team in the mid-'30s, and played with Boston in the late '30s. All four were men of a certain generation, born right at the end of World War I within 31 months of each other—DiMaggio in 1917, Doerr and Williams in 1918, and Pesky in 1919 . . .

"That was something unusual in baseball: four men who played for one team, who became good friends, and who remained friends for the rest of their lives. Their lives were forever linked through a thousand box scores, through long hours of traveling on trains together, through shared moments of triumph, and even more in the case of the Red Sox, through shared moments of disappointment. They were aware that they had been unusually lucky not just in the successful quality of their careers, but also in the richness of the friendships they had made . . .

"For many years, the glue that held them together as friends was Williams; someone that great, one of the very best ever at what they all did, had rare peer power. 'It was,' Pesky once said of him, 'like there was a star on top of his head, pulling everyone toward him like a beacon, and letting everyone around him know that he was different and that he was special in some marvelous way and that we were that much more special because we played with him.'

"He might not, the other three teammates knew, be the easiest man in the world to deal with. He always did what he wanted and never did anything he did not. But to no small degree he was the one who had kept them friends; they stayed close because he willed them to stay close. In a way they had become his family—his real family, the one from his childhood, had been difficult, always causing him more pain than pleasure—and there was an awareness that Ted was always there for them."

Because Williams was the "glue" in this group, I placed his game-worn jersey (from the 1950 season and 1951 spring training) between those of Doerr (circa 1946) and DiMaggio (from the 1950 season and 1951 spring training) for the photograph on the opposite page. (I have yet to find one of Pesky's game-worn jerseys.) The Red Sox regular-season program from 1940, the year DiMaggio joined the team, exemplifies how their lives were "linked through a thousand box scores." In the bottom left of the photo is a ticket to Game 3 of the 1946 World Series. That Series was one of the team's "shared moments of disappointment"; they lost it in seven games to the St. Louis Cardinals. I bought the 1949 pennant, which was sold at Fenway Park during that season, because it represented yet another heartbreak for the Red Sox: They lost the American League crown to the Yankees in the final game of the season that year. Halberstam told the wrenching story in another one of his classic books, *Summer of '49.*

THE YANKEE CLIPPER AND SPLENDID SPLINTER

In *The Teammates*, Halberstam also shares his views on the unique relationship between Joe DiMaggio and Ted Williams, a relationship that evolved from an "unspo-

ken rivalry" during the 1940s and 1950s to one of shared mortality:

"In the late 1990s, as Joe's health began to fail, Dominic got deeply involved in trying to take care of his brother. It was at this point that Ted began to call Dominic five or six times a week, wanting to know how Joe was doing. That of itself was fascinating. Joe had played for the Yankees, Boston's bitter rival, and the great hitters—Joe, who hit in 56 straight games in 1941, and Ted, who hit .406 that same year—had had their own unspoken rivalry. They were at the center of one of the great ongoing debates among baseball fans of several generations, as to who the better ballplayer was, and what might have happened had each played for the other's team, in the other's ballpark. The summary judgment: Joe was the better all-around player; Ted, the better hitter.

"The two had not been close when they played. Joe DiMaggio was the most aloof of men; he held out genuine warmth and friendship not even to his younger brother or his longtime teammates, let alone to Ted Williams, as the one baseball player against whom he was constantly measured. Ted, by contrast, was far more open, far more generous, and far more volatile. After they quit playing his only real connection to Joe, other than through his admiration for him and his love of Joe's younger brother, was the fact that for some 50 years they stood together atop the same pedestal of excellence, honored and celebrated at countless baseball dinners, posing for a seemingly endless number of photographs reflecting baseball's royalty from an earlier age. The byplay between them on such occasions was, more often than not, quite stilted.

"Because they had shared so much of an era, even if they had shared nothing else, their mortality was in some curious way a shared one; if they were linked in life by greatness then they surely would be linked

While Williams (left) was open and volatile. DiMaggio was aloof and cool. Despite their differences, they shared an enormous respect for one another's skills. (7" x 9")

in their obituaries. If Joe, who was nearly four years older than Ted, was dying, then Ted's mortality was at stake as well. The imminent death of Joe DiMaggio meant that an era that belonged to Ted, as much as it did to Joe, was coming to an end. Thus when Joe's health began to fail badly in the fall of 1998, and when it became clear that he was dying, Ted was deeply moved and his regular phone calls to Dominic started, always at the same time of day. As soon as the phone rang, Dominic knew it was Ted calling about Joe, wanting to know how he was, whether he was doing any better, asking what the doctors were saying. When Joe died, Ted took it, his friends realized with surprise, like a death in his extended family."

The "unspoken rivalry" started in 1941, the year that defined DiMaggio's and Williams's legacies. The original black and white photograph taken in the summer of that year captures a warm moment shared between the two legends before the start of a game at Yankee Stadium (upper left in the montage opposite). That year, Gum, Inc., immortalized the Yankee Clipper and the Splendid Splinter in their "Play Ball" series baseball-card set. An original wrapper that housed two cards and a stick of gum lies to the right of the photo; their cards from the set are below the photo. Bats were the key instruments of their rivalry. DiMaggio used the bat in the lower left of the montage during the 1949 All-Star Game played at Ebbets Field, in which he drove in three runs with a single and a double in four trips to the plate, leading the American League to a 11–7 victory. Williams used the other bat during the 1946 season, in which he was named the American League's MVP. By the end of the decade, the rivalry was still going strong: Williams won his second MVP Award in 1949, and DiMaggio led the Yan-

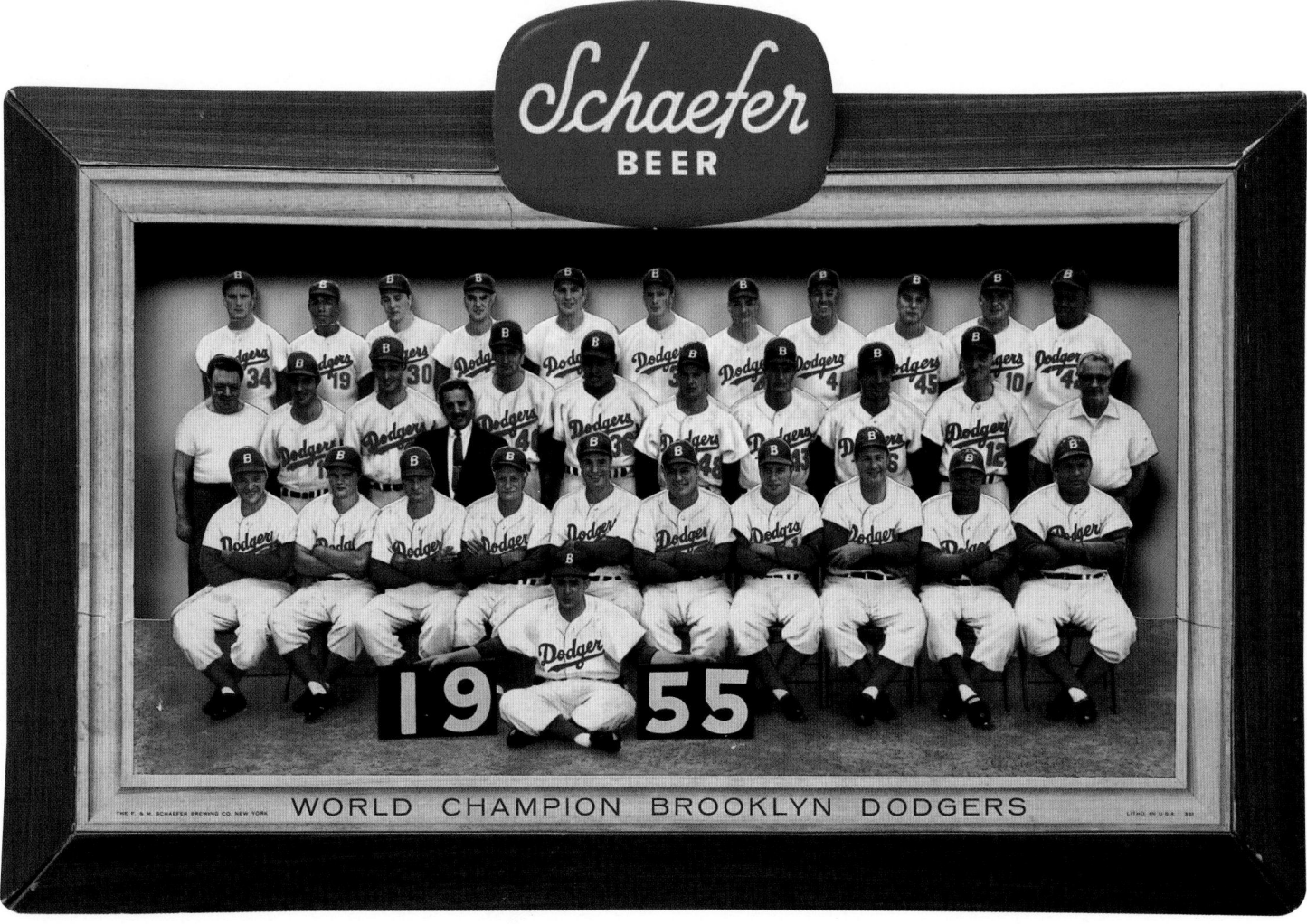

WORLD CHAMPION BROOKLYN DODGERS

kees to World Series victories in 1949, 1950, and 1951. The uniforms displayed with the bats were worn by Williams and DiMaggio during the 1950 season and during 1951 spring training, as indicated by the American League Golden Anniversary patch affixed to the left sleeve on the Williams jersey and the year stitched next to DiMaggio's name on the white strip tag sewn onto DiMaggio's pants.

THE BOYS OF SUMMER

Brooklyn-raised Roger Kahn (b. 1927) followed the Dodgers devoutly as a boy and then covered the team as a newspaper reporter for the *Herald Tribune*, starting in 1952. In 1972, he published *The Boys of Summer*, a poignant and evocative account of his childhood, his hometown, his work, and his team, the 1950s Dodgers. Kahn also wrote about what became of the players in their lives after baseball. In the excerpt that follows, he describes what it felt like to be a Brooklyn Dodgers fan in the 1950s. He goes on to reveal that many of the heroic deeds of the "Beloved Bums" were actually performed without bats or gloves.

"At a point in life when one is through with boyhood, but has not yet discovered how to be a man, it was my fortune to travel with the most marvelously appealing of teams. During the early 1950s the Jackie Robinson Brooklyn Dodgers were outspoken, opinionated, bigoted, tolerant, black, white, open, passionate: in short, a fascinating mix of vigorous men. They were not, however, the most successful team in baseball.

"During four consecutive years they entered autumn full of hope and found catastrophe. Twice they lost pennants in the concluding inning of the concluding game of a season. Twice they won pennants and lost the World Series to the New York Yankees. These narrow setbacks did not proceed, as some suggested, from failings of courage or of character. The Dodgers were simply unfortunate—it is dreamstuff that luck plays everyone the same—and, not to become excessively technical, they lacked the kind of pitching that makes victory sure. In the next decade, a weaker Dodger team, rallying

Schaefer beer saluted the 1955 World Champion Brooklyn Dodgers with this three-dimensional cardboard advertising sign, which was proudly displayed in just about every pub, restaurant, and convenient store within the entire borough.
(24" x 10½", 2½" deep)

The jerseys Robinson and Pee Wee Reese wore during the 1948 season, along with the game-used bat of each member of the team that gave Brooklyn its first and only World Series victory, grace the photo on the opposite page. Nat Fein, a renowned photographer for the *New York Herald Tribune* and winner of the 1949 Pulitzer Prize, captured perhaps Brooklyn's finest moment—the raising of the 1955 World Series championship flag, shown in the lower left corner of the montage.

Two Friends

around Sandy Koufax, won the World Series twice.

"But I mean to be less concerned with curve balls than with the lure of the team. Ebbets Field was a narrow cockpit, built of brick and iron and concrete, alongside a steep cobblestone slope of Bedford Avenue. Two tiers of grandstand pressed the playing area from three sides, and in thousands of seats fans could hear a ballplayer's chatter, notice details of a ballplayer's gait and, at a time when television had not yet assaulted illusion with the Zoomar lens, you could see, you could actually see, the actual expression on the actual face of an actual major leaguer as he played. You could know what he was like!

" 'I start in toward the bench, holding the ball now with the five fingers of my bare left hand, and when I get to the infield—having come down hard with one foot on the bag at second base—I shoot it, with just a flick of the wrist, gently at the opposing team's shortstop as he comes trotting out onto the field, and without breaking stride, go loping in all the way, shoulders shifting, head hanging, a touch pigeon-toed, my knees coming slowly up and down in an altogether brilliant imitation of The Duke.' Philip Roth as Alexander Portnoy as Duke Snider. In the

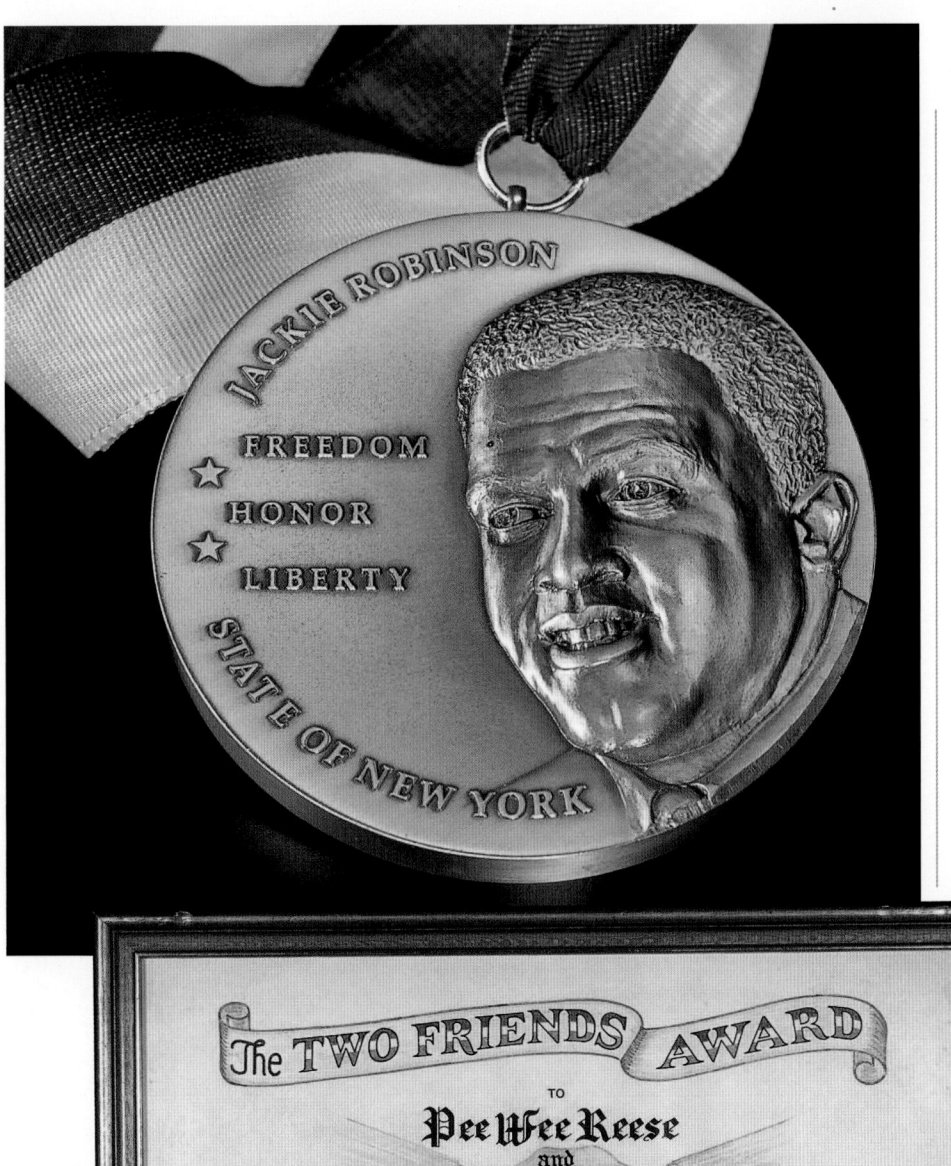

On January 20, 1956, Pee Wee Reese received "The Two Friends Award" certificate (above, 11" x 17", and inset photograph, opposite page, 8" x 10") in recognition of his efforts in helping integrate major-league baseball.

ing in life as becomingly as leaving it. A whole country was stirred by the high deeds and thwarted longings of the The Duke, Preacher, Pee Wee, Skoonj and the rest. The team was awesomely good and yet defeated. Their skills lifted everyman's spirit and their defeat joined them with everyman's existence, a national team, with a country in thrall, irresistible and unable to beat the Yankees . . . .

"[The] dominant truth of the Jackie Robinson Dodgers was integration. They were the first integrated major league baseball team and so the most consciously integrated team and, perhaps, the most intensely integrated team. All of them, black and white, became targets for the intolerance in which baseball has been rich.

"As many ballplayers, officials, umpires and journalists envisioned it, the entity of baseball rose in alabaster, a temple of white supremacy. To them, the Robinson presence was a defilement and the whites who consented to play at his side were whores. Opposing pitchers forever threw fast balls at Dodger heads. Opposing bench jockeys forever shouted 'black bastard,' 'nigger lover' and 'monkey fucker.' Hate was always threatening the team. But the Dodgers, the dozen or so athletes who were at the core of the team . . . stood together in purpose and for the most part in camaraderie. They respected one another as competitors and they knew that they were set apart. No one prattled about team spirit. No one made speeches on the Rights of Man. No one sang 'Let My People Go.' But without pretense or visible fear, these men marched unevenly against the sin of bigotry."

intimacy of Ebbets Field it was a short trip from the grandstand to the fantasy that you were in the game.

"My years with the Dodgers were 1952 and 1953, two seasons in which they lost the World Series to the Yankees. You may glory in a team triumphant, but you fall in love with a team in defeat. Losing after great striving is the story of man, who was born to sorrow, whose sweetest songs tell of saddest thought, and who, if he is a hero, does noth-

On April 15, 1947, opening day at Ebbets Field, 26,623 fans filled the stands to see Jackie Robinson make his historic major-league debut. The fan who held the ticket stub in the bottom right of the photo on page 272 sat in the lower stands. Perhaps the fan wore an "I'm Rooting for Jackie Robinson" pin-back button, like the one below the tickets in that photo. While Robinson quickly

The New York Yankees were not the only team to boast a "Murderer's' Row." Chicago had one as well, and it consisted of some of the era's most formidable sluggers, as shown in this original 1929 autographed photo of (left to right) the Cubs' Rogers Hornsby, Hack Wilson, Charlie Grimm, Kiki Cuyler, and Riggs Stephenson. They would slug their way into the team's first World Series in 11 years, but fall short to the sluggers on Connie Mack's Philadelphia Athletics. (11" x 7½")

proved himself on the field, winning the National League Rookie of the Year Award in '47, he still faced poisonous bigotry practically everywhere he went. Brooklyn captain Pee Wee Reese did everything he could to help his new teammate. Reese's commitment led to a long-standing bond between the two men. (Inscribed on Reese's Hall of Fame plaque is the legend, "Instrumental in easing acceptance of Jackie Robinson as baseball's first black performer.")

W. P. Kinsella has written that "baseball is the chess of sports, the ballet of sports. One has to be a dreamer and equipped with a fertile imagination to be a serious baseball fan." I am eternally grateful for the inspiration that many of the writers mentioned and quoted in this chapter and throughout this book have given me, both as a baseball fan and as a collector. I believe they are some of the most insightful and imaginative dreamers one could ever hope to encounter. May they inspire you, too.

Rogers Hornsby's side-written game-used bat from the 1929 season, in which he was the National League MVP, is shown at near right along with the game-used bats of Hack Wilson, Charlie Grimm, Kiki Cuyler (side-written and vault-marked), and Riggs Stephenson.

THE WONG FAMILY ARCHIVES COLLECTION

277

FEATURED COLLECTORS

Corey R. Shanus—who holds a J.D. and M.B.A. from the University of Chicago and runs a real estate investment and management firm in the New York area—places his left hand on a souvenir that was given to delegates of the Brooklyn Excelsior Base Ball Club in 1859 to commemorate the first meeting of the National Association of Base Ball Players, which was the first ruling body of organized baseball.

A seasoned third baseman and prominent radiologist in the Philadelphia area, Dr. Mark W. Cooper began collecting games and toys related to the national pastime over 20 years ago when he and his wife Lynn purchased The Great American Game by Frantz and Hustler at a flea market. For generations, these artifacts provided adults and children with a great source of home recreation and an entertaining survey of baseball, its rules, and its history.

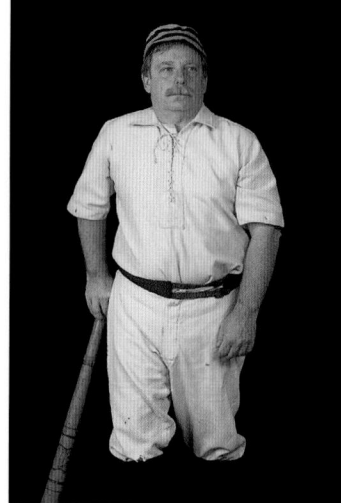

With a collection dedicated to the evolution of the baseball, glove, bat, and catcher's gear, Gregory John Gallacher aptly wears his 19th-century baseball uniform and leans on a "ring bat," which was popular in the 1880s.

The challenge of creating and building things has been a life-long endeavor for Gary Mark Cypres. In the early 1980s he helped grow industrial company Wheelabrator-Frye Inc. into a multi-billion dollar enterprise. After developing his nation-wide travel and mortgage brokerage business from scratch, Cypres built Los Angeles's first sports history museum, which is dedicated to America's three favorite pastimes—baseball, football and basketball.

Brian Seigel, the CEO of asset management firm Emerald Capital L.L.C., kneels down next to the actual sewage manhole cover which served as home plate during street-ball games with his buddies in the summer of 1965. During these games five-year-old Brian first learned the names of many of the stars featured in the T206 set.

A leading ophthalmologist in New Jersey and fervent baseball collector for over 15 years, Dr. Richard C. Angrist sits behind stacks of binders full of detailed documentation providing provenance and authenticity for each item in his treasure trove of some of baseball's most historically significant game-used bats and game-worn uniforms and jerseys.

Let's just call it splendid serendipity that one of the world's most comprehensive collections of World Series scorecards and programs is being preserved by James Clister and his daughter Lauren, who are proud natives of Pittsburgh—the home of the team who played the Boston Pilgrims in the inaugural World Series in 1903.

Dr. Nick Depace's devotion to game-worn uniforms and jerseys began on August 4, 1961, when he saw his childhood hero Mickey Mantle swagger out of the dugout at Yankee Stadium. Depace, a renowned cardiologist in the Philadelphia area, and his son Nicholas share a smile with his other childhood hero—the legendary Willie Mays—during a sports banquet that took place in Atlantic City in October 1999.

After pursuing a distinguished career as one of Denver's leading personal-injury lawyers, Marshall Fogel, who bought his first pack of baseball cards in the summer of 1953, rediscovered his fountain of youth 36 years later, during his first attendance at a National Sports Collectors Convention which was held in Chicago. It was the impetus to one of the hobby's most celebrated collections.

Robert Edward Lifson, a Wharton graduate and founder of Robert Edward Auctions, one of the country's leading sports and Americana auction companies, has been collecting pin-back buttons for over 35 years. According to Lifson, pin backs still foster the time-honored-thrill of discovering previously unknown examples in attics, basements, drawers, antique bazaars, and old shoeboxes throughout the country.

Donning an original Crosley Field ticket-usher uniform from the 1940s, Bruce Spencer Hellerstein—a tax accountant in Denver—stands in front of a ticket window carved into the marble wall in the basement of his home, which forms part of a replica of the grand marble rotunda entrance to Brooklyn's Ebbets Field.

The collection of accomplished film director, producer, and actress, Penny Marshall, exemplifies the breadth of artifacts that commemorate baseball's history. Marshall, who as a child during the early 1950s hailed her Bronx Bombers from the bleachers of Yankee Stadium, typically foregoes Babe Ruth autographed balls and Mickey Mantle bats for some of the game's most bizarre relics.

In the summer of 1952, ten-year-old Charles Michael Merkel shared a bus ride with the entire New York Yankees squad from Sportsman's Park in St. Louis back to the hotel in which the team and Charles's parents were staying. After that memorable ride Charles could never stop loving the Yankees, as well as his baseball cards.

Collecting is a cherished endeavor, especially when shared with your beloved children. Family-business entrepreneur Ron Leff and his two sons Andy and Mitchell have built a remarkable collection together, which includes some of baseball's most prized trophies, jewelry, game-used bats, game-worn hats, photographs, and memorabilia. Andy was forced to stand in this photo because he prefers hockey over baseball.

It has been said that major-league catcher Moe Berg was fluent in seven languages but couldn't hit in any of them. Batting prowess was never part of Berg's talent and it was, in fact, a movie camera, as opposed to a bat, that brought him fame. Retired cardiologist and devout family man Dr. Bill Sear of Atlanta holds the actual "Bell and Howard" once used by the big league's most celebrated spy.

Hobby veteran Bill Mastro stands on the staircase that leads to his magnificent display room of some of the world's finest advertising displays, vintage photographs, and memorabilia. Only perhaps the candy case he saw at Geroloman's back in April 1960 could rival the room's omnipresent eye appeal.

In 1916, William Orville DeWitt started a family legacy in major-league baseball that is now in its third generation. Bill DeWitt, Jr., the principal owner, Chairman, and CEO of the St. Louis Cardinals, sits next to his son Bill DeWitt, III, at Busch Stadium.

Aside from collecting some of the game's most treasured autographed baseball photographs for over ten years, David Bowen, who runs a print media and publishing business in Columbus, Ohio, is a devoted family man and seasoned veteran of fantasy baseball.

Lifelong Chicago Cubs fan Dan Knoll is also one of the hobby's most respected authorities on authenticating game-worn uniforms and jerseys, game-used bats, and vintage baseball photographs. When he is not rooting for the Cubbies or authenticating memorabilia throughout the country, Dan is a devoted husband and father.

Todd McFarlane, the Grammy and Emmy-Award winning producer and director who created the action hero Spawn, played varsity baseball in college and almost made the cut as an outfielder for the Toronto Blue Jays' farm team in 1983. He has been a devoted collector of special home run baseballs for over 12 years.

Stephen Wong, the author of this book, takes his batting stance before a 1975 Little League game in Los Altos Hills, California.

ACKNOWLEDGEMENTS

Poet and philosopher Henry David Thoreau once said, "Go confidently in the direction of your dreams. Live the life you have imagined." This book project was certainly a dream come true and, for the past two and half years, I felt as though I was actually breathing the wisdom of Thoreau. I owe tremendous gratitude to a number of very special people who helped me along the way.

My father and mother were deeply supportive and encouraged me to pursue this project from the very beginning, even though it meant I would most probably be out of work for over two years. Without their lifetime of unconditional love, moral support, and insight, I doubt that I would have had enough courage to move forward with the book.

My sister Adrianna and Ms. Judy Sin (my father's medical assistant for over two decades), like my parents, were always there for me throughout every stage of the project. My wonderful Uncle Sau Wai Lam and Aunty Marie Lam, as well as my two dear cousins Brian and Christine Lam, not only provided me a wonderful place to stay in New York during my research and writing, but also went out of their way to take such good care of me, something that meant a lot to me since I was far away from home.

Initially, one of my major concerns was whether a sufficient number of collectors would actually be willing to be featured in the book. Collecting, by and large, is a private endeavor. But virtually every collector I contacted agreed to participate. I am most grateful to each and every featured collector for believing in this project and allowing me to share with readers their remarkable collections and information about their background and history. Each collector and their family members were exceedingly gracious and hospitable during the photo shoot and interview sessions, and extremely patient and supportive throughout every stage of the project. A number of collectors lent books to me for research and/or went out of their way to send me whatever artifact I needed to serve as a prop for a particular photo shoot.

Some of my dearest friends in the hobby—David Guslani, Bill Mastro, Doug Allen, and David Bushing, in particular—helped me lift this project off the ground, providing invaluable insight, encouragement, and infrastructural support when the project was merely an idea scribbled on a few pages of paper. Each of them

was instrumental in helping me identify and secure the appropriate collections to be featured in the book. Their suggestions in helping me "fine tune" the proposal were invaluable.

Bill DeWitt Jr. not only gave me his friendship and support throughout the project, but he helped me get in touch with Ms. Jane Forbes Clark, Chairman of the National Baseball Hall of Fame and Museum, to write the foreword for the book. It is truly an honor to have Ms. Clark involved with this project, particularly since the Hall of Fame has always been a source of inspiration for the featured collectors in this book.

Tish O'Connor and Dana Levy of Perpetua Press in Santa Barbara were instrumental in helping me prepare a beautiful prospectus. They also provided me with invaluable information and insight into the intricate world of publishing and they were like mentors to me during the early stages of the project.

Whitey Ford, the legendary Hall of Fame pitcher for the Yankees, was so gracious in providing his support for the project in writing, which I proudly displayed in the Introduction of the prospectus. What a privilege it was to have someone like Whitey "go up to bat" for me.

Two very special individuals, both of whom are die-hard baseball fans—Jessica R. Friedman (my lawyer for the project) and Professor Robert Weisberg (my law school professor)—read most of my writing for this book and provided exceptional insight and suggestions to help my narrative and captions appeal to both readers with limited knowledge in baseball history and baseball aficionados.

From the very beginning, my dream publisher was Smithsonian Institution Press ("SIP"). In May 2003, I shared my proposal with Don Fehr, Director of SIP, at the Book Expo of America in Los Angeles. Even though I was a "rookie" author, Don listened intently. After the Expo, he shared my proposal with other senior editors and marketing professionals within SIP, including executive editor Caroline Newman and art director Carolyn Gleason. I want to thank Don, Caroline, and Carolyn and the entire SIP staff, including assistant editor Emily Sollie, for giving me a chance and believing in this project, and for their extraordinary leadership, expertise, and support, throughout the entire project. My friends at Bishop Publishing in White Plains, New York, also provided their extraordinary talent, creativity, and

dedication. The book's designer, Barbara Chilenskas, somehow always knew how to instill elegance into each chapter, and vigilant editors Morin Bishop, John Bolster, and Reed Richardson simply did an outstanding job in vetting the manuscript and getting me back on track when my prose went astray.

In February 2005, The Smithsonian Institution and HarperCollins Publishers formed a publishing partnership to create a distinguished line of high-quality books. This partnership effectively provided HarperCollins the responsibility to implement and oversee the marketing and distribution strategy of this book. To have this book associated with another venerable institution like HarperCollins has been something way beyond my imagination. In particular, I would like to thank Joe Tessitore, Donna Ruvituso, Jean-Marie Kelly, Phil Friedman, George Bick, Beth Mellow, Marguerite Furlong, Tony Valado, and Margaret Pai for their undivided support and expertise in overseeing and marketing this book.

My principal collaborator in this project was photographer Susan Einstein, whose tremendous skill and whose graciousness and compassion as a human being has made all the difference in this book. Over a six-month period, we traveled together to twenty different cities and towns throughout the United States, as well as to Hong Kong, to photograph all the collections featured in this book. There were numerous flights, long drives, checking in and out of hotels with heavy photography equipment, many 14+ hour days of intense photo shoot sessions. One of the greatest pleasures for me throughout the project was to see for the first time a montage shot that Susan produced, rich and lavish as it always is in detail, mood, and feel. I cannot think of a better partner in this project than Susan.

During the project's latter stages, it became evident that some additional artifacts needed to be photographed to augment the look or fill certain holes in particular chapters. Because I was finishing the research and writing in Hong Kong and Susan was based in Los Angeles, I had to hire another professional photographer in Hong Kong who could maintain the exceptional standards set by Susan. I would like to thank Eden Man and Wong Fun Nam of 4D Studios in Hong Kong for their outstanding work and professionalism. I am also grateful to Craig Guyon of Louisville, Kentucky, for helping us take some photographs at the Louisville Slugger Museum.

Brian Bigelow, Scott Emmerling, Laura Harden, and David Murphy of premier auction firm MastroNet provided unfailing assistance at various stages throughout the project. Brian kindly read some of the "collecting tips" chapters when I felt I needed a pair of fresh eyes to review the prose. Scott kindly tracked down a number of images in the MastroNet database that I used as visual props for certain chapters. Laura repeatedly helped me with certain administrative tasks and David helped me photograph a few late-addition artifacts at MastroNet's office in Willowbrook, Illinois, so collectors would not have to send the items all the way to Hong Kong.

I owe a tremendous debt to those friends, fellow collectors, and industry experts who have contributed "collecting tips" essays for this book. David Bushing, David Hunt, Anne Jewell, Dan Knoll, Bill Mastro, Corey R. Shanus, Barry Sloate, and Kevin Struss, provided crucial expertise and insight into collecting some of the major segments of baseball memorabilia. Their advice will be invaluable to both novice and seasoned collectors.

During my research, I relied on some landmark works from some of baseball's greatest scholars and historians. Harold Seymour's Baseball: The Early Years (1960) and Baseball: The Golden Years (1971), Geoffrey C. Ward's and Ken Burns's Baseball: An Illustrated History (1994), John Thorn's and Pete Palmer's classic volume Total Baseball: The Ultimate Encyclopedia of Baseball (1989), and David Pietrusza's, Matthew Silverman's, and Michael Gershman's Baseball: The Biographical Encyclopedia (2000), all served as the project's bible.

Lastly, I would like to thank a number of very special people for their kind friendship and moral support throughout the entire project: Chris Boyd, Paul Brown, Kin Chan, Terence Cheung, Dan Chou, Renee Chow, Thomas Chu, Mr. and Mrs. S. S. Chow, Stephen Chow Chung Yuen and Liat Chen, Choy Peng-Wah, Paul and Mabel Curley, James Direnzo, Alex Fang, Bernard and Virginia Fung, Paula Guslani, Sam and Annie Hanbury, David Hardoon, Clay Hill, Uncle Peter Ho and Aunty Josephine Ho, Bradford Hu and Yuko Kuriyama, Chris Huang and Carol Wong, Tom and Grace Jackamo, Duncan Jepson and Charmaine Li, Alex Karp, Aaron and Shirley Kim, Troy Kinunen, Mr. and Mrs. Alwin Lam, Chi Wai and Kyung Jin Lam,

Irene Lam, Ed Lam, Alain Lam, Tommy and Christina Lee, Mr. and Mrs. Henry Leung, Max Lummis, Ceasar and Davina Luk, Mr. Walter Ma (my godfather), Mark Machin, Will and Cathy McLane, Mr. and Mrs. Robert Miller, Joe Phillips, Sunil Sanghai, Julian Snelder, Colin and Gracie Stewart, Tim Sun, Tony Souza, Jimmy Spence, Cecilia Tamang, Mr. and Mrs. Samson Ting, Patrick and Annie Ting, Karen Ting, Sheldon Trainor, Nissim and Sharie Tse, Alan and Jackie Tung, Wayne Varner, Oliver and Janine Weisberg, Dr. and Mrs. William Wong, my dear cousins Diana Wong, John Wong, Gloria Wong, and Angie Wong, Taylor and Lindsey Wright, David and Zarina Yeh, Raymond and Diana Yin, Laeticia Yu, Mr. Alan Zeman, Kevin Zhang, Bill Zimpleman, Michael Zirinsky and Kelly Fine, the entire staff at Downtown Cipriani's restaurant, Il Mulino restaurant, and the Square Diner in New York, and the entire staff at the Island Shangri-La Hotel Business Center and MAUI Business Center in Hong Kong.

CONTRIBUTORS

David Bushing is one of the world's foremost authorities in authenticating game-used bats and game-worn uniforms and jerseys. He authenticates for SCD Authentic, a leading third-party game-used equipment authentication service which is used by the country's major sports memorabilia auction houses including Sotheby's. Bushing has published numerous articles on game-used equipment and is co-author of the MastroNet Reference and Price Guide for Collecting Game-Used Bats (2001).

David Hunt has been collecting baseball folk art for over 15 years. In 2003 he was a contributor to the baseball folk art exhibition at the American Folk Art Museum in New York. He has conducted appraisals and/or facilitated exhibitions for the Chester County Historical Society, Louisville Slugger Museum, and the National Baseball Hall of Fame and Museum. He is the President of Hunt Auctions, Inc., one of the world's top live-auction firms for sports memorabilia.

Anne Jewell is the Executive Director of the Louisville Slugger Museum in Louisville, Kentucky. She is a summa cum laude graduate of Denison University, where she studied Psychology and Sports Communication, and received an M.A. in Psychology from Wake Forest University.

As a television news reporter she received numerous awards, including an Emmy.

Dan Knoll has been collecting early 20th-century baseball photographs for over 25 years. He is also one of the world's foremost authorities in authenticating game-used bats and game-worn uniforms and jerseys. Along with David Bushing, Knoll co-authored the MastroNet Reference and Price Guide for Collecting Game-Used Bats (2001) and he currently authenticates game-used equipment for SCD Authentic.

Bill Mastro has been collecting vintage baseball cards and memorabilia for 45 years and is widely regarded as one of the world's foremost experts in the field of baseball cards and memorabilia. He brought the concept of major sports memorabilia to a new level by conceiving and creating the first major sports auction conducted by a major auction house with his sale of the James Copeland Collection at Sotheby's in 1991. Ever since then, he has been instrumental in pioneering the Americana and sports memorabilia auction business and is currently the Chairman and CEO of MastroNet., Inc., one of the world's premier Americana and sports memorabilia auction companies.

Corey R. Shanus, who holds a J.D. and M.B.A. from the University of Chicago, is widely considered the hobby's foremost collector of 19th-century baseball memorabilia. Some of his precious artifacts appeared in Baseball: An Illustrated History by Geoffrey C. Ward and Ken Burns.

Barry Sloate holds an M.A. in English Literature from New York University, and has been a collector and dealer of 19th-century and early 20th-century baseball memorabilia since 1982. He has written extensively for some of the hobby's leading periodicals, including Old Judge and Vintage and Classic Baseball Collector. Sloate was also chosen to catalogue the famous Barry Halper sale at Sotheby's in 1999.

Kevin Struss began attending baseball card conventions as a youngster in 1979 and eventually became a partner at SportsCards Plus, a leading sports memorabilia dealer in the Los Angeles area. He has an extremely broad knowledge of vintage baseball cards and has spent the last five years as MastroNet's in-house baseball card expert. He holds a B.A. from the University of California at Santa Barbara with majors in both Economics and Religious Studies.

SELECTED BIBLIOGRAPHY

Angell, Roger. *The Summer Game*. New York: Viking, 1972.

Angell, Roger. *Game Time: A Baseball Companion*. Orlando, Fl.: Harcourt, 2003.

Baumgarten, Linda. *What Clothes Reveal: The Language of Clothing in Colonial and Federal America*. Virginia: The Colonial Williamsburg Foundation, 2002.

Benson, Michael. *Ballparks of North America: A Comprehensive Historical Reference to Baseball Grounds, Yards and Stadiums, 1845 to Present*. North Carolina: McFarland & Company, Inc., Publishers, 1989.

Blom, Philipp. *To Have and to Hold: An Intimate History of Collectors and Collecting*. New York: The Overlook Press, 2003.

Bushing, Dave and Dan Knoll. *MastroNet Reference and Price Guide for Collecting Game Used Baseball Bats*. Oak Brook, IL: Mastronet, Inc., 2001.

Cassidy, Daid. *Uncertainty: The Life and Science of Werner Heisenberg*. New York: W. H. Freeman, 1991.

Colbert, David, ed. *Baseball: The National Pastime in Art and Literature*. Richmond, Va: Time Life Books, 2001.

Cooper, Mark, with Douglas Congdon-Martin. *Baseball Games: Home Versions of the National Pastime, 1860s-1960s*. Atglen, Pa.: Schiffer Publishing, 1995.

Creamer, Robert W. *Babe: The Legend Comes to Life*. New York: Fireside, 1974.

Dawidoff, Nicholas. *The Catcher Was a Spy: The Mysterious Life of Moe Berg*. New York: Vintage Books, 1994.

Dawidoff, Nicholas, ed. *Baseball: A Literary Anthology*. New York: Library of America, 2002.

DeValeria, Dennis and Jeanne Burke DeValeria. *Honus Wagner: A Biography*. Pittsburgh, Pa.: University of Pittsburgh Press, 1998.

Elfers, James E. *The Tour to End All Tours: The Story of Major League Baseball's 1913 – 1914 World Tour*. Nebraska: University of Nebraska Press, 2003.

Enders, Eric. *100 Years of the World Series*. New York: Barnes & Noble Books, 2003.

Feldmann, Doug. *Dizzy and the Gashouse Gang: The 1934 St. Louis Cardinals and Depression-Era Baseball*. Jefferson, NC: McFarland & Company, 2000.

Forbes, Robert and Terence R. Mitchell, *American Tobacco Cards: A Price Guide and Checklist*. Wisconsin: Antique Trader, 1999.

Fried, Frederick. *America's Forgotten Folk Arts*. New York: Pantheon Books, 1978.

Gershman, Michael. *Diamonds: The Evolution of the Ballpark*. New York: Houghton Mifflin, 1993.

Gentile, Derek. *The Complete Chicago Cubs: The Total Encyclopedia of the Team*. New York: Black Dog & Leventhal, 2002.

Golenbock, Peter. *The Spirit of St. Louis: A History of the St. Louis Cardinals and Browns*. New York: HarperCollins, 2000.

Golenbock, Peter. *Wrigleyville: A Magical History Tour of the Chicago Cubs*. New York: St. Martin's, 1996.

Gonzalez, Echevarria, Roberto. *The Pride of Havana: A History of Cuban Baseball*. New York: Oxford University Press, 1999.

Greenberg, Eric Rolfe. *The Celebrant*. Lincoln, NE: University of Nebraska Press, 1983.

Hake, Ted and Russ King. *Collectible Pin-Back Buttons 1896-1986: An Illustated Price Guide*. Wisconsin: Krause Publications, 1991.

Halberstam, David. *The Teammates*. New York: Hyperion, 2003.

Halberstam, David. *Summer of '49*. New York: Perennial Classics, 1989.

Hawkins Joel and Terry Bertolino. *The House of David Baseball Team*. Chicago: Arcadia Publishing, 2000.

Hill, Bob. *Crack of the Bat: The Louisville Slugger Story*. Champaign, Il.: Sports Masters Publishing Inc., 2000.

Honig, Donald. *Baseball When the Grass was Real: Baseball in the Forties Told by the Men Who Played It*. Lincoln, NE: University of Nebraska Press, 1975.

Kahn, Roger. *The Boys of Summer*. New York: Harper and Row, 1972.

Kaufman, Louis, Barbara Fitzgerald, and Tom Sewell. *Moe Berg: Athlete, Scholar, Spy*. Boston: Little, Brown and Company, 1974.

James, Bill. *The Bill James Historical Baseball Abstract*. New York: Villard Books, 1986.

Lipset, Lew. *The Encyclopedia of Baseball Cards: Volume 3 – 20th Century Tobacco Cards (1909-1932)*. New York: Lew Lipset, 1986.

Mastro Fine Sports Auctions catalogues: November 18-19, 1999; November 16-17, 2000

MastroNet, Inc. Sports Memorabilia Premier Catalogue Auction, November 16-17, 2001; Sports & Americana Premier Catalogue Auction, August 22-23, 2002, December 12-13, 2002, August 27-29, 2003; Sports Premier Catalogue Auction, April 23-24, 2003, August 12, 2004.

McCabe, Neal and Constance McCabe. *Baseball's Golden Age: The Photographs of Charles M. Conlon*. New York: Harry N. Abrams, 1993.

National Baseball Hall of Fame and Museum. *Baseball As America: Seeing Ourselves through Our National Game*. Washington, D.C.: National Geographic Society, 2002.

Newhall, Beaumont. *The History of Photography: From 1839 to the Present*. New York: The Museum of Modern Art, 1982.

Neyer, Rob and Eddie Epstein. *Baseball Dynasties: The Greatest Teams of All Time*. New York: W. W. Norton & Company, 2000.

Okkonen, Marc. *Baseball Uniforms of the 20th Century: The Official Major League Baseball Guide*. New York: Sterling Publishing Co., Inc., 1991.

Okrent, Daniel and Harris Lewine, eds. *The Ultimate Baseball Book*. Boston: Houghton Mifflin Company, 1979.

Okrent, Daniel and Steve Wulf. *Baseball Anecdotes*. New York: HarperPerennial, 1989.

Pietrusza, David, Matthew Silverman, and Michael Gershman, eds. *Baseball: The Biographical Encyclopedia*. New York: Total Sports Illustrated, 2000.

Rader, Benjamin. *Baseball: A History of America's Game*. Chicago: University of Illinois Press, 1993.

Rains, Bob. *Cardinal Nation – 2nd Edition*. St. Louis: The Sporting News, 2003.

Rebello, Stephen and Richard Allen, *Reel Art: Great Posters from the Golden Age of the Silver Screen*. New York: Artabras, 1988.

Reidenbaugh, Lowell. *The Sporting News: Take Me Out to the Ballpark*. St. Louis: The Sporting News, 1983.

Reischauer, Edwin O. *"What Went Wrong?"* in James William Morely, ed. *Dilemmas of Growth*. New Jersey: Princeton University Press, 1971.

Ribowsky, Mark. *A Complete History of the Negro Leagues 1884-1955*. New York: A Birch Lane Press Book, 1995.

Ribowsky, Mark. *The Complete History of the Home Run*. New York: Citadel Press, 2003.

Riley, James A. *The Biographical Encyclopedia of the Negro Baseball Leagues*. New York: Carroll & Graf Publishers, 1994.

Ritter, Lawrence. *The Glory of Their Times: The Story of the Early Days of Baseball Told by the Men who Played It*. New York: Macmillan, 1966.

Ritter, Lawrence. *Lost Ballparks: A Celebration of Baseball's Legendary Fields*. New York: Viking Press, 1992.

Robson, Kenneth S., ed. *A Great and Glorious Game: Baseball Writings of A. Bartlett Giamatti*. Chapel Hill, N.C.: Algonquin Books, 1998.

Rubin, Louis D. Jr., ed. *The Quotable Baseball Fanatic*. New York: The Lyons Press, 2000.

Seymour, Harold. *Baseball: The Early Years*. New York: Oxford University Press, 1960.

Seymour, Harold. *Baseball: The Golden Age*. New York: Oxford University Press, 1971.

Simon Tom, ed. *Deadball Stars of the National League*. Washington, D.C.: Brassey's, Inc., 2004.

Smith, Ron. *Baseball's 25 Greatest Moments*. St. Louis, MO: The Sporting News, 2002.

Smith, Ron. *Heroes of the Hall: Baseball's Greatest Players*. St. Louis, MO: The Sporting News, 2002.

Sotheby's sale number 7354. *The Barry Halper Collection of Baseball Memorabilia: The Early Years*. New York: Sotheby's, 1999.

Sotheby's sale number 7354, *The Barry Halper Collection of Baseball Memorabilia: The Modern Era*. New York: Sotheby's, 1999.

Stang, Mark. *Baseball By the Numbers*. Maryland: Scarecrow Press, 1996.

Stang, Mark. *Cubs Collection: 100 Years of Chicago Cubs Images*. Wilmington, OH: Orange Frazer Press, 2001.

Stockton, J. Roy. *The Gashouse Gang and a Couple of Other Guys*. New York: A. S. Barnes & Co., 1945.

Stout, Glenn and Richard A. Johnson. *Yankees Century: 100 Years of New York Yankees Baseball*. New York: Houghton Mifflin, 2002.

Sullivan, Neil J. *The Diamond in the Bronx: Yankee Stadium and the Politics of New York*. New York: Oxford University Press, 2001.

Thorn, John. *Treasures of the Baseball Hall of Fame: The Official Companion to the Collection at Cooperstown*. New York: Villard, 1998.

Thorn, John, et al. *Total Baseball: The Official Encyclopedia of Major League Baseball*. 7th ed. Kingston, N.Y.: Total Sports Publishing, 2001.

Thorn, John, ed. *The Armchair Book of Baseball*. New York: Galahad Books, 1985.

Vecchione, Joseph J., ed. *The New York Times Book of Sports Legends*. New York: Times Books, 1991.

Voigt, David Quentin. *Baseball: An Illustrated History*. Pennsylvania: The Pennsylvania State University Press, 1987.

Wallace, Joseph, ed. *The Baseball Anthology*. New York: Harry N. Abrams, 1994.

Ward, Geoffrey C., and Ken Burns. *Baseball: An Illustrated History*. New York: Alfred A. Knopf, 1994.

Warren, Elizabeth V. and Roger Angell. *The Perfect Game: America Looks at Baseball*. New York: American Folk Art Museum and Harry N. Abrams, 2003.

HQ